PERSONAL
PEAK
PERFORMANCE

Books by Flora Davis

ELOQUENT ANIMALS

INSIDE INTUITION

PERSONAL PEAK PERFORMANCE

How to Make the Most of Your Energy

FLORA DAVIS

McGraw-Hill Book Company

New York St. Louis San Francisco Bogotá Guatemala
Hamburg Lisbon Madrid Mexico Montreal Panama
Paris San Juan São Paulo Tokyo Toronto

First published by Doubleday & Company, 1980

First McGraw-Hill Paperback edition, 1985

1 2 3 4 5 6 7 8 9 FGR FGR 8 7 6 5

ISBN 0-07-015861-4

Library of Congress Cataloging in Publication Data

Davis, Flora.
    Personal peak performance.

    Reprint. Originally published: Living alive! 1st ed.
Garden City, N.Y.: Doubleday, 1980.
    Bibliography: p.
    1. Vitality. 2. Health. I. Title.
RA776.5.D346 1985   613   84-25051
ISBN 0-07-015861-4 (pbk.)

For Mamu

ACKNOWLEDGEMENTS

In researching this book, I had the help of many, many people. Scientists took the time to answer my questions about their research and energists and others talked to me freely about their own energy. I owe particular thanks to: Dr. Andrew Ahlgren, Dr. T. Berry Brazelton, Mary Anne Symons Brown, Sophy Burnham, Dr. Patricia Carrington, Dr. Eliot Chapple, Dr. Stella Chess, Dr. Mihaly Csikszentmihalyi, Lynne DeGillio, Ellie Dylan, Dr. Charles Ehret, Dr. Frederick J. Evans, Dr. Arnold Friedhoff, Dr. Christian Gillin, Jan Gosar, David Hackler, Dr. John Hanley, Dr. Ernest Hartmann, Dr. Sami Hashim, Dr. Donald P. Hayes, Dr. Victor Herbert, Jean Houston, Elaine Kaufman, Dr. Dolores Krieger, Dr. Albert P. Krueger, Dr. Helmut Landsberg, Dr. Richard Lazarus, Dr. Jay Mann, Dr. John Mason, Dr. William McArdle, Cherie McCoy, Dr. William Morgan, Bill Murray, Brian Nakauchi, James Nesdill, Charles Nichols, Dr. Robert M. Nideffer, Louis Nizer, Diana Nyad, Dr. John Palmer, George Plimpton, Dr. Bruce Pomeranz, Dr. Maria Reichmanis, Dr. Marcus Reidenberg, Dr. Jack Richard, Dr. Robert Rose, Dr. Maj-Britt Rosenbaum, Dr. Doris Rothman, Dr. Leah Schaefer, Dr. Hans Selye, Deborah Sewitch, Dr. Baron Shopsin, Susan Shor, Dr. Fredrick Stare, Alexandra Stoddard, Dr. Richard Suinn, Dr. Leonard Syme, Katherine Tennes, Dr. Dorothy Tennov, Dr. Jay Tepperman, Dr. Leonore Tiefer, Dr. Wilse Webb, Dr. Elliot D. Weitzman, Phyllis A. Whitney, and Dr. Marvin Zuckerman.

Though I can't list their names here, I also want to thank those who talked to me anonymously—sometimes for hours—about their own energy problems and solutions.

I am also grateful to Wanda Urbanska, who helped with some of the research and interviewing, and to the members of my writers' group (most especially Anne Barry) who offered many helpful suggestions.

My editor, Kate Medina, provided the kind of guidance and support that writers dream of but seldom get; she should be cloned.

Lastly, I'm grateful to my family for their patience and understanding—especially to Mamu, whose extraordinary vitality first triggered my interest in energy.

CONTENTS

PART II. HOW TO LIBERATE YOUR ENERGY

Healers / Supporters and skeptics / Measuring the
healer's impact / Evidence of a universal energy / Are
we all potentially healers? / How acupuncture works:
the chemical theory / The electrical explanation /
Acupoints / The reality of the senses versus subatomic
realities

Energy: your sense at any given moment
of how much you could do if you chose to

Energy:
Your Untapped Potential

Human energy is an astonishingly complex and powerful phenomenon—and a force that is very much underestimated and often underused.

Many people feel that energy (or vitality) is just a matter of what you eat and how often you exercise, with sundry psychological factors thrown in. Most books and articles on the subject concur.

But there's probably very little that goes on in your body, your mind, or your life that doesn't have an impact on how much energy you have—and how much energy you have affects everything in your life, including your self-confidence and chances of success, your work, love affairs, and your friendships. Energy is one of your most valuable resources—and it's one that you *can* control.

Can you identify the different elements that affect your own energy? Do you know how and why they affect it? This book will tell you what these elements are. It will also show you how to use them to release energy you may never have suspected you had, energy that can be the key to a more productive—and thus very possibly a happier—life.

Making the Most of Your Natural Resource

When it comes to energy, we don't all start out equal. Just as people are born with the potential to grow up tall or short, they're also born with a certain *energy potential*, a quotient that's genetically determined. A few people are endowed with extraordinary vitality; most have less. This fact would seem to set limits on all those who haven't inherited the gift of great energy. However, most of us are born with enough vitality to lead whatever kind of life we wish, for we have much more energy than we regularly use. In fact, most of the time we draw on only a fraction of our true energy potential while the rest remains buried, an untapped resource.

To make the most of your life, you really need to make the most of all the energy you were born with!

Three Famous People with Different Kinds of Energy

To find proof that nobody really needs to suffer from a personal-energy shortage, you have only to look around. If you talk in depth, as I did, to people who lead highly productive lives and seem to have endless energy, you'll soon discover that though some of them apparently owe their vitality to the luck of the genetic draw, others were endowed with a modest amount of energy to start with and simply make the best use of every ounce they have.

Let me cite a few notable examples. Most Americans would agree that in order to survive as the mayor of a metropolis like New York, a politician must have abundant energy. The city itself seethes with restless, nerved-up vitality, with the potential for greatness or degradation. New York City's mayor, Edward I. Koch, is famous for his tireless drive and enthusiasm. He needs both, for he has one of the nation's most complex and demanding jobs. There are endless, frantic pressures on his time. He works an eighteen-hour day, getting up at six most mornings so that he can tackle a tense schedule that's jam-packed with discussions, confrontations, and decisions, not to mention public appearances and private meetings that often last far into the night.

Yet Ed Koch seldom seems to run out of energy. "I love this job," he says often and enthusiastically. He's outspoken, optimistic, and clearly has a formidable amount of energy—so much that a member of his staff notes affectionately, "At times, he reminds me of a fifty-year-old two-year-old!" In fact, his vitality is so extraordinary that it does seem to be a special, inborn gift.

Athlete Diana Nyad's energy is remarkable, too, but in a different way. Diana is the marathoner who swam all the way from the Bahamas to Juno Beach, Florida, in August 1979. During the eighty-nine-mile swim, she had to contend with strong currents, sharks, and stinging jellyfish. She was in the water for over twenty-seven hours with no relief; according to the rules that govern marathon swims, she could never cling, even for a few seconds, to the side of the accompanying boat. Just a year earlier, Nyad had failed in an attempt to swim from Cuba to Florida, but the attempt itself was a remarkable feat, for on that occasion she swam continuously for almost two days—a total of forty-two hours—achieving a distance of seventy-nine miles in rough seas.

To be able to do what she did, Nyad trained hard for nearly a year before each swim, gradually building up her strength, stamina, and energy level. Toward the end of each training period, she was swimming seven hours a day on weekdays and trying for twenty-four-hour stretches on weekends. Diana believes that in athletics the formula for success is not particularly complicated. "You have this much talent," she says. "You put in this much time, and you can measure how good you are compared to everybody else. It's very black-and-white."

Phyllis A. Whitney, the celebrated author of romantic suspense novels, is now in her mid-seventies. Her novels are so popular in the United States that she has yet to have one of them go out of print; she has been writing them at the rate of one or two a year for almost forty years. However, she is not, she says, a person with unusual energy, though she *is* highly organized and very disciplined. Miss Whitney eats lightly but well, exercises regularly (she skips rope for about forty-five minutes each day) and gets plenty of rest. Most of all, though, it's her work that keeps her young. "Activity generates energy," she says.

Are You an "Energist"?

Ed Koch, Diana Nyad, and Phyllis Whitney are all people who seem to have an extraordinary amount of energy and lead full and impressively productive lives. Yet in each case a different kind of energy quotient seems to be involved. New

York's mayor has a vitality and ebullience that are probably matters of basic temperament, which is linked to hereditary traits. It seems likely that Diana Nyad is not too far behind him in inborn energy potential, but she also spends long months in training, gradually raising her energy level and setting new limits on what she can do. Phyllis Whitney is endowed with less of the natural resource, but then energy wells up for her out of a lively interest in life, and she focuses it—the way a magnifying glass focuses a beam of sunlight—through self-discipline.

Are you an *energist* like Koch, Nyad, and Whitney? Energists are people who seem able to use their energy to the fullest. If you are an energist, which type are you? Or do you feel, as most of us do, that your energy isn't really under your control, that you have resources you're not tapping?

If so, there's a lot you can learn from energists like Phyllis Whitney and other individuals in this book, for though they *seem* to have more vitality than most people do, they simply channel what they have in highly productive ways. In fact, they're living proof that you don't have to go through life feeling, "If I only had more energy, I could *really* live!" However much vitality you have, it's enough, provided you understand how your energy works and how to release it, to let it flow to the fullest.

Jawaharlal Nehru, the Indian statesman, once said that life is like a game of cards: "The hand that is dealt you represents determinism; the way you play it is free will." When it comes to energy, we each have been "dealt" a certain potential. What matters in the long run is what you do with the hand you've been dealt.

Provocative Questions and Energizing Answers

This book is the result of several years devoted exclusively to the study of human energy. My obsession with the subject began the way many obsessions do—I fell in love. It rapidly became apparent that the man I cared about had a lot more energy than I did and used all of his to the fullest. (In fact, he has the kind of remarkable inborn vitality that Ed Koch has.) When we began to talk of marriage, I found myself wondering how I'd ever be able to keep up with him. Was there any way I could increase my own energy, or somehow free more of the vitality I suspected I had, so that I wouldn't be worn out or left behind?

I began with several basic questions:

• Is it true that from the time they're born, some people have much more energy than others and that, even so, some of us use whatever we have better than others?

• Where does energy come from?

• Why does it fluctuate so dramatically from hour to hour and from day to day?

• What can a person do to raise his or her energy level?

In tracking down answers to these and similar puzzling questions, I discovered answers to many other questions as well, including some that I'd never even thought of asking. For instance, do you know

• how to cut back on the minimum amount of nightly sleep you "need"?

• what an insomniac's bedtime snack should be?

• why a cocktail hits you harder at noon than it does at six o'clock at night?

• how to keep your energy level up for long periods between meals?

• how to "burn off" anger, anxiety, or depression?

• what colors increase your energy?

• how to stay awake when you feel irresistibly drawn toward sleep?

• how to cope if you're a low-energy person married to an extremely energetic, whirling dervish of a mate?

• how to focus your energy to solve problems creatively?

• that some people experience a personal-energy crisis a few hours *before* a storm begins?

My research into human energy (and the problem of how to augment it) gave me fascinating glimpses into the daily lives of others. I talked to scores of people—some of them famous but most of them not—about their own experiences with energy: the problems they have encountered and the solutions they've arrived at. I also talked with dozens of scientists about recent research that suggests some startling new ideas about energy. I finally came to see that there are two quite different ways of looking at human energy: There is the scientific, theoretical point of view; and then there's the way energy is actually experienced, the physical reality that's familiar to every human being.

What Science Says About Energy

Human energy per se is not a subject scientists are studying directly. From a researcher's point of view, the trouble with energy is that you can't measure it scientifically, any more than you can measure joy, grief, or hunger. You can take note of what people *do*, of course, but often that provides no clue to how much energy, or effort, they put into doing it. There's a great difference between, on the one hand, the person who works hard all day, parties half the night, and then feels exhausted for several days afterward and, on the other, the person who works hard, parties hard, and wakes up the following morning ready to start all over again.

Nevertheless, much research is being done that is directly related to energy, even if that's not what the researchers' primary focus is. I talked with nutritionists, physiologists, sports psychologists, sleep scientists, psychotherapists, endocrinologists, biometeorologists (who study how weather affects the human body), and eventually to a woman who does paranormal healing. Along the way I even read a few books about quantum mechanics!

What Is Energy?

I learned that though *energy* is a word that's used constantly in conversation, different people mean different things by it. To the physicist energy is "the capacity for doing work and overcoming resistance." To the nutritionist it's something produced by chemical reactions that take place in the body's cells as food is processed. To the mystic energy is the life-force, the spark that distinguishes the animate from the inanimate, the raven from the rock.

Most of us mean something more basic when we speak of feeling "energetic," or of feeling sluggish. We're referring to an internal experience, a sense of our own potential to do, think, or be.

This, then, is my definition of the word, what I'll be talking about in this book: *Energy is your own perception at any given moment of your potential for action. It's your sense of what you could do if you chose to.*

What you do—the "action" component of my definition—could be mental or physical, for there are certainly times when one feels physically charged up and mentally dull, just as there are other times when one is highly alert though physically exhausted. But it's all a question of energy—and it's vital to how you feel about, and live, your life.

Know Yourself

The nonscientists I talked with—those who told me their personal stories—were generous with their time and their insights. I learned through many conversations that though most people rarely give much thought to their energy, they refer to it often and are aware of it all the time. And there are certain things they *know* about it (just as there are things you know); they can name some of the factors that boost their energy and some that sap it. I was impressed with how much people know about energy once they stop to think about it. I was even more impressed to learn how very different individuals can be.

For instance, I talked to a number of men and women who said that their energy typically swings from one extreme to the other; it's always either very high or very low, with no in-betweens. One woman explained that stimulation is what she needs to pull herself out of a low period; when she's feeling down, she opts for lots of activity and physical exercise. However, another woman, taking the opposite tack, has learned to use meditation to even out her energy flow and gain better control of her inner forces. Some people were unhappy because they couldn't manage with less than nine or ten hours of sleep at night. Yet, I also talked to a ten-hour sleeper who enjoys every minute of it and

feels that sleeping is one of life's great pleasures (and energizers).

Then there are those who feel that they set their pace for the
whole day by the way they start out in the morning. These individuals, too, can be divided into two camps. Some are off and
running the minute their eyes are open, because they've found
that a slow start means they'll never build up much momentum.
Others ease into the day in an almost gingerly fashion. One
woman actually strives for the calm, dreamlike pace of an underwater ballet because she's found that if something happens to
upset her first thing in the morning—if, for example, her two-
year-old has a temper tantrum before she can get off to work—it
throws her off stride for the entire day.

Then there is Norma, who bolsters her energy continuously
with black coffee (eight to ten cups a day), and Gail, who finds
that half a cup of coffee gives her a jittery sort of energy lift, followed immediately by an energy plunge.

The more I learned, the clearer it became that although
human energy operates according to certain general principles,
to make the most of your vitality you need to know not only
those basic principles but also, and quite specifically, how *your
own* energy works.

I also discovered, as I talked to people, that some had indeed
been able to produce a dramatic increase in their own vitality.
The methods they used were amazingly diverse. For example,
Sharon—one of the reluctant sleepers—took a new job, moved to
a new city, and found that she could suddenly manage on just
seven hours of sleep a night instead of nine. Pamela gave up
martinis before dinner and added three or four active hours to
her evenings. Gail, who became depressed and experienced an
energy crisis when she lost her job, pulled herself out of it by
changing her eating habits (and her self-image): she became a
vegetarian overnight! Ken actually cured his insomnia and made
great energy gains when he gave up the sleeping pills he'd become dependent on. Jay took up yoga and running, lost thirty
pounds, and has felt resourceful *and* energetic ever since!

What Super-achievers Say About Energy

I also talked with a select group of energists, people noted in their respective fields for their accomplishments and their energy. Besides Koch, Nyad, and Whitney, I talked to attorney Louis Nizer and to actor Bill Murray; to author-athlete George Plimpton and to Elaine, the owner of the famous Manhattan restaurant of the same name. I had long conversations with interior designer and author Alexandra Stoddard; TV journalist Ellie Dylan; playwright Sophy Burnham; Jean Houston, a psychologist and one of the leaders of the human potential movement; and Dr. Dolores Krieger, who has taught paranormal healing to thousands of health professionals.

All of these people were highly articulate and each had a particular point of view about energy. By definition they were people who used their own energy to the utmost—they really *had* to in order to achieve what they did. As they talked about their own lives, I learned an enormous amount from them.

The Four Basic Facts

What I learned from all of these sources—the scientists, the energists, and people like you and me—led me to arrive at certain conclusions. Of those conclusions, four are so central to an understanding of energy that they crop up throughout this book. I'll summarize them here because for me these are the *four basic facts* you need to know about your energy to realize its full potential.

1. Nervous Energy Versus "Enerjoy"

"There are times when I feel so revved up that I just have to get up and move around," Laurie told me. "I'm restless, I can't concentrate, I jump at the slightest noise. I'm possessed by a kind of energy that seems entirely unproductive. But at other times everything seems to flow. All day long, whatever I do comes easily and I feel as if I could go on forever."

Virtually everyone I talked to distinguished, as Laurie did, between two kinds of energy: nervous energy and the sort of vitality that simply seems to flow and feels so good! In an interview in *People* magazine, actor Robin Williams, who played Mork on the television show "Mork and Mindy" dubbed the two types *fission* and *fusion*. Those are good labels because when you experience nervous energy you do feel not only tense but somehow fragmented (fission), while with "flow energy" there's a sense that you are really very much together (fusion). I call the fusion kind of energy *enerjoy* since it comes from a deep sense of well-being and its secret is, as Williams put it, that "by being happy you can get energy."

Enerjoy flows; at times it soars. It's the kind of energy we'd all like to have every day, all day! You don't have to drum it up; in fact, effort is often counterproductive. You simply let it flow.

You can learn to liberate this kind of energy, to feel it more frequently.

2. Energy Is a Body Truth

A *body truth* is a personal, internal experience. It begins as a sense impression of conditions in the world outside your skin or of conditions within your own body: you feel cold, hot, tired, hurt, or some such thing. This sense impression becomes a body truth when you assume that other people's impressions are exactly the same as yours, that those who share your circumstances must also be feeling hot, cold, tired, or hurt.

Though this may seem like a reasonable assumption, it isn't always. And because other people also tend to operate on the basis of their own, sometimes very different, body truths, misunderstandings are almost inevitable.

For example: I find a room too warm; you say it seems rather chilly. Impressed by my own body truth, I may decide that you're a sissy, while you, in turn, wonder whether I'm running a fever. Another example: If we both develop stomach flu and I'm doubled over with the same cramps that you're managing to ignore, you may call me a hypochondriac; I, on the other hand, suspect that you're just trying to impress others with your stoicism.

We know reality through our senses, including those that are tuned in to the internal state of our body. We generally believe those senses—in fact, we *need* to believe them to get by in life—and so we often make value judgments and generalizations about others on the basis of our own body truths. But people do experience heat and cold differently, and pain as well, for both physiological and psychological reasons. And, certainly, they experience their energy *very* differently.

Yet we make judgments about people continually that are based on energy, barely realizing that we're doing it. If you can successfully juggle a job, several small children, heavy commitments in the community, and you run in marathons besides, I'm apt to decide that you are "driven." When you discover that I can't manage a similar schedule, you, in turn, may feel that I'm not really trying, that I'm "lazy." We're both wrong. We are simply different.

My research on energy convinced me that it's wise not to leap to conclusions about others—what they "ought" to be able to do or how they "ought" to react—in terms of energy or any other body truth. And yet it's difficult not to leap to conclusions because we all have energy prejudices, which brings me to the third point.

3. Our Energy Prejudices

Americans have mixed feelings about energy. Because we live in a highly competitive society that is very accomplishment-oriented, we value and envy people who seem to have unusual vitality. On the other hand, we sometimes denigrate them as well, insisting that if they're constantly on the go, it's because they're driven by their own private demons. "I'm not high-energy at all," one woman replied indignantly when I asked to interview her. "I'm really not the nervous type." I never said she was!

Many people also equate energy with accomplishment—and that's another bias. As one of my interviewees put it, "Energy is what it takes to do work." It had never occurred to her that it also takes energy to play! Thanks to the Protestant work ethic, Americans tend to get a little grim when they talk about energy and mutter something about willpower. Few people see it as a life-force that's actually brimming over in all of us, or realize that frequently what it takes to release energy is not cranking up but letting go.

Many Americans tend to assume that energy is a masculine trait. Men are supposed to have drive and vitality, though it's all right for women to be passive and subdued. But, of course, neither sex has a monopoly on energy.

It's important to be aware of these cultural biases because they do color the way we think. For example, though times are changing, it's still much more difficult for a man to admit that he's not out there at the high end of the energy spectrum than it is for a woman to admit the same thing. And it's difficult for all of us to realize that even when inner demons are not involved, high energy can be a mixed blessing. A few of the very energetic people I talked to said that at times they felt *too* geared up, as if life was a downhill race and the problem was control.

It's also true that low energy can be an asset in some circumstances. I talked to a psychiatrist who explained, "I sometimes feel as if I operate in a different time frame than other people do. I move more slowly." She also observed that people who move faster and have a lot of energy are seldom introspective; they rarely pause to plan ahead or to analyze their own long-term goals, as she does.

Clearly, both high and low energy can be productive if you accept them for what they are and flow with them.

4. To Get Energy You Have to Spend Energy

This was something I heard over and over again from people who were committed to some form of regular exercise. For example, one jogger said, "If I go out for a run first thing in the morning, I not only feel better and more energetic for the rest of the day but I'm convinced I even think better."

Spending physical energy is one way to increase your vitality;

investing *mental* energy is another. You feel really vigorous when you're deeply interested in the things that are going on around you. You have to be curious; you need to care.

Dr. Stuart Froum, a Manhattan periodontist, once suggested to me that ultimately energy comes from health and from being hungry. I would add that it also comes from belief. Most people barely give health a second thought until they're not feeling well, and then they become preoccupied with getting better or else they simply give in to their illness. Either way, they experience an energy crisis. By "hunger" Froum simply means wanting things badly enough, since our interests, desires, and needs spark energy. As for belief, when you're doing something you enjoy, something you believe is important and, furthermore, you know you're doing it well—*that's enerjoy.*

How My Energy Grew

Beyond the research and interviewing I did, I at times had a third source of information about energy: I tested the things I was learning to see whether they made a difference to me. And there's no question that they did.

A few years ago, when I first began thinking about energy, I realized that only once in my life had I stretched myself to my own energy limits in the area of work. That was back in 1973, when, by plugging away night and day, I managed to write, in the space of just two weeks, one full-length magazine article and two chapters—totaling eighty-four pages—of a psychology textbook. (Normally it would have taken me at least five weeks to do that much writing.) By the time the fourteen days were over, I had developed an annoying twitch in my right eyelid and I was so exhausted that it was an effort just to breathe; but at the same time I felt very good! I wasn't anxious to repeat the experience, but I was pleased to think that just once I'd exerted myself this way to the utmost.

I realize now that in the course of writing this book I have regularly stretched myself that far and even further. I have learned, in fact, exactly how far I can go and for how long before my energy begins to fail. I know that, starting on a Monday,

I can write for two weeks, including two weekends, without a break—for a total of eighteen days—putting in nine to eleven hours at the typewriter every day. Long before the eighteen days are up, I will have developed that twitch in the eyelid, but I know now that it won't do me any harm. However, if I aim for twenty days—in other words, if I try to work right through that third weekend—I'll become so tired and stale that my writing will suffer; so instead I'll take two or three days off and then I'll be ready to start again.

Everyone is different. To some people my maximum energy will seem unimpressive; others may feel it's more than they themselves could manage. The point is that I've moved closer to *my own* top potential where work is concerned. I've asked myself why it happened, wondering which of the many things I've learned about energy was responsible. For as I became energy conscious, I made many small changes in my life. I could name a dozen or more of them, but four seem most significant.

Exercise that Doubles as Meditation

First of all, I finally listened to the exercise enthusiasts, who insist that regular exercise is energizing. I now swim every second or third day. I found that within just a week of starting this routine I did feel much more energetic. Though the time I spend at the pool is time I could spend at my typewriter, it turns out to be worth it.

I also knew from past experience that I could lessen my own tensions—thereby freeing considerable energy—if I meditated regularly. However, I couldn't see any way to work that into my schedule, since I'd been told that I should put in forty minutes a day. Then, while I was researching this book, I learned of a way to meditate in bits and pieces, snatching a few minutes here, a few more there; and, in addition, I began to combine a mantra meditation with my swimming. I found that I could reap many of the benefits of meditation without the heavy investment of a block of time.

Rhythms: Mine and Yours

I also came to accept certain things about myself and the rhythm of my own energy. I learned to live around that rhythm. For example, I realized that I always feel dull and sluggish late in the afternoon, because that's the way my body clock works. Like approximately half of the population, I suffer from something called "postprandial dip," which means that within a few hours after lunchtime my body gears down, as if slacking off for a nap. The problem is worse when I haven't had enough sleep and better when something interesting is going on, but on any day I'm better off if I try not to schedule really demanding work for the late afternoon. I've found that this is a good time to do the grocery shopping or, for that matter, to swim. (When is *your* "down" time?)

Dissolving Emotional Blocks

Exercise, meditation, identifying body rhythms: They all helped me move toward my energy potential, and they are likely to help you, too. However, what nourished my vitality the most was the gradual realization that I lose a great deal of momentum when I put my energy into *not feeling things*—into denying anger, for example. I know now that when I wake up in the morning feeling unaccountably tired and have to force myself out of bed, it's not because I'm depressed; almost always the real problem is anger that I haven't acknowledged and that is lowering my energy and mood. Since I grew up believing that anger is ugly and dangerous, I work hard to suppress mine and that's energy wasted—a double downer. I've learned that if I can just admit to myself that I'm angry and begin to *feel* the emotion, the energy will come flooding back. Sometimes it's nervous energy to start with and that's uncomfortable, but at least the spark is there; the life-force is flowing again.

Many people have no trouble experiencing anger. The particular tactics that would release their energy would thus be quite different. I've simply highlighted here the discoveries I made that mean the most to me.

How to Analyze Your Energy: Where to Find What in This Book

To capitalize on your energy potential, you have to know yourself well and study your own energy, including its rhythms and its ultimate sources in body, mind, and environment. You need to identify the things that give you a lift as well as those that drain you so that you can try to plan your day, or even your life, with such considerations in mind.

Accordingly, the first part of this book will focus on some of the basic facts you need to know to understand how your own energy operates. Chapter 1 sketches four common energy profiles, together with the problems that are inherent in each "type." You'll decide which of the profiles fits you best and what your own energy quotient might be. Also, you'll pick up clues as to how it might feel to *be* someone else, since the way people experience their energy colors the way they experience their lives—and the way you experience them and they experience you. A summary at the end of this and every other chapter will list practical energy tips, and throughout the book important points will appear in italics.

Chapter 2 takes up the old heredity versus environment question and asks: What happens to a person's inborn energy potential on the way to adulthood? Or, in other words, to what extent are your heredity *and* your upbringing responsible for your adult energy level? To turn the tables, we'll also consider whether there are special problems involved in raising a child who is born with an unusually high or low energy potential.

Chapter 3 tackles the ultimate puzzle: Where *in the body* does energy come from? No one really knows the answer to that question, but recent research on brain chemistry and hormones suggests some strong—and surprising—possibilities. We'll also ask: Where does a "manic" patient get his extraordinary energy? Is nervous energy physiologically different from enerjoy? Why does energy fluctuate so dramatically over the course of a day? This chapter is necessarily more technical than the rest of the book, but I hope you'll bear with me; it's important to have a general idea of the way energy works within the body—even if you don't remember every word.

Chapter 4 explores the way your emotions affect your energy and, especially, the way they can block it. You'll find out about the ultimate cause (and cure) of boredom; learn about ways to lift yourself out of a depression; discover how to spend your energy freely in anger when that's appropriate; and learn what to do with angry energy at those times when it would be self-defeating to lose your temper. Along the way, you'll even discover why "nice guys" can make the worst husbands!

Chapter 5 is about body rhythms and the fact that your vitality fluctuates in a fairly predictable way over the course of a day. It's possible to go with the flow, taking advantage of your own energy peaks and living around the lows. Thus, among other things, you'll learn how to identify the time of day at which your energy typically crests; how to cope with a mid-afternoon slump; what to do if you're the sort of person who doesn't really wake up until mid-morning and you're suddenly faced with a series of important breakfast meetings; how to alleviate jet lag; and how to keep your energy up if you're doing shift work.

Liberating Your Energy

Understanding how your energy operates is, of course, only the beginning. Because energy is such an extraordinarily complex physiological and psychological phenomenon, there are literally hundreds of ways to augment it and an equal number of ways in which it can be diminished. In Part II we will consider how you can liberate your energy and tap your full potential.

Leading off Part II, Chapter 6 is, in effect, a guide to intelligent sleeping. It asks and answers such questions as: Can you learn to doze off at will? Should an afternoon nap leave you with more pep or less? How can you prevent insomnia from robbing you of energy? Is there a safe sleeping pill? (New research has come up with a promising possibility.) This chapter contains other intriguing tidbits as well. For example, you'll learn why

American presidents generally sleep well and you'll hear about a woman who dozes off for about an hour a day and can't understand why anybody would need more rest. Imagine having the energy to live a twenty-three-hour day!

In Chapter 7 you'll learn whether, based on available evidence, the following statements should be considered true or false:

- Fluctuations in energy are largely due to diet.
- Most Americans are overfed and undernourished.
- You are only as energetic as your last meal.
- You can increase your energy by dosing up with B vitamins.
- Starches and sugars rob you of energy.

If you answered "false" to most or all of the above, you'll feel comfortable with the rather controversial point of view expressed in this chapter, which also considers whether fat people have less energy than thin ones.

Chapter 8 analyzes various "drugs" people take that directly affect their energy—from uppers such as coffee and amphetamines to downers such as Valium. We'll consider what's known about the way these drugs affect the brain and body and we'll ask whether there's any *safe* drug you can take for an energy boost. You'll also learn about recent research that shows that certain foods actually affect the chemistry of the brain; in some cases they may have an impact on your energy.

Chapter 9 takes up the question: Are physical and mental energy the same thing? Since I've concluded that for all practical purposes they're *not* the same, we'll go on to explore ways to spend physical energy and benefit from it mentally and emotionally. For example, you'll learn that although some runners use running to tune up their energy, others use it to set their creative juices flowing or to burn off anger, anxiety, or depression.

Presenting the other side of the coin, Chapter 10 explains how you can use your mind to galvanize your body and improve your performance in sports. This section describes mental tactics that athletes use—ones that you can use, too—to increase their endurance or insure that they put out just the right amount of effort (as opposed to trying too hard). There are even tactics for turning off negative thinking and others that can help if you have a tendency to freeze up in situations where you're afraid you'll fail.

Many of these mental tricks are as useful off the playing fields as on. You'll also learn that being an extrovert (or an introvert) can give you an edge in certain sports; and that you can use sports and other pastimes to generate enerjoy.

Chapter 11 is about finding the right climate—outdoors and in —for your energy. You'll learn how a falling barometer affects you physically, why the change of seasons is apt to be an energy drain, how to tell whether you're weather-sensitive (and what to do about it if you are). Turning to the climate indoors, we'll first consider the hazards of ion-depleted air and then move on to identify colors that stimulate energy. We'll also discuss some of the little things, part of the very dailiness of life, that can provide you with an energy boost.

Chapter 12 explores the way other people affect your energy. It asks whether energy—and emotions—are contagious; why some people are taciturn while others are terribly talkative and whether this reflects their energy flow; why some of us need lots of contact with other people to maintain our vitality while others crave solitude. We'll also consider this situation: When someone who is central to your life is also a real drain on your energy, what can you do about it?

Other Energies: Nervous, Sexual, Psychic

In Part III we'll take account of the varieties of human energy: We'll look at other kinds of energy that are related to your overall vitality level, though they're not entirely explained by it; in fact, they remain rather mysterious. We'll also pause to explore the way energy differences can affect a marriage and examine energy crises of various sorts—situations in which your energy unaccountably fails.

Chapter 13 is about nervous energy and stress. It describes the way prolonged stress can sap your vitality, but it also introduces people who thrive on a high-pressure life-style and others who cope surprisingly well with personal disasters. What's different about them? What can we learn from them? This chapter suggests a dozen basic tactics for handling stress, so that it won't deplete your energy, including ways to control worrying and blunt the multiple minor hassles that are part of daily living.

Though the most basic energy distinction is between the nervous sort of vitality and enerjoy, there are other forms of energy as well. Chapter 14 deals with sexual energy, asking what it is, why some people have so much more of it than others, and whether lovemaking is a way to generate energy or to spend it. We'll also consider whether people who are fundamentally low in energy are apt to have less of a sex drive, and how a couple who are mismatched in their sexual appetites can negotiate this sexual-energy gap. Finally, this chapter suggests half a dozen ways to liberate your sexual drive and asks: Is falling in love the ultimate energizer?

Chapter 15 describes ways to liberate creative energy. It will tell you how to "incubate" a problem, how to reason and plan in mental images, how to use imagery to end procrastination and dissolve creative-energy blocks, how to dance out a problem, and how to improve your memory by thinking with all five senses.

Chapter 16 focuses on meditation and the way it can generate mental and creative energies even as it takes the edge off nervous drive. You'll find instructions here for simple meditation techniques especially designed for people who haven't the time to meditate—and for people who can't bear to sit still. This chapter will also answer some questions that often puzzle meditators: Are all systems of meditation equally effective? Does it really matter what word you use for a mantra? Is there any advantage to using more than one mantra? Must you meditate for twenty minutes each time or is there any value in doing it for five minutes or less?

Chapter 17 will tell you what to do in an energy crisis—a period when days pass, or even weeks, and for no obvious reason you feel tired all the time. Is the cause likely to be physiological or psychological? When is it serious enough to see a doctor? You'll also learn one medical man's surprising answer to the question: What's the single most common cause of chronic exhaustion?

Chapter 18 explores the way energy differences can affect human relationships, especially marriages. What happens, for example, when someone who has an enormous amount of energy marries someone who has a great deal less? Is this difference a liability or an asset? What is it like to grow up in the same household with a brother or sister who either has much more drive or much less than you do? What about you as a parent with a child whose energy level is so different from yours that you can't begin to imagine what it's like to be inside his (or her) skin? Why, for that matter, do kids always seem to have so much more energy than adults?

Chapter 19 handles the subject of psychic energy, asking: Do humans have "energy fields"? (Some mystics suggest that we *are* energy fields.) Is there a kind of energy that we can't measure, that flows through the body and can become blocked and thereby make you ill? And can that sort of energy be passed along from a well person to a sick one by the laying on of hands?

Your Energy: The Resource You Can Count On

I hope that reading this book will do for readers what writing it has done for me. As you become more energy conscious, hopefully you'll learn a great deal about the way your own vitality flows, liberating it in many different and productive ways (some of them perhaps uniquely your own) and thus live a richer, more successful life.

Energy is not, in and of itself, the one true goal. What counts, in the long run, is what you do with what you have, how you choose to spend it. But whatever your personal values or priorities, there's no question that you'll pursue them more successfully and you'll live more fully and intensely if you have greater access to the energy you were born with.

Energy is a life resource. In a world in which little else seems certain, you can be sure that no one can take it away from you, though old age will eventually temper it. It's a resource that's not affected by changes in the economy or by fluctuations in the dollar. You can not only bank on it; you can spend it freely for a better, happier life.

I
UNDERSTANDING
ENERGY

Four Energy Profiles: Which Fits You?

What is your energy potential? How would you describe yourself in terms of energy? Do you consider yourself high in energy? low? about average? Or does your energy frequently swing from one extreme to the other, so that it's complicated for you to say what it's really like?

On a scale of 1 to 10—if 10 is about as energetic as a person can be and 1 is about as sluggish—where do you think you fit in? 2? 5? 7? 8? How would you rate your *everyday* vitality? What do you think your maximum potential might be? What would you *like* it to be?

Some people will be able to answer these questions easily; many others will not. The purpose of this chapter is to help you arrive at some answers, a sense of what energy "type" you might be, before we go on to learn more about your energy and how you can use it more fully.

The Four Basic Energy Types

I spent over two years talking to people about energy, and it struck me very early in my research that there are really just four basic and quite distinctive energy types; within each category, people generally share the same propensities and have similar problems.

1. A small number of those I interviewed were unusually high in energy. On a 1-to-10 scale, I'd rate them at 9 or 10; their vi-

tality was always one of their outstanding characteristics. I came to think of them as *sprinters*.

2. An even smaller number of the people I talked with were unusually low in energy; they are the *strollers* of this life; on an energy scale they would rate a 1 or 2.

3. Most people fell within that vast middle ground we call "average" (3 through 7); since they set a middling sort of pace, I called them *trotters*.

4. Then there is a fourth group, the *hurdlers*, who swing dramatically between high drive and low.

I didn't conduct a broad statistical survey. As far as I know, no one has ever studied human energy in that way. But when I mentioned my impressions to some of the scientists I interviewed, they agreed that very probably energy is like most other physiological and psychological characteristics—height, intelligence, or optimism, for example—and follows what statisticians call a "normal distribution curve." That would indeed mean that relatively few people would be extremely high or low in energy, just as only a relatively small percentage of the population is extremely tall or short; almost everyone would be middling (except the hurdlers—they swing back and forth and are something of an anomaly).

In this chapter I'll sketch in some energy profiles, variations on the four basic types. Most people will identify easily with one or another. And it helps to know where you fit in, especially if you're not average, to realize that there are others like you, and to see what their problems are and how they've solved them. It helps, too, to understand some of the ways that other people are different from you because those differences can affect relationships (see Chapter 18).

1. The "Sprinters"

GARY: A SPRINTER GREEDY FOR LIFE

Gary is a sprinter. A middle-management executive, he's forty-eight, short, fair-haired, fast-moving, with an incisive and original turn of mind and a formidable amount of drive. Because of that drive, he's forever overscheduling himself, taking on more than any human being could manage; but somehow, by cutting a corner here and reshuffling appointments there, he shoehorns everything in. He goes at projects full tilt and most of the time seems to enjoy himself immensely. "I'm greedy for life," he says.

It's no surprise, then, to learn that Gary feels he's probably a 10 on the energy scale. He explained his reasoning as follows: "I get along on less sleep than most people do, I make more nervous motions, and I pace a lot when I think. At the office I often feel I've just got to get up from my desk and walk around. I'm impatient, too; I like to keep things moving all the time. People I've traveled with have complained that they have trouble keeping up with me, and people who work for me also complain sometimes, though I usually interpret that as a compliment. But, you know, there are times when all that energy gets in my way."

Gary's vitality actually creates several different problems for him. Because he tends to respond immediately to almost any stimulus, he gets a lot of new projects started; however, it's not easy for him to stay focused long enough to finish them, since something new is always turning up to claim his attention. "I constantly cramp my schedule, too, and then have to keep rearranging it," he said. "I try to do a lot of different things at the same time. If I were to sit back and organize myself better, I'd get more done. Also, when I run a staff meeting, my energy sometimes makes me very impatient, so that I really dominate. I've noticed that meetings are sometimes more productive on a day when I'm low in energy, because then my staff gets to have more input."

Gary tackles all sorts of work at a headlong pace. If he washes the dishes after a meal, it takes three people—scraping plates, drying them, and putting them away—to keep up with him, and they all have to work fast. At the office he plunges into his schedule the minute he arrives and the pressure doesn't let up until it's time to go home.

Recently he decided to try slacking off a bit, to see if less speed might, after all, be more efficient; but he found that when he tried to slow down just a little, he immediately became so sluggish that he could hardly get anything done. His speed and intensity are lifelong habits, part of his temperament, and so changes aren't easy to make.

"DEMAND" SLEEPING

Gary's sleeping pattern is completely erratic. He's apt to get four hours of sleep one night and ten the next. Recently he's been experimenting with what one might call demand sleeping. If he's tired at eight in the evening, he'll go to bed for four or five hours; get up and work or read from, say, one to four in the morning; and then go back to sleep until seven. Fortunately, he's the kind of person who can doze off virtually anywhere, anytime, and within seconds if he makes up his mind to it.

Gary drinks a lot of coffee and a fair amount of alcohol. He feels that the coffee helps him concentrate, though it sometimes leaves him jittery, and that the alcohol helps him unwind. Every so often he goes on an exercise binge, and for a week or two he'll get up early to do half an hour of strenuous calisthenics. However, his job requires him to travel a lot, and so the exercise sessions are soon suspended for the duration of a trip to California or France. When he gets home again, Gary usually finds that he has lost his enthusiasm, or he's too tired or too busy to exercise, and so the daily calisthenics are forgotten for the time being.

Gary is actually fairly typical of the sprinters I talked to. Many admitted that they frequently feel impatient, because the rest of the world seems to them to be moving in slow motion. And many agreed with something Gary said: "*I certainly wouldn't wish for less energy, but I'd like to have better control over the energy I have.*" Because sprinters often seem to need activity for its own sake, control can be difficult.

Of course, that isn't true of all high-energy people. When I asked Louis Nizer, the famous attorney, whether he thought there might be such a thing as too much energy, he looked very surprised. He allowed that, theoretically, that might be possible, but only if the person had no ambition to use his energy and didn't know how to get rid of it otherwise. Obviously, Nizer—who paints and writes books when he's not practicing law—has never had any trouble deciding what to do with his own extraordinary drive. (There is more about Nizer in Chapter 2.)

SPRINTERS WITH NERVOUS OVERDRIVE

Though sprinters such as Gary are sometimes hard to keep up with, their vitality is almost contagious, making them stimulating and fun to be around. However, there are other sprinters who create a very different impression: Because of inner tensions, their energy has a jittery quality. The difference is that not only do they have more than the usual amount of inborn vitality, but they have more nervous energy as well.

Take Paul, for example. A lawyer in his mid-thirties, wiry, red-haired, Paul gets up early, goes to bed late, and hardly ever stops moving from the time he rises until he sets. There's no question that he gets a lot done, but there is about him such an air of tension, of irritability barely contained, that he often makes others feel rather uncomfortable. He's the kind of man who always has something jiggling even when he's sitting down.

Marjorie is the same sort of sprinter. A small, intense woman, she's currently managing a large house, two children, and a kennel (she breeds Irish setters). When she complained to her husband a while back that the kennel was getting to be too much for her, he objected. "But think of the psychiatrist's bills if we were to close it down!" He was joking—sort of. He's afraid that if his wife doesn't have enough projects available to drain off her extraordinary energy, she may simply blow apart.

When people feel "driven" by their own energy—when they sense it as an uneasy, simmering inner pressure—it's generally nervous energy that's involved. There's no question that there is such a thing as too much nervous energy, for over the long run it can exhaust you and can actually interfere with the flow of enerjoy. (Chapter 3 has a lot more to say about what nervous energy is, and Chapter 13 describes ways to tone it down.)

Sprinters don't, of course, have a monopoly on nervous energy. Everyone experiences it from time to time, some people more often than others. However, those who are at the top of the scale both in flow-energy and in the nervous sort need to provide themselves with plenty of outlets for all that inner drive.

ARE YOU A SPRINTER?

Though many of the sprinters I talked with were well aware of their own remarkable vitality, others were not, either because they had never given any thought to the matter or because they had grown up in a family where a great supply of energy was simply taken for granted and family members had no sense that their own vitality was out of the ordinary.

How can you tell whether or not you're a sprinter—a 9 or 10 on the energy scale? See if any of the following apply to you:

• You're a sprinter if all your life you've listened to envious remarks from others who complain that they can't keep up with you, or who insist that they can't imagine how you manage to do all the things you do.

• You're a sprinter if you often feel impatient because it seems as if the rest of the world is moving in slow motion.

• You're a sprinter if you often feel that your energy is a force that's right behind you, pushing; that life is a downhill race and the trick is not to lose control.

• You're probably a sprinter if sitting still takes a lot of effort from you, if you think better when you're on your feet and moving around.

A GUIDE TO HIGH-ENERGY PITFALLS

Though the only thing sprinters *invariably* have in common is their abundance of energy, many (but not all) of those I talked with also shared certain tendencies that almost seemed by-products of their unusual energy. Especially on the job, these tendencies are potential pitfalls.

For instance, many sprinters never do just one thing at a time if they can possibly help it. Perhaps because they have drive to spare, they're happiest when they're juggling several tasks simultaneously. One woman explained that at work she likes to keep switching back and forth among several different projects. In the kitchen she operates in much the same way: making dinner, she'll begin the cole slaw, then turn to the chocolate cake, only to abandon it temporarily to wash a few dishes. "I just want to get all those things done," she explained, "and I don't really care how I do them. I work fast and when I think of something that needs doing, I like to get it started right away." That's often not the most efficient way to work, but like a few other sprinters I met, this woman has so much energy that she can usually get away with being less than organized.

Some sprinters have trouble delegating responsibility. They can do the work so much faster than other people that it often seems simpler just to do it themselves. And because of their need to be up and moving, sprinters tend to be too busy to do much long-range planning or to stop periodically and examine their own priorities.

If you're a sprinter with any or all of these tendencies, it pays to be aware of them, because they're often spendthrift ways to use energy.

2. The "Trotters"

KNOWLEDGEABLE YVONNE

As I've said, most people are trotters; their vitality is in the middle range. Trotters occasionally feel that they have so much drive that they don't know what to do with it. They sometimes go through periods when their vitality is down, but ordinarily they take their energy for granted.

Yvonne is fairly typical of the trotters I talked to—with one important exception: *She has unusually clear ideas about the things that energize her and those that drain her.* Though she hasn't yet been able to come up with surefire ways to head off the energy downers, she regularly and intelligently uses what she knows about the things that give her a lift. She's a good example of how a trotter (or anyone else, for that matter) can gain access to more of her own energy potential.

Yvonne is a tall, reserved, dark-haired woman in her mid-thirties, with a low and rather husky voice. In addition to being the head of the history department at a small private school in Philadelphia, she is also the mother of two small children. She commutes to her job from the suburbs.

Yvonne explained that there are three things that are guaranteed to sap her energy: the hay fever she suffers from in the summertime; visits to the Midwest to see her parents; and visits to Pittsburgh to stay with her in-laws. In recent years she has been able to relieve the hay fever problem through medication and by installing air conditioning in her home, but family visits still take their toll. "I tend to sleep a lot when I go home to Michigan," she said. "I never did get along well with my mother and it's a strain being there. And when we visit my husband's parents, there are things that happen that irritate me, and things that are said, especially to the children, that set me on edge. I know I'd better keep my mouth shut, so I do, but I feel draggy the whole time we're there."

KNOW YOUR ENERGIZERS

As for the things that energize Yvonne, the primary one is a marriage that's a source of deep satisfaction. Beyond that, jogging is very important to her. She and her husband get up at a quarter to six every morning to go out and run together. "I find that if I run and then walk to work—it takes me half an hour from where I get off the train—it gives me pep and it's also a way of controlling nervous energy." If she skips the morning run or the walk, she feels as if her motor is racing and she's less productive at work.

Yvonne needs about eight and a half hours of sleep every night. "I'm not really viable if I try to get by on less," she says. On weekdays it's a struggle for her to get out of bed, but on weekends she awakens early and easily. She feels that's a sign that she likes having control of her own time, though it's also possible that on weekdays thoughts of the pressures she'll be facing at work may take that first, fine edge off her energy.

Yvonne also gets energy from working with her hands: sewing, refinishing furniture, and especially playing the piano. At such times she becomes totally absorbed in what she's doing. "Having that as part of the pattern makes all of the pattern open up for me and I can do much more," she said.

Of all Yvonne's energy tactics, what impressed me most was the way she uses her own *momentum* and handles her emotions. She says that her mind is like sludge in the mornings until she runs, but that during the run her energy lifts off and builds up a kind of momentum. Once she's back at home, she tries to move right on with the rest of her day. On the commuter train heading into the city, she briskly tackles paper work that she's brought along with her; if, instead, she relaxes with the morning news-paper, she becomes groggy, loses her momentum, and it takes her a good part of the morning to recover it. Nor is she alone in her need to preserve her precious momentum; others reported a similar early-morning problem.

One of the laws of physics concerns momentum. Newton's first law of motion states that *a body at rest remains at rest and a body in motion remains in motion unless acted upon by an external force.* That law also holds true for human beings: Whether it's physical or mental effort you need to expend, it's often difficult to get started but relatively easy to keep going once you've overcome your own inertia. If you're aware of that fact, *you can get more out of your energy by taking advantage of your momentum, once it's established, and by steering clear of situations in which inertia is apt to settle in.*

As for the emotions, the two notorious downers are depression and anxiety. Yvonne is seldom depressed. "When you're de-pressed, it's as if you've turned your energy inward against your-self," she explained. "I think I'm too much of a survivor to do that." Because her job can be quite stressful at times, she does occasionally feel anxious; however, *she believes that anxiety is energizing.* "The tension builds up," she said, "and then I have to find some place to put it." Anxiety *can,* of course, be paralyzing; it's a matter of degree, of just how anxious you are. But Yvonne is never a victim of the kind of vicious cycle many people be-come involved in. She never allows herself to grow anxious about the fact that she's feeling anxious. Instead, she regards her own jitteriness as latent energy, there to be spent. (More about the emotions and their effect on energy can be found in Chapter 4.)

ARE YOU A TROTTER?

Most people are trotters, about average in terms of their energy. If, as you read the descriptions of sprinters, hurdlers, and strollers, you experience no flash of recognition—an instant when you think to yourself, "But that's what I'm like!"—then it's safe to assume that you're a trotter.

There are trotters who typically operate close to the high end of the energy scale (at 7 or 8) and there are others who are just a shade more vigorous than a stroller would be. I found that most trotters can actually recall periods in their lives when, for days, weeks, or even months on end, they had barely enough energy to get through the day, as well as other periods when vitality surged within them like a flood tide. With no real understanding of what causes either the ebb or flow of energy, they can only think wistfully how nice it would be if the tide came in again.

Yet if you have the kind of self-knowledge that Yvonne has achieved, you can swell the flow of your energy until it rises toward its natural crest.

3. The "Hurdlers"

BETH'S UPS AND DOWNS

Some people are not high, low, or even average in their energy level. They plunge instead from very high to very low and then swing back up again. Everyone has ups and downs, of course, but for some hurdlers the swings are frequent and almost predictable. For others there's no real pattern, but the contrast between the highs and the lows is so dramatic, and the switchover so frequent, that they have no idea what their "real" energy level might be.

Beth is the first sort of hurdler: Her energy swings have a pattern. A single mother, petite, slender, with a mass of curly blonde hair, she is very much aware of the way inertia and momentum operate. "To me," she said, "energy is like a locomotive: It's a force that keeps on going until it bangs into something and stops. Once it has stopped, it's hard to get it going again. I live with a lot of stress and, in a way, I'd be afraid not to, because the stress—having to cope with one deadline after another—keeps me going. I have the feeling that if I really slowed up, I might never get started again."

During her high-energy periods, Beth feels physically good, satisfyingly competent, and she can manage on very little sleep. Recently, while finishing an assignment (she's a free-lance artist) she worked almost twenty-two hours a day for three or four days at a time. "I would go to sleep just as it was getting light outside; then I'd wake up at eight and go out and run—the running seemed to give me energy. I felt very good about myself. I thought, just look what I'm doing!"

Beth slides down from her highs to a middle level and then sinks into a low phase. Though she has never kept a record, she believes that the highs and lows last the same length of time— about a week—and that the transition period between them lasts slightly longer. During her lows, she hasn't the energy for anything beyond the bare necessities of working and living. "Whatever I do then, it costs me more to do it," she said. "I can still get dinner on the table, and if I have an appointment to keep, I get there; I try not to cancel out."

But she can't reach out and start anything new; *new projects always require more energy than the daily routine*—there's a kind of resistance, a hump one has to get over. Mired in her own inertia, Beth feels guilty during her downs, terribly aware that there are many things she should be doing that she isn't. "I feel that if I were the person I'd like to be, I just wouldn't *be* down," she said.

I asked Beth whether her low periods ever occurred over weekends. She wasn't sure. "Sometimes I do spend Saturday or Sunday just lounging around, but that's enjoyable—I don't feel guilty about it. I guess I don't really think of energy as something that's necessary for having a good time. It's only necessary for work. If something is a duty, that takes energy." *Many Americans equate energy with accomplishment and believe it's produced by willpower,* which means that when their vitality sags for no reason they can think of, they tend—like Beth—to blame themselves for not trying harder.

Beth can think of at least one explanation for her lapses of energy, but somehow she blames herself anyway. She believes that her energy swings are related to her menstrual cycle. She suffers from severe headaches and some of them seem to be tied in with her periods and also with her energy lows. "My big headache of the month comes like clockwork four days before my period," she said, "and it drains me of energy and sometimes actually puts me in bed for a day or two."

BLOCKING ANGER BLOCKS MOMENTUM

But apparently that's not the whole explanation, for there are other times when Beth's energy crash seems to be triggered instead by something that happens. "A few weeks ago I had a very heavy schedule," she recalled, "with a lot of things planned, when suddenly my eight-year-old daughter got sick and had to stay home from school. I had to cancel everything and so I started feeling so-so and slid downhill from there. It was almost as if the impetus, the momentum, had been lost. I think part of what started the slide was fatigue from suppressing my anger. I felt very frustrated, but I couldn't take out my feelings on Holly —it wasn't her fault she was sick." Beth's experience is typical of the kind of energy crisis that's likely to occur when a person tries to clamp a lid on strong emotions (see Chapter 4).

When I asked Beth how she got out of a down period, she was quite positive at first that it was all a matter of willpower: "When I'm in a low, I feel helpless, until finally it reaches a point where I see vistas of spending the rest of my life in this down. Then I know I have to do something about it, so I pull myself out. I force myself to start acting as if I'm full of pep and pretty soon I feel better. Holly said to me the other day that *sometimes the way to get energy is to act energetic,* and I agree with her." (Many others, making a similar point, put it slightly differently: To get energy you have to spend energy.)

Nevertheless, when I asked Beth whether, by acting peppy, she could yank herself out of a down on its very first day, she was positive she couldn't. She believes that she has vast energy resources, but that she can't count on being able to get at them. Though she thinks her energy *should* be under her control, to a large extent it apparently isn't.

It's possible that Beth's mood swings have some kind of bio-chemical basis (for more on that, see Chapter 3) or that her menstrual cycle is at least partly responsible (see Chapter 5). But, as always, there are also psychological factors involved.

Beth's guilt over her down periods, for example, is quite striking. When I asked her how, when she was a child, her parents reacted when she was either very high or very low in energy, she couldn't remember, but she did mention that her mother was a semi-invalid, ill with emphysema for as long as Beth could recall. I suspect that, to begin with, a down period threatens Beth because she associates low energy with her mother's serious illness. In addition, it seems likely that when she herself was sick as a child, she felt guilty about it, since a sick child is a terrible strain for a mother without the energy to get out of bed. For that matter, it's a strain on a healthy mother, especially a working mother, as Beth herself can testify.

Then again there's the fact that for her "energy," "work," and "accomplishment" are words that are virtually synonymous. What's more, Beth seems to feel that her lows are almost a form of self-indulgence, an attitude partly attributable to the good old Protestant work ethic. At any rate, when Beth is in a down period she doesn't like herself much; she feels guilty and perhaps a little afraid, and these negative feelings further drain her energy and prolong the problem. In other words, though initially it may be a headache that interrupts the momentum of her energy, *if severe inertia sets in afterward, that happens partly because she's down on herself for feeling down!*

HOW HURDLERS PSYCH UP

Though there is no real pattern to Laurie's ups and downs, they're so dramatic that she can't really rate her energy, and so I consider her a hurdler, too, like Beth. "On your scale, I'm both a 10 and a 1," she explained. Fortunately her energy is more often up than down.

Laurie is a biologist, a tall, slender, elegant blonde in her late twenties. As a youngster she was constantly on the go, and her mother, who complained that she was overactive, once described her as an "interesting but difficult" child to raise. Laurie was frequently so overexcited that she couldn't get to sleep at night, and a doctor finally advised her parents to keep her very quiet from about four in the afternoon on, so that she would have a chance to wind down before bedtime.

Today Laurie's highs are still occasionally a problem for her. "It's scary at times," she said, "like being in a car racing out of control. But mostly it feels good, and the downs are terrible. There are days when I can barely make coffee and all my movements feel slowed down. Everything takes longer to do. I really feel so much better when I'm functioning at a high-energy level that I try to psych myself into it."

What seems to help most is stimulation: getting out and seeing people. *Like everyone else, Laurie needs to have the right balance in her life between gregariousness and solitude, between excitement and tranquility,* to keep her energy flowing (see Chapter 12). "I've also learned that I need variety," she said, "to take on more activities rather than less. And exercise. I take modern dance classes, and after a class I feel very relaxed and also slightly, pleasantly high."

Laurie, like Beth, has strong feelings about her down periods. In fact, she blames her mother for them. "She was constantly at me when I was a child," she explained. "Nothing I ever did was right and it still isn't. She says I don't handle money well, she doesn't like the way I dress or wear my hair, and she doesn't approve of what I do for a living. She's hypercritical. But there was always a double message: She'd also tell me that I was bright, pretty, could have any man I wanted, and so on. So I swung between insecurity—feeling anxious and confused—and self-confidence, and sometimes I still do. When I feel passive, when my energy is low, it's as if my mother's got me down again."

Though Laurie finds the high-energy end of her cycle "scary" at times, her fear of flying isn't really a fear of crashing. "I have a feeling the scariness may be more related to a fear of success," she said, "even a fear of being fully alive." As a child, perhaps, whenever she showed too much confidence her mother cut her down to size, and so she learned to expect low times on the heels of her highs.

ARE YOU A HURDLER?

You are a hurdler if your energy level swings, frequently and dramatically, from high to low and back up again. You may have thought of these as mood swings, from euphoria to depression, but energy is also involved.

Perhaps there's actually a pattern to your ups and downs (though there needn't be), so that you can almost predict when the next low is due; in any case, your vitality fluctuates to such an extent that it's hard for you to say what your true energy level might be.

If you're a hurdler, you may also have a tendency during your up periods to operate at 110 percent of your capacity. Feeling good, you take on more and more projects, becoming busier and busier, until you drive yourself into a state of exhaustion, and then depression and lethargy set in.

It's fairly typical of hurdlers that during their up times they push themselves hard. For some it's just that all that vitality feels so good that it's practically addictive, and, like Beth, they're afraid they'll lose it if they lose momentum. Others appear to be using their energy and activity to hold something at bay—anxiety, perhaps, or a shadowy sense of the meaninglessness of life.

WHY ENERGY SHUTTLES BETWEEN EXTREMES

There are several possible explanations for the hurdling phenomenon. As I mentioned earlier, in some women the menstrual cycle may be responsible; in other individuals psychological factors (such as Laurie's fear of feeling too good) are heavily involved. And *in some instances the cause may be basic brain chemistry.* In highly exaggerated form, manic-depressives also experience mood-and-energy swings, and many psychiatrists now believe that those swings happen because of abnormalities in the brain's internal chemical message system (see Chapters 3 and 5). It's possible that the same chemicals, operating within the normal range, are partly or wholly responsible for the ups and downs of some hurdlers.

HOW TO STABILIZE YOUR ENERGY

Manic-depressives generally rely on medication to control their mood swings, but for most people drugs are, at best, an inadequate strategy with serious drawbacks (see Chapter 8).

Many hurdlers simply accept the fact that they are by nature rather volatile. One man explained that "What helps me tolerate the down times is the conviction that I probably wouldn't have the ups if I didn't have the downs as well." However, that may not be the case. Playwright Sophy Burnham, who used to be a hurdler, found that when she took up meditation it produced a quiet evening out of mood but actually heightened her energy: No longer at the mercy of highs and lows, she found herself operating with calm certainty and a steady flow of energy.

For those hurdlers who are unhappy about their energy swings, meditation is worth trying (see Chapter 16). So is Laurie's strategy: She has learned that to keep her energy up, or to boost it once it has bottomed out, she needs stimulation, contact with other people. However, if you're the sort of hurdler who hits bottom periodically because you've been *over*-stimulated—you've been leading an overpopulated, overtiring life

—your solution might be to retreat from the world during energy dips, to relax, indulge yourself, and marshal your forces.

You may need to experiment with different tactics, to find out what works best for you. One thing is sure, though: It's counterproductive to blame yourself for the low periods, because that will only make you feel worse!

Energy swings are a fascinating phenomenon. Momentum really does seem to be involved, as does inertia, which sets in during the lows. Though most people may not swing from high to low as dramatically and as often as Beth and Laurie do, everyone crashes at times and everyone occasionally rises to the heights. We all have enough experience with the way energy fluctuates to be able to empathize.

4. The "Strollers"

THE BIAS AGAINST STROLLERS

Though it was easy to find sprinters to interview—almost everyone seems to know at least a couple of them—strollers were harder to come by. I suppose it's possible that low energy is rarer than high energy, but I think it's more likely that high energy is more noticeable and envied—plus the fact that most strollers are reluctant to admit they have less than the usual amount of drive.

As I mentioned earlier, there are cultural biases in regard to energy. *Americans admire vitality and tend to think that there must be something "wrong" with those of us who are by nature rather low in energy.* That kind of thinking can affect a stroller's self-image. It certainly affected Martha's.

A tall, thin woman with red hair and freckles, Martha was wearing blue jeans the day I met her for lunch at a Manhattan restaurant. She looked so fresh-faced and young that I'd never have guessed her profession: She's a psychiatrist with a small private practice. She's also the mother of two young children and she's writing a book. Yet, in spite of all that, she considers herself low in energy.

In fact, at that particular time Martha was very impatient with herself because she couldn't seem to get by on less than nine and a half or ten hours of sleep at night (see Chapter 6), and because she didn't have enough energy for all the things she wanted to do. "I have this superwoman facade," she explained, "and I *am* involved in a lot of things, but I'm not working awfully hard at any of them. I have a small part-time practice; I'm puttering along with the book I'm writing; and though I have two kids, I also have a housekeeper and a gardener."

Martha feels that her energy level has set limits on what she's able to do professionally. There was a time when she wanted to lead encounter groups, and as part of her training she was once required to run an actual encounter session. She had had some experience as a group therapist, but she quickly discovered that this was different. A regular group, she explained, is more talky, and the leader is a mere facilitator. An encounter leader has to pour out energy, to maintain the intensity of the emotional experience. As people relive the traumas of their lives, tears flow and anger surfaces; one person's reaction will often trigger something in the next.

"Let's say you put emotional intensity on a scale from 1 to 10," Martha suggested. 'For an encounter group to work, it has to run at 10 the whole time, and as a leader you have to keep it there. That means you must stay right in there with the group; you can't give in to the urge to curl up and take a nap because you're worn out. But I could feel my energy failing at times, and then I'd have to signal my coleader that I was fading fast." Martha now puts leading encounter groups into "the category of things I would like to do if I were somebody else."

Treating private patients can be exhausting, too, though Martha notes that it's tiring the way running is tiring. "It gives and it takes energy," she said. "Actually, I get a lot of energy back from my patients. All the same, I can't be with more than four or five patients a day without feeling very tired, so I limit my practice. That's how many I see."

Martha feels slightly guilty at times because she's not using her medical training to help more people. "I know that you have only one choice in life, to be who you are," she said, "and that the only legitimate question is, are you being the best *you* that you can be? I tell myself that I have significantly helped a handful of people. Though it's not thousands, it's not zero. But then I imagine that other psychiatrists must be treating thousands."

Even when it comes to everyday household chores, Martha feels that her energy isn't really adequate. "After dinner, sometimes I'll sit for a while, looking at all the dirty dishes, thinking, 'Gee, there are a lot of them,' marshaling my energy to do something about them. In the time I spend getting ready to tackle the job, my mother-in-law—who is a very active woman—can finish the whole lot."

Martha can quite happily sit and do nothing for long periods of time. "After every cycle of activity," she said, "I like to sit motionless and cool out, perhaps in the dark, as if I've been overstimulated. But I feel guilty about doing it. It's only when we're out in the country, officially relaxing, that I'm really comfortable about just sitting and watching the grass grow. Our society puts so much value on *doing*," she said wryly.

Martha regards the state of her energy with mixed emotions. On the one hand, succumbing to the American tendency to admire high drive, she feels obscurely ashamed that she doesn't fit the pattern. "We need a group called Low Energy Anonymous," she said. "You know, I could count on the fingers of one hand the people who know how little energy I really have. There may be others out there who are like me, but they wouldn't tell me and I wouldn't tell them. It would be like advertising the fact that you have a low IQ!" Most of the strollers I talked to told me they take pains to hide the fact that they're chronically wound down.

On the other hand, Martha resents all the emphasis on energy and suggests that it may be simply the predictable prejudice of a male-dominated society. She points out that, according to the old stereotypes, *males are supposed to be active and females less so. Is it still the male stereotype that's admired?*

WHERE LOW ENERGY IS AN ASSET

Moreover, it's quite clear to Martha that *there are benefits to being a stroller, just as there are liabilities.* For instance, she has observed that some sprinters overwhelm their children. "My mother-in-law should have been a corporation president," she said. "Instead, she used her drive to control her kids. I think half of being a good parent is knowing when to lay off, though the other half is knowing when to be there for them."

Martha is also well suited to her profession for a number of reasons, and her energy level is one of them. She's not the sort of person who finds it difficult to sit still for hours at a time, listening while patients talk. In fact, patients sometimes remark that they envy her serenity.

She also admitted that she secretly believes she'll live longer because she lives more slowly and doesn't react to "every little thing." And she noted that people who are continually on the run are rarely introspective. They seldom stop long enough to assess the situation thoroughly, or to question their own motives or long-term goals.

Despite all the low-energy benefits she can list, Martha is impatient with her energy level. The truth is, she expects an enormous amount of herself. She'd like to simultaneously commit 100 percent of her energy to her patients, her marriage, her children, and her book. Yet even a sprinter couldn't manage that, and a sprinter would probably spread energy around in a much less balanced way.

Martha can, of course, make better use of her energy by learning more about it. Closing her eyes to the way other people operate, she can experiment until she finds the pace—complete with cooling out periods—at which she herself feels best and is most productive. There are other tactics she can learn, too, from other strollers.

HOW TO MAKE ALL OF YOUR ENERGY COUNT

For instance, Diana pointed out that you have to be well organized to make the most of limited energy.

I asked her a question I've asked of many people: What would you do to boost your energy if you had two weeks coming up that were bound to be difficult? Of all those I talked to, Diana was the only one who mentioned organizing her life in advance. "I'd plan simple meals," she said, "and cook some of them ahead of time. I'd cut out all the extraneous things I handle now. I'd have the car checked to make sure nothing would go wrong with it. Then, when the time came, I'd get enough sleep, I'd have regular meals—I wouldn't skip lunch the way I sometimes do now—and I'd leave time for long, relaxing baths, because that always leaves me feeling better and less nerved up."

Since they don't have an overabundance of energy, it's especially important for strollers to organize their lives, particularly in times of stress. By planning ahead, and by distinguishing thoughtfully between the things that are essential to do and those that aren't, *a stroller can make every last ounce of energy count.*

ARE YOU A STROLLER?

You're a stroller if all your life you've found it difficult to keep up with other people. In most situations you feel tired sooner than others, and even when you're doing as much as everyone else is, it seems to cost you more. Sleep may (or may not) be a problem for you: You may need more of it than most people—and may resent that fact.

You may be a relatively serene sort of person like Martha: Moving along at your own relaxed tempo, you wonder sometimes why other people become so aggravated over little things. Or you might be a stroller with a lot of nervous energy; in that case, you're as likely to react to the little things as anyone else is.

ENERGY TIPS FOR STROLLERS

If you're a stroller and you really feel you were shortchanged on inborn energy, there are several things you can do.

First of all, you should realize that *hoarding your energy won't help.* Since *to get energy you have to spend energy,* you may actually find that the way to tune up your vitality is to get involved in more activities rather than less. Of course, that doesn't mean you should go out and exhaust yourself—you may have to pace yourself more prudently than others do—but you won't experience that marvelous sense of effortlessness, that flow of enerjoy, if you behave as if your own vital forces are in such short supply that you have to hang on to them tightly.

The second point to remember is that you can *make all of your energy count by organizing your life and planning your time*. When you start every day by listing all the things you have to do —numbering the items on the list in order of importance and beginning immediately with number one—you're not only spending your time in the most effective way, you're making the best possible use of your energy. Nonessentials will sink to the bottom of the list, where they either won't get done at all if they're not really important or they'll be disposed of in their own good time.

Another thing you can do is to use your cooling-out periods to examine your priorities on a much grander scale. Ask yourself the following questions: What do I really want to do with my life? Am I doing it, or at least moving in the right direction? If you've been feeling frustrated because you just don't seem to have enough energy to go around, you may feel better once you decide what's important to you in the long run, and what you can realistically do about it now. Then you can *put your energy where your values are*.

Many strollers actually accomplish a great deal. However, they *feel* as if they're doing much less because they're constantly comparing themselves to other people who seem to do as much, or more, with less effort. And that brings me to the last point I want to make: It's important for strollers, in particular, to remember that *what counts in the long run is not how much energy you have but what you choose to spend it on*.

LOW ENERGY—OR JUST AN ENERGY BLOCK?

Some strollers are born with a modest allotment of energy. Even as infants they're less active. They're quiet babies, easy to underestimate (see Chapter 2). But other people function at a low energy level though their potential is actually much higher. Sometimes it's hard to tell them from the natural-born strollers.

For example, there are some individuals who don't seem to put energy into anything they do. Uncompetitive, unassertive, seldom angry, unlikely to become romantically involved (often they have little interest in sex—see Chapter 14), they have apparently learned to suppress all of their emotional responses, and so they've suppressed their energy as well. Others aren't turned off emotionally, and yet they experience an energy shortage that's such a long-term proposition that they can't remember a time when things were different.

A CHANGE OF SCENE LIBERATES UNSUSPECTED VITALITY

Sharon is a good case in point. For a decade, from the time she graduated from college until she turned thirty, she was convinced that she'd been underendowed with energy. Then her life and her vitality both took an unexpected upturn. Two years ago, when I first talked to Sharon about energy, I was surprised to learn that she considered herself a stroller, because I'd thought of her as someone with a lot of drive. A vivacious redhead, Sharon always seems to be lit from within by the glow of good health and her own enthusiasm. When she talks, her words come out with a rush; her gestures are quick, light, and graceful. Two years ago, at the age of twenty-eight, she was already an established magazine writer and seemed very much in control of her life. Yet she herself felt that her energy was woefully low.

"Energy is a real problem for me, and it always has been," she said. "I'm tired a lot of the time. Oh, I know it doesn't show—I make an effort not to let it—but if I don't get nine hours of sleep at night, I can't get up in the morning. I feel draggy all day and I may actually have to take a nap in the afternoon. If a genie offered me just one wish, it would be to become the kind of person who can get by on six hours of sleep. Think what I could get done if I were like that!"

Sharon explained that on junkets abroad she was always the one who headed back to the hotel early to get some rest. At conferences she was apt to fade away quietly in the middle of the afternoon for a nap. And if, at any time, she got only seven hours of sleep for two consecutive nights, she felt irritable and sorely pressed.

For years Sharon had puzzled over her energy problem. "I can't account for it," she said. "I enjoy my work. I'm practically never depressed. I spend an hour or two a day on some kind of exercise—jogging or swimming or squash. I eat a well-balanced diet, I don't smoke, and I don't drink alcohol, coffee, or even tea. My only vice is diet soda, and I go through a six-pack of that every day. I guess the caffeine in it gives me a boost."

During the one period in her life when Sharon felt that she had real energy, she was working for a newspaper on the night shift. "I was on from seven in the evening until 2 A.M.," she recalled, "and then I'd go home and sleep as long as I needed to, so I always had enough sleep. I liked the job, but I think it was the hours that were important, because in my senior year in college I worked as a waitress nights and I really felt good then, too. I guess some people are just meant to be night owls." (That's not true, as you'll see in Chapter 5.)

My first interview with Sharon took place several years ago. Recently I spoke to her again. In the interim she had moved from New York to Atlanta in order to accept a job as a magazine editor.

I was surprised to learn that the move had generated an up-surge of energy that has now lasted for nearly a year. Though Sharon is working long hours, she's actually sleeping less. "I find I can easily get by on seven hours a night for a day or so and I don't have to nap," she said. "I wake up very early without an alarm clock, even on weekends, though back in New York I could barely drag myself out of bed most mornings. You know, if I was a 2 on your energy scale before, I think I might be a 7 now!"

Sharon is at a loss to explain the change in her energy level. It's not that the new job is less pressured; it's quite demanding, so much so that she's exercising less because she has less time, and she has actually gained ten pounds. "Mainly, I think editing is a better job for me than writing was," she said. Sharon had been a magazine editor once before, but it was a job on a brand-new publication and it carried an enormous amount of respon-sibility. She was so overworked that, though she spent her work-days surrounded by other people, she had no time for casual conversation. She sat at her desk, bent over her work, for ten or even twelve hours a day, isolated by the pressure to produce.

At the age of fifteen Sharon had set a goal for herself: She wanted to be a magazine editor. By the time she was twenty-six, she had achieved that goal, and yet she was feeling harrassed, overextended, and not at all sure any longer that this was what she wanted to do with her life. Eventually she gave up her job to become a free-lance writer. Though in many ways the change was for the better, like most free-lancers she found that it was a struggle to make ends meet, and since she was working out of her home and lived alone, it was also an extremely solitary way to live. She thought a lot about getting into television or out of writing altogether.

With the new job in Atlanta, her doubts about the future have faded. "Editing is more of a challenge than writing ever was," she said. "It recharges me to spend my day solving problems, and the job forces me to connect with the other people at the office."

FOCUSING OUTWARD FOR ENERGY

Just as Laurie found that the way to avoid down periods was to get out more, Sharon has discovered that she needs the kind of job that puts her into easy contact with other people, that draws her out of herself rather than demanding that she focus inward. *Many people haven't as much energy as they could have because they're either chronically understimulated or overstimulated.* It's important for everyone to get the right amount of stimulation and the right kind; that's certainly one clue to the change in Sharon's energy.

Atlanta's more relaxed life-style also suits her better. "I was in New York recently and I was struck immediately by the dramatic scale of the city," she said. "I'd forgotten what it was like. I was also reminded that day-to-day living is so much more difficult there than it is in Atlanta. The subways are crowded, everything is more expensive, everyone is in a hurry, and there's more anxiety. Atlanta is so relaxed that, living here, I feel as if I've been freed from a burden. And you know, it's possible, too, that I feel I have more energy partly because now I'm comparing myself with Atlantans rather than with on-the-run New Yorkers."

Of course, all these positive changes add up to the fact that Sharon is much happier now and, as Robin Williams said, "by being happy you can get energy." She is also more focused and less tense, because at long last she knows what she wants out of her working life.

Many people have much less energy than they'd like to have, and some have good reason to believe that they're operating well below their potential. What's particularly interesting about Sharon is the fact that she really believed her energy problem was lifelong. As far as she could remember, the only hint she'd ever had that her potential might be quite high were those two brief periods when she worked the night shift.

Obviously, not everyone can or should change jobs or move to another city. For one thing, a change isn't always an improvement. For another, the problems that are sapping your energy may not be situational at all. There are people who move from job to job and city to city who are always dissatisfied and short on energy, no matter where they are, because what's tying them up are their own deepest feelings about themselves. If you've had a long history of searching for the right job, the right marriage, the right place to settle down, and the search has always been in vain, psychotherapy may be a better solution than yet another move.

However, if you really feel that your everyday vitality is well below what it could be—and if you're very unhappy with your work or your general situation—then it may well require a drastic change of some sort to unblock your energy.

IS YOUR ENERGY BLOCKED?

How can you tell whether you're a born stroller, or just someone with a lot of energy potential that's somehow all tied up?

It's difficult, if not impossible, ever to be sure why a person is low in energy, unless there's a physical cause, such as an illness. Fortunately, in purely practical terms, knowing why isn't important, since the tactics you use to maximize your potential are the same, either way: you need to learn more about yourself and about the things that lift or drain you.

A Summary of Energy Tips

The following are the main energy tips we've touched on in this chapter. (I'll provide similar summaries as we go along.)

1. If you're a sprinter and have so much energy that your problem is control, make a real effort to focus your drive. Don't just give in to the itch to get moving. Take the time to assign priorities and do the most important things first. Resist the temptation to take on more projects than you can handle; whenever it's feasible, delegate authority—even if you suspect that it would be faster to do the job yourself.

2. If you're a trotter, raise your energy consciousness. You might keep notes for a week or so and evolve a highly personal list of things that energize you and those that get you down. Then use what you've learned.

3. If you're a hurdler intent on having more ups and fewer downs, experiment to see whether you need more stimulation or less to keep your energy up or to get it going again when you've bottomed out. You might try meditation to even out those mood swings.

4. If you're a stroller, don't hoard your energy. Go for stimulation, but experiment, too, to find the pace at which you feel the best. Make it a habit to set priorities every day, and think through your priorities on a grander scale as well, so that you can make all of your energy count.

5. If you're very unhappy with your job or your whole lifestyle, changing one or both might unlock your energy.

6. Experiment with momentum to find out how to use yours to best advantage. Learn how to get it going and how to ride with it. People are very different; a fifteen-minute break may be the pause that refreshes for one individual, while for another it's time enough for inertia to set in. Some people can successfully go to extremes: For a time they will *do* intensely, carried along at high speed by their own momentum; then they'll stop and relax completely, before throwing themselves into headlong action again. Others, however, get carried away by their momentum. Because they tend to sail along at 110 percent of their ca-

pacity until they drop, what they must learn is how to ease off before the crash.

Only by experimenting and observing can you learn what works best for you.

High Energy Doesn't Guarantee Success

One last point: *Ultimately enerjoy flows from self-acceptance.* That's why it's terribly important not to misuse the energy scale. It's meant to illustrate ways that people are different, not to point out that some are "better" or "luckier" than others just because they have more energy.

Sprinters definitely don't win all the prizes, nor are strollers to be pitied. (Remember the marvelous old parable about the tortoise and the hare?) Actually, there are lots of highly energetic people who are failures and low-key people who are more successful. To envy someone who seems to have more drive than you do or to look down on someone who appears to have less is, well, it's a waste of energy!

But it helps to know which profile fits you, because in each case different problems come with the territory. It also helps to realize that others may be very different in energy than you are, so that you don't assume that they share your body truths.

Most people say they'd like to have more energy. Thinking of the times when the life-force has blazed up within them, the times when they've had an abundance of vitality and have simply gone with the flow, they're eager to feel that way more often. And though it's impossible to sustain enerjoy indefinitely, most people can achieve it much more frequently than they do—and that's what the rest of this book is about.

But before we come to ways and means, let's take a look at how energy evolves over the years, the way your upbringing can affect your energy potential today.

Energy that "Runs in the Family" . . . or Doesn't

Once you've decided which energy type you are, it's useful to pause and consider how you got that way. Are you a sprinter, for example, because that's the pattern that was laid down in your genes, or did your upbringing somehow energize you?

The heredity-versus-environment question is one that seldom leads to a definitive answer, but it's perennially asked and always fascinating, because to the extent to which something is inherited it resists change, and to the extent to which it's learned it can often be unlearned. In other words, if you assume that you have as much (or as little) vitality as you do because that's what runs in your family, then you must also assume that you're stuck with what you have. But if your energy is a product of your upbringing, then there's a good chance that you can augment that energy, especially if you can figure out how it grew, or failed to grow. Understanding how energy develops could also help you establish for your own children the kind of home environment that fosters vitality.

Many human traits seem to be a product of heredity *and* environment. Energy undoubtedly is, too, so the real question is: How much is heredity and how much environment? *One of the energists I talked with was convinced that energy is largely a matter of heredity.*

Louis Nizer: Succeeding Takes Energy

In the world he moves in, Louis Nizer is noted not only for his skill as a trial lawyer but also for his phenomenal energy. He was seventy-six when I interviewed him and still practicing law, as he put it, "very, very actively." In addition, he wrote books, working mostly on Saturdays, Sundays, and holidays; he had had nine books published. He painted and had sold his own paintings through art gallery exhibits. He wrote music. And he regularly accepted speaking engagements.

I talked with Nizer in his private office at his law firm. It was an elegant and imposing room, big enough so that it seemed a long walk across the thick carpet to the chair beside his desk. With his craggy face, shrewd eyes and gravelly voice, Nizer reminded me of Jimmy Cagney playing a tough but likable ty-coon who came up the hard way. And, of course, Louis Nizer is very much a self-made man. His father owned a small cleaning and dyeing store in the Williamsburg section of Brooklyn, and for many years the family lived in a single room behind the store. Young Louis had to learn to handle himself around the street toughs of the neighborhood. The Nizers were a close-knit family and the parents had ambitions for their only son; yet they probably never dreamed, as they made sacrifices to help him through law school, that he would someday become confidant and counselor to movie stars and statesmen.

Louis Nizer, I soon discovered, has a theory about energy. "I've met people of achievement from all walks of life," he told me, "from presidents to sports figures, and I've found them to be different from one another in every respect except one. Some are honest, some are unscrupulous; some are reflective, some are not; some have a temper and some don't; but what they all have in common is energy—endless energy."

Acknowledging that he, too, is endowed with unusual vitality (on a scale from 1 to 10, I suspect that Nizer's energy rates an 11 or 12), he went on to say that he couldn't claim any credit for it since he inherited it! "I've had it all my life," he explained. "I can still work until two or three in the morning preparing for a case, and my young partners and associates, some of them under thirty, can't keep up the pace."

Nizer believes, as I do, that energy can be one key to a suc-cessful life—but he'd go a step beyond what I would say, for he feels that only those with unusual energy can make it to the top, especially in the national political arena, where campaigning is so arduous. Among politicians he has known, Adlai Stevenson was the only exception to this rule. Nizer noted that where Truman, Kennedy, and Johnson were energized by crowds and campaigning, Stevenson was numbed by them, as well as by hectic schedules that left him so tired he could barely remember what city he was in. "That's the reason he didn't run for President a third time," Nizer said, "even though he was no longer running against Eisenhower."

Of course, Nizer noted, energy is no *guarantee* of success. Among other things, ability and persistence are also important—though *energy is definitely an aid to persistence.* Nizer mentioned Gary Player, said to be the world's greatest golf talent when it comes to getting out of a sand trap. Player acquired his skill partly through persistence and endless practice: He would get into a trap and start hitting balls out of it, and he wouldn't quit until he had sunk five of them in the hole, even if it meant he had to spend the day there. A whole day of whacking golf balls out of sand requires more stamina than most people have.

"Great Energy Is Very Quiet"

Nizer carefully distinguishes between what he calls "natural energy" and the kind that's triggered by the emotions. (Presumably he means nervous energy, a subject I'll come back to in the next chapter.) He mentioned that a flash of anger, for example, is not natural energy. "As a matter of fact," he said, "great energy is very quiet. It's just *there,* like a battery, to draw on." He also believes that people who have a lot of natural energy have less tension. *Tension literally tightens you up, and that tightness and the anxiety that goes with it use up energy.* "If you have a lot of energy," Nizer said, "even when you handicap yourself by being tense, the energy overcomes that."

Tension comes from worrying, and Nizer suggested that people *can* train themselves to worry less. It's a matter of perspective, he said, and he quoted the old saying: "Worry is interest paid on trouble before it becomes due." The calamities we anticipate probably occur only about 1 percent of the time, he maintained, and in any case worrying won't prevent them. Noting that we all suffer sorrows, aches, pains, and diseases, that they're part of life "and that's perspective too," he suggested that we take ourselves less seriously. Obviously, that's easier said than done, and he acknowledged this, explaining that he wasn't "preaching any perfection. I worry, despite everything I say, and everybody else does too. But you can *reduce* worrying—that's the point—by having a true perspective." Tension wastes energy but perspective reduces tension: It boils down to the fact that *your approach to life partly determines how well you're able to use the energy you were born with.*

As for the way Nizer manages his own energy, he not only maintains a demanding schedule but—like other high-energy people—he likes to do several things at the same time when he can, and he does this quite successfully. "Sometimes, while watching television and playing cards, I've simultaneously written a few pages of a book," he told me. This isn't as impossible as it sounds, for it seems he always thinks things through carefully before he begins to write, and "what I've thought through I can write down. It doesn't matter what else I'm doing at the time. It's part of a lawyer's training to be able to operate on several levels at once. I draw faces and heads of people while I'm in the courtroom; sketching doesn't distract me—if anything, it helps me concentrate." Anyone, he said, can learn to operate on several levels simultaneously.

Reaching Beyond Your Limits

Though Nizer's vitality is indeed phenomenal, it's clearly his approach to life that liberates his energy and allows him to tap its full potential. *Many people do less than they could because they believe they're already doing all they can do, but Nizer sets no such limits on himself.* He believes that most people use no more than 10 or 15 percent of their natural capacities, that we all have inner resources we haven't even begun to explore. As proof, he cites the physical feats people sometimes manage under hypnosis and the marvels of the human brain.

An incident in his own life illustrates what you can do if you believe in, and draw on, the untapped powers of the mind. Years ago, while Nizer was undergoing minor surgery in a dentist's office, the surgeon accidentally cut his carotid artery, in effect slitting his throat. However, immediate packing staunched all bleeding, and so the wound wasn't discovered at the time. Several days later, when the packing was removed, the artery gushed, and the surgeon was visibly frightened. In fact, as Nizer was being rushed to the hospital in a taxi, he saw from the look on the dentist's face that the man believed him to be bleeding to death. However, he also realized that if he became panicky his heart would beat faster and accelerate the pumping action of the artery, so he forced himself to remain calm. He closed his eyes, relaxed every muscle in his body until he was completely limp and still, and he even breathed as softly as he could. By the time he reached the hospital, the bleeding was beginning to slow down and soon afterward it stopped of its own accord. "That was self-discipline and perspective," he explained.

Nizer describes this incident in his most recent book, *Reflections Without Mirrors*. In the same book he also writes, "Sheer will can triumph over great odds. He who will not be beaten can't be beaten." When I read that, it struck me that Nizer's achievements are due to his natural vitality, his belief that he has almost boundless inner resources to call upon, and to the fact that he knows so clearly who he is and what he wants from life.

You Can Outgrow Your Energy

Louis Nizer is probably right in saying that many—but not all —of the world's super-achievers *are* people born with the gift of unusual vitality. He's definitely right in his assumption that this sort of inborn energy doesn't guarantee success. It doesn't even guarantee a fully energized adult, for sometimes intense, highly active children grow up to be human slugs. Other youngsters spend their childhood perpetually on the sidelines, watching, and yet they develop into adults who lead extraordinarily productive lives. Clearly, a lot can happen to energy on the way to adulthood.

The Case for Heredity

It's also quite clear that energy *is* partly hereditary, since *energy differences exist at birth and even earlier.* Any woman who has borne two or more children knows that in the womb some babies are much more active than others. Almost from the moment of birth infants make their energy felt: Some are tiny, bright-eyed insomniacs, never really still except when they're sound asleep; others are remarkably placid and seem to swallow the world with their eyes, though they're not given to moving around much. It's possible to spot the energy extremes—the sprinters and the strollers—while the child is still in the bassinet, and to make a pretty fair guess at the energy potential of many trotters as well. In fact, the energy level is so apparent in babies and seems to be such a fundamental aspect of personality that over the years a number of child-development experts have focused on it. In *Infants and Mothers,* for example, Dr. T. Berry Brazelton, the eminent Harvard pediatrician, describes in detail the early development of three basic types of infants: active, average, and quiet. When I asked him why he had picked energy as *the* distinguishing feature, he explained that it's the trait that's apt to bother mothers and fathers the most. Presented with an infant who is extremely active, some parents feel inadequate while others are delighted to have such a lively offspring. Similarly, the solemn, quiet baby disappoints some parents, while others will say enthusiastically, "She's such a good baby!" Thus, *the baby's energy type—and the way the parents react to it—can shape relationships within the family from the beginning.*

The Impact of the Family Environment

Parents bring their own energy prejudices to the business of raising a child, and these prejudices play a role in the child's development and in determining his adult energy level. For example, parental expectations about sex roles are often significant. Parents are more likely to be disappointed in a low-energy baby if that baby is a boy, since boys in this culture are supposed to be vigorous and assertive. Conversely, a couple may feel quite disconcerted if their infant daughter metamorphoses into one of those driving, never-still-for-a-moment toddlers, since that doesn't fit the culture's definition of "feminine." When parents believe that their child is somehow not quite normal, the child often comes to believe it too. The inner tensions that result take their toll in energy.

Parents also work from another prejudice: their own body truth. On a gut level and in ways that may never be verbalized, a mother who is a hurdler understands, and resonates with, the tempo at which her hurdler son operates. Conversely, a stroller who has a sprinter for a son may never really understand the boy's need to be in almost perpetual motion.

Furthermore, parents have positive and negative feelings about their own energy, and those feelings can affect the way they react to their children. A high-energy mother who has a high-energy daughter will be proud of her and will encourage her to make the most of her vitality—provided the mother herself feels good about her own strong inner drive. If, instead, she has always felt that she's almost a freak because she has too much "nervous" energy, then she won't be pleased to see her "problem trait" reproduced in her child.

Then again, some parents equate a lack of energy with ill health and pass along this prejudice to their children. One man I talked to recalled that he had had rheumatoid arthritis as a child. "As I began to recover," he said, "I learned not to complain when I felt tired, because my mother always took any lapse of energy as a sign that I'd taken a turn for the worse. She was forever warning me that I mustn't tire myself or I might get sick again." Many years later he discovered, with a sense of incredulous relief, that he *could* actually push himself to the limit with no ill effects.

If, when you were a child, your parents felt that you had too much energy or too little, or if they worried aloud every time your vitality flagged, there's a good chance that their attitudes still color your feelings about yourself and your energy; I'll have more to say about that a little later on.

Energy—and the Rest of Your Temperament

Energy doesn't operate in a vacuum. Other human traits also appear to be hereditary and are present at birth; they determine how a child spends her (or his) energy and how manageable she's likely to be. Some youngsters are simply born "difficult": They're harder to live with and harder to raise than most children. Their energy, in combination with other traits, plays a part in their problem, though not in quite the way you might expect.

According to a pioneering study that began in 1956 and was still going strong almost twenty-five years later, *there are nine traits that collectively form a person's basic temperament.* These traits were identified by Drs. Alexander Thomas and Stella Chess, a husband-and-wife team of psychiatrists on the staff of the New York University School of Medicine. Thomas and Chess followed a group of over a hundred children from infancy through young adulthood, chronicling the way their basic traits developed and ultimately jelled into an adult personality.

Energy Differences at Birth

Though none of the traits are labeled "energy," two seem to correspond in different ways to the inner force we're concerned with in this book. First of all, Thomas and Chess kept tabs on each child's "activity level"—a term that simply refers to the fact that even as babies some children move around much more than others. They also recorded "intensity of response," a measure of the amount of energy a child invests in the things he does. In *Your Child Is a Person,* a book they wrote with Dr. Herbert G. Birch, Chess and Thomas explain: "One baby may open his mouth for a second spoonful of food he likes without any other movements. This is a response of mild intensity. On another occasion he might open his mouth, turn toward the dish, and strain actively toward the spoon with his whole body. Such a response is one of high intensity. The child of preponderantly low intensity smiles gently, but his vigorous companion chortles, gurgles and kicks when he is happy." The more intense youngster also cries more loudly when he's hungry or uncomfortable.

Though it would seem logical to assume that high activity and intensity go together, Chess and Thomas actually found that this was not the case. Dr. Chess said, "The degree of physical motion and the degree of internal steam did not have any real correlation. You could have easygoing kids running around at great speed as well as high-intensity kids running around." Whether we think of intensity as a form of mental or emotional energy, the fact remains that *some youngsters seem to feel things more and want things harder than others do.* Some also express these feelings intensely; this driving quality is there from birth. (Other children who feel deeply may express very little; it's part of a parent's job to understand that the response is still there.) Intensity is undeniably one facet of energy. The fact that it's not wedded to the need for physical activity suggests that energy is indeed a complex phenomenon and that *there certainly is more than one kind of energy.*

Intensity, rather than a high activity level, can, in combination with other traits, make a child hard to live with. That fact was brought home to me by talks I had with two mothers who had youngsters of about the same age. Both kids were unusually active, but there the similarity ended. One was definitely a handful to manage, whereas the other wasn't.

Highly Energized Children

"Dana is adopted," her mother, Terry, said. "She was six months old when we got her and it was immediately obvious that she had tremendous energy. She was completely bald in the back because she was always moving; she moved by arching her back and sliding on her head. Though she slept more than other babies did—I guess she just wore herself out—whenever she was awake she was very, very active."

Dana is nine now and she's still an energetic and noisy child. "I enjoy her," Terry said. "She's really fun. But I have friends who don't like to be around her because she won't sit still and she hates to be ignored."

Dana needs constant activity and company, so Terry has worked hard to provide her with playmates and things to do. "Otherwise," she said, "she'd wear me out." An after-school play group that features sports has been a godsend. It has also helped Terry to structure her daughter's time, something she feels is important for very active children. Thus, Dana is in school until three, has the play group from four to six, then does her homework and has dinner. Afterward she's allowed an hour of television and then it's bedtime. She reads for about half an hour in bed, but even after that it usually takes her an hour to fall asleep; she has always had a tendency to become so wound up that she has trouble letting go.

Dana is a very intense child. "She's extreme in everything," Terry said, "not only in her energy but in her emotions as well. She's either so angry you wouldn't believe it or she's overly loving, kind, and generous. She's one of the most affectionate children I've ever met—she doesn't do anything moderately."

Terry has put a lot of effort into trying to teach her daughter to direct her energy in constructive ways. "She does a lot of random running around," she said. "She'll get all involved in playing wildly with the dog, so that she forgets to get dressed in the morning. She gets sidetracked easily, too, and then she becomes upset because she doesn't have time to do her homework properly. I tell her she has to try to plan ahead and concentrate on one thing at a time.

"I'm a teacher and so in school I see many children who have too much undirected energy. I have a feeling that's how Dana could have turned out, too. It's the way she used to be, but she's much better now and actually she's doing fine in school."

Adam: Active but Independent

Adam, who is now seven, was also a difficult baby. "I thought he was hyperactive," his mother, Stella, said, "because he wasn't a sleeper." However, she eventually decided that if he was difficult it was partly because he had colic and partly because he couldn't focus very well—he had a lazy eye—and that was very frustrating for him.

Adam is not quite as intense as Dana, but he certainly is as active. He's one of those youngsters who did everything early. By the time he was nine months old he was not only walking but running. He was a fast mover, a child who tended to fidget, and he was extremely verbal. Stella feels that it made a vast difference that he was also an independent youngster with an impressive attention span. "Adam always found something to do," she said. "As soon as he was old enough to play in his crib, I could sleep late if I wanted to and he would busy himself with his toys. When he learned to ride a bike, he rode it and rode it. When he was in his room, he'd get out all his books. He loves music, too, and he'll listen to it by the hour."

Stella was delighted with Adam's independence and encouraged it. "At a very early age he'd ask me for an ice cream and I'd give him a dime and say, 'Go buy it,' and he would. If he was hungry, I'd say, 'Make yourself a sandwich.' He's been getting his own breakfast of cold cereal since he was three and a half. He developed confidence—he learned that he could do things for himself—and I think that's the whole key."

What Makes a Child Difficult?

Though both Dana and Adam are unusually active, Dana has obviously been a more difficult child to bring up than Adam. Her intensity is part of the problem, that "internal steam" that Dr. Chess spoke of.

In some ways, Dana fits the profile of the "difficult child." Chess and Thomas found that their nine traits tended to group themselves into three distinct patterns, and that two-thirds of the youngsters they studied fitted one or the other of these three patterns—they were either "easy," "difficult," or "slow to warm up."

Here is the complete list of the nine traits:

• Activity level

• Intensity

• Regularity (e.g., some infants eat and sleep on a regular schedule from the beginning while others remain irregular and unpredictable for a long time)

• Approach or withdrawal as a response to new situations

• Adaptability to change
• Sensory threshold level (i.e., how sensitive the child is to bright lights, loud noises, and so on)
• Positive or negative mood
• Distractability
• Persistence and attention span

Difficult children combine five of the nine traits in a particular way: They tend to be intense, irregular, negative, slow to adapt, and they generally react to new situations by drawing back. In other words, the baby's "internal steam" makes itself felt in negative moods and in resistance to change and to anything unfamiliar; and he's unpredictable in his sleeping and eating habits besides! Basically he's very vulnerable because he finds it so hard to cope with change.

Though the difficult child is not necessarily super-active, Dr. Chess noted, "If you have a highly intense child who happens not to like things more often than he likes them, and he also happens to be highly active, he's even harder to cope with." Such children are a real challenge to most parents.

Difficult Infants Are Born, not Made

In the Chess-Thomas study, the researchers found no evidence that the difficult child's traits were produced by parental ineptness. Some children had parents who managed them well, while others were handled badly. Some parents also had other children with different temperaments and were much more relaxed and effective with these easier siblings.

However, though temperament is what makes some children, from birth, more difficult than others, *personality itself evolves as upbringing modifies temperament.* This is nicely illustrated in the case histories of two of the study's difficult children.

Roger was lucky: His father saw him as "lusty" rather than "difficult." He cheerfully described to the researchers how loudly his son howled when confronted with his first bath, new foods, or strangers. Another man might have felt overwhelmed, but Roger's father, who was the quiet sort himself, felt that he had been something of a pushover as a child. He was very glad he had a son who was never going to duplicate his behavior. Thus, accepted for what he was and handled with patience, Roger thrived, gradually becoming less negative. Like some other difficult children in the study, he developed into a youngster with an enormous enthusiasm for life—the internal steam now definitely representing an asset.

David was both difficult and highly active, and his parents found him a trial. When he was a baby, he would fuss and cry for a week after any change in routine. As a toddler, he was into everything, and his parents were constantly at him to "sit still . . . stop running . . . don't touch." Unfortunately, he was the sort of child who just had to be on the move.

Faced with so many prohibitions and unable to comply with many of them, David became even more negative and rebellious. He was no fun to have around and his parents, guiltily aware that they felt differently about him than they did about his younger brother and sister, found it harder and harder to insist that he behave himself. As David grew older, personal demoralization and discouragement gradually blocked his energy; by the time he was seventeen, he was obese, apathetic, and low-active—sluggish, to use Dr. Chess's word.

Answering the Heredity-or-Environment Question

Psychologist Donald O. Hebb once remarked that we are 100 percent innate and 100 percent acquired. Personality is a joint product of inborn temperament and upbringing and, as should be clear by now, an adult's energy level is too.

More important, if a born sprinter like David can grow up to be a thoroughly de-energized adult, then *energy owes enough to upbringing to be very much subject to change.* Since the vicissitudes of life seem more likely to rob you of vitality than to invigorate you, it follows that many people really can hope to liberate their energy and lead a more vigorous life.

How to Take Your Own Energy History

As noted earlier, your basic attitudes do help to determine how much energy you have available. One thing you can do, then, to increase your vitality is to examine those attitudes, to see if some of them are getting in your way. In fact, you might take a kind of energy history, somewhat the way doctors take a medical history, to try to pin down exactly how you feel about your energy and why. Here are some of the questions you should ask yourself:

• How did your parents feel about your energy? Did they complain that you had too much? too little?

• Did they feel (and do you) that it's unfeminine for a woman to have a lot of drive, that a man *ought* to be vigorous and active? How did such prejudices affect you and the way you feel about yourself?

• When you felt low in energy, did your parents panic and assume that you must be sick? Do you tend to panic in the same circumstances today?

• Do you have the feeling that you're fragile physically, that you must be careful not to overspend your energy?

• What about your angry energy? Were you expected not to have any? Or was it all right to feel angry as long as you kept a tight rein on your behavior?

• What were you expected to do with your sexual energy? Did you dare admit that you had any?

• Do you feel fragile emotionally? Does it seem risky to experience emotions too intensely, to want things too badly?

Most people are stronger and tougher than they think they are and—as Louis Nizer said—have inner resources they're not even aware of. *When you believe in yourself—in your strengths and resources—you extend your reach and free your energy.*

Raising Children to Be Fully Energized Adults

As a parent, there are several things you can do to help your children realize their full energy potential.

1. Recognize what your own energy prejudices are and accept your child as she (or he) is.

2. If she's a stroller or relatively low in energy, don't underestimate her. Many people, including parents, mistake low energy for low intelligence. There's no connection at all.

3. If she's a sprinter, realize that she may have a real need to be up and moving, that it may be genuinely difficult for her to sit still for any length of time. Channel her energy into sports or other vigorous activities if you can.

4. Some youngsters have a tendency to get carried away by their own intensity: They become more and more excited and then don't know how to unwind. Dr. Brazelton has suggested that when such a child is an infant, parents should carry her often in a restraining sling; feed her in a dim, quiet room; rock her and allow her extra suckling; and teach her how to quiet herself by sucking her thumb. With older children it's sometimes helpful to structure their time and to set aside a quieting-down period at the end of every day.

5. As for the difficult child, from their studies Chess and Thomas have developed some definite ideas about how to handle her. First of all, whenever it's at all possible allow her to take her time and become familiar with a new situation before insisting that she get right into it. Equally important, try not to respond to her intensity, when it's expressed as a tantrum, by allowing her to become a tyrant. It's tempting to give in to such a child, or else to do battle constantly. Some people feel terribly guilty about their child's "bad" behavior, convinced that they themselves must somehow be to blame, and so they're either punitive or appeasing—or they vacillate between the two. If you can be firm, steady, patient, and consistent for a long enough period (the figure Dr. Chess mentioned was five years), the difficult child will gradually improve and become less negative, and problems will subside.

6. Whether she's difficult or not, you can help your child to distinguish between what she feels and how she behaves. You can explain to her that anything she feels is acceptable, but that you have definite expectations about her behavior: that it's all right to feel angry, for example, but it's not all right to throw a temper tantrum. The idea is to acknowledge—and protect—that internal steam while insuring that it's released in acceptable ways.

Tracking Energy to its Sources in the Body

I've suggested both in this chapter and in an earlier section that nervous energy isn't the same thing as the kind of energy that flows and feels good.

Now it's time to consider how the two might be different and why, to look for physiological explanations for the energy experience. The next chapter will take up such questions. Because it concerns the physiology of energy, Chapter 3 is necessarily somewhat technical. I've presented in considerable detail the evidence that supports my conclusions about what energy really is and why it's so important in your life and mine. You'll be reading about brain chemicals and hormones, and about current theories regarding mental illness and stress. However, you won't need to master all the details to follow the major points in my argument —or to understand how they apply to your own energy.

3

The Physiology of Energy:
Your Body and Brain

What *is* energy? Where in the body does it come from? Why do some people have so much more energy than others—and how are those high-vitality people different from everyone else? Is nervous energy physiologically different from enerjoy? And why, for most of us, does vitality fluctuate so dramatically from moment to moment and from day to day?

Physiology: Where the Clues Come From

Intriguing and important though they are, these are difficult questions, for science supplies no ready-made answers. Energy has never been fully investigated by researchers, partly because there's no way to record and measure it and so there's no way to experiment with it scientifically. Yet if we're to have better access to our own vitality, we *need* to understand the physiology of energy: to pin it down, as far as this is possible, to specific anatomy or body chemistry or internal processes of some sort—to where it "comes from" in the body. And there *are* clues that suggest tentative answers to the questions I've posed.

To begin with, there are the experiences of people who suffer from an energy disorder, from a disease whose primary symptoms include an excess or dearth of energy. I'll introduce two such men shortly, each of whom has suffered in a very different way from an energy excess. Other clues come from the medical literature, especially from recent research on brain chemistry. And, finally, there are clues that are simply body truths that reflect the way people describe their own energy experiences.

The conclusions I've drawn, based on these sources, are all

quite speculative, but they do suggest certain approaches to maximizing the energy you have.

Locating the Energy in Your Body

What is energy and where is it "located"? It seems clear to me that *energy is a whole-body phenomenon.* In fact, there's probably very little that goes on in your body or mind that doesn't affect your energy in one way or another, though some things have a much greater impact than others.

At any given moment your sense of your own energy—of your potential for action—depends on your state of health; on whether you've had enough sleep; on your blood sugar level; on the demands you're making on your body and whether you're physically fit to handle them; on the time of day (night owls, for example, typically haven't much energy first thing in the morning); on how much stress you're under and how well you handle it; on the *mood* you're in; on how motivated you are; and on other things as well. We'll talk about all of these factors in the chapters to come, but in the meanwhile, as far as the answer to our question is concerned, the implications are obvious: *Your energy is the sum total of hundreds of ordinary bodily events, and it's also determined by mood and mind—it's generated simultaneously in every corner of your being.*

What Gives Sprinters Their Edge?

However, all of the features just mentioned are transient, related to the way energy fluctuates but not to inborn differences. They supply no explanation for the fact that all their lives some people have so much more vitality than others.

Where *do* sprinters get their energy? Are they physically different in some way from those of us who can't match their pace?

Many people would suggest that energy differences are a matter of basic metabolism, that vitality itself is actually a product of metabolism. Knowing that the cells of the body burn food with oxygen to produce something nutritionists call "energy," they conclude that perhaps some people have bodies that burn it more efficiently: Because these people have a higher rate of metabolism, they have more energy.

However, the fact is that the basal metabolic rate (BMR) varies only slightly among normal people. What's more, though the question is not one that has been systematically researched, several endocrinologists assured me that there's no evidence that people who have a slightly higher BMR are higher in energy as well. In any case, the "energy" produced by metabolism operates at the level of the individual cell, and though it certainly does play a part in the overall experience of energy, that part isn't the starring role that many people imagine it to be.

But if metabolism isn't the answer, it's possible that brain chemistry is. For if energy is a kind of continuum stretching from very low to very high, then out beyond the sprinter at the high end of the scale are the manic-depressives—at least while they're in a manic state. Since many psychiatrists today believe that manic-depression is caused by an imbalance among chemicals in the brain, it seems very possible that *the same sort of chemistry that produces mania might, in a less volatile mix, provide sprinters with a life supply of unusual energy.* Of course, brain chemistry could also help to explain the energy swings of the hurdlers.

What is it like to be manic, to have too much energy? Is there really any similarity to the sort of energy high that all of us experience at times? I learned a great deal about mania from a conversation I had with a lawyer.

The Manic High

Max is a hard-working junior partner in a small law firm, and he's highly thought of by his colleagues. Only his close friends know that he's manic-depressive, for these days he takes a drug called lithium, which keeps his moods and energy within the normal range.

While he was in college, Max endured one bleak and lengthy period of depression, but he recovered completely when he was treated with antidepressants. The dimensions of his problem didn't become clear until he was in his late twenties and had a manic episode.

"For a while there I was euphoric twenty-four hours a day," Max recalled, "and the energy I had was extraordinary. I had my first job with a law firm then, and I was working long hours, but I was also writing a novel on the side. I found I could work every night until 4 A.M., grab an hour or two of sleep, and then get up and start all over again. I felt fantastic—powerful, creative, bursting at the seams. Even my eyesight and hearing seemed sharper than normal, and I was sure I was extraordinarily intuitive—I seemed to know things about people without ever being told.

"Of course, afterward I realized that some of what I did and said during that period was pretty crazy, but at the time, when people tried to slow me up, I got very impatient. I didn't understand what was wrong with the rest of the world because I was sure there was nothing wrong with me."

Eventually Max crashed: The mania subsided and he sank into a deep, almost paralyzing depression. This time, when he went to see a psychiatrist he was diagnosed as manic-depressive and was put on lithium.

What Mania Is Like

The normal person oscillates between activity and rest, but the manic has little interest in rest. In fact, he often seems to be entirely unaware of his own physical needs because of the way his mind is racing. His energy and his emotions are out of control.

Nevertheless, he isn't disconnected from reality in the way that a schizophrenic is, but may instead function, at least for a time, at the absolute top of his form. Usually he feels euphoric, expansive, omnipotent; and if he's intelligent to begin with and succeeds in channeling all that energy, he may be capable of prodigious things.

However, mania manifests itself differently in different people. According to Dr. Baron Shopsin, a psychiatrist who treats manic-depressives—and heads the Affective Disorder Research Treatment Unit at New York University Medical Center—though one patient may experience great joy and have great charm, another may feel mounting anger, his energy fueling an astounding rage. But either way, the manic is almost certain to come into conflict eventually with family, colleagues, and friends. "Sooner or later," Dr. Shopsin said, "the manic construction worker is in there telling the construction chief that he's an idiot, or the manic lawyer will call the judge a fool. They can't gauge the consequences of what they say and do. They are often litigious and spend money excessively. Mania frequently leads to family alienation and divorce, and perhaps difficulties with the civil law authorities."

In addition, some patients begin to feel frightened as the mania swings toward its peak. They know they're high and they're afraid they're going to crash. One man described the experience to Dr. Shopsin as "riding the bonsai rail." That's what surfers call the huge waves of Hawaii; they're supposed to be the ultimate ride—but they're also the ultimate crash.

If mania is an unparalleled energy high, depression at the other end of the cycle is an energy low that's about as low as it's possible to get. Some more fortunate patients will dissolve out of a high into a period of normal living that may last for months or even years before depression sets in. Others crash quite suddenly: After months spent in a state of constant euphoria, with no warning they'll wake up one morning feeling totally inert and depressed. While in a manic phase, one young woman began looking for a better job, became engaged, signed a lease for an apartment she couldn't afford, and charged hundreds of dollars' worth of new furniture to her account. Then she swung abruptly into depression and attempted suicide.

Giving up Mania—with Mixed Feelings

Today manic-depression is a treatable illness. Patients like Max can be maintained on lithium so that their mood swings are tempered and brought within a normal range. For psychiatrists such as Dr. Shopsin, lithium has seemed at times to pose a moral question, at least in regard to patients who are artistic or creative. "Before the lithium," he explained, "they might feel worthless for six months of the year and be completely unproductive, but during the next high they'd make up for it. When we normalized their behavior and mood with lithium, they'd come back to us saying that they were no longer creative during their high periods. However, over the years we found that for many of them it was worth the trade, that if they were truly talented they'd start to get their highs from sitting down and beginning to create and feeling good about what they were doing, like almost everybody else, rather than having to feel high *before* they could create."

There's a moral in that observation. Most of us know that it's easier to produce when you're feeling really good: A little bit of euphoria can take you a long way. But in most people's lives euphoria is a fairly rare occurrence. One way to make it happen, though, is to invest a lot of effort in some challenging project, whether it's writing a novel or reupholstering a chair. *Creative work, when it's going well, often generates joy and soaring energy.*

Mania Is a Matter of Chemistry

Though not every psychiatrist agrees, Dr. Shopsin is completely convinced that the so-called mood disorders and schizophrenias are indeed caused by a chemical imbalance in the brain. "I don't think environmental factors have anything fundamental to do with it," he said. The disorders seem to represent a hereditary biochemical defect. There have been reports of twins separated from birth who developed psychotic symptoms at almost exactly the same point in time when they reached their twenties or thirties. Dr. Shopsin also mentioned a recent Belgian study of manic-depressives who were adopted at birth: Where the disease seemed to "run in the family," it was to be found in the original biological family but not in the adopting family.

In addition, Dr. Shopsin pointed out that heavy doses of an amphetamine (which seems to ignite energy) will produce symptoms similar to, or identical with, those of mania, while a drug called reserpine can produce severe depression. If the symptoms of a disease can be duplicated by chemicals introduced into the body in the form of drugs, it seems reasonable that disturbances in the body chemistry—specifically, in the neurotransmitters within the brain—might be the cause of the disease itself rather than a mismanaged childhood or some emotional conflict.

The Chemistry of Inborn Energy

If mania is caused by brain chemicals gone awry, and sprinters owe their edge largely to chemistry, then there's a broader implication as well. *It's very possible that all of us derive our basic energy level, our inborn potential, primarily from the brain's ingredients.* Dr. Shopsin and other psychiatrists and brain researchers I talked to believe that's probably so. They suggested that the genes may prescribe a particular balance of the various chemical regulators of the brain, and that this balance, which presumably varies from person to person, largely explains why people are so different in their energy level right from the moment of birth.

However, though your potential at birth may be mostly a matter of brain chemistry, over the years emotional traumas and other events could alter that chemistry and your potential along with it. In addition, *at any given moment your energy level really is a whole-body phenomenon, the sum of many factors overlaying that basic biochemical potential.*

How Is Energy Built into the Brain?

If we assume that brain chemistry has a lot to do with inborn energy, then the logical question is: Which chemicals and which brain mechanisms are involved?

For answers we can look again to theories that have been developed to try to explain manic-depression. Most of those theories do focus on the brain's chemical signaling system. (While the material that follows may seem complicated, stick with me for a few pages. The research does appear to add up to a rough picture of the way your energy potential may be built into your brain. In order to understand this, you really do need to know a little bit about how brain chemicals work.)

The average human brain weighs three pounds and has about a hundred billion nerve cells, or *neurons*. To the naked eye, of course, each of those cells is no bigger than a speck, but under a microscope most neurons look like the stringy root of a plant. Each has a single nodule (the *cell body*) that trails a long, branching stem, its *axon*. The axon's diameter is measured in thousandths of a millimeter, but it can be anywhere from a tenth of a millimeter to more than a meter (about thirty-nine inches) in length! Within the brain, neurons are densely packed, entwined in a kind of cerebral snarl that's really a highly organized communication network.

Many people believe that the brain's nerve cells communicate with one another by electricity. Actually, nerve impulses are transmitted partly by electricity and partly by chemistry. In each nerve cell, near the axon's end points, a chemical called a *neurotransmitter* is stored. When an electrical signal sizzles along the length of the axon, it triggers the cell so that the transmitter chemical is squirted out into the *synapse*—the minute gap that separates the cell from its neighbors. The transmitter diffuses across the synapse and its individual molecules connect with *receptors* on the surfaces of neighboring cells.

Receptors are large protein molecules embedded in the cell's outer membrane that project into the synapse. The surface of each receptor has a particular shape, as do the molecules of the transmitter substance. When the shape of the transmitter molecule matches the shape of the receptor, the transmitter fits into the receptor the way a key fits into a lock. Once that connection is made, mechanisms within the receiving cell are triggered, a new electrical impulse may be generated, and the original signal is passed along.

Meanwhile, the receptors and the synapse must be cleared for action and the transmitter disposed of or the system will become clogged and will respond to new signals slowly or not at all. The transmitter chemical is thus rapidly deactivated. Either it's broken down by other chemicals, called *enzymes*, right where it is or it's sucked back into the original cell to be broken down or recycled.

The Chemistry of Moods and Dreams

So far several dozen different neurotransmitters have been discovered in the human body, and undoubtedly there are many more to be found. Most neurons seem to be specialized in that they make only one kind of transmitter; there are nerve cells that manufacture dopamine and others that produce serotonin, norepinephrine, and so on.

The neurons that make a particular transmitter generally occur in clusters or form pathways within the brain. Since scientists are familiar with the geography of the brain—they know pretty well which areas control which human functions—once they've localized a transmitter they can guess some of the functions it might be involved in. In addition, by determining how various drugs affect transmitters, and combining that information with the way those drugs affect the body and behavior, researchers gather more information. Thus, they can say, tentatively, that the ebb and flow of serotonin seems to control the onset of sleep; that norepinephrine probably plays a part in dreaming and emotional responses; that dopamine neurons apparently help to determine how good you feel, how aroused you are, and how well coordinated.

Furthermore, scientists have developed theories to explain the way malfunctions in the chemical system might produce certain illnesses. They're fairly sure, for example, that Parkinson's disease, which manifests itself in muscle tremors, is caused by the loss of brain cells that make dopamine. Recently some researchers have also suggested that if the elderly move more slowly and have slower reflexes and less energy than they had when they were younger, it may be because in old age the brain has less dopamine.

Visualizing the Brain's Energy Mechanisms

As for manic-depression, some scientists believe that the swing into mania occurs because the brain is producing too much of a transmitter such as norepinephrine or serotonin, and that the plunge into depression happens because suddenly, instead of generating an oversupply, the brain begins to produce too little of the same substance. However, there's no real agreement as to exactly which brain chemicals might be involved, and many of the experts now say that this explanation is much too simple.

They point out that the brain's chemical transmission system is so complex that there are many steps at which something might go wrong. Cells could be hypersensitive, for example, and over-react to a perfectly normal chemical message. Either the enzyme that dismantles the transmitter might be in short supply or the mechanism that sucks it back into the sending cell could be faulty. In either case the transmitter would linger in the synapse, and that would have much the same effect as if too much transmitter had been released to begin with. There are also things that could go wrong within the receiving cell after the transmitter has connected with the receptor.

Then again, in manic-depression the fault might lie in the brain's electrical signaling system, or in aberrations produced by some of the myriad other chemicals present in the brain whose functions we don't yet understand.

It follows that any of these mechanisms could also be responsible for the sprinter's inborn abundance of energy—or for anyone else's energy potential. Your brain may produce more than the usual amount of a crucial neurotransmitter—or less; it may be especially sensitive (or not so sensitive) to some transmitters; it might make a lot or a little of a crucial enzyme that dismantles a crucial transmitter, and so on.

Obviously, it's too early to draw specific conclusions about the biochemistry of manic-depression or energy potential. However, once you're aware of the way brain chemistry works, it becomes easier to understand how your energy potential might be prescribed within your brain.

For our purposes, what's important is the fact that *many researchers do feel that brain chemistry holds the explanation for the manic's mood and energy swings, and so it may well explain inborn energy differences, too.*

Locating the "Nervous" Energy in Your Body

Let's turn now to the question of nervous energy: Is it physiologically different from enerjoy? I believe it is. Actually, most of us know from our own experience that the two kinds of energy do feel very different. Enerjoy feels good and seems to depend largely on *mood*. Nervous energy, on the other hand, can be unpleasant. It makes itself felt as hyperalertness, tension, a restless drive to be up and moving; sometimes we experience symptoms of anxiety as well. Nervous energy seems to be a reaction to stress; I'll have more to say about that later.

Beyond the evidence of my senses and yours, I have another reason for believing that nervous energy arises from different sources than enerjoy. I'm persuaded by conversations I've had with a man who has suffered, as Max has, from an excess of energy. Peter's experience was completely unlike Max's, and his difficulty was created by a different sort of bodily malfunction.

The Hyperthyroid High

Peter is a tall, thin business executive in his forties. Twenty years ago he was diagnosed as hyperthyroid, which means that his thyroid gland was producing too much thyroid hormone. His condition was uncomfortable and dangerous, so he was given radioactive iodine, which killed off part of his gland. Unfortunately, the treatment destroyed too much tissue, leaving him *hypo*thyroid (his body now produces too little of the hormone), so that he now has to take thyroid supplements daily. The medication is quite benign, he says, except that occasionally it seems to get out of balance: He begins to feel that he's taking too much or too little, and he has to adjust the dosage. Just recently he decided it was time to cut back, since he was feeling too keyed up and was finding it hard to sleep.

"When you're getting too much thyroid hormone, you feel energetic, of course, and that's better than feeling down, but it's not pleasant," Peter said. "You breathe more shallowly, you feel your heart beating fast, your hands tremble, you sweat a lot, you're always thirsty, and you feel very, very nervous. The symptoms are just like the symptoms of anxiety. In fact, it's always hard for me to sort out at any given time whether I'm anxious about something, whether I'm taking too much of the medication, or whether it's both."

When he's taking more thyroid supplement than he needs, Peter has too much jittery, nervous energy. However, his energy high is not at all like the sense of boundless, flowing power that Max has experienced, nor is Peter's problem due to brain chemistry.

Most people can remember times when they felt euphoric, powerful, bursting with energy, and other times when they were strung out on nervous drive. Such experiences are like briefer, paler versions of the energy highs that Max and Peter described. It seems quite possible that mania is caused by a malfunction of a brain system that normally generates energy and good feelings, and that hyperthyroidism is a malfunction in a body system that normally contributes some of the steam in nervous drive. If that's so, then *enerjoy and nervous energy must be as different physiologically as are mania and thyroid disease.*

Energy Fluctuations: The Mood Factor

Let's consider the fourth question now: Why does energy fluctuate so? Since vitality is a whole-body phenomenon, it's affected by many different factors, most of which are frequently in a state of flux, from your blood sugar level to your need for sleep. The most important factor is undoubtedly mood. Your emotions have an overwhelming impact both on enerjoy and on nervous energy, though in each case different physiological mechanisms are involved.

Enerjoy ebbs and flows with mood: That's a body fact most

people are aware of. When you're feeling good about life in general and yourself in particular, you almost always have a lot of energy as well, whereas depression saps vitality.

Your moods, in turn, are related to the chemistry of your brain, probably to particular neurotransmitters. For instance, scientists have discovered that rats will repeatedly and eagerly perform tasks that will earn them a quick fix of norepinephrine or dopamine; apparently these chemicals are a source of pleasure. Perhaps in some way they mediate energy as well. It's too early to be able to say just how mood and energy might be linked in the brain, but it's possible to suggest *why* they may have become linked in the course of evolution. It's in the interest of survival for humans to experience an uprush of energy and the urge to move out and explore at times when they're feeling particularly good, and to lose that urge when they're feeling badly.

What Makes Energy Fluctuate?

Nervous energy often makes itself felt in the wake of some strong and perhaps negative emotion: It's there at times when you're feeling frightened, angry, anxious, or merely excited—keyed up in anticipation of some event. There may be other times as well when you're fluttery with nervous vitality, though you can't imagine why; but even then some emotion has almost certainly triggered your energy, whether or not you can identify the feelings involved.

For *nervous energy seems to be a response to stress.* When people describe it, the symptoms they report—tension, restlessness, perhaps a rapid heartbeat and a vague sense of apprehension—sound very much like the bodily changes that are part of the famous fight-or-flight response.

The human body responds continually and automatically to the world around it. Evolution has cleverly designed it so that although it ordinarily idles along in order to conserve its resources, when danger threatens it gears up quickly for maximum effort. The heart beats faster, blood pressure rises, more blood flows to the muscles; metabolism also speeds up; there's more sugar in the blood; the mind becomes more alert; and many other physical changes occur.

This useful phenomenon is known as the fight-or-flight response because it prepares a person either to fight or to run away. The response may be triggered within the brain, but it's orchestrated by the endocrine glands,* which pump hormones into the bloodstream that carry the emergency signal to individual body cells. I believe *it's the general gearing up produced by those hormone signals that we experience as nervous energy.*

It's quite clear that *some hormones do have a major impact on your energy.* Because the glands are constantly at work, pumping their products into the bloodstream, it's not easy to single out any one of them and describe the exact effect it has on energy. However, we can draw some conclusions from pathology—from the experiences of people like Peter, who produce too much or too little of a particular hormone. There have also been experiments in which volunteers were given synthesized hormone in the form of a pill or an injection and bodily changes were recorded. Furthermore, in recent years new and sensitive techniques have been developed by which scientists can record minute amounts of hormone in blood samples, spinal fluid, or urine, so that they can measure the normal endocrine response under various conditions.

The Hormone Story: The Thyroid "Upper"

Thus, we know that the chemical messengers produced by the thyroid gland are among those that gear you up to meet an emergency. Thyroid hormones not only speed up metabolism throughout most of the body, but they also increase the rate of blood flow, the heart rate, respiration, and they stir up the intestines as well. They boost the activity of most other endocrine glands and they even accelerate the mental processes. In addition—and most important for our purposes—they provide an energy boost.

Though Peter found an excess of thyroxine distinctly uncom-

* The endocrine system includes the pituitary, parathyroid, thyroid, and adrenal glands, plus the thymus, pancreas, testes, ovaries, and placenta.

fortable, some people actually become addicted to it. New York endocrinologist Dr. Jack Richard explained, "When hypothyroid patients (those whose gland produces too little of the hormone) are allowed to adjust their own dosage of the medication, sometimes, if they're feeling a little tired, they'll boost the dose. Then the body adjusts and they find that even on the new dosage they're feeling tired again, so they'll boost it some more." They may wind up eventually taking massive amounts and using the medication the way others use amphetamines.

The Adrenaline Assist

Energy is also affected by epinephrine, sometimes called adrenaline. At times of crisis it's turned out in quantity by the pair of adrenal glands located near the kidneys, thus priming the body for action: It mobilizes blood sugar and speeds up the heart. Epinephrine can also increase the metabolic rate by as much as 100 percent. In fact, a shot of synthetic epinephrine produces such a rush of energy that for a few minutes afterward individuals feel capable of doing things they couldn't ordinarily do —such as feats of strength and clear thought. These people are apt to feel very alert and keyed up, though there's an optimum level; too much epinephrine can be downright disorienting.

The Cortisol High

The adrenal glands produce several other hormones as well, including cortisol, which clearly has an effect on energy. Cortisol closely resembles the drug cortisone; in the past, when cortisone was used in much larger doses than it is today, it often (but not always) seemed to generate energy and short-lived euphoria. This suggests that the body's own supply of cortisol may have a similar effect. Certainly, when the adrenal glands overproduce it, the result is an energy high, and when cortisol is in short supply, as it is in Addison's disease, the individual experiences overwhelming fatigue.

Cortisol is a hormone that has been closely studied, and so we know quite a lot about it. We know, for example, that cortisol production, like epinephrine production, increases during emergencies; and that your cortisol level is apt to respond even more dramatically when you're anticipating something stressful than it does while that something is actually happening to you. In other words, as a high school senior stands backstage waiting to give the valedictory address, her adrenal gland pours out cortisol; but while she's actually delivering the speech, the gland is less active. The cortisol level also climbs whenever a person is trying really hard.

Obviously, it's useful to have a hormone response that begins to tune up the body even before action is necessary, one that's psychologically triggered by apprehensiveness, anxiety, or fear!

How to Reset Your Tension Level

However, cortisol doesn't just surge in times of stress. Research has demonstrated that it also responds rapidly and sensitively to a variety of everyday events. For example, one study showed that in a patient who was hospitalized cortisol levels dropped over weekends, apparently because his surroundings were quieter then. Researchers have also reported that young adults who sat through a distressing war movie reacted with a rise in cortisol, while others who watched a Disney nature film showed a drop. Apparently, cortisol shifts up and down, shadowing our daily routine, responding to the small things we do that build or ease tension. Knitting, meditating, a back rub—all might lower cortisol production. Such activities may affect other hormones as well, for endocrine expert Dr. John Mason believes that the various glands function together as a closely co-ordinated system. It's possible, then, that someone who is chronically nerved up might be able to use everyday activities to tune down the endocrine system and bring nervous energy under better control.

Managing Moods to Manage Your Energy

To sum up: *Your energy fluctuates with your feelings.* Enerjoy depends on mood, and nervous energy is ignited by the emotions.

Those statements may sound like bad news if you're someone who feels helpless in the face of your own emotions, as many people do. It may seem to you that joy, anger, fear, and other feelings wash over you in waves; with each shift of emotions your energy surges or subsides, but you have no control over this internal turmoil.

However, there are ways to live more comfortably with your emotions and to tame fluctuating moods—and the energy fluctuations that go with them.

Emotions Are Information

The first thing you can do is to recognize that, uncomfortable though they may be at times, feelings are useful and necessary. We know that's true because evolution equipped us with a brain designed to generate emotions. In fact, Dr. Arnold Friedhoff, of the Department of Psychiatry at New York University School of Medicine, believes that brain chemicals operate as a kind of "psychostat," responding sensitively to situations much as a thermostat keeps adjusting furnace activity to maintain room temperature at the required setting. "If you're walking down a dark street at night," he explained, "you may experience a certain level of fear that has protective value. In that situation or in any other the psychostat makes you more or less alert, more or less apprehensive or attentive. It sets a tone against which things happen."

No one is a closed system. We respond constantly, physically as well as mentally, to the things that are going on around us. Our emotions exist to direct and focus that response: They provide a kind of running, nonverbal, gut-level commentary on events, playing into internal systems that mobilize our resources in anticipation of need.

Emotions also serve as a form of reward and punishment: They insure that we will do again the things that are good for us —and make us feel good—while avoiding the things that are bad. And in the welter of confusing detail that's the normal human ambience, emotions also tell us what to pay attention to and what to file away in our memories for future reference. They flag for us matters of importance.

In other words, emotions are information. It helps if you can learn to think of them that way, for many people are thrown off balance not by their primary emotions but by secondary ones, by the feelings they have about their feelings. They're afraid of their own anger, ashamed of the clammy pricklings of fear, apprehensive when they discover in themselves symptoms of anxiety. But *accepting your emotions is the first step toward managing the mood-and-energy connection.*

How to Achieve Perspective

The second step is to pay more attention to what you're telling yourself as problems arise, for what you tell yourself often determines what your feelings are. That's what perspective is all about, as Louis Nizer knows so well (see Chapter 2).

For instance, if your boss is in a foul mood and dresses you down for no good reason, there are any number of things you can tell yourself about what happened. You might decide that his behavior is intolerable and that you'll have to quit your job. Or it might occur to you that the man simply doesn't like you; if you're the sort of person who needs to feel liked, that insight could be devastating. Or you could shrug off the whole incident, simply making a mental note to try to steer clear of your employer on days when he's in a bad mood. The right response here is the one that reflects the reality of the situation, for *you achieve perspective when your emotions jibe with reality.*

Emotions Can Be Misinformation

Too often, however, your feelings whisper "Danger!" when there is none, or you flare into a fit of rage when mild annoyance is all that's called for. Dressed down by your boss, for example, you might feel as helpless and as overwhelmingly angry as you used to feel when your father yelled at you, and so you overreact.

Everyone responds to situations on the basis of past experience, but sometimes, in an almost automated way, you repeat a pattern—perhaps one learned in childhood—that may not be at all appropriate to present circumstances. You feel jealous, angry, put-upon, or threatened—and you may or may not realize that the feeling is exaggerated or doesn't fit the facts of the matter at all.

You can't break out of such a pattern until you understand where it came from, and that, of course, is what psychotherapy is all about. *Psychotherapy is a time-consuming but often highly effective way to learn to liberate and manage your emotions—and, through them, your energy.*

Quick-Energy Tips

1. If nervous energy is a problem for you, remember that it does exist for a purpose. The people I've talked to who seem to feel most comfortable with it all think of it as a resource. "Even when I can't decide why it's there, I find it handy," one man told me. "I can always find a way to turn it to use." It seems, then, that "Where shall I put it?" is a logical and constructive response to a flush of nervous energy.

2. You can tone down excessive nervous energy by making more room in your life for the ordinary activities that you find soothing: reading, warm baths, knitting, long walks.

3. Remind yourself that perspective is important. Tune in often on your own thoughts and test some of your hazy, half-formed conclusions against reality. One of the best ways to gain

perspective is to talk things out regularly with friends or to keep a diary. Problems seldom loom as large once they're out in the open.

Blocking Emotions Blocks Energy

I mentioned earlier that *often it's the emotions you have about your emotions that create problems for you.*

The worst sort of energy blockage occurs when you have such strong feelings about your feelings that you try to shut off certain emotions altogether. Frightened of your own competitive drive, or ashamed of your anger or jealousy, you try to blot out those feelings by damping down the bodily sensations that betray their presence and by shutting down your mind. Some people are so successful at this that they're totally unaware that their jealousy, anger, or competitiveness exist.

But that kind of success can dull your vitality, for you can't flow with your own energy while you're preoccupied internally with the job of turning off the feelings you're determined not to have.

If you want to liberate your energy, the most important (and the most difficult) step you can take is to liberate your emotions first. And that's the subject of the next chapter.

4

The Thrust and Drag of the Emotions

Boredom

"I'm suffering from terminal boredom," a stockbroker sighed. "I don't like my job or the cultural scene. I've been a broker for the past six years. It's a living and fairly exciting in one sense, but I'm working for upper-class people who are looking for a free ride and there's no serving, no love. It's a fairly brutal business and the people I work with are materialistic. At times I feel a kind of despair."

His energy level, he said, is low. Because of the frustration he feels, he's enormously tense, and so he's exhausted. Not knowing what else to do, he simply lives with the situation. The boredom itself is "a nullity, a deadness. Tediousness and repetition—nothing seems satisfying. Then I sink into depression. Boredom and depression are similar—one resonates into the other—and when the boredom becomes severe, I cross the line into despair."

Still, he considers himself fortunate compared to some of the brokers he works with. "There are guys in the office who are divorced and their boredom is *global*," he explained. "They go fishing or sailing for relief, or they use fast cars or partying, but mostly they have affairs. That's the big solution around here: the affair."

He himself is fortunate because he has a good marriage and "a bit of creative activity, something I can do." He has written several short stories that have been published. Unfortunately, that brought in very little money, but he states emphatically that writing is not boring at all! It's a challenge, and afterward there's something to show for it, an end product that will give pleasure to others. He'd like to make his living writing fiction, but for the moment he sees no way to manage that. Wistfully he notes, "If you're quickened by what you're doing, you don't feel bored or despairing."

Like many other Americans, this stockbroker is caught in a well-padded trap. He has a job he doesn't enjoy, but he can't afford to leave it. His boredom is a sign that he needs to take some action, if he possibly can, that will get him out of the trap.

But is that *all* that's going on here? I think not, for boredom is often caused by an energy blockage. It happens because you've deadened yourself, shut off your emotional energy to keep from feeling some particularly painful emotion. At the root of the broker's problem, then, there may be anxiety or rage that his life has turned out as it has, as well as the despair that he does acknowledge.

To Free Your Energy Feel Freely

When you block your emotions, you block energy. No one knows exactly why that's so; in fact, there's no scientific proof that it's true. However, most psychotherapists I know would be ready to swear to it.

Perhaps the physiological explanation lies in the fact that almost any emotion generates arousal as the body gears up for action of some sort. It may be costly, in terms of energy, to suppress that arousal or repress your awareness of it.

Be that as it may, *one of the most dramatic ways to release your energy is to allow yourself to feel more freely.* Sometimes, as people grow older and as circumstances change, they simply become freer. Sometimes it takes years of psychotherapy. Either way, fundamental personality changes must occur, and they don't happen easily or overnight; but when they do begin to happen, the flow of energy and of good feelings can be phenomenal.

When You Damp Down Rage, You Damp Down Energy

Anger is probably the emotion most often repressed. You can feel the urgent energy in anger, the drive to strike out, to *do* something. Yet many people almost never give vent to that energy. They're unable to strike out or even to talk back—and, what's worse, they're unable to feel their own anger either. They've learned in childhood that it's "not nice" to get mad, that if they do they'll be rejected and no longer loved. Some are actually frightened that if they were ever to lose their temper, they'd go completely out of control. Others are afraid even to think angry thoughts, because they're still haunted by the childhood fantasy that by wishing someone harm you can actually hurt them.

Women have a harder time dealing with their rage than men do and are more likely to repress it, because nothing in our culture condones anger in a woman. A man is supposed to be somewhat aggressive and is expected to defend himself at times, but it's never all right for a woman to lose her temper unless she's willing to be thought unfeminine or a shrew.

Yet anger is part of the human condition. And so, if you're the kind of person who almost never feels angry, you might do well to ask yourself whether that's because you never *allow* yourself to feel angry. Furthermore, the next time you wake up in the morning feeling terribly tired for no particular reason and slightly depressed, you can consider the possibility that you're actually angry about something, and that you're depressed because you're deadening that angry energy. If you can connect with the feeling and can tolerate the whine and crackle of your own rage, even just for a few moments, usually your energy will ignite and the depression will disappear.

What's more, contradictory as it sounds, the key to behaving reasonably is acknowledging—and allowing—your own *un*reasonable emotional responses. Emotions are often far from reasonable, but if you close your mind to them because of that, then you're off guard and you may act on those shadowy feelings without ever intending to. If you're angry, for example, and you're also unaware of your anger, you're apt to take out your feelings on the person you're angry with in subtle, underhanded ways; or you may instead bend over backward and become a kind of doormat for this individual, because you're ashamed of your anger or frightened of it—though you may be as unaware of those feelings as you are of the anger itself.

Later in the chapter we'll consider how you can get in touch with your anger and what you can do with it once you've identified it. But before we come to that, let's look briefly at other emotions.

Fatigue: A Sign of Depression

Anger is not, of course, the only emotion people try to stifle. Jealousy, resentment, and guilt are often rejected, too. Thanks to our culture's sexual stereotypes, there are many women who can't admit to themselves that they're strongly competitive; and many men who must deny fear and every other sort of vulnerability. When you clamp a lid on any kind of emotional energy, you lose some of your internal momentum.

But what of depression, which is surely one of the most uncomfortable emotions humans experience? It would seem absurd to talk about the "emotional energy" there, since fatigue is one of the sure-fire signs of depression. Yet many psychotherapists believe that depression is simply anger turned inward.

Betty: Deserted and Bone-Weary

Last year Betty suffered through a period of severe depression. At the time anger seemed the least of her problems. "I was totally inert," she said. "I couldn't even have worked up the energy to feel annoyed."

Betty's depression began when her husband of fifteen years left her for another woman. Though at first she tried to carry on as before, she soon developed early-morning insomnia. She would wake up at 5 A.M. feeling remarkably fresh but unable to get back to sleep no matter how late she'd gone to bed the night before. Soon some worry would begin to nag at her, and in the drab predawn hours it would loom larger and larger. By the time it was seven o'clock and her teenage children were beginning to stir, Betty was feeling so badly that she could barely drag herself out of bed.

As her depression deepened, she found herself incapable of making even the simplest decisions. She had trouble concentrating and she was supersensitive, apt to burst into tears over nothing. She felt hopeless and empty, but mostly she was just bone-weary: Even brushing her teeth sometimes seemed too much of an effort. Eventually she reached the point where she didn't care about anything anymore. She didn't even care if she never felt better.

Finally a friend talked Betty into seeing a psychiatrist, who prescribed an antidepressant. It took several weeks to work and there were unpleasant side effects—she felt dizzy when she first woke up in the morning and sometimes her vision blurred—but the depression began to lift. The pills were necessary, the doctor said, before psychotherapy could help, because she'd been so down that there was no way to reach her.

Crisis intervention theory holds that *if a person gets the right kind of help while she's in the midst of a crisis, she may emerge from it stronger than she ever was before, and (I would add) more energized*. Certainly, that's what happened to Betty. Through therapy her rage at her husband surfaced at last, and she began to feel less like a helpless victim. She came to see that, far from being over, her life was in some important ways just beginning, and that her task now was to figure out what she wanted *for herself*.

Recently Betty found a job and has begun to take evening courses in accounting. "I'm on the run twelve hours a day now," she says, "and it's hard for me to believe that just a year ago I felt so tired that I spent most of my time in bed. When I look back, I'm actually glad about the divorce. It was a terrible thing to go through, but because of it I've become someone I would never otherwise have been."

Depression Is a Circuit Breaker

Though it feels like a *failure* of energy, depression is actually a *blockage of energy*, just as boredom often is. People who are depressed may seem totally inert, but lab tests show that usually their muscles are in a state of constant tension. The body is, if anything, hyperaroused.

Susan B. Shor, a New York City psychotherapist, runs self-help groups for depressives. Her theory about depression is that *it's actually a protective device, a kind of circuit breaker that people use when they're suffering from emotional overload.* "Depression is a nonemotion that masks emotion," she explained. "It's a state of nonfeeling numbness. Usually, if you take a patient's history, you find that the depression was preceded by such a massive amount of emotional input that the person simply closed down because the flow of energy felt too intense.

"The classic theory is that depression is anger turned against the self," she continued, "and I wouldn't disagree with that for a minute. Too much has been asked of such people and not enough has been given, and so they feel depleted and angry even though they're not aware of their rage. When you take away the depression, they react in one of two ways. Either they experience enormous sadness—and that's different from depression, because they do feel something—or they feel enormous anxiety."

Depression and anxiety often go together. Shor says she rarely sees one without some trace of the other. "It's like a continuum," she explained, "and so when a person is mostly depressed you treat the depression, and when they're mostly anxious you treat the anxiety. Most people are in the middle, with a constant shift back and forth, which makes sense if depression *is* a circuit breaker, to protect against the anxiety."

Homework Assignments that Lift Depression

In the beginning Shor gives her patients permission to *be* depressed rather than trying to talk them out of it. Gradually she helps them realize that they don't have to be depressed all the time, that they can experiment with letting feelings in. The task of the therapist, as she sees it, is to make sure that as the depression lifts "the energy that's coming in, that nervy buzz, seems manageable; to help the person realize that it's not going to wipe them out."

Susan Shor is the director of Project Connect, which offers group therapy for depressives. Patients are screened first and then assigned to a group according to the level at which they're able to function, so that the severely depressed are in one group and the mildly depressed in another.

At each meeting the members share their experiences and also design homework, tasks carefully created to build self-confidence and stretch coping skills. The assignment might be to say "no" to somebody; to ask someone for help; to do something mother wouldn't like. One woman whose husband had left her decided to go home and cut up her wedding gown. At the next session she brought in the pieces in a huge envelope and dumped them out—along with some of her repressed rage.

In other groups the general level of depression is so severe that such tasks are beyond the members. Shor might start by asking: "Can you clean out a closet? a drawer? half a drawer?" These seem small things to do, but the person who manages to put the sock drawer to rights knows that when she comes back to the group and reports success she won't be laughed at, because the others realize that reorganizing a drawer is a major accomplishment for someone who feels so low that she doesn't even want to get dressed in the morning. The next time out she may be able to take on a task that's more demanding.

Energy Tips for the Depressed

All of us feel depressed from time to time, but sometimes the feelings linger, settling in like smog. Shor suggested that the person who is having a bad time of it because of a divorce, a death in the family, or for no reason she can think of can help herself in several ways.

The first thing to do, she said, is to reach out to someone else who has had a similar experience, because "I've never met anyone who was really depressed who hasn't felt like a freak. You believe that if anyone really knew how you sleep all the time, refuse to answer the phone, and turn down invitations, they'd think you were crazy. To have just one person say, 'I went through the same thing,' is an enormous help."

You can also set yourself some tasks that are confidence-building: Clean out your house and your life, both literally and symbolically; take a course; do something you've always wanted to do; stretch yourself. The goal is to get back to the point where you feel you have some control over your world. Get angry: Instead of being down on yourself, heap some of the blame onto others.

If none of this works, or if the problem is so severe that you simply can't get going, find professional help. Remember that the right kind of help at a time of crisis can bring you through feeling revitalized and stronger than ever!

Anger Problems

Anger and energy are intimately related, for anger can mobilize and focus energy. There's nothing more invigorating than justified rage.

Most of the time anger is a gut response to the feeling that you're in danger, that you're threatened in some way or about to be hurt or abandoned. The person who is continually angry, then, is usually someone who feels especially vulnerable. Easily threatened, he has learned to hide his vulnerability by striking out at others in retaliation—or sometimes in anticipation of what he suspects they're about to do to him.

People who can't control their temper have one sort of anger problem. People who can't express their anger have another—and they're often at the mercy of those whose angry energies flow freely. In fact, those who *can* explode sometimes deliberately use their anger to intimidate people who can't. One woman recalled, "Last year I had some problems with my son's teacher, and at one point I lost my temper and really told her off. Afterward I felt awful. I never lose my temper and, anyway, I was overreacting. But my ex-husband said to me, 'It won't do any harm if you get a reputation for being the kind of parent who makes waves. They'll listen faster the next time you've got a complaint.' I realized then that *he's* never ashamed of being angry. In fact, sometimes he blows up for strategic purposes if he thinks that getting mad will get him what he wants."

Less Angry Often Means Less Sexual

But for those who bury their anger there are worse penalties than being intimidated by people who can rage freely. *When you learn to hold back your angry energy, you learn to hold back your energy in giving, getting, and lovemaking as well,* according to Dr. Doris Rothman, who runs "anger workshops" that have proved highly popular. Dr. Rothman explained that if a child is taught that she must not hate, the next time she has a strong feeling of any kind she may try to hold it back, suspecting that she's not supposed to feel that way either. And so she grows up to be a person who is not only cut off from her anger but from her other emotions as well.

Dr. Rothman, who runs The Institute for Experiential Learning and Development in Lawrenceville, New Jersey, sometimes uses Bioenergetic techniques in her work on anger. Bioenergetics is based on the belief that everything you do and are is expressed in your body. In fact, as you grow up your fears, tensions, anger—your attitudes—are preserved in locked-in muscular patterns and in breathing patterns that can block the easy flow of energy. Thus, rather than trying to change the personality by reaching it verbally through the mind, Bioenergetic therapy works through the body by using body awareness and special exercises to root out self-damaging traits and attitudes. However, Dr. Rothman is eclectic in that her anger workshops operate on both nonverbal and verbal levels.

Though most of those who attend the workshops come because they have trouble expressing their anger, one or two out of every ten participants are *splashers,* people who can't keep their temper and explode frequently. "Often splashers are well aware of the negative effect they're having on other people," Dr. Rothman explained. "They realize that their marriages are in trouble,

or that their children are afraid of them. Usually they're very
loving people—because those who have angry energy tend to
have other kinds as well, and when they love, they love just as
explosively—and so they're deeply concerned."

Feelings Never Need to Be Justified

The first point Dr. Rothman tries to get across at a workshop is
that emotions simply *are.* If you're like most people, from the
time you were very young others assumed the right to judge
your feelings, to say whether they were good or bad, until eventually you, too, believed that you must justify and rationalize
your emotions. But your feelings are your own and they don't
have to be justified. They're always "correct" *for you,* even when
they're based on a misinterpretation of something that happened,
because they're there and they're all the information you have to
go on.

You need to own your feelings, Dr. Rothman says, "and when
you own them that begins to take you back to your body, while
going back to the body also takes you to your feelings."

Where Is Your Anger Located?

Thus, the next lesson she teaches in workshops is the one on
how to recognize the symptoms of anger—because many people
can't. Actually, anger produces different symptoms in different
people. Dr. Rothman noted, "Depression is more consistent—it's
almost always located in the chest, though some feel depressed
all over. Fear is usually a fluttering in the gut—which is where
the expression 'yellow-bellied' comes from. But when I ask about
anger, people locate it anywhere from the top of the head right
down to the toes."

The Consequences of Bottling Up Rage

It's important to be able to identify your own anger and to
allow yourself to experience it, because those who bottle up their

rage are apt to develop psychosomatic symptoms, as well as an energy deficit. They suffer from headaches, earaches, eye irritation, sinus trouble, and acne. (Dr. Rothman calls it "the breaking out of the angry skin".) Tension in the jaw leads to grinding the teeth at night, and then there are arthritic aches, backaches, ulcers, colitis, constipation, high blood pressure, and more.

We often say of others that they're "a pain in the neck" or "a pain in the ass." Dr. Rothman has found that if someone who is suffering from a real pain, located in the neck, can just identify the person who's symbolically a pain—can say aloud, for example, "Mother, *you* are the pain in my neck"—often the ache will disappear on the spot!

Denying anger has psychological consequences as well. To begin with, anger that hasn't been dealt with typically turns inward and produces depression. "There's no such thing as depression or even grief that doesn't have anger in it," Dr. Rothman said. "In fact, sometimes grief and mourning drag on for years because the anger has been overlooked." The person who is bereaved feels as outraged as an abandoned child and longs to ask, "How could you die and leave me when I wasn't ready for you to die?" But this hardly seems reasonable and so the very thought is suppressed.

The person who buries anger is also likely to behave like a victim, and victims are hard to take. As Dr. Rothman said, "They can make you feel so guilty when they keep apologizing all over the place, walking around as if they're in a swamp of misery. They're so irritating, and yet if you do or say anything nasty to them *you're* the aggressor."

In addition, those who can't express anger are apt to develop marital problems. "A relationship can die because of a lack of energy," Dr. Rothman said. "A couple can bore each other to death. Sometimes a woman will come to me, very unhappy with her marriage, and she'll say, 'I don't know what's the matter with me to feel this way. My husband doesn't drink, he doesn't chase other women. No matter what I do he tolerates it. He's such a nice guy.' And I say, 'They're the worst kind.' Because those 'nice guys' don't give any feeling to the relationship. They're never angry, but they're never anything else either. 'Whatever you want to do, dear,' they say, and it's like living with a sponge. They let you pick the fights, so it's all your fault. Their crime is one of omission, a lack of energy and of giving and sharing."

What to Do with Angry Energies

Dr. Rothman believes that *it's important not only to acknowledge your anger but to put it where it belongs.* You can tell people that you're angry with them and why without becoming a splasher; and you can learn to say "no" when it's appropriate instead of being a doormat. People who begin to use and appreciate their own healthy, aggressive energy usually find the experience exhilarating. "That man was rude to me and I told him I didn't like it," one woman said delightedly. "He was so surprised. I've been feeling good about it all day." Another woman, deserted by her husband when their baby was just six months old, at first felt as if she were teetering on the brink of a frightening drop into depression. "I discovered that I could help myself," she said. "Whenever I began to feel terrifically low, I'd pick up the phone and call someone who didn't know what Tom had done, and I'd tell them. Just talking about it made me angry all over again and produced a jolt of energy and a lift in the way I felt. I couldn't unload my anger on Tom because he'd disappeared, but letting it out to other people made me feel better."

Of course, there *are* situations where you'll actually do yourself harm by expressing your anger openly—when your boss is a tyrant, for example, and you can't afford to lose your job. Many people invent outlets for themselves in such situations. One woman Dr. Rothman knows actually keeps a voodoo doll in her desk and whenever her boss does something outrageous she stabs it with a pin. Others jog off their anger, burn it off playing tennis, or pour their indignation into a good cause.

How to "Exercise" Your Rage

In her workshops Dr. Rothman teaches several exercises that serve as anger outlets and general energy releasers. For people who have never been able to express their anger these exercises provide firsthand experience with rage; and for the splashers—those who express anger too often—there's some practice in containment.

For the first exercise you need a tennis racket and a bed. You stand facing the bed with your feet planted a comfortable distance apart, toes pointing slightly inward, knees loose. Hold the racket in both hands and raise it overhead as you take a deep breath; then slam it down on the bed and, as you do, exhale and make some sort of sound. "Ahhh" will do, though you might want to curse instead, talk to someone, or grind out the word "die!" Keep your feet firmly on the floor and put your whole body into the swing. As soon as the racket hits the bed, raise it overhead once more, inhaling as you do so, and slam it down again. Keep flailing the bed until you're completely exhausted and your anger is spent. It's important not to stop too soon, because if you do the aggressive energy you've built up may spill over later onto some innocent bystander.

In the second exercise you simply substitute fists, raised overhead, for the tennis racket. For some people using fists is too real, too close to what they'd like to do or are afraid they'll do; a tennis racket is somehow at one remove and so is a better starting place. Aside from that, the exercises accomplish much the same thing and require the same procedure: the wide-set stance, exhaling on the downstroke, making sounds, and aiming for total exhaustion.

Dr. Rothman doesn't recommend either a tennis racket or fists for the splashers, those who are in fact likely to strike out, either physically or verbally. For them she suggests a third exercise using a bath towel. You fold the towel in half first and roll it into a cylinder; then you grasp it in the middle with both hands held close together. Squeezing as hard as you can, you begin to wring it, standing all the while with feet apart, toes in, knees loose, and breathing slowly and deeply. "You hang on for dear life; you wring in one direction; and you hold the wring until you're exhausted, all the while breathing deeply and making sounds or talking," Dr. Rothman said.

As you do this, you should feel the angry energy rise like a wave within you, crest, and then finally subside. If you've been afraid that if you ever really let your anger go you'd never get it under control again, that you might kill someone or be destroyed by your own rage, the towel exercise is for you. "It's a magnificent thing," Dr. Rothman said, "to find out just how angry you can be when you let go and to learn that you *can* contain it, because you're bigger than your rage. You become like a battery as the angry energy flows up and down through your system."

Some splashers discover that a towel can be their best friend. When they're furious and afraid they might lash out, they go off alone somewhere to do some towel wringing; afterward they tackle the issues with the people they're angry at. Nonsplashers can eventually graduate to the towel exercise, though for those who are too frightened even to use the tennis racket the towel, with its comforting sense of anger contained, is actually a better starting place.

"All three techniques are basically ways to put you fully in touch with your energy," Dr. Rothman said. "If it's blocked, they help you get it moving. If it splashes out, they help you contain it. *The best thing is to be the container of your angry energy and use it constructively, so that you neither hurt yourself by repressing it nor hurt others by exploding.*"

Murder by Imagination: It Frees Energy

Dr. Rothman also has another technique she teaches that is nonphysical. She calls the wipe-out fantasy "one of the most sophisticated ways to deal with anger." In the fantasy—the idea originated with Milwaukee therapist Dick Olney—you totally destroy the person you're angry at.

Almost everyone fantasizes. Some people learn as children to control their behavior, but as they do they find an outlet for forbidden feelings in fantasy and thus discover a way to release emotional energy. However, others grow up feeling that a "sinful" thought is just as bad as a sinful deed, and so they struggle to control their own thinking, shutting down their minds whenever they detect "bad" thoughts or images. But *true freedom of thought*, Dr. Rothman said, *is feeling free to think or imagine anything, because you know that fantasy is not the same as real-ity.* "My mind is totally free," she explained, "when I can say, 'There is nothing I will not permit myself to think.'" People who grow up with no outlet in fantasy are more likely to develop psy-chosomatic illnesses and they're also more likely to vent their hostile impulses in disguised ways, for you can only control a desire to hurt or humiliate if you know that it's there in the first place.

Because some people are uneasy about controlled daydream-ing, Dr. Rothman approaches the wipe-out fantasy through a series of preliminary exercises. She begins by asking workshop participants to close their eyes and imagine a rose: to see the color, smell it, explore the texture and the thorns, and sense the way it feels as they pick it up and throw it. Next she moves on to comical imaging, inviting participants to imagine turning her into a pretzel, or to fantasize tickling her. Switching to something slightly humiliating—which therefore smacks of the forbidden—she suggests that they picture her delivering a lecture on physics while nude.

Next she may suggest that in their imaginations they com-pletely demolish the room they're in; then they're to throw imag-inary rocks at her—which is a totally different experience than throwing that imaginary rose, for one tends to cringe a little in sympathy as the mental missiles fly. Finally they move on into wipe-out fantasies, perhaps starting with a politician they de-spise but have never met and graduating to someone they're re-ally angry with. Dr. Rothman does not suggest that beginners immediately polish off a person close to them, such as a parent or child, since some find that too disturbing.

Whatever method of annihilation the individual chooses, Dr. Rothman insists that the body be totally destroyed before the fantasy is over, so that no trace of it can ever be found. She says that otherwise the imaginary victim has a way of coming back to imaginary life. Instructed to get rid of the body, many people become extremely creative. One woman ground up her step-mother's corpse and then stamped the residue into the ground. A week later she reported that she had a mysterious pain in her heel. It turned out that when she put her victim through the grinder, a single gold tooth survived. Her attempt to trample it into the ground apparently produced the pain in her foot, a pain that disappeared as soon as she replayed the fantasy and disposed of the tooth as well.

"Fantasizing is the greatest device I know for strengthening the ego," Dr. Rothman said, "for mastering the distinction between reality and unreality. *A wipe-out fantasy invites you to take charge of your own aggression even as it releases blocked energy.*"

Energy Tips for Those Who Stifle Anger

1. Try to figure out what your own anger feels like. Where in your body is it located? If your rage frightens you, you may actually experience it as the flutterings of fear. Or your only clue may be a lack of energy, a mild depression. Once you've identified the symptoms of anger, watch for them as you go about your daily life.

2. The first question to ask yourself when you know you're feeling angry is, "Can I put that assertive energy where it belongs?"

3. If expressing your anger would be self-defeating, look for an outlet for the energy. Try a wipe-out fantasy, beat up a bed, strangle a towel, or go out for a run or a brisk walk. Don't try to rein in the energy; let it flow—you'll feel better for it.

What Are Your Peak Hours for Energy?

Freeing your feelings is one way to free your energy, and for those who habitually hold in their emotions it's the method most likely to produce dramatic results.

Another way is to learn more about how your energy operates, to identify your daily peak times and the hours at which your vitality is usually low. Energy flows according to its own schedule; its comings and goings are predictable to a surprising extent. Once you know what to watch for, you can tune in to this subtle inner rhythm and make the most of it. There is more on how to do that in the next chapter.

5

Learning to Flow with Energy Rhythms

"My getting-up time is always the same," Beth said. She's a commercial artist who works on a free-lance basis. "Whether I go to bed the night before at nine or at two in the morning, I'm up at seven—I seem to be incapable of sleeping any later than that. I also do my best work first thing in the morning, so I feel frustrated when I can't make an early start. If I have to spend the morning in the dentist's office or something like that, it's hard for me to get going in the afternoon. When I have a really difficult assignment to handle, I try to start work as early as possible. Ideally, I'll get up at five so that I'm well into it by six-thirty."

Marion's energy flows according to a completely different schedule, for Marion is extremely sluggish early in the day. "I can't stand people who are cheerful at breakfast," she told me. "At that hour of the morning I'm barely conscious myself and conversation is beyond me. At eight in the evening I'm an entirely different person. In fact, I seem to develop a second wind around dinnertime, and I can keep going for half the night with no trouble at all. Actually, all week long I go chronically short on sleep, because at midnight or one o'clock I'm just not tired; then on the weekend I make up for what I've missed by sleeping until noon or later."

For everyone there is a pattern to the daylong flow of energy, but that pattern differs tremendously from one person to the next. There are day people and there are night people, and it's not just a matter of preference. You're one or the other, depending on the way the internal rhythms of your body are orchestrated.

The human body is like a river: Though outwardly it may look the same, it changes constantly over the course of a day. From moment to moment hormones and other biochemicals ebb and flow like tides; enzymes that are present at noon are conspicuously absent at midnight. Furthermore, blood pressure, heart rate, body temperature, blood sugar level—virtually all of our internal systems—swing through cycles roughly twenty-four hours long, with fairly predictable peaks and troughs. At any given instant, then, the individual is the sum of his inner rhythms. The body with which he meets a crisis at four in the morning is in many important ways different from the one with which he would have handled the same situation at four in the afternoon.

Unaware of all this, most of us treat our bodies as if they were machines that operate in precisely the same way at all hours of the day. In particular, we either ignore the normal flux of energy or actively struggle against it; but it's possible to learn to flow with it instead. The energy payoff that comes when you do can be like the difference between paddling against the current and coasting with it.

Finding Your Own Peak Energy Period

All of us have a peak period daily, a few precious hours during which vitality crests and we're at our most alert and efficient. The exact timing of the peak varies from one person to the next, but once you know when yours generally occurs you can try to plan your day accordingly. You can schedule demanding tasks for the hours when you usually feel most vigorous and tackle routine matters while your energy is low.

Many people find that it's relatively easy to identify their own prime time once they know that such a thing exists. Both Beth and Marion know when theirs is. However, someone who wants to be more scientific about it—and who is willing to spend the time and go to the trouble—can pin down the peak more exactly with the help of an ordinary thermometer. (I'll explain the procedure a little later in this chapter.)

Why a thermometer? It seems that, for whatever reason, energy echoes the body temperature rhythm; and though we assume that 98.6 degrees is a normal body temperature, your temperature actually varies about a degree and a half every day. It's generally lowest between one and four in the morning and highest in the late afternoon and evening—this is true even if you run a fever. Strenuous activity briefly heats the body, but that's no more than a kink in the normal cycle.

Scientists don't actually talk about energy in relation to temperature rhythm, since "energy" is a word that has never been adequately defined from a researcher's point of view. However, various studies have demonstrated that both fatigue and efficiency mimic the body temperature cycle: In the normal course of a day, the cooler your body is, the more tired you feel; conversely, in your warmest moments you're more alert and efficient—your psychomotor performance, to use the proper terminology, is at its zenith. Scientists know that's so because they've tested subjects at regular intervals over the course of a day on tasks such as card sorting or multiplication problems, recording their temperature at the end of each task. As the temperature increased, so did efficiency.

All this means that your lowest ebb occurs as your temperature bottoms out in the wee hours of the morning. You feel more tired then than at any other time—though if you stay up past sunrise you'll begin to revive as you warm to the new day. The body is also most vulnerable during those dark hours of the night: Allergies tend to flare up then and accidents happen. More people are born and more die.

The Mid-afternoon Slump

On the other hand, most of us are least tired and most efficient during the afternoon and evening, when the temperature crests in the peak period. It seems, then, that it would be smart to schedule an important meeting or a crucial exam for the afternoon, if possible, rather than the morning—it would be, that is, if it weren't for the postprandial dip.

Approximately half of those individuals who have been tested by psychologists regularly experience a mid-afternoon slump called postprandial dip. Postprandial means "after a meal," but it's a misnomer since the dip doesn't seem to depend on when or what you ate. It simply happens, manifesting itself as a measurable drop in efficiency that begins sometime between about 2 and 4 P.M. and lasts a couple of hours, with a drop in temperature to match. Though there's no universally accepted explanation for it, a sleep expert I talked to suggested that the natural rhythm of human sleep may include an afternoon nap and that the dip is simply the body easing off in anticipation of that nap. Dr. Wilse B. Webb of the University of Florida called attention to something we all know: In subtropical countries an afternoon siesta is an assumed part of the day. It's also the last bit of sleep babies give up and it tends to reappear in the elderly.

For some people the postprandial dip is a real problem. Jim, for example, is a graduate student struggling to finish his thesis. He complains that in the middle of almost every afternoon he falls asleep over his books. If he has had enough sleep the night before, he may simply nod off a few times, but if he's been up late he conks right out. Either way he loses time and becomes very impatient with himself.

If, like Jim, you suffer from postprandial dip, you'll be better off if you can simply accept the fact that a mid-afternoon slump is part of your normal pattern. You can, of course, try to counteract it in various ways. You may be able to stave it off with coffee, for example. However, getting up and moving around works even better, and if you don't have to spend your afternoons conforming to office protocol, you have other options as well. You might try running in place. One woman I talked to said that letting out a few war whoops really revives her. You can also use the time to run errands or do something else that keeps you moving and makes few mental demands; or you can always give in and take a short nap, knowing that your sleepiness will pass before long, that it's not a sign that you're worn out and washed up for the day.

How to Chart Your Peak

Returning to that peak period, to identify your own high point, you can chart your temperature over the course of a day. To get an accurate picture, you'll need to take temperature readings at least six to eight times at two-hour intervals, preferably with a rectal thermometer, since it's more accurate than the oral version. (If, instead, you check your temperature on a haphazard schedule, leaving the thermometer in place only briefly each time, you're apt to find that there's no identifiable pattern.)

Two other points are worth noting. It's best to choose a day when you can remain relatively quiet, since activity raises the temperature. A stroll to the corner to pick up a newspaper can boost the thermometer reading by half a degree or more. And there's a bit of controversy about temperature cycles in women. Some research suggests that a woman's temperature rhythm may shift substantially over the course of a menstrual month, though other studies have indicated only minor changes.

Are You a Lark or an Owl?

If you're like most people, you'll find that your temperature-energy peak occurs in the afternoon or early evening; the exact timing varies, depending on whether you're a lark or an owl, since there are two quite distinctive patterns. As sleep expert Dr. John Hanley put it, *There's a large group of larks who take all day to go to sleep and a small group of owls who take all day to wake up.*

More specifically, larks are people who wake up quickly and easily in the morning to a body that has already begun to warm up; their temperature rises, peaks, and then falls relatively early; their prime time for energy is apt to occur at around three in the afternoon. As for the owl, he's generally sluggish in the morning, for at the moment of awakening his temperature still lingers near its nighttime low. It may not crest until 6 or 7 P.M., and he's still full of energy in mid-evening. Marion, of course, is an owl. However, few people fit either the lark or the owl pattern exactly, for there are large individual differences.

Survival Tactics for Owls

The nine-to-five world seems to have been designed by and for larks, and owls sometimes have a hard time reconciling themselves to it. I often hear people say that they simply can't function before ten in the morning or that they can never get to sleep before one. "If I could just work the night shift, that's what would suit me best," Janet told me. "Then I'm sure I'd have more energy. But who ever heard of a nursery school teacher who worked nights?"

However, no one is really born to work the night shift, for the energy-fatigue cycle isn't permanently linked to particular hours of the day. That's just as well, since otherwise someone who moved from New York to London, say, might forever afterward have to live with a body that felt like 4 A.M. in mid-morning. Fortunately, just as a mechanical clock can be reset, the energy cycle and the other internal rhythms can shift backward or forward in time in response to certain outside-the-body cues. These cues include the normal daily cycles of light and darkness, warmth and coolness, eating and fasting. Our reaction to light, in particular, is absolutely basic—it's the most important factor—though we create our own individual light-dark cycles when we close our eyes while asleep and then open them upon awakening.

You can place sleep anywhere you want within the twenty-four-hour day, just as long as you place it there regularly; once the new pattern is established, the other body rhythms will begin to adjust. Obviously, then, if a night owl like Janet were to switch to staying up half the night and sleeping all morning, within a short time her temperature-based energy and efficiency rhythms would change as well. She'd find that she was waking up at noon with her body still cool and her energy low. She'd put in a sluggish afternoon rather than a sluggish morning, and her peak period for work or whatever would occur at midnight or even later! If this suited her life-style, it might be all well and good, but it seems clear that it would affect the *timing* of her energy rather than her basic energy level.

Furthermore, an owl whose mornings tend to be terribly demanding would probably do better if she went to bed earlier and then got up earlier and lingered over breakfast to give herself a chance to warm up. Though at first this might go very much against the grain (many owls love to sleep late in the morning), once the new rhythm was established it should pay off.

Owls who can manage their own time can go with the energy flow and schedule less demanding tasks for the morning hours and more difficult ones for late afternoon. I know a corporate executive who spends his mornings handling the mail and other routine matters and who schedules dinner meetings whenever he can. Still another owl friend is fortunate enough to have a husband who's a lark. Ever since their children were small, she has buried herself sleepily in the New York *Times* at breakfast while he copes with the kids.

However, other larks and owls who become involved with one another feel that their differing energy schedules are a liability rather than an asset. Herb, for example, nearly gave up on Phyllis because he couldn't tolerate the hours she kept. They lived in different cities and spent their weekends together. For a while it seemed that they were woefully mismatched, since by ten-thirty at night he could barely keep his eyes open, while there was no way she could fall asleep at that hour. The next morning he was up with the sun, impatient to get on with the day, and irritated because it took her half the morning to come to. He felt that there was something vaguely immoral about sleeping late, and she once referred to him as a "party pooper." Neither of them recognized that body truths were involved.

In spite of their differences, Herb and Phyllis eventually married—and discovered, when they started living together, that their problem solved itself; for once Phyllis began to get up at six-thirty every morning with Herb rather than at eight, as she used to, she, too, couldn't keep her eyes open after ten-thirty at night. Their body clocks had been operating on different schedules. Of course, she still played owl to his lark—her days got off to a groggy start and he was never at his best in the evening—but they stopped using dire words like "incompatible."

Predictable Mood Shifts

I've dwelt at length on temperature rhythm because it's closely related to the normal flux of energy. However, there are many other body rhythms as well, and knowing about some of them can save you both aggravation and energy.

Certain moods, for example, fluctuate in a fairly regular fashion. Anxiety and depression are generally worse in the morning than in the afternoon, so if you start the day feeling terrible, you can be fairly sure you'll feel better later on. Irritability peaks twice a day, at dinnertime and in the wee hours of the morning —possibly because those are the times when the blood sugar level is lowest. Even this small ration of predictability may make your own moods and those of others easier to tolerate.

Alcohol: The Most Intoxicating Hours

You may save yourself the price of a hangover if you take into account the fact that the body metabolizes alcohol differently at different times of the day, probably because of those enzymes and other biochemicals that are present in abundance at some hours and scarce at others. At any rate, cocktails consumed in the evening are apt to be much less intoxicating than the same number of drinks downed at noon or at one in the morning, because from about two in the afternoon until midnight alcohol is cleared from the bloodstream relatively quickly.

Foods that Soothe or Stimulate

Coffee and tea also affect the body differently, depending on when you drink them, and recent research suggests that the timing of foods may be significant as well. Scientists have learned, through research on animals, that high-protein meals encourage the body to produce a particular succession of brain chemicals that are normally present while one is awake, whereas high-carbohydrate meals favor the synthesis of a chain of chemicals that are associated with sleep. (For more about food and brain chemistry, see Chapter 8.) To Dr. Charles Ehret, a senior scientist at the Argonne National Laboratory, this suggests that a breakfast of sugary cereal would tend to send one back to sleep—or would, at any rate, take the edge off one's energy—while a steak dinner might act as a stimulant at a time of day when many people prefer to wind down. Dr. Ehret suggests that a sensible alternative is to have a high-protein breakfast, dinner at midday, and a light supper of pancakes.

In a brief, ill-fated experiment I tested this regime to see what would happen to my energy level. The first morning I had a steak sandwich for breakfast, but since I'm never very hungry at that hour I only ate half of it. At noon I had a regular dinner, though a small one. By seven that evening I was ravenous, and the breakfast food I'd planned to eat wasn't at all appealing, especially since the rest of the family were dining as usual; so I gave in and had my third "dinner" of the day. The same sort of thing happened the next day, and on the third day I dropped the experiment. Habit was simply too strong for me. Other people might do better.

There's also another reason for switching to big breakfasts and small dinners: If you're trying to lose weight, it apparently helps to do more of your eating earlier in the day. In a University of Minnesota experiment volunteers consumed two thousand calories a day, all at one meal. For a week they had that meal at breakfast time, then for another week they had it as dinner. During the breakfast week they lost significantly more weight; this apparently wasn't because they got more exercise after the morning meal, since people who were hospitalized and inactive who tried the same lopsided regime got similar results. Of course, few of us would want to force down two thousand calories at a single sitting, but logic suggests that if the body uses food more efficiently earlier in the day, then a less drastic routine—one that calls for a sizable breakfast and a very skimpy dinner—might still be a help to the dieter.

Coffee and Tea Can Reset Internal Body Rhythms

As for coffee and tea, they are, in a sense, drugs, though they're drugs that people have been taking down through the ages. The folklore of many countries includes stories about the discovery of one of these beverages; usually a religious leader or mystic is given credit for it. Coffee and tea, and cocoa as well, contain substances called methylated xanthines—specifically caffeine, theophylline, and theobromine. The xanthines affect the body's biological rhythms by turning on certain key enzymes, though the exact effect they have depends on the time of day at which they're consumed. Experiments with animals indicate, for example, that if you drink coffee at breakfast you're probably setting your body clocks back, so that various rhythms will peak later in the day on subsequent days: If your prime time for energy was ordinarily at around three in the afternoon, it might occur later. Coffee drinking in the evening seems to set the clocks forward, so that rhythms peak earlier for the next few days. In mid-afternoon, between about two and five, caffeine sets body clocks neither forward nor back.

It may sound as if you could easily reschedule your peak energy just by guzzling coffee at the right time of day. However—for reasons I'll come to in a little while—Dr. Ehret believes that it may be dangerous to keep resetting the body's clocks.

Jet Lag: Physiological Bedlam

Normally the body's various internal rhythms fit together efficiently, the interplay of the different peaks and troughs well suited to the lives we lead. *If, however, you change your sleeping and eating schedule by a few hours—perhaps because you've flown across several time zones—the body's rhythms are thrown askew.* What's more, they stay that way for many days because some cycles adjust to the new time schedule much more slowly than others do. The result within the body is a kind of physiological bedlam, which translates as extreme fatigue and a feeling of confusion. This rather common energy crisis is, of course, known as jet lag.

The neatest explanation I've found for the way jet lag operates was supplied by Professor John Palmer of the University of Massachusetts at Amherst. In his lively textbook, *An Introduction to Biological Rhythms,* Palmer describes the adventures of a hypothetical Italian who flies to New York, arriving in time for a 2 P.M. business meeting. As he sits down at the conference table, it's 8 P.M. Rome time, which puts him at his daily peak of efficiency; since the Americans he's negotiating with are in the midst of their own postprandial dips, the meeting turns out well for the Italian. However, later on, when they all adjourn for dinner, he's practically wiped out by a couple of drinks—hardly surprising since, according to his body, it's now past midnight and alcohol has a more potent effect then. Finally arriving back at his hotel at 1 A.M. New York time, the Italian is surprised that he has trouble sleeping. By then it's 7 A.M. in Rome and so his body has warmed up once again and is ready for a new day.

For anyone who flies often, jet lag is one of the unpleasant realities of life. Most seasoned travelers develop their own tactics for coping with it. There are, in fact, two schools of thought: Some people believe in making allowances for jet lag, while others are of the plunge-right-ahead-and-ignore-it persuasion.

How George Plimpton Copes with Jet Lag

Up to a point George Plimpton makes allowances. An energist who writes, edits, lectures—and travels a lot—Plimpton is perhaps best known as the author who realized many men's dreams when he signed on for a time as a professional baseball player in order to write a book (*Out of My League*) about his experiences. He has also done a stint as a pro football player (*Paper Lion*) and a pro golfer (*The Bogey Man*). In fact, in his varied career as a participant-journalist and amateur sportsman Plimpton has: fought a bull; gone several rounds with fighter Archie Moore; lost a tennis match to Pancho Gonzales; sat in as a percussionist with the New York Philharmonic; performed as a trapeze artist, lion tamer, and clown with a circus; and more. His friend Robert

Kennedy once said of him, "If I wanted to be President, which of course I don't, I'd still *rather* be George Plimpton."

Travel has long played a big part in Plimpton's life. He explained that nowadays when he flies coast to coast he tries to ease himself gradually into the new time pattern. Arriving in California from New York, for example, he'll go to bed quite early the first night, and then an hour later on each successive night until he has made up the time difference and is turning in at his usual hour. This doesn't prevent jet lag, but it's some help. Plimpton noted ruefully, "The jet-lag problem seems to increase as one gets older. I don't remember being bothered by it when I first started going across the continent, but now I find I really need a 'day of adjustment,' just lolling around and letting my energies catch up with me, as if they were on a plane coming along later."

As for the flight itself, since he can't abide luggage claim areas, Plimpton avoids aggravation and saves energy by traveling light, "even if it means being somewhat threadbare at the other end. If my bag is too bulky to go under the seat, I'll take enough out of it so that it does, and I'll hold a suit, a pair of shoes, and some manuscripts in my lap during takeoff.

"The air trip is fine for working," he continued, "because you're trapped for the duration. I've written at least two or three books' worth working on airplanes. I do much better in a plane than at home. Send me aloft for best quality! Of course, it's a very expensive way of getting one's words down."

Though his books are delightful, highly literate, and witty, Plimpton says he'd rather do almost anything else than write, than have to squeeze words out of his head. "The great disciplining agent," he said, "is the fact that if the story doesn't come in, the editors are going to drop you, or your reputation is damaged. The consequences are that you stay awake working twelve, fifteen, twenty hours at a time, as if you were saving yourself from drowning." He thinks writers are motivated by the same thing that motivates the athlete: fear of humiliation.

Plimpton doesn't believe he's endowed with more energy than others. However, the people he compares himself with are famous jet-setters such as David Frost and Ethel Kennedy. He suggested that people who accomplish a lot are actually driven by necessity. "They set themselves too many things to do and then feel victimized by them," he said. "I think the responsibilities, the pressures of cosmopolitan living, especially if you're successful, are huge." But on a more positive note he added, "When you take on responsibilities you become focused, committed to them, and then your energy level goes up."

How Aircrews Cope

Aircrews who fly regularly across time zones have more experience with jet lag than anyone else. Two flight attendants I talked to agreed that it's not something you get used to—in fact, as George Plimpton said, coping becomes harder as you grow older. (Scientists have also taken note of that fact, though they haven't been able to explain it.)

When I talked to him, Jim Nesdill had been working for TWA for four years. At first he dealt with jet lag by trying to ignore it. A typical layover in Switzerland would get Jim into Geneva in the morning, after working a night flight, and he'd immediately take a train out into the country. Later, an afternoon nap revived his energy, and he was usually in bed by ten that night. "But then," he said, "I'd wake at two and couldn't get back to sleep." In the long run that kind of schedule takes its toll. Jim eventually changed his habits and took a nap when he first arrived at his layover city.

Brian Nakauchi, a TWA flight attendant since 1975, told me that instead of attempting to ignore jet lag, he coped by keeping to his home schedule as much as possible. When he was in Europe, he left his watch set on New York time and he let his appetite tell him how much to eat and when. Arriving in France at 8 or 9 A.M. local time (the middle of the night in New York) Brian generally took a four-hour nap before he got on with the day.

"Most new international flight attendants have trouble with the job at first," he said. "In the first few months they get sick a lot. My solution is to keep my body as strong as possible. At home I run a couple of miles every day. In Europe I try to do five miles a day. I can sightsee as I run."

How to Combat Jet Lag

Whether you should try Jim's old way and forge ahead as if jet lag didn't exist, or go with Brian and George Plimpton and make allowances for it really depends on how your own body reacts. Some people *have* to make allowances. Either way, there are a few simple energy-saving "don'ts" that medical researchers agree are worth noting.

Don't eat too heartily during the flight or immediately after arrival, since your digestive rhythms are bound to be out of sync with the meals you're putting down. Don't have much to drink during the flight because alcohol combined with the altitude can make you feel very tired. (The plane is pressurized to the equivalent of five thousand feet above sea level.) In addition, alcohol is dehydrating; since the air in the cabin is very dry, that's another reason to avoid drinking too much. Don't smoke, or at least cut back as far as possible; smoking, like drinking, will heighten your fatigue since, combined with the altitude, it drastically reduces the amount of oxygen circulating in your bloodstream.

Researchers have also suggested that if it's very important for you to function well immediately upon arrival, you can try to preadapt your body to the time change by gradually shifting your sleeping hours *before* you leave home—much as Plimpton shifts them after he has arrived. Thus, if you're flying east, you start several days before the flight and get up a little earlier each day and then go to bed earlier that night. Flying west, of course, you get up and go to bed later.

An Eating Plan that Eases Jet-lag Fatigue

An alternative method is to tackle the jet-lag problem by using an eating plan that Dr. Ehret has worked out, one that takes advantage of the resynchronizing abilities of the xanthines and the eat-and-fast cycle. Here's how the plan works. Let's say you're flying from New York to Paris on a Wednesday evening. You want to set your body clocks ahead, then, by six hours. Beginning on the preceding Sunday, alternate feasting with fasting, consuming large meals on Sunday and Tuesday and eating lightly on Monday and Wednesday. This variation on the normal eat-and-fast cycle helps to swing certain key enzymes into line; it also forces the body to dip into its reserves of glycogen, a starchy substance stored in the liver and tissues that's readily converted into biochemical energy.

On Wednesday avoid carbohydrates completely except for fruits and fruit juices. Don't touch tea or caffeinated beverages before six in the evening. In the period between six and midnight, which often coincides with the early part of the flight, drink several cups of black coffee or strong tea to nudge those clocks forward. Skip the meal provided by the airline and stay as quiet as possible until seven or eight in the morning, Paris time; then have a high-calorie, high-protein meal without coffee or tea. This will encourage the synthesis of those daytime biochemicals and, in addition, your buildup of glycogen reserves will now occur according to Paris time. (If your flight doesn't land until mid-morning, ask to have your dinner from the night before heated and served as a breakfast.) Later in the day have a large high-protein lunch and a high-carbohydrate supper and go to bed early.

Coming home, you're hoping to set your body clocks back. Ehret suggests that you drink several cups of coffee or strong tea before noon and then keep away from coffee, tea, and alcohol after that. Eat lightly during the day and on the plane. Set your watch to home time and stay active during the hours when you'd be active at home. Once again, when it's breakfast time in New York have a high-protein, high-calorie breakfast, followed by a high-protein lunch and a high-carbohydrate dinner.

Dr. Ehret's program has been tested on soldiers flying east from the United States to Europe. Their internal rhythms were recorded before, during, and after the flight; afterward their performance on various tasks was also tested. When they were compared to a group of soldiers who made the same flight but did not follow the program, it was clear that the Ehret plan made a remarkable difference.

Energy Crisis on the Night Shift

If jet lag is sometimes hard to handle, shift work can be just as much of an energy drain since it, too, jars rhythms out of sync. If an individual, after switching to the night shift, reorganizes his life so that he's consistently sleeping days and working nights, his body will gradually adjust. However, many shift workers sleep days during the week and then on weekends they try to switch back to sleeping nights, so as to be up and around when everyone else is, which tends to prolong the discomfort. Sometimes, too, shifts are rotated and switched back and forth at such frequent intervals that there's no hope of adjusting. All this is a growing problem, since almost ten million Americans are involved in shift work.

The scientists who study sleep have as hard a time working shifts as anyone I know. In addition to the fact that at irregular intervals they're up all night "running" a subject in the sleep lab, there's the exquisite irony that this form of shift work requires them to stay awake in order to watch while someone else sleeps. Inside the lab's soundproof bedroom, the subject—wired up to machines that continuously record his brain waves and various other functions—dozes and dreams, while the researcher outside who is monitoring the machines downs quantities of black coffee in an attempt to stay alert.

Debbie Sewitch, a very tall, dark-haired young woman with an air of quiet competence, was a postgraduate student doing sleep research when I interviewed her. For about a month one summer she ran subjects in a sleep lab three times a week, working an eighteen-hour "night" each time. "I'd get to the lab at nine at night," she recalled, "and finally finish up at three the next afternoon. I was home and in bed by four and I'd sleep until one in the morning. Then I'd get up and try desperately to stay awake until at least seven, so that I could do my sleeping again during the day, because the following night I had to be back at the lab. You know, I don't think anyone has studied the personality changes that go along with shift work. Certainly, I knew I was changing and changing fast, though of course it wasn't a permanent thing.

I suspect that people on shift work often become jumpy, erratic, and irritable—or perhaps ecstatic and flighty instead."

Some people seem to cope with shift work—or jet lag—much better than others. Perhaps they're not locked into their daily cycles as firmly as most of us are, and so their rhythms may adapt more easily. Or perhaps, as Dr. Ehret suggested, some of them are already chronically desynchronized to such an extent that shift work (or jet lag) makes very little difference to them. Normally hyperactive or perhaps even quite irritable, they simply become a little more so.

Scientists who study biological cycles have been suggesting for years that it may actually be a rather dangerous thing to have chronically skewed rhythms. In fact, a recent California study of over two thousand American workers found that those on a rotating shift had more accidents than others and were also more apt to develop a variety of medical and psychological problems ranging from colds, cramps, and chest pains to fatigue and nervousness.

Ehret points out that even those of us who don't do shift work and seldom jet anywhere are constantly shifting our rhythms around because of the coffee and tea we consume and the irregular hours we keep. As he explained it, it's as if we're continually experimenting with many different synchronizers applied simultaneously. "No one has studied the effects of multiple synchronizers on a human population," he said, "so we can't really claim that the sky is falling; but indications are that we should show some concern." He cites research on the lowly tomato plant—for plants and animals have their internal cycles too. Ordinarily, the warmer it is, the more tomatoes the plant produces, and of course it's warmer while it's light and cooler at night. You'll remember, too, that both the light-dark cycle and the warm-cool cycle are natural synchronizers, capable of resetting body clocks. If, then, experimenters substitute a regime that's first cool and light and then warm and dark, the plants become stunted, grow tumors, and die. Lab animals, if kept desynchronized, also live shorter lives.

Nevertheless, at this point in time no one is really sure what effect the lack of synchrony has on *human* health—let alone human energy—in the long run. Therefore, I don't think any of us needs to become compulsive yet about bedtime or meal hours, though it's probably better to be more regular rather than less. And, certainly, if I had something coming up that was bound to lay siege to my energy, I would train for it beforehand by keeping hours that were as regular as possible.

Revitalize by Flowing with Your Free-running Rhythm

If I could opt out of the nine-to-five world for a while, I'd try drifting with my own free-running rhythm: That's definitely an energizer. For, though most of us function normally according to a twenty-four-hour day, we do it mostly because of habit and social pressure. *Left to our own devices, we might generally live a day somewhat longer than twenty-four hours.*

We know this because scientists, curious to see what would happen if all known synchronizers were removed, have persuaded volunteers to spend weeks or sometimes months in windowless isolation, with no clues to the passage of time. Some have taken up residence in caverns deep underground; others have lived in bunkers or in soundproof suites at a university. Under such conditions most people begin to go to bed a bit later each night, and to get up later and later as well. They settle into living a day that's regularly about twenty-five rather than twenty-four hours long. Scientists call this naturally emerging rhythm the *free-running rhythm.* Plants and animals kept in isolation—in constant light or constant dimness—show a similar tendency to lengthen or shorten the twenty-four-hour day.

The Laboratory of Human Chronophysiology at Montefiore Hospital in New York City has an ongoing time-isolation project that's fairly typical of experiments on free running. Paid volunteers live alone in a windowless, air-conditioned, three-room apartment at the hospital. They're deprived of all time cues for the duration of the experiment: They have no clock, telephone, or TV set, and though they're visited often by the research staff, they're allowed no outside visitors, no mail, and no newspapers. They do have records and books available and they can read, write, work and, of course, request a meal whenever they feel hungry. Some have stayed in isolation for as long as six months.

For the first few days after a subject checks into the suite, the Montefiore researchers hold him to a time-entrained day while they measure baseline rhythms—in sleep patterns, hormones, temperature, and so forth. Then time cues are removed and he's turned loose, allowed to choose his own hours for sleeping and eating. The only way he can do that is to tune in to the needs of his body, something most of us seldom do. Instead, we go to bed at a certain hour because we know we'll have to get up the next morning; we eat to *prevent* ourselves from becoming hungry.

Cued by body time rather than clock time, within a few days all subjects develop a new daily rhythm. Most live a day that's about twenty-five hours long, but there have been some subjects who have actually adopted a forty-eight- to fifty-hour day, sleeping for a long period just once every two days and spacing their meals accordingly.

Subjects usually report that it feels good to free run—to settle into your own natural rhythm. Dr. Elliot D. Weitzman, chairman of the Department of Neurology at Montefiore Hospital and director of the Laboratory of Human Chronophysiology, explained, "They're not happy to be in isolation. They're delighted when the experiment is over and they can go out and do things and see people again, but while they're free running they often report that they feel very healthy and full of energy. An internal feeling of well-being, of alertness, vigilance, and clear thinking is very characteristic."

There are people out in the real world who deliberately free run and others who should probably try it, for the free-running rhythm is apparently stronger in some people than it is in most. Years ago, Dr. Wilse Webb speculated that somewhere among the human population there must be individuals who find it uncomfortable to have to live a twenty-four-hour day. Eventually scientists began to hear about a few blind people who periodically suffered energy-crisis symptoms rather like those of jet lag. For several weeks at a time they would find that they were drowsy and inefficient during the day and had trouble sleeping at night. When their body rhythms were recorded, it turned out that, deprived of the potent light-dark synchronizer, they were indeed cycling according to a "day" longer than twenty-four hours; thus, though sometimes they were in sync with the sighted world, at other times their bodies were registering night while it was day.

There are also sighted individuals who *choose* to free run when given an opportunity to set their own hours, apparently because they feel more comfortable that way. Dr. Webb knows a free-lance computer programmer who does this. But abandoning the twenty-four-hour day would leave most of us uncomfortably out of sync with the working world and with family and friends.

Nevertheless, Dr. Webb believes (as does Dr. Weitzman) that whenever people manage to escape from schedules they tend to lapse into their free-running rhythm. On weekends, for example, many of us phase shift a bit. We go to bed later each night and get up later in the morning; then we feel out of sorts when we have to wrench ourselves back into line on Monday morning. During vacations we're even more inclined to succumb to the body's preference for a longer day. However, there's generally a limit to how far we'll phase shift, because otherwise we'd soon reach the point where we were up all night and sleeping all day; so for a while we free run and then we settle into a new schedule —this one self-imposed.

The very concept of free running has built-in appeal. It's a chance to escape from the tyranny of rigid schedules, a way to get in touch with the body's underlying rhythms. Some years ago I experimented with free running in a limited way, though at the time I didn't know that this was what I was doing. We were on vacation, sharing a summer house with friends, and I suggested to the children—ages five, six, and eight—that we hide all clocks and watches. We would get up when we no longer felt tired, eat when we were hungry and not before, go to bed when we were sleepy, and generally tune in to what our bodies were telling us. The children liked the idea of learning to listen to their bodies instead of the clock.

Unfortunately, their bodies told them different things. On the first night two of the children sat up happily until nearly eleven; the third youngster, six-year-old Tara, unwilling to go to bed alone, sat up with them, though she had to struggle to stay awake. The next morning she woke inexorably at seven, her usual hour, and then roused the other kids, who dragged themselves out of bed complaining. The same thing happened the second night, and the third, until all three children were exhausted. Though we had escaped the mechanical clock, I hadn't reckoned on the fact that we all have our own biological clocks, and on the body truth that they can operate differently! Tara was a lark and so all of her internal rhythms nudged her toward that 7 A.M. awakening, while the other children were of the owl persuasion and so were primed to wake later and enjoy the evening hours more.

It's tempting to conclude that free running is the "natural" way to live, especially since it seems to be so energizing. However, as Dr. Weitzman pointed out, "Living in an entraining society is actually a very natural life for humans. There has always been a rhythm of nature all around us that we had to live with." Even primitive people presumably got up with the sun and retired to their shelters when darkness fell; they learned that there were times to plant and times to harvest, times when it was safe to hunt and unsafe times as well; and so they must have scheduled themselves much as we do. Free running, then, is not a way to get back to nature. All it does is unmask the hidden rhythms we all harbor, rhythms we normally entrain every day to our lifestyle.

Nevertheless, the next time you're on vacation you might try escaping the twenty-four-hour day as an energy experiment. Put all clocks and watches out of sight. Sleep when you're sleepy and eat when you're hungry—depressurize and listen to your body for a change. After a while you should begin to feel remarkably well and fully charged with energy. However, if yours is a particularly demanding job, it might be best to begin easing yourself back into a normal schedule a few days before your vacation ends in order to soften the shock of re-entry.

Body Rhythms and Manic-Depression

The discrepancy between the free-running rhythm and the twenty-four-hour day seems to create few, if any, problems for most people. However, it may be different for the manic-depressive, for researchers are beginning to suggest that this cyclical disorder (see Chapter 3) may be caused by abnormal biological rhythms.

The evidence so far is spotty but suggestive. For example, in one group of manic-depressives whose rhythms were recorded half were drifting away from the twenty-four-hour day. Furthermore, scientists from the National Institute of Mental Health successfully treated one such patient just by adjusting her bedtime!

The patient was a fifty-two-year-old woman who ordinarily cycled from manic to normal to depressed to normal and back to manic again in about forty-three days. The researchers first "synchronized" her to a twenty-two-hour day, since that seemed to be her natural rhythm, and as a result she went through the shortest depression period she'd had in years. Figuring that perhaps, like someone with jet lag, she was trying to sleep when her body was wide awake, and vice versa, the scientists then advanced her sleep schedule so that she was going to bed six hours earlier than she had been. The change worked like an antidepressant drug and the effects lasted for two weeks. As they wore off, the researchers again advanced her by six hours and again won her a two-week respite. However, on the third try the technique didn't work, possibly because she was by then almost back on her original schedule, since her bedtime had been pushed forward by a total of eighteen hours. Curiously, it usually takes about two weeks for antidepressants or lithium to take hold with a manic-depressive. What's more, recent studies indicate that the so-called tricyclic antidepressants speed up the cycles of mania and depression, while lithium slows them down.

From all of this, some scientists have evolved a new theory to explain manic-depression. They suggest that the body may have one biochemical clock that regulates the daily rise and fall of body temperature and also governs dreaming sleep, and another that controls nondreaming sleep. Perhaps in the manic-depressive the two clocks are drifting out of sync, so that brain levels of powerful chemicals that ought to balance one another—one of them rising as the other falls—peak and fall simultaneously and, in the process, cause mood swings and the other symptoms of the psychosis. It's an ingenious hypothesis, and only time and careful research will prove it out one way or the other.

Rhythms of Alertness and Daydreaming

In addition to the twenty-four-hour rhythms discussed so far, the body also harbors cycles that are both shorter and longer. Dreams, for example, occur every ninety minutes or so all night long. *There are also several daytime rhythms that seem to peak once every ninety to one hundred minutes: stomach contractions, alertness, daydreaming, and the urge to converse.* (For more about the conversational rhythm, see Chapter 12.)

The studies that have been done of the rhythm of daydreaming are particularly intriguing. In one experiment volunteers sat alone for ten hours in a room from which virtually all distractions had been removed. Every five minutes a whistle blew and the person wrote out a summary of what he'd been thinking about for the last five minutes. When these records were analyzed, the researchers discovered that virtually everyone cycled regularly—every ninety minutes or so—from reality concerns to daydreaming: from times when they were busy making plans, thinking about real problems, and examining their surroundings to times when they reported fantasies and bizarre thoughts and images. In a follow-up study eight volunteers carried tape recorders and timers around with them while they went about their business. Every ten minutes the timer buzzed and they dictated into the tape recorder an account of their thoughts for the last ten minutes. Despite all the distractions of a normal daily routine, the daydream rhythm surfaced once again.

A Basic Rest/Activity Cycle?

The fact that dreams and daydreams occur roughly once every ninety minutes is intriguing. It's almost as if the dream rhythm continues beyond sleep, making itself felt at regular intervals as a tendency to fantasize. Many years ago veteran sleep researcher Nathaniel Kleitman suggested that there may be a basic rest/activity cycle that affects the central nervous system throughout the twenty-four-hour day. During the night it controls the alternation of dreaming and nondreaming sleep. During the day it sees to it that the mind shifts gears periodically, becoming more or less fanciful, more or less alert. It's possible that the same central control mechanisms are involved in both the daytime and the nighttime ninety-minute cycles, though there's no proof that this is so.

From a practical point of view, it's handy just knowing that those ninety-minute daytime rhythms exist. If you enjoy daydreaming, for example, then when you become aware that fantasies are welling up—strange, vivid, creative—you may want to pause and savor them while the daydream cycle is at its peak.

As for the alertness cycle, when you feel that you're really focused on your work and that the alertness rhythm is cresting, that may be the time to resist the temptation to take a break. On the other hand, as you sense your concentration slipping, you can ease off for a few minutes rather than forcing yourself to persevere, since you know that in short order you'll be feeling mentally sharp again. People who have trouble falling asleep can also take advantage of the alertness cycle by heading for bed while the rhythm is at a low point and they're feeling muzzy-headed and drowsy; for if they wait until the cycle begins to swing upward again, it will bring with it a second wind and sleep may prove elusive.

The Menstrual Cycle

Among the body rhythms that cycle over a period longer than 24 hours, there is, of course, menstruation. Statistically, the average menstrual month is not 28 days long, as most people assume it is. It's closer to 29.5 days—which is the length of the interval between successive new moons. Obviously, this cycle, too, has its synchronizers; in fact, some years ago a doctor discovered that an ordinary electric light could often regularize irregular periods, perhaps by standing in for moonlight. If a woman left a lamp burning at the foot of her bed all night, every night, from the fourteenth through the sixteenth days after the onset of her last menstruation, it apparently triggered ovulation, for within a few months her period was usually right on schedule.

For most, but not all, women, energy waxes and wanes in a predictable way throughout the menstrual month. They tend to feel more alert, happy, outgoing, competent—and are least sensitive to pain—during the first half of the month, with the good feelings at a peak at about the time of ovulation; during the second half of the month they're less alert, happy, and so forth. In addition, women who have a problem with premenstrual tension often actually become somewhat depressed and irritable just before their period starts and for the first few days afterward. These mood swings don't happen to everybody; some women don't notice any difference at all, while others actually feel a welling up of energy just before their period begins. In fact, since a sexually active woman can only be positive that she's not pregnant while she's menstruating, that's a good time for many.

Obviously patterns vary. At any rate, any woman who is aware that her own energy does flow in some predictable way over the course of her menstrual cycle can plan to capitalize on her "up" days, the time of the month when her vitality is naturally highest. (Men probably have no similar long-range mood-and-energy cycle; attempts to identify one have come up with contradictory results.)

About Biorhythms

There are other long-term body rhythms as well. However, most scientists do not include among these the three cycles postulated by proponents of Biorhythms. This very popular theory maintains that everyone has a physical-abilities cycle that peaks once every twenty-three days, an emotional, good-feelings cycle that crests once in twenty-eight days, and a thirty-three-day intellectual cycle. All three are supposedly set in motion at the moment of birth and all are said to be useful in predicting up and down days and approaching crises. The researchers I talked to were convinced that Biorhythms have no scientific basis, that they're really a form of numerology. As one man explained it, the real body rhythms don't cycle with machinelike regularity from the moment of birth; they're more like the menstrual rhythm in that they are different from one individual to the next and even in the same individual from one day to the next. Furthermore, their timing can be thrown off by stress and, in fact, often is.

Why Do We Have Body Rhythms?

What causes biological rhythms? A minority opinion maintains that rhythms are imposed from outside the body by geophysical forces, subtle tides from space that can't yet be measured, though we can see their effects in the ebb and flow of the earth's magnetic field or in changes in gravity or barometric pressure. However, most scientists believe instead that every individual body cell probably has many different kinds of clocks, and that the body's timing results from a complex interaction of cellular, hormonal, and neural rhythms that are synchronized (under normal conditions) by environmental cycles of light and dark.

Why do we have body clocks? Some researchers have suggested that plants and animals developed cycles of their own to take advantage of the fact that they existed in a rhythmic environment in which day followed night, warmth followed coolness, and so forth. Going further back, Dr. Franz Halberg and Dr. Andrew Ahlgren of the University of Minnesota believe that even the very first single-celled creatures had to have whole arrays of rhythms if they were to exist at all, each particular cycle adapted both to the environment and to all the organism's other internal cycles. Some of these cycles evolved to match environmental cycles, but life was basically rhythmic from the beginning.

Early humans must have found rhythms handy things to have. Not only do body cycles tend to peak at times when they're most apt to be needed, but long before there were clocks they provided us with internal cues to the passage of time, a way to anticipate events such as nightfall or the daily forays of particular animals.

With the invention of mechanical clocks, electric lights, and the development of civilization in general, we began to lose touch with biological time, until today we most often ignore or override our internal cycles. Many times it's all to the good that we can do this, but undoubtedly we pay a price in stress and ultimately in energy.

If you can learn to tune in to your rhythms and ride with them more often, you'll cut down on the stress. You'll also be using your own internal momentum in a unique way to make the most of your energy.

Energy Tips

1. What are your daily peak hours for energy? Once you've pinpointed your own prime time, schedule yourself accordingly.

2. When you suffer from mid-afternoon slump, try coffee or brisk physical activity to revive yourself; or else use the time to do tasks that don't demand much concentration; or nap if you can.

3. If you're a night owl facing difficult mornings, get up earlier to give your body a chance to come to. And whenever you can, schedule tougher jobs for late in the day.

4. Save energy by anticipating your own mood cycles: Expect to feel somewhat irritable at around dinnertime and in the wee hours of the morning. If you wake up anxious or depressed, remind yourself that you'll probably feel better later on.

5. Hangover prevention: Remember that the drinks you down with lunch will hit you harder than the same number of drinks would at six in the evening.

6. Dieter's tip: Do more of your eating earlier in the day to lose weight faster.

7. As an experiment, try switching to high-protein breakfasts and high-carbohydrate suppers to see whether that gives your energy a lift.

8. To combat jet lag, ease into the new time schedule gradually. Leave your watch set on home time for a few days. Let your appetite tell you when to eat and how much. Shift your bedtime by just an hour every night, even if that means that for a few days you're going to bed very early (or very late) according to local time.

9. During the flight itself don't overeat or overdrink, and avoid smoking.

10. If you're crossing time zones and it's important for you to be in top shape immediately on arrival, begin adapting before you leave home: Shift your bedtime gradually, starting a few days before the flight. And try the schedule of fasting/feasting that Dr. Ehret recommends.

11. If you're working the night shift, don't give in to the temptation to revert to sleeping at night on the weekends.

12. When you have a grueling schedule coming up, prepare for it ahead of time: Be as regular as you can in your eating and sleeping habits in order to get your body rhythms solidly in synchrony.

13. While you're on vacation, drift with your free-running rhythm for a real energy high. Put clocks and watches out of sight and listen to your body. Sleep only when you're tired and eat only when you're hungry.

14. Flow with your alertness cycle whenever you can. Make the most of alertness peaks; when you feel your concentration slipping, ease off for a few minutes. Head for bed at night while the cycle is at a low point.

15. If you're a woman and your energy ebbs and flows in a predictable way over the course of the menstrual month, plan ahead: Take advantage of the times when you can expect to feel most vital.

The Basic Facts About Energy: An Instant Replay

The last five chapters have covered the basics of human energy —facts you need to know to understand how your own energy operates. To summarize briefly:

• In Chapter 1 you were invited to figure out what your energy profile is and how it has affected your life.

• Chapter 2 explored the heredity/environment conundrum and concluded that, though your energy level is originally determined by heredity, as time passes environment has a massive impact on that level. As an adult, then, you may be operating far below your potential.

• Chapter 3 suggested that the two kinds of energy are physiologically different; that your inborn potential for enerjoy is probably determined by the chemistry of your brain; and that nervous energy is basically a response to stress.

• Your emotions are the most important determinant of your daily energy level. Chapter 4 explained how repressing emotions can repress energy.

• Chapter 5 pointed out that fluctuations in the energy level are caused, in part, by the ebb and flow of the body's myriad internal rhythms.

All this, of course, is just the beginning, because many other factors also affect your energy. Food and drugs do, and so does the amount of sleep you've had, the shape you're in, the weather, and even the people you're with.

The next section will look at all of these factors in the light of recent research. We will scan that research for practical tactics that you can use to liberate energy.

Sleep: A Prerequisite for Vitality

In the next chapter, we'll take up the subject of sleep. For the past twenty years research on sleep has flourished. In labs around the world scientists have been studying the sleep of volunteers—insomniacs, average people, and those with special skills—for some people can fall asleep at will, while others catnap for an hour or two every night and feel that this is all the rest they need. Sleep and energy are obviously related. Sleep research suggests some novel strategies for augmenting energy.

II
HOW TO LIBERATE
YOUR ENERGY

6

Sleeping Tactics

• Do people who need a lot of sleep need it because they're basically low in energy?

• Can you train yourself to get by with less sleep or to doze off at will?

• Should a nap leave you with more pep—or less?

• How can you prevent insomnia from robbing you of energy?

• What can you do if your need for sleep is excessive?

Researchers have come up with some surprising answers to these questions, answers that for many people will have immediate practical value. For the connection between sleep and energy is quite straightforward: *If you don't get enough sleep, you won't have enough energy!*

What Kind of Sleeper Are You?

When it comes to sleep, individuals are again very different. There are long sleepers and short sleepers; there are those who can catnap anywhere, anytime, and those who have to go through an elaborate bedtime ritual if they're to sleep at all; there are some who must be in bed by ten and log eight hours of solid sleep if they are to function normally the next day, and others who can forgo a whole night's sleep with few apparent ill effects. Some of these differences may well be hereditary, programed in the genes.

At any rate, the old assumption that *everyone* needs eight hours of sleep a night is far from true. It helps, then, to know what kind of sleeper you are and what your particular sleep needs and problems might be, so that you can be sure the sizable proportion of your life you're investing in sleep is providing the maximum assist to your energy.

Two kinds of people have sleep problems: those who would like to spend less time sleeping and the insomniacs who yearn to spend more time at it. We'll consider both problems in this chapter, and we'll also ask whether napping is a reliable source of energy.

How Much Sleep Is Enough?

Unquestionably, some people need more sleep than others. Since sleep and energy are so clearly related, you might suppose that strollers, who have less-than-average energy, would also log more hours in bed. My talks with strollers turned up no evidence that this is true, nor does it seem to be true that sprinters are inevitably short sleepers.

However, I did find that those strollers who *are* long sleepers—who can't function without nine or ten hours of sleep a night—are apt to be very unhappy indeed.

Martha: Too Much Sleep

In 1978, the year I first met Martha—the low-key psychiatrist mentioned in Chapter 1—she had just made an appointment for a work-up at a sleep clinic, because she was so unhappy about the fact that she couldn't get by on less than nine hours of sleep a night.

Martha first became sleep conscious when she was pregnant back in 1973. She discovered then that to feel well she needed ten hours of sleep every night. However, the pregnancy seemed to explain that; in fact, through the next four hectic years of coping with two small children (she had a second baby in 1975) plus a job, that ten-hour requirement seemed logical and temporary, and so it didn't bother her. But in 1976, when her life began to settle down, she realized that nine hours was still her minimum and she began to wonder.

"I couldn't really remember, but I couldn't believe I was always like that," she told me, "because if I had been, how would I have survived my internship, when I sometimes had to work forty-eight hours at a stretch? So I had medical tests done, and I found there was nothing physically wrong with me. Since, as a psychiatrist, I know that people who are depressed sometimes do a lot of sleeping, naturally that possibility occurred to me, too. But though I do feel down at times, mostly I'm up, and the amount of sleep I need doesn't change much, no matter what my mood."

At that time Martha seldom went to bed at the same hour for two nights running. "I start to poop out at ten-thirty or eleven," she explained, "but my husband likes to stay up until one and so I try to stay up with him if I can. Lately he's been away on business for part of every week, which means that half the time I go to bed on my schedule and the other half on his."

When Martha got less than nine hours of sleep, by around three the next afternoon her urge to nap became almost irresistible. If she drank coffee she could postpone sleep, but then she felt sluggish and grouchy. She became very frustrated when she needed to sleep but couldn't, and unhappy, too, because it was so hard to control the napping.

"Do you know, I nap more than my three-year-old does," she said. "I sometimes fall asleep at parties, too, and I have trouble meditating, because unless I've had both a nap *and* some coffee, the minute I begin to relax I doze off."

And yet, though she felt guilty about her naps, Martha also enjoyed them very much. "The moment of falling asleep is extremely pleasurable to me," she said. "I can watch myself doing it: There's a kind of click inside my head and I know I'm asleep. There's something almost sexual about that release of tension—it's nearly orgasmic."

After an initial work-up at the sleep clinic, Martha was asked to take a nap in the laboratory while wired up to an electroencephalograph, a machine that records brain waves through electrodes stuck to the scalp. Though her sleep, as recorded, looked normal, the psychiatrist working with her felt she might have a very mild case of narcolepsy all the same. (Narcolepsy is a disorder characterized by brief, uncontrollable attacks of sleep.) So he prescribed a stimulant for her, a medication often used for narcoleptics, who are generally advised to take it three times a day. When Martha took one pill just once, it kept her up for thirteen hours and she felt better for a week afterward.

"I call it my magic pill," she said. "I take it now only about once every two weeks, at times when I'm really sleepy and yet I need to function at my best. It works within twenty minutes and it makes me feel alert but not driven." She's had only one negative experience with the drug: Once she took it not because she was sleepy but because she was in a bad mood and she thought it might help. It left her hyperalert but not happier.

Martha suspects that for her the really significant thing about the magic pill is not its physical impact but the fact that it has made her see her problem differently. Now that she no longer feels helpless in the face of her own fatigue, she's not so focused on sleep. "I may still get as many hours of it," she said. "I'm not sure because I've stopped counting. On some days I still nap, though on others I don't. But the main thing is that I don't feel so badly about it now."

When you feel anxious about a problem and helpless to deal with it, the difficulty will often balloon: Suddenly it seems like the focal point of your life. The same sort of thing sometimes happens to people who develop insomnia (a subject I'll come back to later). The point here is that *when something comes along that proves to you that you're not helpless after all, the problem often ceases to be a problem.*

Self-induced Jet Lag?

However, there may also be another explanation for Martha's difficulty. I talked to two different sleep researchers about her and both suggested that if she got up at the same time every morning and went to bed at about the same hour every night she might feel better, since it's possible that she creates a kind of chronic jet lag for herself by keeping irregular hours. (As you'll see later in this chapter, a haphazard bedtime can also generate insomnia.) As it happens, because her husband stopped traveling, Martha's sleep pattern stabilized at about the same time that she discovered the magic pill. I suspect that both the pill (or simply the knowledge that it was available to her) and the new schedule helped.

Incidentally, neither of the sleep researchers found it surprising that Martha has sleeping difficulties now that she didn't have when she was an intern. Most people are more flexible in their sleep needs when they're young and can survive the occasional sleepless night much more comfortably than when they're older.

How to Spend Less Time Sleeping

If, like Martha, you feel that you're doing more sleeping than you want to—and perhaps more than you need, going by past experience—the first thing to do is see a doctor. A change in your need for sleep could be a sign that something is physically wrong (see Chapter 17).

It could also be a sign of depression. People who are depressed sometimes do a lot of sleeping, and it's possible to be mildly depressed and not realize that that's your problem. Or you may be understimulated—perhaps life isn't demanding enough of you—or it's demanding too much and you're using sleep as an escape. If you're resorting to sleep for any of these reasons, then you'll need to solve the basic problem before you can expect to expand your waking time and have more energy.

If none of the above applies, then you might take a look at the hours you've been keeping: Is your bedtime so irregular that your body rhythms are chronically askew and you're always tired? If so, your solution is obvious.

Unless you're a bona fide narcoleptic and under treatment by a doctor, leaning on pep pills is no answer. You might, like Martha, get a psychological boost from knowing that you had pills available, but for many people the temptation to abuse such drugs is just too great (see Chapter 8).

However, you can *train* yourself to manage on less sleep. The trick is to cut back gradually, shaving off only about fifteen minutes at a time, and then living with the new regime until you're comfortable with it—even if that takes a week or so—before paring back again. People who have gone slowly enough have been able to cut their sleep requirements by as much as 20 to 30 percent, dropping from eight hours, say, to five and a half or six. However, researchers warn that at the lower figure you probably won't feel or work quite as well, and that this tactic is likely to work better for those whose sleep needs are fairly flexible to begin with.

You have one other alternative, of course, and that's to accept the fact that you're simply a long sleeper. Thanks to our culture's emphasis on doing, many Americans assume that the goal is to hit a kind of balance: Get just enough sleep to function at an optimum level, without spending a moment more in bed than is absolutely necessary. But *sleep may have psychological benefits that we can only guess at.* Furthermore, some people sleep for the fun of it!

Sleep Is a Marvelous Place to Be

Mary Anne Symons Brown, a free-lance copywriter, rated herself an eight or nine on the energy scale. She said emphatically that she needs a lot of sleep—ten hours a night—and she often naps besides. "Without sleep I'm a dead man," she said. "When I travel or go to a convention, if I try to get by on four or five hours' sleep a night I have a life-span of about forty-eight to seventy-two hours. After that I'm a zombie—constipated, ornery—you know, the Archie Bunker syndrome."

What struck me immediately about Mary Anne is that she doesn't mind needing all that sleep. In fact, to her sleep is simply a marvelous place to be. "How can anyone *not* like sleep?" she asked. "It's free, it's nonfattening. I adore sleep—sleep and baths are my religion. In tense times I've used it as a release valve. It's one of the grand miracles of nature that if you're upset about something you can go to sleep and wake up feeling much calmer and better able to deal with the problem. You may see it in a new perspective, too, and that's true even of the crossword puzzle. I often go to bed stymied and wake up and immediately find five new words. During tough times, or if I'm depressed, I take a nap or sleep late; sometimes I actually sleep all day.

"Sleep is also the only time when I'm alone with my thoughts. Even if no one else is home, if I'm awake I'm externally stimulated—I'm busy reading or working or whatever. The only time I'm internally stimulated is when I'm sleeping. It's a nice little cave to have; nobody else can come there."

Mary Anne always dreams—and in color—crazy dreams that are sometimes shocking and unpleasant but always creative and strange, and she can always remember some. The dreams are probably part of the reason she enjoys sleeping. As a child she used to program herself to have "the Margaret O'Brien dream" about being invited to a Hollywood party. For a while she ran that one through night after night.

I think one crucial difference between Martha and Mary Anne is that Mary Anne has always had the kind of flexibility that Martha has to get from her magic pill. If she has a deadline to meet, Mary Anne can work through the night. She can function, if she has to, on very little sleep for two or three days. Perhaps that's why she's comfortable about spending ten hours out of every twenty-four in the arms of Morpheus. Of course, it also helps that she enjoys sleeping and, even more to the point, that during her waking hours she's the high-energy sort.

Martha feels that she's been shortchanged on energy, and that undoubtedly colors her attitude toward sleep. People who find that they have neither the time nor the drive to do all the things they badly want to do are apt to resent time-outs beyond the eight-hour night. But sprinters who need a lot of sleep are much less likely to complain about it. Some say their waking hours are crammed so full that they've earned their rest. Others, like Mary Anne, feel that sleep bestows all kinds of benefits that are seldom recognized.

If that's true (and I suspect it is), then long sleepers of all energy types might as well follow Mary Anne's example and count their blessings!

Are You a Short Sleeper?

The average person needs seven and a half hours of sleep a night. However, *sleep experts consider it quite normal to need nine or ten hours—or to be able to get by regularly on just an hour or two!*

According to Dr. John Hanley, a California psychiatrist and sleep scientist, the world's champion short sleeper is a woman in her seventies who puts in about seventy minutes a night. "She's convinced that's all the sleep anyone needs," he said, "and all her life she's found it difficult to believe that other people are so lazy."

Nor is she unique. Runners-up have been reported. For example, a recent Australian study turned up several people who typically sleep for only two to two and a half hours a night. One man admitted that he also lies down for twenty minutes at noon every day. When asked if he felt particularly tired around noon, he said no; it was just that he'd promised his doctor he'd rest then, because the doctor was worried that he got so little sleep! Napoleon is also regarded as a true short sleeper, though he needed three or four hours a night. On that little sleep he could get up and simultaneously eat breakfast, play chess, and direct a battle.

Very short sleepers who are talented and creative tend to be extraordinarily productive. Those who aren't as gifted usually hold both a day and night job. Several researchers have tried to determine whether there are consistent personality differences between short and long sleepers. One study reported that short sleepers are more efficient, ambitious, self-confident, energetic, and that in general they're psychologically healthier; but another study found no real differences between the shorts and the longs. Dr. Hanley pointed out that both studies looked at variations within the usual range of sleep needs (six and a half to eight and a half hours) rather than at the extremes. He also noted that, personality differences aside, the life-style of someone who habitually sleeps only four hours a night *has* to be radically different from that of someone who sleeps nine hours.

Short sleepers are generally admired and envied by their friends, for, as I mentioned earlier, many people believe that the less one sleeps the better. In fact, those who are driven to achieve often feel that sleep is a complete waste of time. Thomas Edison certainly thought so: He was delighted when he invented the electric light, because he hoped that, since it banished darkness, it might actually eliminate the need for sleep.

Sleep: A Body Truth

Sleep is one of those body truths: We're all quite different in our needs and habits, and yet we tend to judge others on the basis of our own bodily experiences. Short sleepers frequently have no patience with long sleepers. People who like to wake up early often seem to feel that it's in some way immoral to sleep late. People who prize every waking moment are amazed to find that others sleep for the fun of it.

Such attitudes *can* lead to trouble. One couple I know had a running battle for a while because her child (it was the second marriage for both of them) kept waking them early in the morning. This made him very angry, which she thought was unreasonable. It took both of them a while to understand that once he was awake in the morning he was awake for good and was unable to fall asleep again, while she felt it was one of life's supreme luxuries to be awakened early and know that she could roll over and sink back to sleep for another half hour or so.

Flexibility was at issue here, and flexibility is one of sleep's features that seems to vary a great deal from one individual to the next. At any rate, the moral of the story is: *You simply can't assume that other people are exactly like you in their sleep needs, energy, or anything else.*

Varieties of Insomnia

As every insomniac knows, lack of sleep is a monumental energy downer. In fact, when I described Martha's problem to Dr. Hanley, his reply was, "Think how insomniacs would envy her!

There's a huge segment of the population who would give anything to be able to sleep."

Insomnia comes in several varieties. If you have a problem with insomnia, it helps to know what kind of insomniac you are, since different methods of treatment are often recommended for different types.

The Hard-Core Insomniac

You're a hard-core insomniac if you *always* have trouble sleeping. Whether your life is going well or poorly, whether it's a weekday or a weekend, whether you go to bed early or late, you virtually never get the sleep you need.

Dr. Hanley believes that some insomniacs owe their sleeplessness to an unknown physical disorder. He explained that physiologically such people are alike in certain ways: At night they have a higher body temperature than most people, a faster heart rate, and increased resistance to peripheral blood flow. (Normally, with the onset of sleep more blood begins to flow to the body's periphery.) When they do finally succeed in sleeping, they do less dreaming and spend less time in a deep sleep. No one knows why these differences exist, but they seem to indicate that this kind of insomnia, at least, can't be put down to emotional problems.

The usual responses to hard-core insomnia are medication—under a doctor's continuing supervision—or stoicism. Dr. Hanley has found that many patients prefer to do without medication. He explained, "I have a surprising number of patients who will settle for a regime of exercise, no stimulants, and the assurance that they have a true physiological complaint that's treatable but not curable."

Poor-Quality Sleep

Some insomniacs complain about the quality of the sleep they get rather than the quantity. They seldom sleep well. A pharmacist I talked to explained that he wakes up at the slightest noise and that even on nights when nothing awakens him he sleeps restlessly. His wife added that he starts every morning by commenting on how well or how badly he slept the night before.

One way to improve the quality of the sleep you get is to exercise early in the day. Studies have demonstrated that strenuous exercise can increase the amount of deep sleep you have—the kind that feels most refreshing. However, since physical activity alerts the mind even as it fatigues the body, it's not a good idea to schedule a workout for the evening hours.

The Sleeper Who Forgets to Breathe

Some people who experience poor-quality sleep probably have apnea, which has only recently been recognized as a form of insomnia. The victim—usually someone who's a nightly snorer—simply stops breathing from time to time. Soon he becomes uncomfortable from the lack of oxygen and as he gasps for air he awakens briefly. If this happens often enough in the course of the night, he's bound to feel tired in the morning, though he may not remember the awakenings.

Though apnea can be severe and even life-threatening, those are the rare cases. In fact, a recent study conducted at the University of Florida demonstrated that normal, healthy men who are asleep will often stop breathing for anywhere from ten seconds to almost a full minute—without doing themselves any physical damage. The same study confirmed that men are more likely to develop apnea than women, just as they're more likely to snore. To date, no one can explain apnea or snoring, and there's no easy cure for either.

Insomnia that Comes and Goes

If you have this kind of insomnia, your sleeping problems follow a regular cycle. For three or four nights in a row you feel extraordinarily sleepy at around eight or nine in the evening, but then you revive and by bedtime you're wide awake and sleep is impossible. Then suddenly the problem clears up and for a week to ten days you're tired at a normal hour. But then the first phase reappears and you begin to conk out at eight or nine again, only to be wide awake afterward.

To Professor Frederick J. Evans, of Rutgers Medical School, this pattern suggests that your internal rhythms are free running and are cycling according to a "day" that's longer—or, for some, shorter—than twenty-four hours (see Chapter 5). Dr. Evans, who is also director of research at the Carrier Foundation in Belle Mead, New Jersey, explained that when a person is out of sync with the twenty-four-hour day, his body will ease off, in preparation for sleep, at a different hour each night. That's why you sometimes feel tired enough to sleep at bedtime, though at other times you don't.

Some people create a similar sort of insomnia for themselves by keeping highly irregular hours. Their internal rhythms are thrown askew—just as they are with jet lag—and the body becomes confused and may be primed for action just when it's time to go to sleep.

Whether your problem is self-generated or not, scientists believe that the way to treat it is to "anchor" your wake-up time, because there's some evidence that this is the best way to swing internal rhythms back into line. You get up at the same time every morning no matter what—even if you've been up half the night, even if it's the weekend or you're on vacation. For a few days you may feel very tired, but then, as your rhythms stabilize, sleep should begin to come more easily.

Trouble Falling Asleep Versus Trouble Staying Asleep

Some people wake up very early in the morning and are unable to doze off again. They get up at their usual hour, having had much less sleep than they need, and feel groggy and low in energy for the whole day. Depression is often the cause of this sort of sleep problem—as it was with Betty (see Chapter 4). In general, the best way to treat it is to treat the depression.

Others take hours to fall asleep: they may toss and turn for half the night before finally dozing off. This kind of insomnia is extremely common; most people can remember nights when they've been too excited or too upset to fall asleep. Usually the problem persists for only a day or two. For some people, however, it becomes chronic. Often they're the people who have looked for a solution in sleeping pills.

Sleeping Pill Problems

Many doctors today agree that sleeping pills are safe to use for a few days at a time. Someone with frequent bouts of insomnia might actually be happier just having them in the house, since knowing they're there may make him less anxious about his sleep problem. However, he'd be wise to make up his mind to use them no oftener than once or twice a week.

The difficulty with barbiturates is that you build up a tolerance to them, so that you need to take more and more to do the same job. If you take a pill every night, for a week or two the drug will work beautifully; but then it will begin to lose its effectiveness and you'll once again find yourself lying awake at night. You may be tempted to increase the dose; if you do, there will again be a brief improvement, followed by a return of the insomnia. This cycle can be repeated again and again until you're heavily into barbiturates, can't manage without them, and still can't sleep, because now the drug is a direct cause of your insomnia. If you try to give it up, what little sleep you get will be riddled with nightmares, for barbiturates suppress dreaming and the minute they're withdrawn there's a kind of dream rebound.

In recent years a different kind of drug called flurazepam (the trade name is Dalmane) has become popular, but it, too, has drawbacks. Though it has little effect on dreaming, it eliminates deep sleep. It also lingers in the body for days and accumulates; it can thus affect daytime co-ordination and the ability to drive a car, for example—especially after you've had a drink or two.

Nondrug Solutions

There are a number of ways to combat insomnia without resorting to medication. As I mentioned earlier, many people find that strenuous physical exercise early in the day makes a difference.

Meditation can be helpful, too. Those who meditate regularly often report that they doze off faster than they used to and sleep more soundly; some meditators can actually manage with less sleep. Professor Robert Woolfolk of Rutgers University actually taught a meditative technique to a group of severe insomniacs who had been taking an hour and a quarter (on the average) to fall asleep at night. At the end of a month their average was down to just half an hour. (For more about meditation, see Chapter 16.)

Recent research also suggests that by eating a big, starchy meal at bedtime you *may* be able to increase brain levels of the natural chemical that induces sleep (for details, see Chapter 8). If you swallow a couple of aspirins with the meal, that could help, too. Researchers have long known that aspirin somehow promotes sleep, and some of the experts are now beginning to suggest that it may do so by helping tryptophan—a substance that's in the food you eat—to reach the brain, where it's converted into that sleep-inducing biochemical.

The Common-sense Alternative

But perhaps the best solution is the common-sense alternative. It can, in fact, be combined with meditation, exercise, or midnight meals. It was first explained to me by Mary Anne. Although she really enjoys her sleep, she also has an occasional bout of insomnia. At times she'll wake up at 2 A.M. and find that she can't get back to sleep. When that happens, she remembers the advice she once heard from a doctor: "If you can't sleep," he said, "get up and do something. Tell yourself your body doesn't need sleep right now. The next night go to bed at your usual time—don't turn in early just because you had insomnia the night before. Even if you can't sleep on the second night either, if you keep to this schedule you'll exhaust yourself within a few days and there's no way you'll be able to stay awake." And so, when she can't sleep Mary Anne gets up and stays up all night—or at least until sleep becomes irresistible. But in any case, a little bit of insomnia is never likely to snowball on her: *She'll never become so anxious, worrying about whether she'll be able to sleep tonight or not, that she can't sleep.*

Napping

Turning now to the subject of napping, we must start once again by noting how very different people are. Some can fall asleep almost anywhere, anytime, and wake a short while later feeling immensely refreshed. Others insist that if they nap they feel groggy for the rest of the day. Recent research again suggests that there are different patterns for different kinds of nappers.

A few years ago Professor Evans, together with colleagues at the University of Pennsylvania, undertook an extensive study of nappers and napping. Aware that some people nap enthusiastically while others never do it, he decided to find out whether the sleep of regular nappers was different in any way from the sleep of people who disliked daytime dozing. So he brought subjects into his laboratory in the middle of the day and asked them to go to sleep while he recorded their brain waves and other bodily reactions.

The habitual nappers Evans rounded up fell into two subgroups. Some said they slept in the daytime only when they had to make up for lost sleep or wanted to store up sleep in anticipation of a late night. He called this group *replacement nappers.* Others liked to nap as often as possible regardless of whether they needed the sleep or not. These he called *appetitive nappers;* he found that 30 percent of his nap group were appetitive. Both kinds of nappers seemed to be able to control the sleep process, to fall asleep at will; perhaps because they knew they could control it, they tended to keep irregular hours.

It's not exactly a soporific experience to be hooked up to an electroencephalograph in a laboratory, to sleep wearing a kind of topknot of brightly colored wires that are glued to your scalp. Nevertheless, even the non-nappers were, for the most part, able to fall asleep. Surprisingly, when Evans looked at his data he found that the sleep profiles of non-nappers and replacement nappers were quite similar. The data on both showed the kind of sleep that usually occurs early at night and recorded a gradual transition from the lighter to the deeper stages. The appetitive nappers were different: They repeatedly danced from drowsiness into light sleep and back up again in the course of the laboratory hour. It's very likely that they experienced a lot of what's called hypnagogic imagery—the fragmented, often bizarre fantasies that occur in that dozing-off period at the beginning of sleep.

"We're not sure what function napping serves for appetitive nappers," Evans told me. "And in fact that may differ from one person to the next." Perhaps they use naps to reduce tension or anxiety, or as a defense mechanism—no one really knows. But it seems clear that to some extent *they nap for the psychological benefits, like the ones Mary Anne described, rather than because of fatigue.*

Despite the fact that the sleep of the antinap faction looked so much like the sleep of the replacement group, in other important ways the non-nappers were quite different from both kinds of nappers. All subjects had their temperature taken before they tried to sleep, and those who made a habit of napping turned out to have slightly lower temperatures than those who didn't. You may remember from Chapter 5 that temperature and alertness cycle together. Professor Evans suggested that either nappers have a temperature rhythm that's a little different—somewhat lower in mid-afternoon than the average person—or else it's more under their control. In other words, perhaps they can somehow tune down their bodies just as they tune down their minds in preparation for sleep. It's possible that non-nappers, on the other hand, have sleep-related rhythms so pronounced and inflexible that they can only drop off easily at night, after the temperature and allied cycles have begun to swing downward. This is speculation, however, since no one has yet looked at the biological rhythms of non-nappers over the course of a whole day.

Evans' study proved that *non-nappers aren't just prejudiced against daytime sleep, for many of them paid for that laboratory nap with a lapse in energy and efficiency.* All subjects woke up feeling muzzy and disoriented, but for the habitual nappers this muzziness dissipated within just a few minutes; they did well on various tasks they were tested on after their nap, and they slept well that night. The non-nappers, on the other hand, stayed groggy for a long time, and for the rest of the day their performance was below par. They were also less active than usual and slept poorly that night. Dr. Evans has no idea why they reacted as they did, but the moral of the story is obvious. "Some people," he said, "just shouldn't nap."

Can You Will Yourself to Sleep?

The most important difference between nappers and non-nappers was the fact that nappers could fall asleep at the drop of an eyelid, not just in mid-afternoon but almost anytime, anywhere. Professor Evans believes that *many nappers may have the ability to control their own consciousness in other ways as well.* He has found, for example, that individuals with good sleep control also tend to be highly hypnotizable.

Many people still believe that hypnosis is a power the hypnotist wields, but actually it's an ability that resides in the subject. One out of every four adults can easily experience hypnosis, one can't be hypnotized at all, and the other two fall somewhere in between. Hypnotizability is related to the ability to concentrate, to focus the attention. In general, people who are very hypnotizable also like to daydream and are inclined to get so caught up in their fantasies that they lose track of what's going on around them.

It has also been reported that those who are hypnotizable learn to meditate more easily than others. Evans himself has found that while they're asleep they'll respond to suggestions (that they move a leg or an arm, for example) without any sign in brain wave tracings that their sleep has been disturbed; in some way they've apparently retained a degree of contact with the outside world.

Evans believes that all of these related abilities probably share some kind of central control mechanism. However, though they overlap, they're probably not entirely interchangeable, for not everyone who has good sleep control is hypnotizable, though the reverse does seem to be true—those who are easy to hypnotize can almost always control their sleep.

Hypnotizability may be inborn. At any rate, Dr. Evans says that it doesn't seem to be particularly learnable. No one knows yet whether sleep control can be taught, but Evans is trying to find out.

How to Nap for Energy

Many people can rarely make time during the day for sleeping, but for those who can *napping is such a promising source of energy that it seems worth experimenting with.* You'll never know whether you're a napper or a non-napper until you've tried it a few times. Do remember, though, that everyone feels groggy when he first wakes up. The definitive questions are: How long does the grogginess last? How do you feel for the rest of the day?

If you *can* nap productively, then you can use napping to make up for lost sleep; or if you're expecting to have a late night, you can actually store up sleep in advance. There are limits, however. Dr. Evans believes that if you reduce your nighttime sleep by more than 20 or 30 percent, then even if you nap you'll feel the effects.

Catnapping is one way to cope with mid-afternoon slump: It's the line of least resistance. And for the appetitive napper, if a brief dalliance with sleep releases tensions, it may be extremely energizing. However, since no one really knows why appetitive nappers nap, if you're one of them you can only judge by the way you feel. Bear in mind, too, that some people nap to procrastinate. If that's your pattern, you'll have to work out for yourself whether the psychic benefits of the nap are worth whatever price you ultimately have to pay for the procrastination.

Why Do We Need Sleep?

Why is sleep so necessary for energy and comfortable functioning? Despite years of research, nobody really knows the answer to that question. From our own experience most of us would testify that sleep is restorative; yet how it restores us or what bodily mechanisms turn it on and off remains a mystery.

Dr. Wilse Webb has a theory about why sleep exists or, in other words, how it contributes to the organism's survival. He believes that any animal runs smaller risks if it remains hidden and inactive (i.e., asleep) for part of the day. Hence, sleep may have evolved at some fairly early stage in the history of living creatures.

But that really doesn't explain why, after a night's sleep, we wake up feeling revived and re-energized; or why some people seem to sleep for different reasons than others, and to derive different benefits; or why some people need so much more sleep than others; or whether sleep control can be taught.

Undoubtedly, we'll learn the answers to some of these questions in the not-too-distant future. Once we know them, we may find that it's possible to spend less time sleeping and do it so efficiently that we get the same results. Some people will rejoice at that prospect. Others—those who enjoy sleep—will probably be totally uninterested.

Energy Tips

1. If you're spending too much time sleeping, ask yourself whether it's because you're depressed or because you're using sleep to escape from a life that's too empty or too full. Or could it be that you keep such irregular hours that you're chronically tired? In each case, to sleep less you'll have to tackle the underlying problem.

2. If you're a long sleeper longing to extend your waking hours, try reducing your sleeping time very gradually: Shave off just fifteen minutes of sleep and then give yourself time to adjust before you cut back again.

3. Whatever your own sleep needs, remember that other people's needs may be genuinely quite different.

4. To combat insomnia try meditation and getting more exercise. Avoid coffee, tea, Coke, and other stimulants. Be as regular about your hours as you can be; in particular, try to get up at the

same hour every day, even on weekends. Experiment with starchy snacks at bedtime.

5. When you can't sleep at night, get up and do something until you're too groggy to stay awake. The next day wake up at the usual time and don't turn in early that night. Hang on to your perspective: Remember that nobody can stay awake forever and that once you're tired enough sleep will become irresistible.

6. If you must take sleeping pills, don't do it more often than once or twice a week—unless you're a hard-core insomniac under a doctor's close supervision.

7. If you've become hooked on sleeping pills and are taking them in heavy doses, go to a sleep clinic or a sleep specialist for help. You need to be weaned gradually.

8. Experiment with napping to find out what kind of napper you are.

9. If you're a replacement napper, use napping whenever you can to refurbish your energy when you've gone short on sleep, or to store up sleep in anticipation of a late night.

10. If you're an appetitive napper, sleep when you can for the psychic benefits.

Nourishing Your Energy

It's plain common sense: To make the most of your energy you not only have to get enough sleep but also have to feed your body well, since if you're undernourished—or overnourished and overweight—your vitality will be affected.

But when it comes to food, common sense is often left far behind. In fact, a whole mythology has grown up about food and energy. Many people are sure they know what to eat for a fast jolt of energy or what vitamins to take for long-range results; yet much of what they "know" is a fallacy.

7

How to Eat for Energy

If you knew you had two weeks coming up that were going to be a severe drain on your energy, what steps would you take to help yourself cope?

Over the last few years I've asked scores of people that question. Almost all of them mentioned, among other things, that they'd make some changes in their diet. Apparently many Americans feel, half guiltily, that they're not eating quite what they should; they assume that if they were more virtuous nutritionally, they could have more energy.

Food does affect vitality, of course, and there *are* ways to increase your energy in terms of what you eat. But they're not the ways that many of us think of first. In general, you can't get extra energy by improving your diet, popping vitamin pills, or swearing off sugar and "unnatural" foods. It would be nice if the energy equation were that simple, but it's not.

When it comes to nutrition and inner drive, most Americans today worry about the wrong thing. *In this country an energy shortage is much more likely to come from overnourishment than undernourishment.* Too many calories—and too much weight—are what really drag energy down.

Nutritionists' "Energy" Versus What We Call Energy

Quite a number of fallacies about food and energy are widely accepted as facts. The confusion arises partly because nutritionists who talk about "energy" don't mean the same thing that the rest of us mean when we speak of being "full of energy." For the nutritionist energy is something produced by the chemical reactions that take place continually in the body. Every human cell is like a miniature chemical processing plant: Within it compounds that began as foods are built up into different substances and then are torn apart again. Much as the tearing apart of molecules of coal in a coal fire releases energy in the form of heat and light, this process of tearing apart within the cell releases biochemical energy. Though some of it is used up as we move our muscles and go about our daily business, more goes to power the innumerable cellular processes by which the body maintains itself.

In the normal course of events, then, you're full of biochemical "energy" all the time; but you're not aware of it any more than you're aware of other microscopic events that take place within your cells. Of course, if you're starving to death, or if you've been on a crash diet that requires you to eat nothing but sardines or grapefruit, you'll be very low in energy; even on a normal diet you may, from time to time, feel the effects of changes in your blood sugar level. Nevertheless, the dramatic fluctuations in vitality that we all experience from hour to hour and from day to day seem to be due, for the most part, to factors other than diet. *You are what you eat, but you are* not *only as energetic as your last meal.*

If You Judge What You Eat, That Affects Energy

Yet most of us can cite a few dramatic success stories. We've met people who reformed their eating habits and promptly achieved new health and vigor; however, improved nutrition is seldom the explanation.

Take Gail, for example. A tall, rangy blonde in her late twenties, Gail works as a publicist. For her, as for most of us, food is a loaded subject. She grew up with strong but ambivalent feelings about nutrition, because her mother was always on one crash diet or another. "I remember the banana diet, the grapefruit diet—there was always something," she said. "Mother believed that if she could just lose twenty pounds, that would solve all her problems. Unfortunately, she expected the rest of the family to diet along with her. If she wasn't allowed to have anything but bananas for dinner, then the rest of us had bananas too."

As an adult, Gail swung between extremes, between periods when she was very conscious of what she ate and made a real effort to eat sensibly and periods when she binged on ice cream and Hostess Twinkies—luckily without gaining much weight. Three years ago she quit her job because she had another, better position lined up, and went off into the wilderness on a camping trip with friends. For ten days she lived a Spartan existence and ate only the simplest, most nourishing foods. She came home lithe, tanned, and vigorous—to discover that her new job had fallen through.

Disillusioned and angry, she resorted to ice cream and Hostess Twinkies again, plus jolts of coffee during the day to keep her energy up while she hunted for a job. However, after about two months she rebelled. "I felt as if everything in my life was out of control," she said. "There wasn't much I could do about being unemployed, except to keep looking until I found work, but I could do something about the way I was eating. I knew all that sugar wasn't doing me any good, and I wanted to get back to that terrific sense of physical well-being that I had at the end of the summer."

And so Gail became a vegetarian overnight. The change in her diet couldn't have been more dramatic or more complete. Along with meat, she cut out sugar, refined flour, alcohol, coffee, tea, and soft drinks. Suddenly her freezer was empty of ice cream. Bottles of vitamins lined her shelves—encapsulated virtue—while bean soups simmered on the stove and the smell of fresh-baked bread filled the apartment. She took up jogging and in a short time was feeling fit, healthy, and self-confident again. And, of course, she found a good job.

In the years since she became a vegetarian, Gail has not been sick once. Even when everyone around her is sniffling and sneezing, she hasn't come down with a cold. She thinks the way she eats makes a difference, but she's not entirely sure. "Sometimes it occurs to me that I may be like the alcoholic's daughter who grows up to be a teetotaler," she said. "Perhaps I'm reacting against my mother and yet applying the same sort of magical thinking to the way *I* eat. However, I'm more consistent than she ever was and my food habits are certainly healthier."

I believe that Gail's new diet was actually a symptom of an important inner change rather than the sole cause of all the good things that followed. When you load up continually on food that you believe is bad for you, in a way you're punishing yourself, behaving as if that's what you deserve. If Gail began to treat herself better at mealtimes, it was because—for whatever reason—she now valued herself more. That change in her attitude was definitely an energy boost.

Becoming a vegetarian was an important step, because it snapped her out of a self-defeating frame of mind. She'd been feeling like a helpless victim of circumstances—and of her own food compulsions. When she changed her diet, she took charge of her life in a drastic and significant way; afterward, whenever she sat down to eat, she was reminded of her newfound strength and willpower.

For many people mealtimes are like acts in an endless morality play, a drama about sin and redemption, self-destructiveness and self-control. Thus, every bite they eat partakes of vice or virtue and so becomes an additional reason to like or dislike themselves —and, of course, the way you feel about yourself has a tremendous effect on your energy.

Are You Overfed and Undernourished?

You may be wondering how I could possibly rule out improved nutrition as the explanation for Gail's new lease on life. I'm certainly not arguing that her diet isn't healthier now; I simply doubt that it had any short-term effect on her energy other than the psychological impact.

One of the more popular fallacies about food is the belief that many Americans are both overfed and undernourished, that because we supposedly subsist on a diet of fast foods and junk foods, we're not as healthy and energetic as we could be. Actually, all of the nutritionists I've talked to are convinced that very few Americans are malnourished, except those who are too poor to be able to afford fresh fruits and vegetables. Dr. Victor Herbert, chief of the Hematology and Nutrition Laboratory at the Veterans Administration Hospital in the Bronx, New York City, told me that anyone who manages to have one serving of fresh, uncooked fruit or juice a day, or one serving of a fresh, uncooked vegetable will be well enough nourished, if aside from that she eats as most Americans do.

In its long-range effects the typical American diet leaves much to be desired because it contains too much cholesterol and too many calories; but it's certainly nourishing enough to sustain energy, for even fast foods are relatively nutritious. A cheeseburger with lettuce and tomato includes all four of the basic food groups; its real drawback is the fact that it's loaded with fat. Junk foods, though they're apt to cause tooth decay, are often fortified with vitamins and minerals. The body also averages out its nutritive needs over a period of weeks or even a month, so *as long as you eat a varied diet you're not likely to run short of food "energy."*

What *is* a good basic diet? In their book *Eat OK—Feel OK!* Dr. Fredrick Stare and Dr. Elizabeth Whelan spell it out this way: Adults need two servings of meat, fish, poultry, or cheese daily, plus two servings of fruit, two of vegetables, and several servings of whole grain or enriched bread or cereal. (The size of the serving will depend on your weight—and vice versa.) Adults should have one or two glasses of milk as well, or some cheese; children and women who are breast-feeding or pregnant need even more milk.

The Placebo Theory of Nutrition

Because food nourishes the psyche as well as the body, it all boils down to this: If you reform your eating habits, it may make only a marginal difference nutritionally, but you may indeed feel reinvigorated for a variety of *other* reasons. Thus, as long as the new diet is a sensible one, the change may be a good idea.

Actually, I'd go even further than that. Most people have a few "magic" foods they believe in, things that, for no nutritional reason, *seem* particularly comforting to eat or feel energizing. I think it's a good idea to know which foods have magic powers for you and to use them when you need them. I call this the placebo theory of nutrition.

We're most apt to reach for magic foods when we're not feeling well. For some people comfort is a bowl of chicken soup. Others treat colds with rare steaks and hot toddies, or restrict themselves to ginger ale and salty crackers whenever they experience that feeling of fatigue and vague malaise that most of us get from time to time. Hangover cures run the gamut. I know one man who combines the scrapings from burnt toast with black coffee and honey.

For many people breakfast is another time for resorting to special foods. One woman told me she'd had Wheaties for breakfast almost every single morning since she was two, "and if I have to have something else, I go through the morning feeling vaguely uneasy, as if something is not quite right." I have to confess that I myself have a passion for oatmeal, the gray, lumpy kind. Sometimes at ten o'clock at night it occurs to me that in just ten hours I'll be sitting down to oatmeal again, and I can hardly wait. I have no desire to have oatmeal at any other meal; for me it's the only way to start the day.

Life is complicated and there are few simple solutions—and perhaps that's part of the appeal of magic foods, "health" foods, and offbeat diets: We could all use a little magic in our lives, a pill we could take or something to munch on that would miraculously confer on us a new ability to cope. Unfortunately, some of the things people believe are magic aren't as harmless as Wheaties and oatmeal or black coffee with toast scrapings. I'm thinking of the current enthusiasm for megavitamins.

Vitamin Fallacies

The belief that vitamins can boost your energy if you take them in heavy doses is one of the commonest food fallacies. More and more people today are treating themselves with food supplements—vitamins and minerals—apparently on the principle that if a little is good for you, a lot must be even better. Actually, a lot can be dangerous.

Yet many Americans have been persuaded by the claims of the vitamin gurus. Gail, for example, is an enthusiastic convert. She's convinced that the government has set the recommended dietary allowance (RDA) for the various vitamins and minerals far too low. The RDA, she told me, "represents how much of the vitamin you need to keep from developing a deficiency. But there's a gray area between deficiency and the best possible nutrition, and if you're in that area, you might not be feeling bad—you might be getting just enough of various vitamins—but if you had more, you could be feeling even better. Besides, people are so different that what's enough for one person may not be nearly enough for another."

Unfortunately, almost everything Gail "knows" about vitamins is wrong, according to top American nutritionists. The fallacies become clear if you look at the basic facts about the way the body processes vitamins.

There are thirteen vitamins in all: A, C, D, E, and K, plus the eight that make up the B-complex group. Humans need to consume all of these in small amounts to stay healthy. Each was, in fact, discovered because people who weren't getting enough of it developed symptoms of the deficiency.

Vitamins do not in themselves provide food energy, but they do make it possible for us to use efficiently the food we eat; they act as catalysts—they increase the speed of various chemical reactions though they're not themselves consumed in the process. Without vitamins some of the body's biochemical events would happen very slowly, if at all.

Nevertheless, most vitamins can't catalyze anything on their own. First they must combine with substances called apoenzymes, which are manufactured within the individual cells. When a cell is making apoenzymes at its maximum speed, and they're combining with vitamins as fast as they're made, the cell is said to be "saturated" with that particular vitamin. Obviously, once the whole body is saturated, any excess vitamins can't act as vitamins at all. So, like any other chemical or drug you ingest, they're stored or they circulate in the bloodstream. As drugs they *may* be good therapy for certain conditions—I'll come back to that point in a little while—but, like any other medication, they should be prescribed by a doctor and treated with caution.

As for the RDA, Dr. Herbert explained that it's not based just on what prevents deficiency. It's determined by looking at the range of individual variability and then adding a safety factor above that. Thus, the RDA for vitamin C for adults is forty-five milligrams. Five milligrams would prevent deficiency, and it takes only thirty-nine milligrams a day to saturate the cells. And there's no evidence that saturation is desirable; in fact, though for some vitamins (like C) it seems harmless, with others it's downright dangerous. Dr. Herbert explained, "Saturating with minerals is harmful, and saturating amounts of vitamin D can be lethal."

In Megadoses Vitamins Can Deplete Energy

Obviously, you can *overdose on vitamins; when that happens, one of the milder symptoms is fatigue.* Others can include headaches, diarrhea, anemia (vitamin A), calcium deposits in soft tissues such as the kidneys (vitamin D), or muscle weakness and a tendency to bleed (vitamin E).

Some vitamins are soluble in fat, while others dissolve in water. The fat-soluble vitamins (A, D, E, and K) are more dangerous, since any excess is stored in body fat, where it can act as a toxic chemical. Vitamin C and the B-complex vitamins are water soluble, so they're eliminated from the body more rapidly. Even so, they can cause problems.

Vitamin C, for example, apparently promotes bladder and kidney stones when taken in megadoses. It may also destroy B$_{12}$ and cause the bones to lose calcium. Diabetics and heart patients need to be wary of it, because megadoses can distort the results of urine tests diabetics are sometimes required to take; they can also counteract the effects of blood-thinning medications often used in the event of a heart attack or stroke. In addition, people who suddenly stop taking megadoses of vitamin C sometimes develop rebound scurvy, which manifests itself as bleeding gums and sores that won't heal. Thus, if you decide to give up vitamin C after you've been taking large doses regularly, it's advisable to taper off rather than going cold turkey.

Beyond their potential for harm, vitamins in megadoses are expensive and unnecessary, for though there *are* people who do need vitamin supplements (I'll come to them in a minute), most healthy individuals don't. And yet the vitamin gurus recommend taking food supplements in doses that are more than ten times the RDA, promising great benefits if you follow their advice. Some insist that B vitamins can give you extra energy, for example, despite the fact that research has not backed up such claims. *Though people who have a vitamin B deficiency do tire easily, when B vitamins were added to the normal, balanced diets of healthy working people who did different types of strenuous physical work, they had no effect whatsoever.*

Vitamin C: Pros and Cons

Vitamin C is perhaps the most controversial food supplement, since the evidence on the benefits of megadoses is contradictory. Studies indicate that vitamin C has no power to prevent colds, as is often claimed, though in large enough doses—about two hundred milligrams or more a day—it does seem to reduce cold symptoms by about one third. Larger doses have no greater effect. Apparently, vitamin C acts as a drying agent and does what a mild antihistamine can do. Since in mega amounts it does have those unpleasant side effects, an antihistamine seems preferable.

However, though vitamin C seems to be ineffective against the common-cold virus, it's possible that in certain circumstances it may help to ward off some kinds of cancer (though it may promote others). Some researchers recommend that we wash down our morning bacon and our noontime hotdogs with orange juice, because bacon and hotdogs both contain preservatives that can be converted by the body into cancer-causing substances called nitrosamines. Vitamin C seems to forestall that conversion; partly for that reason it's often added now to bacon and hotdogs.

Who Needs Vitamin Supplements and Why?

Though most of us have no need for a vitamin supplement, that's not true of everyone. Even in this overnourished day and age, there *are* people who are likely to develop particular kinds of vitamin deficiencies.

Heavy drinkers, for example, are often deficient in some of the B vitamins; very heavy drinkers apparently have an even more serious problem, for one recent study showed that people who have six or seven drinks a day, even for as short a time as two weeks, begin to suffer from starvation no matter how much they eat and no matter how well balanced their diet is. Under conditions of alcohol abuse, the small intestine pours out fluids and flushes food from the body before vitamins and minerals can be absorbed.

Heavy smokers may need to increase their intake of vitamin C. However, Dr. Herbert believes that drinking an eight-ounce glass of orange juice daily is probably all it takes. Women who are on the Pill tend to harbor less than the usual amount of several B vitamins as well as vitamin C. Nevertheless, according to Dr. Herbert, if a woman has one serving a day of fresh, uncooked fruit or fruit juice, or one uncooked vegetable, she'll make up the difference. He also pointed out that women on the Pill are less likely to have an iron deficiency than most women, for they lose less iron since their menstrual bleeding is reduced.

Postoperative patients, old people who eat poorly, and pregnant women may all need vitamin supplements—and some dieters do, too. If you cut your food intake by half, you are probably cutting out too many vitamins. In all cases, an ordinary multivitamin that supplies no more than the RDA is likely to be sufficient.

Getting the Most from the Vitamins in Food

There are many people who don't fit into any of these categories. They take a multivitamin daily as a form of nutritional insurance, because they suspect that their diet isn't as well balanced as it could be. This does no harm, according to Dr. Herbert. At worst it's a waste of money. However, as a cheaper form of insurance, you might observe a few simple rules when buying or preparing food to make sure you get the full benefit of all the vitamins that are naturally there.

• When buying fruits and vegetables, choose fresh or frozen rather than canned ones, since canning can reduce the vitamin content drastically.

• Treat fresh produce with respect. Keep it well wrapped in the refrigerator and try to eat it within a day or two. Make your salads at the last minute and chop vegetables just before cooking. Don't leave them to soak, since some vitamins will be leached away. Cut them into large rather than small pieces to preserve more of the vitamin content; pressure-cook or steam them in as little water as possible.

• Choose whole grain breads and cereals rather than refined ones; select brown rice instead of white.

Vitamin Therapies of the Future

As I mentioned earlier, it's possible that in the future vitamins will be prescribed in large doses *as medication* for certain conditions. For example, preliminary research suggests that a variant of vitamin D may be effective against osteoporosis, a condition in which a breakdown of bone sometimes occurs in women as their ability to absorb calcium decreases with age. There's also evidence that a synthetic analog of Vitamin A can cure the sort of severe acne that doesn't respond to the usual therapies. Note, though, that in both cases the drug being used—and it *is* a drug—is not the ordinary vitamin that's sold over the counter but only a substance similar to it.

The Carbohydrate Controversy

Another food fallacy that's prevalent today is the idea that carbohydrates (starches and sugars) can rob you of energy and that, in fact, the way to have more pep is to stick to a high-protein, low-carbohydrate diet.

By now the case against carbohydrates has been stated many times over in books and in the press. The argument goes this way: If you eat something sugary, the level of sugar in your blood will rise quite rapidly, providing you with an energy boost; but then insulin goes to work to remove the excess sugar from the blood and convert it into a starch called glycogen so that it can be stored. In many people the insulin supposedly overshoots the mark and removes too much sugar, creating a sharp dip both in the blood sugar level and in energy. The individual may then feel tired, anxious, depressed, even dizzy, and her heart may begin to pound. When these symptoms are accompanied by very low blood sugar, which plummeted as a result of what was eaten, the condition is called *reactive hypoglycemia.*

People in the early stages of diabetes sometimes develop this sort of problem, but actually reactive hypoglycemia is relatively rare. *Most medical authorities agree that for most people eating sugar does not precipitate an energy crisis.*

Yet many Americans are mistakenly convinced that they have hypoglycemia. It's a simple, nonthreatening explanation for vague and uncomfortable symptoms. The recommended treatment is convenient and nonthreatening too: small, frequent meals and a diet that's high in protein and low in fats and carbohydrates. For people who really do have reactive hypoglycemia, the new eating pattern restores energy, but others who try an extreme carbohydrate-free diet because they think they have a blood sugar problem—or because they're trying to lose weight, or they believe all those proteins will give them extra energy—often begin to feel pretty low after the first few days. One problem with a diet that's essentially limited to meats and some fats is that it's terribly monotonous. Those who follow it soon begin to eat much less out of sheer boredom, and for this and other reasons fatigue soon sets in.

Foods to Hold off Hunger and Fatigue

Most people don't have hypoglycemia. In fact, even if they fast for a day or two, they don't develop any of its florid symptoms. *However, from time to time everyone has experienced what one might call a "normal" energy dip due to a normal dip in blood sugar.* You've skipped breakfast and lunch is late, and suddenly you begin to feel tired and distinctly irritable.

There are, of course, any number of reasons for feeling tired and irritable, but if you have something to eat and in short order start to feel much better, chances are that low blood sugar was partially to blame.

It's possible to make yourself fatigue-proof, at least where that sort of energy dip is concerned, by taking into account the real, physiological facts about blood sugar. Dr. Fredrick Stare, the eminent Harvard nutritionist, explained that whenever you eat any kind of food, there's a prompt rise in your blood sugar level. How big the rise is depends on how low the level was to begin with and how much you eat. How fast it happens depends on whether the food is protein, fat, or carbohydrate, because sugar is digested more rapidly, protein is slower, and fats take longer still. More specifically, if, first thing in the morning, you have a cup of coffee with two or three spoonfuls of sugar in it, in a few minutes your blood sugar level will start to rise. If instead you have an egg with toast and a glass of milk, the rise will begin in ten or fifteen minutes but the level will remain high for much longer.

Obviously, if you have to last a long time between meals, proteins and fats will sustain your energy better than carbohydrates. Something like peanut butter is an especially good bet; since it contains carbohydrate, protein, *and* fat, the digestive process continues in a slow and sustained way over a period of several hours. A cheese sandwich ought to work well for the same reason. What do you reach for if you're already feeling the effects of a blood sugar dip? A candy bar *is* faster acting, but only by about five or ten minutes.

Dieter's Tip: Try a "Scientific Nibble"

Dieters can use the facts about blood sugar in a different way: You feel hungrier when your blood sugar is low and not so hungry when it's high, so if you start a meal with a relatively high sugar level you'll probably eat less. Thus, Dr. Stare recommends what he calls "the scientific nibble" (as opposed to the "common nibble," which is simply a snack between meals). When you nibble scientifically, you take time out thirty to forty-five minutes before you expect to eat and you help yourself to something that would ordinarily be part of your meal. If lunch is to include a tuna fish sandwich, for example, have half the sandwich at a quarter past eleven in the morning to dull your appetite; then satisfy your hunger with the other half at twelve. You'll eat less and, what's more, experience has shown that you won't crave dinner any sooner. You can shrink your dinnertime appetite in the same way. However, once any meal begins, you have to discipline yourself. Some people feel obliged to clean up their plates whether they're hungry or not, and even after nibbling they will eat a huge piece of steak—just because it's there. It's better to cut it in half and save half for the next day.

Breakfasts that Sustain Energy

A third tactic is so obvious that I hesitate to mention it: Have a decent breakfast to avoid a blood sugar dip during the morning. In his book Dr. Stare reports a study done some years ago at the University of Iowa. Researchers recorded reaction time, maximum work output, and muscle tremor in people who had had no breakfast, in some who had had only black coffee, and in others who had eaten moderately or heavily. They found that the subjects who skipped breakfast did poorly and those who had had black coffee did worse. The best performances were turned in by those who ate moderately.

For health and energy upkeep, the best breakfast is one that's heavy on protein and includes fruit and a small amount of fat. Once again, the idea is to choose a combination that will be digested in a slow, sustained way, so that you won't begin to feel hungry and low in vitality late in the morning. It's possible that a high-protein breakfast is an energy plus for another reason as well: Some scientists believe that protein may be something of a stimulant (see Chapter 5). At any rate, here are a few breakfast suggestions:

• Try a sliced, fresh orange with a toasted English muffin spread with peanut butter, or have one of the high-protein ready-to-eat breakfast cereals with low-fat milk.

• Blend low-fat milk with fresh (or frozen) strawberries, a

sliced banana, and a dash of vanilla extract. Drink this very filling milkshake with a buttered bran muffin.

• Begin with a tangerine, a wedge of cantaloupe, or a bowl of fresh strawberries. Add a slice of toasted raisin bread spread with cottage cheese and topped with a dollop of jam.

• Eggs with toast and orange juice are also a good combination, or you can always try a small hamburger on a bun, or a grilled cheese sandwich, plus fruit, for a less traditional breakfast.

Carbohydrate Loading for Stamina

Some athletes increase their stamina by taking advantage of the bodily mechanism that governs the way starches are stored. In the course of a race a marathon runner or swimmer needs to draw on reserves of glycogen stored in the muscles; her body converts this starch into glucose to keep her blood sugar up and to fuel the activity of the cells.

Some marathoners use a technique called "carbohydrate loading" to increase their stores of glycogen before a race. It works this way: First schedule one day of really strenuous exercise; next, for about three days eat a low-carbohydrate diet; then, for the last three days before the race load up on carbohydrates—spaghetti, bread, pastries, whatever appeals to you. By first reducing your own starch content and then pouring it on you can persuade your body to deposit more than the usual amount of glycogen in the muscles. However, there's one drawback: Because the glycogen bonds to water, some people find that carbohydrate loading leaves them feeling heavy and sluggish—literally waterlogged.

The technique is of no practical use to those who put out a moderate effort for a long time or a maximum effort for a short time—in other words, it's no help to tennis players, weight lifters, or runners who don't compete in marathons because they never reach the point where they've used up their normal glycogen stores.

Energy Tips

1. The best way to eat for energy is to stick to a balanced diet. If you aim for variety and include fresh fruits and vegetables, you can't go far wrong.

2. Know what foods have "magic" powers for you and use them when you need comfort or an energy boost.

3. If you're a woman and are on the Pill, have at least one serving a day of fresh, uncooked fruit or fruit juice, or one serving of an uncooked vegetable. Heavy smokers should down eight ounces of orange juice daily.

4. Anyone on a really stringent diet probably needs to take an ordinary multivitamin; in any case, stringent diets, if continued for any length of time, should be supervised by a doctor.

5. To get full benefit from the vitamins naturally present in food, buy whole grain breads and cereals rather than refined ones, brown rice instead of white, and fresh or frozen fruits and vegetables rather than canned. Eat fresh produce within a day or two. Chop the vegetables into large rather than small pieces at the last minute. Cook them in as little water as possible.

6. For a stick-to-the-ribs meal that will sustain your energy for a long time, choose a combination of foods that's high in protein but includes carbohydrates and some fat as well.

7. Dieting? To curb your appetite "preview" your next meal: Eat a small portion of it thirty to forty-five minutes head of time.

8. If you run in marathons, try carbohydrate loading. Studies indicate that it really does increase glycogen stores.

Overweight? Eat Less for More Energy

For many people the best way to get a really dramatic energy boost is to eat less—and lose weight.

An estimated fifteen million Americans are obese, which means that they weigh at least 20 percent more than they ought to. Most of them know from long experience with dieting—losing and regaining pounds—that there's an inverse relationship between weight and energy: Beyond a certain point, the heavier you are the less energetic you feel. They know, too, that *it's marvelously revitalizing to lose a significant amount of weight.*

Obesity interferes with energy in several different ways. First of all, if you're overweight it's more of an effort to move around: Ordinary activities cost you more in energy. Thus, people who are too heavy are generally much less active than their thin-to-middling colleagues.

Then again, energy springs from self-confidence, and fat people often lack confidence. It's difficult to feel good about yourself when you've a heavyweight trapped in a culture that strongly disapproves of corpulence to the point of actually discriminating against those who are fat.

Furthermore, studies indicate that the obese apparently have higher base levels of insulin than normal-weight people, and that their bodies also release more insulin in response to a meal. This is significant, because not only is insulin the hormone that removes excess sugar from the bloodstream for storage as glycogen or as fat, but the effects of insulin can also make you feel lethargic and sleepy.

Incidentally, an insulin abnormality is *not* the root cause of obesity. Instead, it seems to be the other way around: Getting fat distorts the insulin system. This was demonstrated in an experiment conducted in a Vermont prison. When convict volunteers deliberately overate for a period of several months, they not only gained weight but also developed the fat person's typical insulin pattern.

The Fatter You Are, the Fatter You Become

It's clear that once you begin to put on weight, you're caught in a vicious circle. You feel low in energy—because of the insulin problem, because it's more of an effort to get around, and because you're not pleased with yourself—and so you become less active. The less active you are, the fewer calories you burn, and the fatter you become. *Obesity is a self-perpetuating disease.*

Obviously, fat prevention is enormously important. However, for many American adults it's already too late for that. Shedding pounds is the only option, and that's not easy to do. Most diets amount to nothing more than a trip on the seesaw: The individual loses weight only to regain it as soon as he goes back to "normal" eating again.

Obesity is a stubborn problem. Until recently there was very little hope of a cure, that is, if you define "cured" as someone who has slimmed down and then has maintained a normal weight for at least five years. Even today only 10 to 15 percent of all patients who are treated recover from obesity, according to Dr. Sami Hashim of the Obesity Research Center at St. Luke's Hospital in New York. That may sound like depressingly few successes, but Dr. Hashim noted that ten years ago the rate was probably less than 5 percent. He believes that if things are looking up it's because clinicians now have a better understanding of what causes obesity and of how to treat it. In addition, good obesity clinics have been opening at hospitals and universities all over the country.

Success Story: Elaine's

One of the most impressive success stories in recent years features a rather remarkable energist. Elaine Kaufman is the owner of Elaine's, a Manhattan restaurant that's almost a legend because of its celebrity clientele. Writers, film people, theater people, and Wall Street movers and shakers are all inclined to gather of an evening at Elaine's, drawn both by the food and by the personality of Elaine herself. Years ago she was described to me as a big, feisty woman with a quick intelligence and a sharp tongue. Very much overweight, she was said to be somehow larger than life. She had a tremendous presence—in her body, her voice, and her manner.

Early in 1979 I began to hear that Elaine had lost vast amounts of weight with the help of the clinic at St. Luke's Hospital. Late in April she agreed to an interview.

When I arrived at the restaurant during the quiet time just after lunch, a diminutive, dark-haired woman was waiting for me. At first I took her to be an assistant of some sort, for it was impossible to believe that this was the redoubtable Elaine. She was quite short and had alert brown eyes behind her large glasses. I'd heard (and she later confirmed) that she'd lost over 150 pounds, but the new Elaine seemed to weigh less than 150 pounds in all. Half of what she'd been was no more!

Before she went to St. Luke's, Elaine had tried "everything" to lose weight. She'd been on many different diets, and for twenty years, off and on, she'd taken amphetamines in an effort to suppress her appetite. "All they do is make you hungrier," she noted now, "because they increase your anxiety."

She was referred to St. Luke's because she had torn cartilages in her knee. Her doctor wanted to operate but was afraid the knee wouldn't heal afterward because she was so heavy, so he wanted her to bring her weight down. When she went to St. Luke's, Elaine didn't know what to expect. She wasn't really primed for such stunning success, but she explained, "I do everything with the same intensity, whether it's working, or playing, or losing weight. So I kept on losing and losing until in the end it turned out that I didn't need the knee operation after all."

One of the first things the doctors did at St. Luke's was to ascertain, using a special machine, what percentage of her body mass was fat, because throughout her treatment they'd have to be careful that the fat was all she lost, not muscle and other tissue. They also checked her heart and her health in general, since it's a strain on the body to lose substantial amounts of weight.

Elaine lived at the hospital for the first three months because she was on a very stringent diet and so had to be under constant surveillance. She was allowed a mere 420 calories a day, in the form of low-fat cottage cheese, fish, skinless chicken, and veal, together with salads and other vegetables. Even though she was eating very little, she never felt really tired or debilitated; for its "energy" needs, her body mostly burned its own stored-up fat. After a while her feelings about eating changed. "Meals were no longer the high points of the day," she said. "They began to seem no different than washing my face or brushing my teeth. But at the same time I had to learn how to feed myself emotionally, so that I wouldn't require so much food."

Psychotherapy helped with that. "You don't overeat because you're starving," she explained. "It's insecurity that makes you

need so much food. You have to learn to understand what you're
doing and why."

As a child Elaine Kaufman was actually rather slight. Her
problems with food didn't really begin until she was an adult
coping with the multiple stresses of a demanding life. "I was
anxious, insecure; I had no self-confidence and no ego," she recalled.

Before she got into the restaurant business Elaine tried a number of different things: She was in market research for a time;
she sold stamps, cosmetics, and used books. She was never very
successful until, sixteen years ago, a friend showed her the restaurant she still owns. "I knew for what I had, for my character,
it would be perfect," she said. She wasn't referring to her skill
with foods—that's almost assumed—but to other things. "I'm a
good listener," she explained. "I have street intelligence. I have
read excessively, more than some of the people who come in
here. And I've done self-exploring, so I can understand what
people are talking about and how they're feeling."

Elaine brought to her restaurant venture the intensity that's so
characteristic of her. She did all the ordering herself, insisting on
absolutely fresh foods. If a dish required a particular ingredient,
she'd never substitute. And every dish that came out of her
kitchen had to meet her own exacting standards, which meant
that she had to taste everything. Under the circumstances, overweight was something of an occupational hazard.

But that was only part of the problem. It was stress that did
her in, for Elaine is a very hyper sort of person. "I can get high
just on conversation," she said. "That's part of doing everything
intensely." And so the pounds piled up. Eating eventually became a kind of reflex for her. "I remember once," she recalled,
"we were having a party here and there was a tray of homemade
cannolis. I wasn't thinking about what I was doing and I saw my
hand go out to them. It was as if it weren't attached to my body,
as if it didn't belong to me."

It took Elaine a little over a year to shed 150 pounds, and
when I spoke to her she had maintained a normal weight for
about five months. Surprisingly, she no longer had to struggle to
keep from overeating. During her stay in the hospital, and in the
months that followed, she'd absorbed a new eating pattern and

had built different habits. The thing she had to watch out for now was that when she became too absorbed in what she was doing she sometimes *forgot* to eat. "I've learned that it's important to eat three times a day," she said. "Otherwise you become tired and you begin to feel anxious, and then you're ready to eat just about anything."

In her new, thin persona, Elaine found that customers who hadn't seen her for a while often failed to recognize her. "The other night," she said, "an man came over to me and asked, 'When does Elaine come in?' I said, 'She comes in seven days a week,' and he said, 'Thanks' and walked away without ever recognizing me. That sort of thing happens all the time." She had also been getting a lot of mail from people who had heard about the weight she lost and were inspired to try the same thing themselves. "I've been amazed at the reaction," she said.

Anyone who has managed to lose even just ten or fifteen crucial pounds knows the sense of accomplishment and the elation that come with success. For a while it feels as if you've been issued a whole new body. You're so much lighter that it's a pleasure just to get up and walk across a room. Of course, these perceptions soon fade as you begin to take the new body—and the new energy—for granted.

How a Dieter Can Be a Successful Loser—Without Losing Energy

People like Elaine who have a lot of pounds to lose are more likely to succeed if they have the help of a good obesity clinic. Those with less severe problems may find that some of the tactics used by clinics are helpful.

For example, before they get down to the serious business of dieting, patients at St. Luke's are usually asked to keep a food diary for a week. (Elaine didn't have to do this since she was to be hospitalized for several months, with her food intake entirely under the control of her doctors.) In the diary patients record their normal eating pattern, writing down not only what they eat but the time, place, and circumstances, their emotional state, and what situation they're reacting to if they overeat. "The idea," Dr.

Hashim explained, "is to microscopically dissect out their eating behavior. They write down in the diary how fast they eat, who they're with, whether they're watching television during the meal, and much more." When the patient eventually sits down to analyze the diary with a therapist, many things become clear. She may suddenly realize that because she watches TV during meals she usually doesn't notice how much she eats; or that because she uses huge plates any helping looks small to her. If she eats fast, she may not be giving her brain time to register the fact that her stomach is full, and she'll be advised to put her fork down between bites.

It may also turn out that the cocktails she has before dinner relax her so much that she eats more than she otherwise might. Or if she tastes as she cooks, she may discover that the calories have been adding up there. And if she tends to do her grocery shopping late in the afternoon, when she's feeling a little hungry, she may be buying all kinds of high-calorie items that she'd resist if she shopped on a full stomach. If she then brings them home and leaves them around in plain sight, the end will be almost inevitable. Many people find that the best way to forestall food binges is to keep no cookies in the cookie jar—or, better yet, no cookies in the house.

Overeating is not a simple problem. It's the end result of a chain of activities that begins when the food is bought at the market; and so every link in the chain is worth examining. The goal, Dr. Hashim explained, is "to normalize the situation so that the individual is eating in response to hunger, not in response to other things."

A Diet to Keep Up Your Spirits and Your Energy

Fad diets that drastically restrict one kind of food, such as the popular low-carbohydrate diets, are inevitably a drain on your energy. Your body needs a balanced regime to operate normally. A highly restrictive eating plan is also a mistake psychologically, because if the diet feels like a punishment for past sins, you'll find that you're constantly coming up with excuses to escape the punishment. There will be days when you depart from your diet because you have something to celebrate, and other days when you feel you simply must comfort yourself by going off it.

A diet should have variety and should include enough of the things you like so that you won't feel deprived. You may indeed have to give up cheesecake and chocolate mousse, but you can go on having potatoes, bread, spaghetti, and other starches in reasonable amounts, together with lots of fresh fruits and vegetables and lean meats. When you're picking a diet to follow, look for one that emphasizes a balanced regime and a slow, steady weight loss. The Weight Watchers' diets are generally good. I like the Wise Woman's Diet, which is published in *Redbook* magazine at regular intervals.

Most people can lose weight, up to a point, without too much difficulty. The problem is that they always gain it right back again. It seems pretty clear that *to maintain a weight loss you have to make some significant changes in your life-style*. Briefly, here are a few suggestions.

Tips: How to Develop a Low-calorie Life-style

1. Use your diet to retrain your eating habits. That means you must eat regularly and have balanced meals. The problem with fad and starvation diets is that the minute you've reached your weight goal and go back to normal eating again, you fall right back into your old bad habits and regain the weight.

2. Learn less fattening ways to prepare food. The clinic at St. Luke's actually offers cooking classes for patients. Such classes are excellent motivators, but similar information is also available from Weight Watchers and in the Wise Woman's Diet in *Redbook*.

3. Retrain your tastes. The clinicians at St. Luke's work to convince patients that skim milk, diet margarines, and other low-calorie foods are preferable. Re-educating tastes is a slow business: When you've got your mind and your mouth set for homogenized milk, the skimmed sort can seem thin and uninteresting, but with time your perceptions change until the homogenized variety tastes strange.

4. It helps to diet with a friend, as a family, or you can join a

group like Weight Watchers. The group approach is a very effective one for many people.

5. If at all possible, "fatproof" your household. This tactic, as described by Dr. Alvin Eden in his book *Growing Up Thin,* drastically reduces the temptations in your life. You simply go through your kitchen and throw out all the junk foods—candy, cookies, sodas, ice cream, all the high-calorie items that have relatively little nutritive value—and you refuse to give them house room ever again. If the only way to have ice cream is to go to the store and buy some—by the scoop—you're virtually certain to eat less of it.

6. Get involved in sports or community affairs, or take lessons in something you've always wanted to learn. New interests not only take your mind off food but help you evolve a more active and satisfying life in which eating plays a less central role.

Drugs: Uppers and Downers

Though there's no food or diet that's guaranteed to magically increase your vitality—the best way to get extra pep from your diet may be to eat less, not more—there *are* things you can consume that will give you a real lift. There are certain drugs that will ignite energy and others that are guaranteed downers. What's more, new research suggests that it may be possible to increase the brain's supply of some important neurotransmitters *by what you eat!* Though it's too early to draw conclusions from this research about what the proper "brain foods" really are, the prospects are fascinating.

Let's move on, then, to consider the drugs that affect energy—and the foods that may reach the brain.

8
Drugs: The Now-and-Future Energizers

If you're facing a deadline and you have more work to do to meet it than you have time or energy available, should you opt for the kind of energy boost that amphetamines can supply? Or would it be safer to simply shore yourself up from hour to hour with black coffee?

If you're tense, anxious, and strung tight with nervous energy, does it do any harm to "solve" your problem temporarily with tranquilizers or turn to a dry martini for relief?

There are many drugs available today that can affect your energy, substances that will take you up when you're feeling down and others that will bring you down when you're hyped up on nervous drive. Often, when people take such drugs they're primarily intent on manipulating their mood: They want to feel good, or at least to feel less badly. But sometimes it's the energy impact itself that they're interested in, and generally that impact is a hoped-for dividend.

Virtually all of today's energizing and tranquilizing drugs have serious drawbacks. None of them are any kind of answer for someone who's simply feeling draggy, or who is too keyed up. Nevertheless, people *do* take them for just those reasons and so they're worth a brief survey here.

Also worth surveying is the new research on how such drugs affect the brain, for scientists are finally beginning to understand some of the mechanisms involved and are able to guess at others. Their work sheds a little more light on the complex ways in which energy operates. It also suggests that *in the near future*

*we may be introduced to a new generation of drugs that can ig-
nite or dampen energy.* Let's look at the brain story first.

Stand-ins for the Brain's Own Chemicals

Chapter 3 described the brain's neurotransmitters and suggested some of the things that can go wrong as one nerve cell
transmits a chemical signal to another. However, the brain has
other methods of internal communication as well.

In 1973 scientists announced a discovery that touched off a
new era in brain research: They had learned that morphine molecules plug into receptors on some brain cells as neatly as if
receptor and molecule were meant for one another. Researchers
were, of course, quite sure that the human brain would never
have evolved receptors just to accommodate an extract from the
opium poppy. Convinced that the body itself must produce a
chemical with molecules structurally similar to those of morphine, biochemists began looking for "the body's own opiate"—
and in short order discovered several likely candidates that were
all closely related chemically. One of the most promising of these
is *beta endorphin,* a peptide* manufactured in the pituitary
gland and in the brain. Like morphine, beta endorphin relieves
pain and generates euphoria—and unfortunately it, too, appears
to be addictive.

The brain contains many other peptides as well; over two
dozen of them are currently being investigated. Scientists already have a strong suspicion that a peptide known merely as
"Substance P" causes the experience we feel as pain. There are
probably other peptides that stimulate, tranquilize, or produce
pleasure or distress. Some may, in fact, balance one another, like
opposing forces, to establish a kind of mental and emotional
tone.

Peptides appear to operate over much longer distances than
do neurotransmitters, which have only to cross a minuscule synapse from sending to receiving cell. It's not at all clear how the
peptides and the transmitters interact. Opiate receptors occur

* Peptides are composed of amino acids, which are also the building blocks
of proteins.

right on the nerve cell terminals that release certain neurotransmitters. Some scientists suggest that the opiate may serve to
modulate the activity of the transmitter—in effect turning the
volume up or down. It might instead constitute a separate signaling system—or it could do both.

To get down to specifics, let's consider how just a few of the
more popular stimulant and tranquilizing drugs affect energy,
what their drawbacks are, and what's known about their effects
on the brain. At the end of this chapter we'll also consider the
likelihood that some food substances directly affect the chemistry of the brain—a finding that is already suggesting new drug
therapies.

Amphetamines: The Drugs that Ignite Energy

People usually take amphetamines (they're also known as
speed) for the flare of energy they touch off. It's a nervous sort of
energy, and many people actually find it unpleasant, but they
resort to uppers anyway because the drug does get them moving.
Speed may, in fact, make it practically impossible for them to sit
still.

However, individual reactions vary. Mara usually felt good
when she took an amphetamine. She used the drug in college
whenever she was so anxious about something—such as a term
paper she had to write—that she couldn't seem to get going.
Amphetamines boosted her over the hump, so that she could
not only make a start but usually could bulldoze right through to
the end. As she worked, she was convinced that the paper she
was writing was absolutely brilliant; but, judging by the marks
she got, her professors seldom agreed with her, for she did better
with papers she wrote without benefit of speed.

Mara sometimes felt quite jumpy while she was on the drug; it
gave her the equivalent of coffee nerves. However, this seemed a
small price to pay, since she was also joyful, self-confident, and
full of loving kindness. "And I'd get so involved in things," she
said, "simple things, but they'd hold my interest for hours. One
day I sat on the floor playing the guitar and singing the same
song over and over again, from nine in the morning until five in

the afternoon. When I came out of it and realized what I'd done, I found it more than a little frightening."

After she graduated from college, Mara gave up taking speed. She never became addicted to it, though some people do, just as some overdose on it. An amphetamine overdose can be deadly, and when it doesn't kill it can create an amphetamine psychosis, an abrupt departure from reality that looks very much like paranoid schizophrenia.

Amphetamines apparently increase the activity of norepinephrine and dopamine, two of the brain's neurotransmitters. Because speed literally speeds up their transmission, and because an amphetamine psychosis mimics schizophrenia, some scientists believe that schizophrenia itself may be caused by a disorder in these transmitter systems. However, others insist that this is, at best, an oversimplification; very recently a team of researchers suggested that a chemical called phenylethylamine (PEA for short) just may be the body's own amphetamine!

Cocaine is very similar to amphetamine in its effects. It's more trendy, though, and people in the film world sometimes speak of it as their "chief energy source." The cocaine high is relatively short—it lasts about twenty minutes—and it's said to be more subtle than an amphetamine high; but an overdose of coke can produce a psychosis that resembles paranoid schizophrenia and it can be lethal.

Tranquilizers

The tranquilizer Valium is *the* drug of the turbulent present, the one most often prescribed today in the United States. For those who suffer from anxiety it offers relief—but with significant drawbacks.

Ilona, for example, began taking Valium a few years ago, at a time when she was unemployed and was feeling tense, anxious, and unhappy. She took the drug at night to combat insomnia, but sometimes she also took it during the day. However, it soon became clear that its effect on her was definitely unhealthy. "I'm terribly sensitive to drugs—I overreact to almost everything," she said, "and Valium knocked me out. While I was taking it, I felt as if I were moving in slow motion. I was tired and yawning all the time, and I had no positive outlook—I didn't really care about anything. I felt somehow disconnected from the things that were going on around me, and unfocused, like a badly tuned TV set." So after a couple of weeks she gave up the drug.

However, a few months ago Ilona got out the Valium again because she was having nightmares almost every night. She decided that she'd use it only at bedtime, but she soon found that it left her with a distinct hangover the next day. She's teaching grade school now, and she was actually falling asleep during the reading period. "Some of the time I was so spaced out that I didn't care whether the kids killed each other right there in class," she said, "but at other times I was overemotional; I'd cry at the drop of a hat. I finally made up my mind that I'd just have to put up with the nightmares; I preferred them to the way I felt on Valium."

The Body's Own Tranquilizer

We all feel anxious at times and it's an unpleasant experience. Tranquilizers do suppress the symptoms and so they may seem like an easy solution. However, they have at least two major drawbacks. First of all, recent studies indicate that Valium may be addictive not only in high doses but even, when used regularly, in smaller doses. Secondly, as Ilona discovered, tranquilizers can make you quite groggy.

In the past few years researchers have been hunting avidly for a new drug that will tranquilize without sedating, and there's every reason to think they'll soon find one. They already know that just as the brain has receptors for morphine to plug into, it has receptors that fit Valium, Librium, and chemically similar drugs. Thus, it stands to reason that *the brain not only manufactures its own opiate but also makes its own tranquilizer*. It may even make an anxiety-*generating* substance as well.

The receptors that Valium connects with occur in clusters. The problem with Valium may be that it attaches to all the receptors in the cluster rather than selectively plugging into just one or

two of them. In other words, Valium may be like a master key
that turns too many locks, including some that are tranquilizing
but others that have a sedative effect and may, perhaps, be the
very receptors that alcohol and barbiturates affect.

If scientists can come up with a substance that binds to some,
but not all, of the same sites as valium, they may be able to produce
a more effective tranquilizer with fewer side effects.

Whether that will be a boon to all or just a bigger temptation
for most is a question worth asking.

Curing Symptoms Can Be Risky

Thanks to recent research, it seems clear now that evolution
designed the brain to be self-balancing: to respond with anxiety,
for example, when anxiety is appropriate, and then to turn the
anxiety off. But occasionally the brain's balancing act fails. In
some way the individual is traumatized. Psychologically and
chemically he experiences profound internal shifts, becomes too
anxious, and can't find his way back. At such times many people
resort to drugs. Unfortunately, most mood-altering drugs have
serious drawbacks, except as temporary expedients. They're
clumsy stand-ins for the brain's own substances.

It seems likely that in the near future scientists will succeed in
identifying and synthesizing quite a few of the brain's biochemicals; we may fall heir to a host of new drugs that do what today's stimulants and tranquilizers do—but do it much better. I
suspect that this will be a mixed blessing.

When a person is emotionally off balance—when he's knotted
up with anxiety, exploding with nervous energy, or is depressed
—it *may* be because his biochemistry has simply malfunctioned,
but most often his emotions are at the root of the reaction. If he
tackles his problem by taking stimulants or tranquilizers, he
won't solve it. What's more, if the drugs are so effective that they
actually abolish his symptoms—with no irritating side effects—he
will no longer even feel the need to solve the problem.

Nobody ever said that life was never supposed to be difficult,

Nobody ever said that life was never supposed to be difficult, tense, or uncomfortable. In doing away with discomfort and tension, you may actually prevent learning and growth. *When you lean on drugs, even if you come closer to realizing your energy potential, you may fall far short of your full* human *potential.*

Alcohol: The Lift Before the Letdown

Stimulants and tranquilizers are recent inventions. However, the desire to manipulate mood and energy is probably as old as humankind. Furthermore, if we include alcohol, cigarettes, coffee, and tea among the substances we consider to be "drugs," then it becomes clear that most Americans have an ongoing relationship with one kind of drug or another. The pros and cons of such involvements vary with the particular substance.

Pharmacologists classify alcohol as a depressant. However, Dr. Arnold Friedhoff of the New York University School of Medicine explained that the word "depressant" is misleading, since drinking doesn't make people depressed—in fact, quite the opposite. What alcohol depresses is the central nervous system (CNS). It puts a damper on CNS activities and, in the process—particularly when used in moderation—it somehow releases energy and good feelings, though if you drink enough alcohol, of course, you'll go to sleep or pass out.

But even if you don't sleep, the lift you get is short-lived. The glow fades quickly and once it's gone you're apt to feel tired and irritable. Pamela, for example, found that if she had two martinis (sometimes three) every night with dinner, she could count on feeling relaxed and happy at least once a day. However, the rest of the evening was generally wasted, because once the good feelings wore off she was too tired to do anything more ambitious than stare at the television set. She tried to cut down to just one martini, or one glass of wine, but she discovered that one of anything swept away her willpower. Pamela finally went on the wagon because she felt that alcohol was getting too much of a hold on her. When she did, she found that she had added several active hours to her day. She also felt so much better about herself that she was completely revitalized!

Cigarettes: Lighting Up a Tranquilizer

Scientists are still trying to explain the mechanisms behind the effects that cigarettes have. They do know that nicotine interacts with some of the acetylcholine receptors (acetylcholine is a neurotransmitter) and that it has an impact on the autonomic nervous system and on other transmitters as well.

Cigarettes are considered stimulants because they increase the heart rate and raise blood pressure, cardiac output, and blood sugar level. However, they seem to calm those who become addicted to them. One study found that though smokers were generally more nervous than nonsmokers, they felt less nervous while smoking and reacted less strongly to stress. Nonsmokers, on the other hand, responded to stress the same way after they lit up as before.

It's not surprising, then, that when a smoker quits he's apt to feel extremely jittery and tense for a while. George recalled, "For the first two weeks, I felt as if all my energy was going into denying myself cigarettes and into coping with anxiety and tension. But then gradually it began to get easier. I found I was remarkably clearheaded and I stopped coughing. When I discovered that I wasn't getting winded as fast either on the tennis court or in the swimming pool, I suddenly began to feel absolutely terrific: healthy, smart, in control. Now *that* was energy!"

As for marijuana, like alcohol it is a euphoriant. It sharpens perceptions—you sense things more vividly—and occasionally distorts them. It stimulates the appetite, but it's also apt to leave you feeling drowsy. In addition, when some people smoke pot they become so focused on their own inner world that they have no energy for anything else. In fact, a loss of energy in someone who's very much into marijuana is a danger signal, a warning that he's abusing the drug.

Coffee: A Mild Upper

In general, coffee has a mild stimulant effect on the brain. Though the mechanisms by which it achieves that effect are still somewhat mysterious, scientists do know that through a chain of biochemical events caffeine increases the concentration of an important substance (cyclic AMP) that turns on many cells so that they do what they were designed to do. Some of the cells affected make particular hormones; others are brain cells of the sort that play a part in emotional states and in alertness.

Researchers have also reported that caffeine appears to attach to the same brain receptors that accept Valium. No one can say yet what that means, but one theory holds that by occupying those receptor sites caffeine blocks the action of the brain's own natural tranquilizing chemical, and so it may promote a mild anxiety.

There's a body truth worth knowing about coffee: It affects different people very differently. Norma, for example, admits that she uses caffeine as a kind of crutch to prop herself up from hour to hour. A free-lance writer who works at home, she's almost never without a cup of coffee. "I'm embarrassed to say how much of it I drink," she said. "I suspect it's eight to ten cups a day. But, you know, I seldom have coffee nerves. Once in a long while I feel jumpy and restless, and usually what's different on those days is that I stayed up quite late the night before. Of course, the later I stay up the more coffee I drink. Then if I sleep for just a few hours, the next morning all that caffeine is probably still in my system."

Gail's reaction to coffee is entirely different; she can't drink it at all anymore. She used to have five or six cups during the course of a day, but she was always aware that for her caffeine was a mixed blessing: Though it gave her a real lift, it sometimes left her feeling tense, scattered, and jittery; and once the effects wore off, she felt let down and more tired than ever.

Three years ago, when she turned vegetarian, Gail gave up caffeine in all its guises; she stopped drinking coffee, soft drinks, and teas, except the herbal ones. Six months later she reconsidered her decision and concluded that there was really no reason why she shouldn't have the occasional cup of coffee as long as she kept her consumption down; but when she tried it, she found that even half a cup gave her the jitters. "I seem to have been cured of coffee drinking for life," she said.

How is it that one person can't tolerate coffee at all while another can down eight to ten cups a day with no apparent ill effects? Dr. Marcus Reidenberg of Cornell Medical Center in New York has done research on coffee drinking. He has found that people are very different in the way they metabolize coffee—how much caffeine they absorb and how fast they eliminate it. Thus, two people who drank the same amount of coffee from the same pot might wind up with quite different amounts of caffeine circulating in their bloodstreams. Dr. Reidenberg suspects that there may be differences in the brain's sensitivity to caffeine as well, so that even if blood levels were the same the effects might be different.

In addition, he explained that *coffee is like most drugs that act on the central nervous system: People do develop a tolerance for it, so that the same amount does less and less for them* and they have to increase the dose to get the equivalent effect. If the drug is withdrawn, they lose their tolerance after a while; when they try coffee again, it has a greater impact. That explains why Norma only suffers from coffee nerves when she increases her already high level of caffeine consumption, and it also explains why Gail can no longer comfortably drink coffee at all.

Caffeine is mildly addictive; if people who drink more than five cups a day are forced to do without, even for twenty-four hours, they sometimes suffer withdrawal symptoms—usually just a headache. If Norma ever decides to give up coffee, then she'd be well advised to taper off gradually.

Is It Safe to Drink Coffee?

Whether or not Norma *should* give it up or cut down is another question. The experts are still debating just how safe coffee is. On the one hand, it *is* a drug; in fact, you can kill yourself by drinking too much of it. However, in order to succeed you'd have to gulp fifty to a hundred cups of coffee, one right after the other; suicide by caffeine is therefore seldom, if ever, attempted. As Dr. Reidenberg said, "Too much of anything can make you sick."

People with heart trouble, especially those who have an irregular heartbeat, are often advised to steer clear of coffee, because in high enough doses it speeds up the heartbeat and increases the force of the contraction. Moreover, Dr. Charles Ehret of the Argonne National Laboratory believes that caffeine throws off the timing of the body's internal clocks (see Chapter 5).

On the other side of the question, there's no real evidence that coffee, consumed in normal amounts, has ever done damage to normal, healthy people. Though there have been a few studies that suggested that it's harmful, Dr. Reidenberg pointed out that it's difficult to separate the effects of drinking coffee from those of cigarette smoking, since so many people do both. Where researchers have been able to examine the effects of coffee alone, they've failed to find evidence that it's damaging. It probably helps that caffeine doesn't linger long in the body. By the time three to five hours have passed, half of it is gone, and during an average night's sleep it's completely washed from the system, so that we start the new day caffeine-free.

To date, then, though coffee isn't entirely in the clear (perhaps nothing that affects the body so profoundly really could be), there doesn't seem to be any reason for a person with a healthy heart to give it up. But if you want to make intelligent use of the kind of energy boost it can provide, there are two facts worth keeping in mind.

The first is that there are vast differences in the way people react to caffeine. For that reason, you have to look to your own body truths and adjust your intake accordingly. If coffee often leaves you jittery and uncomfortable, then it's totally irrelevant that others can drink it by the gallon with no ill effects.

Secondly, be aware that the more you drink the more you'll need to drink to get an extra energy boost. It's easy to get into a kind of coffee spiral until, like Norma, you've built up a mild dependency to the point where security is a cup of coffee close at hand. If you need extra energy, there are dozens of ways to get it that have a more lasting effect.

Food for Sleeping

Turning now to recent studies of foods that affect the brain, we find that although the research is rather new, in one area it seems close to being of practical use. All protein foods contain small amounts of an amino acid called tryptophan. In the brain tryptophan is converted into serotonin, a transmitter that appears to moderate pain and anxiety and is involved in the onset of sleep.

As we've seen, sleep (or the lack of it) affects energy. Research suggests that tryptophan may turn out to be a mild, safe sleeping pill. Dr. Ernest Hartmann, director of the Sleep Laboratory at Boston State Hospital, found that a one-gram dose of tryptophan—about as much as you'd get in a large meal—helped normal people fall asleep faster. It reduced lying-awake time, on the average, from twenty-three minutes to just twelve, and those who ordinarily took the longest to fall sleep got the most benefit. Tryptophan has also proved helpful to the kind of insomniac who has trouble getting to sleep. It produces drowsiness, but you can't knock anyone out with it; and in a month-long trial it didn't distort the normal pattern of sleep the way most sedatives do. It's cleared from the body quite rapidly—though it helps people stay asleep early in the night, it seems to have little effect later on.

Insomniacs who would like to try tryptophan can always experiment with their diet. Researchers haven't yet done the necessary studies on diet and sleep; however, from animal experiments we do know that the way to get tryptophan to the brain is to pile on the carbohydrates, not the proteins. Though protein foods contain tryptophan in small amounts, they also contain other amino acids in abundance that easily beat tryptophan to the entry sites in the brain's capillary system and block them. Therefore, the best way to increase brain serotonin is, paradoxically, to have a meal that's high in carbohydrates and low in protein—a big, starchy meal late in the evening, for example. The carbohydrates stimulate the insulin response, and then insulin removes the competing amino acids from the blood, permitting tryptophan to reach the brain.

Food for Energy?

A high-protein meal may do nothing much to increase the cerebral supply of tryptophan, but it does increase the amount of tyrosine circulating in the blood, and tyrosine (another amino acid) also reaches the brain, where it seems to be converted into dopamine and norepinephrine. Norepinephrine is believed to be a key to regulating blood pressure; and already rat studies indicate that tyrosine lowers blood pressure. It could also turn out to be something of an upper if it works the way amphetamines do, for they apparently increase levels of both norepinephrine and dopamine in the brain. If tyrosine has a similar effect, then science will have confirmed what many people believe—that protein has a special ability to energize. (See Chapter 5 for more on that theory.)

Food and Memory

Acetylcholine is yet another brain transmitter. The substance it's made from is choline, and choline, in turn, is contained in lecithin, which is found in egg yolks, soybeans, and liver. Lecithin is also an additive; as such, it's part of many processed foods. People who eat a varied diet can easily consume ten times as much lecithin one day as they do the next, and no one is quite sure what that means in terms of the way we live and behave. However, acetylcholine seems to play a part in memory, sleep, co-ordination, and perhaps in mood as well.

Working with doses of choline far higher than people normally get from food, researchers have begun to test this substance for medical applications. So far, lecithin looks quite promising as a treatment for tardive dyskinesia, a movement disorder that often afflicts those who have taken antipsychotic drugs. Choline has been of some help to people suffering from a form of progressive senility known as Alzheimer's disease. And an intriguing set of experiments suggests that choline may do good things for someone who has trouble memorizing.

The memory experiments, like so many, were done mostly on college student volunteers, so the subjects were people who were actually pretty good at memorizing. Nevertheless, some were better than others. All were asked to learn lists of words and, in general, the students who were the poorest at doing this under normal conditions—when they'd been given no drug—showed the most improvement when they took choline.

Next, further studies were done using scopalomine, a drug that blocks acetylcholine and interferes with memory. Again, the students who had the poorest memories under normal conditions had the most trouble learning lists of words while under the influence of scopalomine. Dr. Christian Gillin of St. Elizabeth's Hospital in Washington, D.C., and the National Institute of Mental Health was one of the scientists involved in this study (with Drs. Sitaram and Weingartner). He speculated that perhaps some people have a good, strong acetylcholine system while others don't. Those who don't might be more responsive both to drugs that interfere with acetylcholine and to those that promote it.

Research on brain foods is young. It will undoubtedly lead to new drugs, but it's hard to say what impact it might have on the way we eat. It seems possible, though, that *some time in the future we may know what foods to consume to give ourselves just a bit of an edge while studying or while trying to fall asleep— and even what to eat for an energy edge.*

Energy Tips

1. Take stimulant and tranquilizer drugs only under a doctor's supervision and as a temporary expedient. Don't use them as a substitute for solving your basic problems. Be aware that it is easy to become dependent on such drugs.

2. The potential dangers of cigarettes, marijuana, and alcohol are too well known to go into here. Suffice it to say that if you're hooked on any of these substances, one way to boost your energy dramatically is to give it up! You may go through an energy crisis while you're adapting to the change, but the aftermath is pure enerjoy.

3. Watch out for the coffee spiral: If you reach for a cup of coffee every time you need an energy boost, it will take more and more coffee to give you the same lift.

4. If you have trouble getting to sleep at night, you might experiment by having a very late starchy dinner or a hefty bedtime snack.

Another Kind of Stimulant: Exercise

It seems a simple enough equation: You take in "energy" in the form of food and spend it in the form of exercise. However, just as there are misconceptions about food and energy, there are misunderstandings about exercise. Perhaps the most common is the belief (held chiefly by the sedentary) that activities such as jogging and calisthenics are entirely a matter of energy outgo. People who exercise regularly know that exercising is a way to increase vigor.

In fact, the truth of the matter, as we've said, is that, in general, *to get energy you really have to spend energy!*

9

Exercise:
Using Your Body to Fine Tune Your Mind

Energy that Lasts . . . and Lasts

On August 13, 1978, twenty-eight-year-old Diana Nyad waded into the ocean off Ortegosa Beach, Cuba. She was determined to make it to Key West, Florida, the hard way: by swimming the 103 miles, an accomplishment that would win her the world's distance record for open-water swimming—if she succeeded.

Waiting for Nyad offshore was the *Cleopatra*, a huge metal cage mounted on pontoons and equipped with its own motors. Forty feet long, twenty feet wide and eight feet deep, it would enclose her throughout the swim in order to protect her from sharks.

Diana had estimated that the crossing would take about sixty hours, or two and a half days of steady swimming. She would not sleep for the duration. And, according to the rules of marathon swimming, she couldn't cling, even for a few seconds, to the side of the cage. Treading water wouldn't help her either, since it, too, requires an expenditure of energy; and if she did it from time to time, it would be more mental than physical rest. Once every hour those aboard the cage would blast a police whistle to call her in for a cup of hot glucose, extended to her at the end of a long pole. During the worst times, when her energy and spirits were lowest, a pacer would slip into the water with her to keep her company.

By the time she was twelve hours out, Diana's muscles were pounding from the strain, but that was only to be expected. Later the sea grew rough and six-foot waves crashed against the

Cleopatra. Inside the cage the backwash was fierce and Diana became seasick. Then she was stung by jellyfish, and her tongue grew so swollen from the salty water that she couldn't close her mouth around it. At times she hallucinated and saw spiders in the water. But still she kept going.

At dawn of the third day she had been swimming for almost forty-two hours and had covered seventy-nine miles. However, she had also been blown forty miles off course! It was clear that even if Diana swam for another fifty hours, she wouldn't make Key West, so she was pulled from the water exhausted and in tears.

Despite the fact that she didn't reach Florida, Diana's determined attempt was an extraordinary example of human endurance and energy. How can anyone swim without resting for forty-two hours—nearly two days—in rough seas? Where does the energy come from?

Diana Nyad: Incredible Stamina

Three months before her Cuba swim I interviewed Diana Nyad in the New York apartment she had borrowed from race-car driver Janet Guthrie while Guthrie was away at the Indianapolis 500. Nyad turned out to be a middle-sized young woman with a thatch of sun-bleached brown hair and a light dusting of freckles across an upturned nose. Her body was her most distinctive feature, for it's a classic swimmer's body: deep-chested, slim-hipped, substantial but without a pinch of fat anywhere.

Born in New York City and raised in Florida, where people tend to take competitive swimming seriously, Diana began to train as a sprinter when she was ten years old. She didn't get into marathon swimming until 1970, when at the age of twenty she entered a ten-mile race on Lake Ontario and set a new women's record for the distance. In the ensuing years she raced in the Suez Canal and the Nile, the Bay of Naples and the North Sea, among other places. She circumnavigated the island of Manhattan, stroking twenty-eight miles in less than eight hours; she was the first person ever to swim across Lake Ontario the hard way, from north to south, battling strong currents from the Niagara River for the last five miles.

The record for long-distance swims actually stands at an astounding 281 miles, but it was set by an Argentinian who swam *down* the Parana River. Rivers are less turbulent than oceans, and the river current can actually be a help. At the time Diana decided on her Cuba project, the record for the longest swim in open water was 60 miles across Lake Michigan. Thus, she felt with good reason that if she could swim the 103 miles from Cuba to Florida, it would be "the greatest endurance feat in history." She would have to make every foot of progress on her own, with no help from currents and no protection from the shore. In May, when we talked, she estimated her chances of succeeding at about fifty-fifty.

Before the Cuba swim, Diana had decided that it would be her last, that she was ready to give up long-distance swimming. Her new goal was to become the top woman squash player in the United States. However, she had other dreams as well, for Diana is more than just a superb athlete. A Phi Beta Kappa college graduate on her way to a Ph.D. in comparative literature, she had written two books, including *Other Shores*, which is autobiographical. She had also finished a screenplay and she thought that someday she'd like to write a novel. Nevertheless, she wasn't ready to take literary goals too seriously since, as she put it, "Life outside the world of sports is more complicated. In athletics the formula is easy. You have this much talent, you put in this much time, and you can measure how good you are compared to everybody else. It's very black-and-white."

She made it sound simple, but actually it takes experience and self-knowledge to compete in marathons: An athlete must know how to pace herself and pay out her energy intelligently. It also takes a complex character, driven by complex needs, to shoot for glory and a world's record in long-distance swimming, for in this sport every achievement almost inevitably comes on the heels of prolonged pain, and cash rewards are virtually nonexistent. The pain seemed less important to Diana than the fact that she had been able to push the human body—her own body—to feats of endurance that to most people are unimaginable. Courage, strength, an indomitable will: They're old-fashioned words, but they're part of Diana's frame of reference. Still, up to a point, as she said, the formula *is* simple: Take one natural athlete and train obsessively, gradually pushing the body's limits further and further.

How to Train for Endurance

It took over a year of training to prepare Diana for the Cuba swim. She started slowly. For the first few months her schedule called for workouts on weight machines twice a week; in addition, every day she ran ten miles in the morning, covering the distance in about sixty-two minutes; she swam two hours of sprints; she jumped rope for half an hour; and she spent three or four hours playing squash—not because squash was part of training for the swim, but with an eye to the future.

By the time I interviewed her, Nyad was pushing herself much harder. She was still working out with weights several times a week and skipping rope for half an hour a day, but she'd given up running, and squash was down to an hour a day, because she was now swimming for six to eight hours daily in local pools.

Inevitably, the stepped-up schedule had changed her sleeping and eating habits. Ordinarily Diana only needed about six hours of sleep a night, and that was true even when she was in the early stages of training. But once she was swimming for six hours a day or more, her sleep needs escalated and she found that she couldn't get by on less than nine hours a night. "Even then, I'm so exhausted that I sometimes fall asleep at the breakfast table or conk out over the research I'm doing for my new book," she said.

A Marathoner's Diet

As for food, the day I interviewed Diana—I arrived just after lunch—I found her tucking away a jelly doughnut and orange juice. Eyeing the doughnut, I asked her if she did carbohydrate loading, as marathon runners often do (see Chapter 7). She pointed out that the best runners rarely run for much more than two hours, even in a twenty-six-mile marathon. At that time she was already swimming six to eight hours a day in preparation for a swim that might last for more than sixty hours. "So if I were going to load on carbohydrates, what would we be talking about?" she asked. "I'm already eating a tremendous amount." In fact, so far that day she had consumed five thousand calories, and before she went to bed that night she'd be up to eight thousand. By the time the Cuba swim rolled around, she would be downing nine thousand calories daily. (A woman of her size who was not an athlete would normally have about two thousand calories a day.)

In general, Diana aimed for a varied diet, heavy on both protein and carbohydrates, and she liked raw food. She used to get up at four-thirty in the morning. Before going off to swim she'd down four raw eggs with a glass of orange juice while standing at the refrigerator. It was simply faster and easier to have them raw than to cook them. However, she had subsequently read that eating eggs raw is risky, because of bacteria they may contain, so she had taken to cooking her breakfast. Her favorite dinner was steak, uncooked just because that's the way she prefers it. "I like to have a two-and-a-half- to three-pound raw sirloin for dinner," she said. "I chop it into tiny cubes and dip them in soy sauce."

The week before the Cuba swim, Diana would virtually stop training to over-rest and overeat; at that time she planned to pour on the carbohydrates, partly because they're easier to digest but largely because she would need to gain 10 pounds. The extra weight would represent food energy, and she'd lose it and more during the swim. The time she raced in Lake Ontario, she was in the water for 20 hours and dropped from 130 to 111, losing 19 pounds, which is, as she said, rather serious. That swim was particularly difficult because the water was so cold that, in producing its own heat, her body burned up a great many calories of energy—and flesh. Afterward she was hospitalized briefly and needed crutches for a few days because she was so stiff. Still, she never seriously considered giving up her sport.

Endurance Events: The Pain—and the Ecstasy

Pain is an assumed part of almost any long-distance swim. In fact, it's a given in the lives of many professional athletes and top amateurs. Diana admitted, "Nothing about a marathon swim is enjoyable until I can see with my own eyes that I'm about to finish, which happens when I'm about two miles out. What is enjoyable is having gone through it, to touch the other side and be so thoroughly spent, so 110 percent exhausted. It's a rich feeling to have been that strong physically and mentally."

She explained that swimmers talk about a progression from hurt, to pain, to agony, to ecstasy. "If you're not in condition," she said, "you can swim to the point where you hurt a little bit. If you really work out for a couple of months, you may actually feel pain before you collapse. Push further than that, dedicate yourself to the sport so that it's almost a full-time occupation, and you can reach agony; and if you can reach agony, you have the potential for feeling ecstasy." She tolerates the pain, she said, because she knows the formula: She knows she can't get to the ecstasy without going through the pain.

Mind Games to Ease an Ordeal

There is mental as well as physical pain, for depression is a major hurdle on a marathon swim. Diana explained, "It would be much easier for me to swim 103 miles in a pool, not only because I wouldn't have to battle rough seas but because I would always know exactly how far I still had to go. If I'm in the middle of some lake or in the ocean, nobody in the boat can tell me that."

Depression generally strikes when she's been in the water about eight hours. The uncertainty about the ordeal ahead is part of it, but low blood sugar is another factor. For the first eight hours or so Diana can successfully keep her blood sugar up by drinking hot glucose once an hour, but after that the feedings can't keep up with the rate at which she's burning calories.

Along with extreme fatigue and depression, Diana must cope with bouts of delirium. She pointed out that marathon swimming really amounts to sensory deprivation. Goggles cover her eyes so that she can barely see; she wears several bathing caps to conserve body heat, so she can hear very little; and there's nothing to feel except the water that envelops every inch of her body. Cut off from ordinary sensations, from contact with the world outside her skin, she's left alone with her thoughts. *A long swim is not only a physical challenge but a mental one as well.*

On swims that last no more than twenty hours, Diana said, she daydreams as much as possible to take her mind off her discomfort. She might, for example, have a fantasy about playing a brilliant game of squash. "I actually play the game, point by point," she said. "I can feel my legs run up and feel myself hit the ball. Sometimes I wake up from it absolutely shocked that I'm not really on the squash court."

The danger with fantasies is that, as fatigue builds, they can turn into hallucinations, like the spiders in the water during the Cuba swim. They can also leave Diana so disoriented that she no longer remembers where she is or what she's supposed to be doing. Consequently, she knows that after fifteen or twenty hours she must try hard not to daydream any longer. "That's unpleasant," she said. "Without the fantasies it's harder not to focus on how badly I feel, and not to keep wondering why I'm doing the swim in the first place."

Short of the danger point, Diana holds her fantasies in check by simultaneously playing counting games. She knows that six hundred strokes will carry her a mile unless it's a very long or a very cold swim, so by counting her strokes she can judge how far she has come. Often, instead of counting strokes she counts choruses of the song, "Row, Row, Row Your Boat." At eight strokes to a chorus, seventy-five choruses make a mile. While she "sings" in her mind and counts, she indulges in dreams of glory and perhaps childhood memories; the counting game keeps the fantasies relatively faint and distant. (Out of curiosity I tried Diana's system one day while swimming; I found that it's a bit like trying to carry on a conversation and watch television at the same time. It certainly occupies the mind completely.)

"I always joke that when I finish a swim I feel as if I've spent six months on a psychiatrist's couch," Diana said. "I think that anyone confined for a long period, virtually unable to hear or see, would inevitably go through an extremely intense mental experience. When I finish a swim I usually know very clearly what I want to do with my life and what I don't want to do anymore. I think you mature quite a bit, mentally and emotionally, during a long swim."

For Peak Energy, Focus Both Body and Mind

Diana's training program and her accomplishments illustrate quite clearly the relationship between food and sleep needs, on the one hand, and physical energy and endurance, on the other. They also illustrate the way mental energy inevitably interacts with physical energy.

Americans are culturally programed from an early age to think of mind and body as separate entities, the mind somehow inhabiting the body. We are only belatedly beginning to realize that the two are so intimately related that it's impossible to understand one without taking into account what's happening to the other. To a large extent, people actually think with their bodies. If you *imagine* moving a finger, the muscles in that finger will begin to generate faint bursts of electrical activity even though your hand remains perfectly still. If you think about listening to a voice, muscles in your middle ear will react—even though no one is speaking. Similarly, the state of the body affects the mind. A person suffering physical pain can't think very clearly. Someone who downs a cup of strong coffee or a slug of Scotch feels the effects in his head.

To dramatize the fact that body and mind are parts of the same whole, some psychotherapists have begun to speak of the "body-mind." Some also believe that physical and mental energy are simply different manifestations of the same inner force.

However, in the minds of most people physical and mental energy are distinct from one another. They're experienced differently and so they're defined differently as well. When Americans speak of physical energy they usually mean vigor, vitality, the urge to be up and moving. When they talk of mental energy they're referring to alertness, quick thinking, and the ability to concentrate.

A number of the people I interviewed also remarked on the fact that physical and mental exhaustion feel quite different, which was interesting, since exhaustion is the opposite of energy. One man recalled an evening when he came home from work mentally worn out and unable to concentrate, too tired to tackle his tax return or even to read over the owner's manual for his new car; and yet it felt good to get out that night and play ball with his kids. He noted that it's also possible to be so utterly spent physically that all you want to do is sit, though at the same time you're feeling very alert mentally.

Up to a point it makes sense to distinguish between the energies of mind and body. Certainly, thinking isn't the same thing as moving around. It's also useful at times to look at physical and mental vitality separately, just as it can be useful to consider the motor of a car apart from the steering mechanism. One isn't going anywhere without the other, but they do operate differently.

I'm convinced that *the times in our lives when we're most effective are the times when physical and mental energy are both perfectly focused on the task at hand.* That's peak energy and it's a rare experience.

Physical Exercise Ignites Mental Energy

Short of such peaks, however, there are ways to use physical drive to get your mental energy flowing, and vice versa.

By spending *physical* energy you can clear your head, focus your thinking, and free creative forces. You can generate a new surge of power in mind *and* body. You can also use your *mental* energy in some unexpected ways to focus and intensify your physical drive.

Let's look at some of the ways in which mind and body interact, first considering what the body can do for the mind and then —in the next chapter—examining what the mind can do for the body.

A Way to Recharge Your Energy Anytime

Most Americans think of exercise as a way to spend energy, and yet whenever I talk to sports addicts—to people who are heavily involved in running, swimming, biking, or squash—I hear the opposite: that *exercise produces energy.* In fact, a Chicago lawyer I'll call Jay insisted that energy is self-generating. "Up to a certain extreme point," he said, "the more you put out, the more you get back."

Now in his middle thirties, Jay was the sedentary sort until about seven years ago, when he began doing yoga exercises. He started because of a vague, guilty feeling that he was out of shape, but then he continued because he enjoyed it. Eventually he began running as well. Now he starts every day with a half-hour run and every second day follows that up with thirty-five minutes of exercises.

"For me, running is primarily a way to start the day feeling good," he said. "But sometimes I run at night as well, because I've discovered that when I come home from work I have two alternatives. I can either sit down, drink two martinis, and face an increasingly drowsy evening—and that's fine, because I work a pretty hard schedule and most nights I feel I deserve time off; or I can jolt my body with jogging or yoga—and if I do that, I feel ready to start a whole new day. In other words, in the baggage I carry around with me in life is a technique for recharging my batteries, for generating new energy whenever I want to, and I'm delighted to know it's there."

Of course, it's light-to-moderate exercise that's energizing; the marathon runner feels far from vigorous at the end of a race. Still, all of the sports enthusiasts I talked with agreed that exercise begets energy, and almost everyone had a theory about why. I was told, for example, that "the human organism was meant to be an active, foraging animal, so when the body is finally used as it was intended to be, good things happen." Others suggested that physical fitness leads to increased energy, or that a charged-up circulation is responsible. A number of people, noting that their minds were clearer after exercise, put it down to an increased flow of oxygen to the brain.

However, Professor William McArdle, director of Applied Physiology at Queens College in New York City, was doubtful about most of the popular theories I'd come across. He explained that alertness probably can't be credited to a shot of oxygen to the brain, since the brain's overall oxygen consumption doesn't change much with exercise. As for the fitness hypothesis, we develop and maintain the muscles and cardiovascular system our life-style requires. The requirements of a sedentary person are quite different from those of an athlete, but his body will still be adequate to meet most of the demands of his everyday life, and he'll only feel short of energy and stamina if he does something that's unusual for him, such as climbing several flights of stairs. "The body is a beautifully regulated organism," Dr. McArdle said. "If you have big muscles and a good, big heart, and you don't use them, you lose them; the body reabsorbs what you don't need. You can lose quite a bit of your physical fitness within just five to ten weeks."

There are, of course, other ways in which exercise might generate energy, for vigorous activities such as running and swimming certainly do cause profound changes in the body. When a woman sets out on her morning run, in short order her heart begins beating faster, her blood pressure rises, her blood sugar level goes up, and glands become more active. Adrenaline is released, as is cortisol. (You may remember that adrenaline helps the body gear up in an emergency, while cortisone, which is synthetic cortisol, can induce euphoria.) Some scientists suspect that there may also be changes in brain chemistry, in the activities of those crucial neurotransmitters.

That, of course, is speculation; however, even if we don't know exactly how exercise generates energy, there doesn't seem to be much doubt that it does. "I run," Professor McArdle said, "and I've felt it, too."

Running for Therapy

Vigorous activity can also liberate energy in another way. *Apparently exercise helps some people get rid of anger, anxiety, and depression—all of which can sap vitality.*

Jay, for example, has used running to burn off anger. "There are situations sometimes when you're very angry, but staging a confrontation would be a self-defeating thing to do," he explained. "When I've got something like that going on, sometimes while I'm running my mind will project to what a confrontation would be like. I imagine what I'd say and I think how I'd feel. It's a way to vent anger, and if I do it two or three times, then I'm through with it."

Another man I talked to has used running to counteract anxiety. Don, an insurance broker, is lean, dark-haired, fortyish, with an attractive smile. There was a time when he was hamstrung with anxiety to the point where he couldn't cope with his life. He went into therapy and it helped a lot, but when it came time to stop seeing the therapist he found that, though he was better, he wasn't 100 percent well. Just about then he began running. "I told myself that now it was going to be different," he recalled. "No more tranquilizers. If I had any problems, I'd put on my shoes and run. And I found that my level of stress, anxiety, and depression went right down, even though in the beginning I was doing only a mile and a half a day. There's no question that therapy did more for me than running has. Running, like tranquilizers, doesn't solve any basic problems; but it does make it easier to cope, and at this point it's all I really need."

In the years since Don took up running it has come to play a substantial role in his life. When I talked to him he was averaging ten miles a run, which meant that, with warm-ups before and after, running was eating up about two hours out of every day. However, it literally got him away from things that made him anxious; while he was out on the road or on the indoor track at the Y he was free. "You'd have to be able to keep up with me to give me grief," he said.

Today some therapists are beginning to use exercise to treat anxiety, because studies show that it produces results. Professor William P. Morgan, director of the Sports Psychology Lab at the University of Wisconsin, explained, *"After a vigorous workout there's a decrease in anxiety that we can measure in the lab.* We look at the level of adrenaline in the blood, at blood pressure and heart rate, and we also get self-reports on how people feel. There's no doubt that exercise improves the state of mind, but the question is why. I think ultimately we may be able to demonstrate that brain chemicals such as serotonin, norepinephrine, or the endorphins are changed with exercise and that's why people feel better, but we're a long way from being able to show that now."

How to Outrun the Blues

Exercise also seems to be good for depression. One man who jogs regularly told me, "Running is definitely a mood elevator. If I'm really feeling bad about something I'll go out and run." Nor is running the only form of exercise that's an antidepressant and energy reviver. In a study done at the University of Virginia, students who complained of depression were instructed to work out vigorously three times a week for ten weeks. Some wrestled while others jogged, did exercises, or played tennis or softball. All improved except the softball group, though the joggers improved the most. It seems possible that softball simply isn't vigorous enough to have an effect.

Another study, done recently at the University of Wisconsin, compared running with psychotherapy. Though it was only a small-scale pilot study, results suggest that *for treating depression running may even, in some cases, be as effective as therapy.* Individuals who came to a college clinic because they were depressed were assigned either to ten weeks of running therapy, ten weeks of psychotherapy, or to unlimited psychotherapy. The joggers were trained in the art of running by a leader who at first ran with them three times a week. During these runs talk about depression was discouraged. If a patient persisted in discussing it, the leader suggested that she focus on her running or on her breathing instead. At the end of the experiment, the running patients and those in *limited* ten-week psychotherapy showed the most improvement. A year later most of the joggers were still running and were free of depression.

Running Tips for Beginners

At a symposium I attended, Roger Eischens, who was the running leader in the Wisconsin study, explained that when he teaches jogging he puts his emphasis on technique, so that his trainees will focus on the running experience rather than on achieving a certain distance or speed. On the first day he tells his runners to focus initially on their breathing and to try to deepen it. Four or five breaths later he suggests that now they pay attention to making their run smooth. That leads them to do it right, coming down on the heel and then pushing off gently with the toe. He also works on economy of motion and on keeping the spine erect. "Regardless of fitness level, if they can do all of that they can feel what experienced runners feel," he said. He also stops them before they can tire; in fact, the early sessions alternate running with walking, as trainees learn how to pace themselves by paying attention to their breathing rate and noticing whether or not they can still talk easily. If they can't, they're pushing themselves too hard. Eischens notes that when runners drop out it's often because they tried to do too much too soon.

Therapists in other parts of the country have also been experimenting with the running treatment. Some of them actually jog with their patients, while others simply prescribe the exercise. Professor Robert Brown of the University of Virginia has pointed out that running gives the patient the power to help himself, which has to be significant, since people who are depressed tend to feel both trapped and helpless.

Running: A Positive Addiction

Like most mood elevators, running can turn into an addiction. "We think of it as a positive addiction," Professor Morgan said, "because of the benefits, but the hard-core exercise addicts are not very different from any other addicts. They may forsake their job, their family, and they can get to the point where they need more and more exercise to get the same effect. For the runner that means the five-mile run becomes a ten-mile run and one a day may become two. If they can't run for any reason, they sometimes suffer an exercise-deprivation crisis and become irritable and moody. For some the need is so great that they insist on running even when they've injured a foot or leg."

Withdrawal Symptoms in the Exercise Addict

Withdrawal symptoms are one of the classic signs of addiction. Psychologists are finding it difficult to study them in exercise addicts; most are unwilling to give up their sport even temporarily —even when they're paid for abstaining. One experimenter finally had to settle for people who exercised only three times a week rather than daily, but after a month's deprivation even subjects in this group reported an odd cluster of symptoms: They weren't sleeping as well and they were experiencing increased sexual tension and a greater need to be with others.

Don recently suffered a withdrawal crisis when he had to stop running for almost two months because of a foot injury. His symptoms took the form of insomnia and depression. "When you suddenly stop running and you've been doing six to ten miles a day, it's like losing a friend," he explained. "You come down a long way." Don tried swimming instead and that helped, but overall his two months without running were so uncomfortable that once he was able to run again he cut down on the amount of time he was investing in it. "To stay in condition, you only need to do a couple of miles a day," he said.

Getting High on Exercise

Vigorous exercise can precipitate a surge of energy and good feelings, the kind of experience people usually describe as "getting high." Again, no one knows why this occurs; in fact, some doubt that it does. There are runners, for example, who insist that they've never been high while running, though others say it happens almost every time.

Psychologists point out that there's a definitional problem here, for the term "runner's high" has been used to describe everything from a simple feeling that the body has warmed up and is being used as it was meant to be to an almost delirious euphoria. A tentative taxonomy of runner's highs, then, might include the following:

• Lift: a rare experience in which the legs feel like strong springs. Swimmers talk of "glide," which is similar.

• A feeling that one has emptied out and time has slowed down; a sense of peace.

• Delusions of power: the conviction that the runner could leap over cars if he wanted to. (Hyperventilation—rapid breathing that overoxygenates the blood—may be responsible for this.)

• "Drunken" euphoria: the individual giggles, tap dances, calls out to passersby—all because he feels so good.

• A kind of Zen high that comes from running in beautiful surroundings and drinking them in. Skiers report similar experiences.

• The high that comes with second wind, after the body has settled in, when breathing becomes easier and the runner is sweating nicely. Dave Hackler, a public relations executive who has been running for twelve years, explained it this way: "With second wind sometimes I get the feeling that things are just right. Suddenly everything is in tune and I feel I could run the rest of the way around the world if I wanted to."

• The high that happens one to three hours *after* a run. Dave said, "I get a kind of euphoria. If I run at three or four in the afternoon, it happens at five or six, and I sit there grinning, feeling sorry for everybody else in the world." Don reported a similar experience: "The best feeling is about an hour afterward," he said. "You're so much more relaxed than everyone else, and you feel that you've *done* something."

The Psychological Payoff

The exercise enthusiast who sticks with his sport sometimes comes to feel that his body, his psyche, and even his identity have changed significantly. As a result, *he likes himself better, and that's bound to be energizing.* As Don put it, "These days I don't envy anyone; I don't want to be anyone but me."

For Jay there was a definite change in physical appearance. "Weight has always been a problem in my family," he recalled. "Both my parents were quite heavy, and though I was never tremendously fat, I used to be somewhat overweight and that affected my whole view of myself.

"I never dieted deliberately, but in a positive way when you start running you become very aware of what you eat. Doing good running is so important to me now that I don't want to do anything that will interfere with it, so I don't overeat or load up on rich foods.

"Anyway, between the yoga, the running, and the change in my diet, over the last seven years I've lost about thirty pounds and that has had a profound effect on the way I see myself. I feel quite presentable now—I don't go into situations feeling defensive. I guess it boils down to self-esteem."

Jay's self-image has changed in another way, too. Because he has stuck with the exercise and has lost the weight, he now sees himself as someone with the self-discipline to persist until he gets what he wants. He said, "I've showed myself that if I want to do something I absolutely can do it. The facts don't always bear that out, but inside I feel that way, and I think half of doing things is just believing that you *can* do them."

For many middle-aged men and women, the body changes that exercise can achieve have another meaning as well. In this youth-oriented culture most people assume that after the age of twenty-one it's all downhill: You're doomed to a spreading waistline and failing powers. The discovery that you can reverse the process, that you can train until your body is agile and sinewy again, can make you feel almost immortal.

Body Confidence Liberates Energy

There is also another kind of body confidence that's a by-product of fitness. Eventually you begin to suspect that you may have the physical ability to cope with almost any situation. Don told me, "I don't worry about getting mugged because I could outrun most muggers. And I know that I don't absolutely have to have air conditioning or even a roof over my head because I run no matter what the weather. I could probably set out right now and walk to Florida if I wanted to. I have everything on board that I need. That's confidence—knowing that you can see yourself through most situations.

"We're all dependent on the system. But the paycheck can stop; people let you down. Running is a model activity, I think, because you learn that you can do some things all by yourself. You have all the equipment you need. What frustrates people most is not having a choice; we all hate to sit and wait for the other shoe to drop. *In a way, running gives you the sense that you have control over your life.*"

Psychiatrist John Sours has said that runners—and this may apply to other exercise addicts as well—are people who don't want to depend on or believe in anything but themselves. For them running symbolizes autonomy. It's a religion without priests or a deity, a therapy without therapists, a cult with no guru.

Running for Creative Energy

The last, and perhaps most unexpected, thing that vigorous exercise can do for the mind is to free creative energy.

Solitary, semiautomated forms of exercise such as running and swimming inevitably provide you with time to think, with a chunk of the day when you're not pressed by immediate problems and have no distractions. People tend to use this thinking time in several quite different ways.

For some, the kind of ruminating they do while they're on the road (or traveling to and fro in the lap lane) is a far cry from mundane, logical thought. The running itself requires just enough attention to forestall the orderly monologue that dominates consciousness most of the time. Thus, the runner is free to immerse herself in a state of reverie somewhere between dreaming and daydreaming, and to connect with deeper levels of consciousness.

Many simply enjoy the reverie for what it is. Dave said, "When I jog, I let my mind run free. I fantasize and it's very pleasurable." Others take advantage of insights that occur during running. Jay said, "I never set myself a problem to work on while I'm running. That would be counter to the spirit of the thing. But running is a chance for reflection and so I let my mind drift, and I find that I resolve a lot of problems that way without really trying. For example, if I have to fathom out a trial strategy, the solution will often come to me while I'm running."

There are others who deliberately use their exercise time to do problem solving; most of the time *their* thinking is apt to be logical and coherent. Don began to write poetry at about the same time he started running, and now he uses his hours on the road to work on poems. The finished product has an unmistakable runner's cadence, captured in short lines and strong rhythms.

I myself have discovered that going swimming is not a bad way to write a book. Every afternoon I set myself a problem—how to structure a chapter, perhaps, or how to weave in an interview—and then I head for the pool and start plowing up and down the lap lane. I find that I can concentrate better and think more clearly underwater. Perhaps it's because there are fewer distractions; all I can see is the bottom of the pool, and I can't hear anything. Perhaps it helps that the water relaxes me. *Like most people I think better when I'm relaxed.* Whatever the explanation, I'm delighted with the process.

The idea of combining problem solving with running or swimming makes some people indignant. They use their exercise time to get away from problems, not to meet them head on. Still, there's no reason why a sport can't be used in different ways at different times. Don, for example, ran in marathons several times a year, and to him the race itself was somehow a creative act. "I trained for it for months beforehand," he said. "I spent hours planning my strategy, deciding how fast to run over certain stretches of the route so as to have enough energy left to finish. Then there were all the unexpected things that happened during the race itself, things that could help you or hold you back—injuries, or running for a while beside someone who was fun to talk to. I finished feeling exhausted but absolutely great. I told myself I hadn't done anything, really, except run twenty-six miles, but I felt as if for a while I'd *been* my own poetry."

Energy Tips

1. If you're a runner (or a swimmer, or any sort of exercise enthusiast), the next time you're feeling low in energy try a run (or a swim, or whatever) for an instant pick-me-up.

2. Are you the sedentary sort? To boost your energy dramatically, experiment until you find *some* form of vigorous exercise that you really enjoy and then make it a regular part of your schedule.

3. When you're feeling anxious or depressed, don't just sit there—do something. Get out and run, or go swimming, or whack a tennis ball around. Use your physical energy to get your mental and emotional drive going again.

4. If your sport is a solitary one, such as running or swimming, you might use it at times for problem solving. Define the problem for yourself before you start out and then just let your mind ramble. Mull things over in a very relaxed way and see what you come up with.

What Your Mind Can Do for Your Body

When you spend physical energy in vigorous exercise, you're doing a great deal not only for your body but for your mind and your psyche. But that's only the beginning, because there are ways to return the compliment and use mental energy to improve your performance in sports.

Tricks of the Mind that Energize the Body

How can you use your mind to increase your endurance? To make sure you put out just the right amount of effort (as opposed to trying too hard)? To improve your skill and co-ordination?

How can you combat a tendency to freeze up in situations where you're afraid you'll fail?

What can you do to improve your ability to concentrate? When you're distracted, much of your energy is diverted from the task at hand.

Can you use sports to generate enerjoy?

Most people assume that sports are something you do with your body, something requiring physical energy. However, you can make better use of that energy—and, in fact, you can augment it—if you can also bring your mental energies to bear.

Top athletes have always relied on tricks of the mind that they discovered for themselves. Recently sports psychologists have begun to study some of these mental tactics, as well as others borrowed from behavior therapy, and to teach them on ski slopes, in swimming pools, and on tennis courts. *Some of the techniques they've focused on are particularly interesting since they can be used not just in sports competitions but in other situations as well.*

Daydreaming for Endurance

Just as some people exercise partly because they like to dissociate—to let their minds drift freely—others dissociate in order to exercise more, to increase their endurance.

Diana Nyad does this when she fantasizes or plays counting games to distract herself from her aching body and from depressing thoughts. Many runners use similar tactics during a marathon when they come up against "the Wall," a sudden onslaught of pain that often occurs at about the twenty-mile mark in a race. It is a signal that the body has depleted its reserves of food and energy and is beginning to experience real stress. Muscles pound with fatigue, fingers and toes sometimes start to tingle, and the runner may feel queasy and light-headed.

Once they hit the Wall, many marathoners make a great effort to think hard about something other than their own acute discomfort. One runner reported that at such times he does math problems in his head; another imagines that he's listening to Beethoven. A third handles Heartbreak Hill—a gradual but demanding climb that occurs at about the twenty-mile mark in the Boston marathon—by imagining that he's a child again, riding in the cab of his father's locomotive. His legs become the pistons driving the wheels and his breath is the engine's steam.

Dissociating: The Pros and Cons

Dissociating is quite common among ordinary marathoners, according to Professor William P. Morgan of the University of Wisconsin, who once worked with runners entered in the Boston marathon. However, when Morgan got the chance to study the running elite—the twenty-four top distance runners in the United States—he learned to his surprise that none of them dissociated and most denied that there *was* a Wall. In fact, they told him that the key to avoiding pain is to read your body continually as you run, which is the opposite of dissociating, and to adjust your pace accordingly. Though the elite might tune out periodically during training runs just for the pleasure of it, during a race they were generally very much tuned in.

When he tested elite and ordinary runners on a laboratory treadmill, Morgan found that at ten miles an hour the elite had an easier time of it: Their hearts didn't beat as fast and they consumed less oxygen and produced less lactic acid, the exercise metabolite that tires muscles and makes them hurt. In other words, for them the physiological cost was less. Morgan concluded that during a race top runners can *afford* not to dissociate.

For the average runner, however, dissociation does offer a way to increase endurance, though there are risks involved. The runner who tunes out is more likely to forget his strategy and overextend himself too early in the race; he's also more apt to suffer an injury or heat stroke, or to develop hallucinations. Morgan suggests that the marathoner use dissociation sparingly in races to get through temporary pain zones; as a general rule, though, he should monitor his body closely whenever he's really pushing himself.

Beyond endurance sports, dissociation is handy in other situations as well. It's particularly useful in the dentist's chair to take your mind off your discomfort, and it offers an escape at times when you're in danger of being bored to distraction—when you're riding a long-distance bus, for example, and you've brought nothing along to read. Of course, in cases like that dissociation is simply an important-sounding name for daydreaming.

How to Psych Yourself Up or Down

Often it's simply assumed that to do their best athletes need to be "psyched up"—hence, locker room pep talks and coaches who insult, threaten, and punish players, doing whatever they can to build up tension before a competitive event.

However, many sports psychologists recognize that it's possible for athletes to be overaroused as well as underaroused. Though there are times when players aren't excited enough and somehow can't fully commit their energy to the event, overexcitement and trying too hard may be even more common. The person who is overexcited is apt to be less co-ordinated and doesn't react as quickly and smoothly.

As W. Timothy Gallwey and Robert Kriegel point out in their book *Inner Skiing*, there seem to be two kinds of fear. One primes the body for combat or escape by producing a useful jolt of nervous energy while the other sets up tensions that actually reduce stamina. Muscles become so tight that the individual can't move smoothly. He may forget to breathe, and he's apt to dwell on dire thoughts.

It seems likely that the difference between the two types of fear is largely a matter of degree. In fact, *there's probably an optimum level of arousal in sports.* Below it we don't try hard enough and above it we're overaroused, anxious, and inefficient. Since that optimum level differs from one person to the next, the trick in competitive sports (or in almost any situation) is to know yourself well enough to be able to gauge your own level of arousal—to know whether you're over or under, and to know what to do about it.

If, for example, on the morning of a tennis match you're feeling somewhat slow, dull-witted, or stale, there are a number of things you can do to psych yourself up and ignite your energy. You might go for a short run or volley with a friend for a while just to get yourself moving; or you might strike up a conversation with the competition if that's likely to raise your hackles. Different tactics work for different people. One Olympic-caliber athlete spent the time between fencing matches pumping up his level of hate for his next opponent. Then there was the skier who discovered that he skied more aggressively if he let out blood-curdling yells as he schussed down the slopes.

On the other hand, if on the day of the big event your heart is hammering and you feel so tense and edgy that it's hard to concentrate, you need to psych down, to relax.

Relaxation is highly touted these days, for sports psychologists have learned that *top performance often seems to be correlated with a kind of letting go.* The athlete who surpasses herself, perhaps setting a new record, is apt to remark afterward that she's amazed that she did so well, since at the time it all seemed so easy that she hardly felt she was making a real effort at all.

California track coach Bud Winter is often quoted on the subject of relaxation. He believes so firmly that fast running is relaxed running that he tells his sprinters to run at four fifths of their top speed rather than all out. He suggests that this makes physiological sense, since for every leg movement one muscle must contract while an opposing muscle releases. Thus, the tension generated by an all-out effort could prevent opposing muscles from letting go quickly and completely.

How to Manage Anxiety During Competition

Many people find it very difficult to relax, especially during competition. Some become so anxious that they don't perform as well as they did in training. To deal with this sort of problem, Professor Richard M. Suinn, head of the psychology department at Colorado State University, has developed a procedure he calls *anxiety-management training*. To start with, he teaches the individual to relax his body at will; for this he uses an abbreviated version of Progressive Relaxation, a technique developed many years ago by Dr. Edmund Jacobsen. While lying down in a quiet place, the trainee is instructed to tighten and then relax various muscles, paying close attention to what both tension and relaxation feel like. He might begin by clenching his left fist, for example, and then move on to the left arm before proceeding to the right fist. Gradually, and at a slow, steady pace, he works over all of the major muscle groups in the body, including those in the face.

After several such sessions the trainee is usually ready to skip muscle-tensing and try immediately for all-over relaxation. Once he can achieve this, Professor Suinn asks him to relax and then to imagine that he's in a competitive situation such as skiing or running a race or whatever. As he feels tension again, he's to allow it to build but then to reinduce the controlled relaxation to directly reduce the tension.

With enough practice, most people can learn to let go and relax when they spot signs of tension in themselves during competition. To help the process along, Professor Suinn sometimes links the relaxation experience during training to a particular cue. The individual learns to trigger relaxation automatically by taking a deep breath, for example. Once Suinn used a visual cue instead—the symbol, "7-"—for the Colorado State ski team. He had it put on the backs of all the racing helmets, so that as the team rode up on the lift they'd tune down in response to the "7-" on the helmet of the skier in front of them.

There are, of course, many nonathletic situations in which a person might need to psych herself up or down. Facing an important job interview, for example, she may realize that she's feeling tired and dull-witted. At such times it's helpful to get up and move around, to jog or do calisthenics or anything else that will set the internal juices flowing. Rehearsing the interview beforehand is another tactic; get a friend to play the role of the interviewer and play him, perhaps, as a crisp, stern, and demanding character in order to get your adrenaline flowing.

At the opposite extreme, if you need to psych *down* in order to cope well with an interview or some other challenge, you can try meditation (see Chapter 16) or Progressive Relaxation exercises. *It's so useful to know how to relax your body at will that everybody should probably be trained in one method or the other.*

Saying No to Negative Thoughts

Occasionally tension develops suddenly in the middle of a race or meet, arriving on the heels of some dire thought. The tennis player locks onto the idea that she's about to lose the set, so she doesn't focus on the next serve. The skier, knowing that a rough patch is coming up, can't think of anything except falling.

It's not easy to turn off negative thoughts, and many people simply don't know how to do it. As a friend of mine once pointed out, if you're forced to sit in a corner and then you're told not to think about a white bear, it becomes almost impossible to keep that bear out of your mind.

However, it helps a lot if instead of concentrating on *not* thinking about a white bear you think hard about a brown one. And so Professor Suinn, who is convinced that most people can't focus on two different thoughts simultaneously, supplies his athletes with positive, neutral, or coping thoughts to substitute for their intimations of doom. For example, a swimmer who is worried about tiring fast might switch to the positive, prerehearsed thought that she's close to the finish line and will soon be able to relax. Neutral substitutes work equally well. Suinn trained one skier to react to negative thoughts by immediately telling himself, "Stop!" Then he conjured up in his imagination a piece of music that had a strong, driving beat and focused on skiing to the beat.

A negative thought can also be turned into a cue that will trigger a coping response. Sometimes a marathon runner will suddenly realize that his leg muscles are beginning to tie up. He can be trained to react to this not with an anguished "Oh, no!" but by immediately reminding himself that it has happened before, and by then taking measures to cope with it—perhaps shortening his stride or trying to loosen up.

As we go about our daily lives, we're all prey to negative thoughts at times. People who are in stress situations are especially vulnerable: the man who's in the midst of a messy divorce or the woman who has just been fired from her job. If you realize that you've fallen into the habit of dumping on yourself, or of anticipating failure, *it's worth rehearsing positive, neutral, or coping responses so that you'll have them ready to substitute whenever you catch yourself thinking negatively.*

"Thinking" with Your Body

A few top athletes have always known about mental rehearsals, the tactic Richard Suinn calls "body thinking."

High jumper Dwight Stones is one example. The key to whether or not he clears the bar is the run he makes up to the bar. According to sportswriter John Jerome, Stones stands back and rehearses that run in his mind before every jump. He bobs his head as he concentrates, so that watchers can almost see the run's sequence as he plans it: five sprinting steps in a straight line, then five more steps in a tight, banked curve and a takeoff with body turned slightly away from the bar, so that he soars over it head first, face up. Each time Stones tries the high jump, he follows the same path to within a fraction of an inch; he has worked out a precise formula. Since it takes incredible concentration to reproduce that formula exactly, a mental rehearsal helps.

Pro golfer Jack Nicklaus is another athlete who uses body thinking. In his book *Golf My Way* he wrote, "I never hit a shot, not even in practice, without having a very sharp, in-focus picture of it in my head. It's like a color movie. First I see the ball where I want it to finish, nice and white and sitting up high on the bright green grass. Then the scene quickly changes and I 'see' the ball going there: its path, trajectory and shape, even its behavior on landing. Then there is sort of a fadeout, and the next scene shows me making the kind of swing that will turn the previous image into reality."

As I mentioned earlier, *we think with our muscles as well as our minds*. Professor Suinn reports that if you place electrodes over a skier's leg muscles, with wires leading to a recording pen, and then ask him to mentally rehearse in detail what it's like to ski a particular trail, his legs may remain completely still but electric impulses from the muscles will send the pen skittering, registering a jump here, a rough patch there, reproducing the whole run right down to the final massive effort as he brakes at the end.

Small wonder, then, that mental rehearsals can improve co-ordination and timing. However, Professor Suinn believes they're even more effective if an athlete has had relaxation training, for the imagery becomes much more vivid when the body is relaxed. People are not only able to see movies in their minds, they're able to hear, touch, feel their muscles tensing, experience emotions—all without moving an inch. One swimmer reported that when she mentally dove into a pool the cold water was a shock; simultaneously the filmstrip in her head switched from black-and-white to color.

Suinn is also convinced that body thinking works best when it's employed to solve a specific problem. For instance, he has used it to identify errors in a case where a skier didn't really know why he'd fallen during a race. Instructed to stand back mentally and watch himself perform, he suddenly realized what his mistake had been. Body thinking can also be used to eliminate an error by rehearsing a sequence that is error-free. To accomplish this the individual is told to *feel* himself going through the motions rather than to observe himself. In fact, error detection is the only problem Suinn tackles by advising the athlete to stand back and watch.

Mental rehearsals are handy in other situations as well. They're a good way to make a first attempt at a risky new skill. You can also use them to practice concentrating despite distractions from onlookers, or to run through, far in advance, the way you'd cope with a particular problem if it occurred—an awkward landing after a ski jump, for example. *Body thinking can also help musicians, dancers, typists, and anyone else trying to learn a physical skill.*

The Power of Concentration

In his book *The Inner Athlete* California psychologist Robert M. Nideffer asserts that an individual achieves top performance only when his feelings and thoughts are totally concentrated on the event he's involved in, when physical and mental abilities are integrated. Nideffer suggests that for most of us this happens so seldom that when we do manage it it's a real high.

The Far East's martial arts, such as karate and aikido, aim for just such an integration. To break a board in a single blow with the edge of his hand a karate master must be able to focus all of his attention on a spot several inches below the board. As he concentrates on driving his hand through the wood to that spot, he overcomes the instinctive tendency to flinch at the last instant as hand crashes into board.

Similarly, the aikido expert who can keep his arm so rigid that two strong men can't bend it achieves this by mentally directing all of his energy out through the tips of his fingers. Most people, determined to keep their arm straight, will tense forearm and biceps, but those are the wrong muscles to use. When the aikido master concentrates on sending his energy out to his fingertips, he automatically relaxes his biceps and instead flexes the triceps muscle in the back of the arm, producing maximum resistance.

Obviously, the ability to concentrate can make an immense difference in how you perform any task, and that's as true of someone trying to hit a golf ball as it is of a karate master or of a person adding a column of figures. *When you're distracted your energy is fragmented and much of it is diverted from the task at hand.*

Distractability is the enemy, then, in sports as in other things. Here, too, sports psychologists are beginning to point up tactics that can help. For example, some players create minor rituals to promote concentration. Professional tennis player Brian Gottfried always goes through the same motions before he serves: He rubs the ground with the toe of his shoe, bounces a ball, looks at the balls in his hand, picks one, pockets the other, and then finally serves. All these small activities concentrate his attention; they help him shut out distractions created by the crowd or by his own reaction to the previous point.

However, concentration is more than just a matter of focusing your mind on a single thing. It's a surprisingly complex phenomenon, for, as Nideffer points out, attention can be channeled in several different ways: It can be focused broadly or narrowly and it can be turned inward or outward. Martial arts instructors tell their students that they must learn to broaden or narrow their focus at will; and, of course, it's also vital to be able to switch back and forth from inward concerns to outward ones, from planning your strategy, for example, to executing it.

When you broaden your focus and direct it outward, ideally you allow your mind to "touch everything evenly," as martial arts students put it. That means that if you're an aikido master surrounded by half a dozen opponents who are out to lay you flat, you are continually—evenly—alert to every movement each one of them makes. You are also exhibiting a broad outward focus when, on the football field or in any place where a lot of things are going on simultaneously, you can easily keep track of most of them.

A narrow external focus, on the other hand, is good for breaking boards with a karate chop or for archery, target shooting, bowling, tennis, or golf, because these are sports where there are very few cues to keep track of and in which responses (such as the tennis serve) are almost reflexive once you set them in motion.

For planning strategy—weighing up all the elements of a situation and predicting possible consequences of various actions—you need a broad internal focus, while a narrow internal focus is what makes it possible for marathoners to dissociate, to tune out pain by tuning in to fantasies instead.

"In most situations that people find themselves in," Dr. Nideffer explained, "they need a fairly broad focus of attention while they're assessing the situation or determining a course of action, but once they decide to take action they need to narrow their attention." That rechanneling of mental energy isn't always easy. Nideffer has found that most people have a predominant *attentional style:* They're basically broad external or broad internal, or else they tend to focus narrowly whether their attention is turned outward *or* inward. The super-performers among athletes and in other professions are generally able to manage an attentional shift from inward to outward, or broad to narrow, with ease. However, the average person under pressure plays to his own greatest strength whether that's appropriate or not. Thus, if he's a broad internal whose strength is an ability to plan strategy and the situation calls for fast, decisive action instead, he may be out of luck.

What Is Your Attentional Style?

How can you tell what your own style is?

• You're an *external* if you're observant and responsive to what's going on around you. You may also have a tendency to react first and think later.

• You're an *internal* if you're introspective—a brooder, a daydreamer, or a planner. It's possible that you're often so distracted by what you're thinking about that you lose track of what's happening around you.

• Yours is a *narrow* focus if you find it easy to concentrate, to rivet your attention on some object or mental task and shut out all distractions. You may, however, have a tendency to zero in on the trees and miss the forest—to grapple with one small aspect of a problem while neglecting the larger view.

• Your focus is *broad* if you can usually see all the angles in a situation and all possible solutions—perhaps to the point where it's often hard for you to settle on a single plan of action.

To turn to a concrete example, Lucy is a broad internal—broad because she's good at developing complex strategies and internal because she does a lot of woolgathering. Squash is her game, but she feels she'll probably never be very good at it because she can't seem to stay focused on the ball. Even as she dashes to hit it, she's replaying the last point in her mind or planning the move after this one. However, Lucy comes into her own on the chessboard, where her ability to work out a battle plan serves her in good stead. She always reviews the game afterward, noting her own mistakes, and she rarely makes the same mistake more than once.

Alan is a broad external. He's a grade school assistant principal. Thanks to his attentional style, he can keep track of most of what's going on in a room full of noisy youngsters. At a party Alan can be involved in one conversation while eavesdropping on another, but if someone asks about the score of the ball game, though the TV screen is on the other side of the room, Alan can not only answer the question but can provide a summary of most of the last inning! He's also good at finding money—on the street, in the grass, under the seat in a movie theater—in public places where other passersby have missed it. When Alan is under pressure, however, his mind-set sometimes becomes a problem, for he has a tendency to react without thinking first.

Carolyn's focus is predominantly narrow. She's a high school student who is serious about ballet and puts in long hours of practice. She has few other interests—a fact that worries her parents—but her teacher feels that her talent and single-mindedness (a symptom of narrow focus) will carry her far. However, her attentional style also has its disadvantages, for when she makes a mistake in dance practice or elsewhere she has a way of compounding the error by locking in on negative thoughts. As she silently scolds herself, her tension plays havoc with her co-ordination.

Obviously, attentional style is as relevant in other areas of life as it is in athletics, and Dr. Nideffer, an instructor at the California School of Professional Psychology in San Diego, runs workshops for business executives, police officers, and graduate students, as well as for athletes. He has found that even where people enter professions well suited to their attentional style, if they're not flexible enough to shift focus when that's necessary they can run into problems. Police officers, for example, tend to be broad externals who are good at reading the environment. That's the kind of skill they need to have, and yet, as Dr. Nideffer said, "The problem we nail them for is not think ing before they take action"—a liability that goes with the mind-set.

Similarly, business executives tend to be broad internals who are good at analyzing. When they make a mistake under pressure, it's generally the mistake of being *overly* analytical—and failing to take action.

As for those who focus narrowly, Dr. Nideffer said that in careers that demand real dedication narrowness is a good thing. A person whose energy is sharply focused generally has great self-discipline and the ability to follow through on goals she sets. If her career is her total identity and she's successful at it, her narrow focus will be an asset; but if life—or her family—begin to make other demands on her, then her style may become a liability. In addition, in the business world a narrow focus can create serious problems; as Dr. Nideffer explained, "These people tend to lock in on a way of approaching a problem that has worked for them in the past and then they fail to respond to new input; they can be very frustrating to work with."

Learning to Shift Gears Mentally

If you have problems that seem to originate with the way you focus your mental energy, then it's worthwhile to try to retrain yourself in order to become more flexible.

There are several ways to do this. Meditation is among the training methods that Nideffer recommends. It's good for those who need practice in looking inward or in narrowing their attention, since meditators are generally taught to retreat from the outside world and to try for "one-pointedness": to concentrate on their breathing or perhaps on a mantra, a word repeated over and over again. Surprisingly, meditation can also be good for people who need to practice focusing outward, for some variations are actually a way to make broader contact with the world outside your skin. Lucy discovered this one day when she was experimenting with a walking meditation, repeating a mantra silently to herself as she strode along. After a while the mantra began to fade, becoming quieter and quieter, until finally her mind was completely still and silent. Suddenly she was sharply aware of colors, sounds, and the feel of the pavement beneath her feet. For a change she was flooded with perceptions because her attention was not only broadly focused but entirely external. "It felt great," she said, "and I couldn't help wondering whether some people notice all of those things most of the time, since they're not always off somewhere inside their heads, daydreaming or worrying, the way I am."

There are other retraining methods as well. With mental rehearsals you can use the privacy of your own head to practice deploying your attention in different ways. If you tend to choke up in competition because of anxiety and to zero in on some detail (perhaps on the golf course the nearby sandtrap fills your awareness as you tee off), relaxation training may help; for *anxiety narrows your focus and relaxing broadens it.*

Which remedy you resort to will, of course, depend on your particular problem, but here are a few examples:

• If your game is tennis and you often play poorly because your own thoughts distract you—you're turned inward, worrying about the next point or about something totally irrelevant—you can try doing some of the things that baseball players do to keep their attention from wandering. Keep up a running conversation with your partner or opponent; while you're waiting for him to serve, bounce a little on the balls of your feet or flex and unflex your free hand—do something to stay physically involved. You might also try meditation to practice narrowing your focus.

• If you're a tennis player or golfer and your concentration is easily disturbed by spectator chatter or by whatever else is going on around you (you're a broad external), it may help to rehearse your game mentally, complete with distractions, and practice tuning them out. Once again, learning to meditate will give you experience in shifting mental gears.

• On the other hand, if your focus is too narrow—on the basketball court, for example, all that fast-moving confusion overwhelms you, so that you're slow to react—relaxation training may be the answer, since your focus will broaden once you're more relaxed.

There's still a lot to learn about the phenomenon of attention, especially about our ability to focus broadly and to do several things at once. Some people seem to manage this more easily than others, but it *is* a learnable skill. With long and arduous training, researchers have actually been able to teach people to write from dictation while reading stories—and to understand both what they've written down and what they've read.

If someone can be taught to do that, then certainly the distractible tennis player and the would-be basketball star who can't quite keep track of the action can also learn new ways of focusing their mental energy.

How to Generate "Deep Flow"—and Enerjoy

Everyone experiences peaks of efficiency and good feeling from time to time. For fifteen minutes, an hour, or even most of a day your concentration seems to flow effortlessly. Whatever you're doing, you do it smoothly and well and you're totally involved in it. What's more, both mental and physical drive are perfectly focused on the same goal.

This phenomenon has been studied and described in detail by a Chicago researcher, who calls it "deep flow." I find his work fascinating, because enerjoy is clearly one element in the flow experience and because it seems fair to say that *whatever produces deep flow will also generate enerjoy.*

The researcher, Dr. Mihaly Csikszentmihalyi, is an associate professor of human development at the University of Chicago. Some years ago he became interested in activities that are their own reward—in the things that people do not for money or fame or power but for the fun of it; and so he set out to discover why some of us become so passionate about pastimes such as chess or rock-climbing.

He soon learned that the incentive in such activities is something he came to call the "flow" experience, because flow was a word his interviewees often used (just as many of the people I talked to spoke of flow when describing times of peak energy). Apparently there are different degrees of flow, from the brief flicker of pleasure a man may feel as he lights a pipe to the waves of euphoria (deep flow) that a climber sometimes feels as he scales a difficult rock face.

From flicker to euphoria, flow experiences have certain features in common, and in his fascinating book *Beyond Boredom and Anxiety* Professor Csikszentmihalyi describes half a dozen of them.

• To begin with, by definition flow is its own reward—no others are necessary. As one rock-climber put it, "The purpose of flow is to keep on flowing."

• During deep flow the individual becomes completely involved in what he's doing. Action and awareness merge until he has no distracting thoughts. A chess player described it this way: "The game is a struggle, and the concentration is like breathing—you never think of it. The roof could fall in and if it missed you you would be unaware of it." *Most people seem to crave this kind of total concentration.*

• Flow also involves a narrowing of consciousness. Attention centers on a limited area. For the chess player there is only the chessboard; for the rock-climber the rock face becomes almost a self-contained universe where past and future no longer matter. One climber said, "When I start on a climb, it's as if my memory input has been cut off. All I can remember is the last thirty seconds, and all I can think ahead is the next five minutes. . . ."

• The person in deep flow is no longer conscious of himself. Though body awareness may actually increase and the chess player is sometimes very aware of the workings of his mind, what's lost is the kind of self-consciousness that usually gives you a minute-by-minute reading on how you're doing in relation to the rest of the world.

• Flow presents the right balance between skills and challenges: The individual must stretch himself, but he's not worried about the outcome. Anxiety occurs when a challenge is too great. Boredom happens when a situation isn't challenging enough. Flow takes place somewhere between the two, at the point where skills are tested—and prove adequate.

• A flow experience also makes coherent and noncontradictory demands and provides unambiguous feedback. On the chessboard or the rock face the rules are clear and a mistake is usually immediately obvious.

Though he doesn't consider it one of the main characteristics of flow, Dr. Csikszentmihalyi also mentioned that a surge of energy occurs. And, as I suggested earlier, during flow physical and mental energies—mind and body—are completely integrated; the individual is aware of no difference between them.

Where to Find Flow

You can learn to recognize flow when it's happening to you—and to value it and seek it out. *Most of the activities—the sports and games—that are considered recreation have flow potential, but flow also occurs in other situations.* In fact, people actually find it in the most unexpected places.

For instance, actor James Coburn seemed to be talking about flow when he explained, during an interview, why he likes to drive fast sports cars. "I drive to be proficient," he said, "and, in a way, to relax. It's a total experience for me and my attention is totally on what I'm doing. I also play the flute. They're opposite activities but they give the same effect."

Public relations man Dave Hackler often experiences flow when he's at work building a model ship inside a glass bottle. "There's something about using your hands in a creative way that's a release for me," he said. While he's working he's so absorbed in what he's doing that he loses track of time. He recalled, "Once I worked for two or three hours and when I stopped I suddenly realized that all I had done during that time was to tie two knots."

It's the piano that provides Yvonne with deep flow. When she plays, her commitment to the music is so total that her children (they're preschoolers) can't bear it, for they feel shut out. *Creative efforts often generate flow*—as Sunday painters and people who write music or poetry can testify.

Lovemaking can be a flow experience, and so can meditation. Disco dancing can lead to flow. Bettina explained, "On a really good evening I can get out on the dance floor and forget who I am and everything that's worrying me and just let the music move me."

Some people get flow from what they do for a living. Surgery, for example, requires complete concentration. Each operation also has a clear beginning and end. The medical team is provided with feedback throughout—the surgeons know from minute to minute whether things are going well or badly. That means the circumstances are just right for flow.

Unfortunately, many other occupations rarely provide that optimum balance between challenge and control that leads to flow: the clear-cut, short-term situation that exactly matches the worker's skills. Instead the individual is apt to be either under-utilized or overworked, bored or anxious. Often he's not entirely clear about what's expected of him and feels he has little control over what happens.

If there's seldom an opportunity for deep flow in *your* working life, that's all the more reason to look for it outside your occupation. To choose an activity that's likely to provide flow, look for these features:

• Pick something that's a manageable challenge now and that will continue to be a challenge as your skills improve. Most sports and games, for example, can be enjoyed by people with almost any level of ability. Even beginning chess players and rock-climbers can experience flow provided they choose their opponent or their rock face with care.

• The activity should also present you with what psychologists call "a limited stimulus field"—like the tight little world of the chessboard or the rock face. Such limitations help you concentrate—as does the physical danger involved in climbing.

• The activity should challenge you every minute that you're involved in it, leaving you no time to feel bored or anxious. From beginning to end it should so engross you that you live only in the present moment.

• It should make clear demands and supply unconfusing feedback. You should always know what's required of you and how you're doing. You should be able to measure your progress, either because you're up against competition or because there's an obstacle to overcome.

• The outcome should be open-ended, unpredictable, but *you* should still have the power to determine it.

How to Conjure Up Flow in Unlikely Places

You can probably learn to be in flow more often even if your life doesn't abound in opportunities for it; for some people are adept at flowing under the most unlikely circumstances.

To become one of them you must learn to apply to everyday situations the tactics that sports enthusiasts take for granted. In rock-climbing, for example, the same rock face may bore one climber, make another anxious, and put a third into flow. However, the person who is bored can return to flow by finding a way to increase the challenge, or by handicapping himself and so reducing his skills; and the person who is anxious can return to flow either by decreasing the challenge—by tackling an easier climb—or by training and increasing his skills. Similarly, in a nonrecreational situation where a task has become routine and boring, you can revive interest by aiming for elegance or absolute precision. Where a job seems overwhelmingly difficult, you can train until your skills are equal to it.

"When you study workers, you find that even with boring jobs some people enjoy them," Dr. Csikszentmihalyi said. There is the waitress in the fast-food restaurant who gets to know her steady customers *and* makes a game of remembering how they like their hamburgers or their coffee. There is the typist who tries to see every business letter as a chance to break her own past record for speed and precision. Dr. Csikszentmihalyi believes that all jobs should provide opportunities for flow, but he also believes that in situations that don't, people can learn to generate their own flow.

"It's not as easy to find flow in a dentist's waiting room as it is to get it from playing touch football," he said, "but it can be done." And so you have the patient who looks at the paintings and the furniture and makes a game out of trying to guess the personality of the dentist; or who strikes up a lively conversation with the receptionist; or who simply closes his eyes and begins to meditate. He may experience relatively shallow flow under the circumstances, but that's better than anxiety or boredom.

The ability to generate flow probably comes down to the abil-

ity to concentrate and to tune in to your environment. The people who pay attention to the world around them and who continually see opportunities for action there can enjoy themselves almost anywhere.

Flow is worth having because of the intensity of the deep-flow experience and because of that tide of energy that comes with it. More important, perhaps, flow is confidence-building. And if it happens often enough, those good feelings may spill over into the rest of your life.

Energy Tips

1. In situations that call for sheer endurance—perhaps you're swimming a long distance or occupying the dentist's chair—daydream to tune out discomfort.

2. But when you compete in marathons, pay attention to your body and to the terrain most of the time. If you hit the Wall, dissociating or fantasizing will take your mind off the pain, but remember that it's risky to tune out for too long.

3. If you face a challenge and you're feeling listless and dull-witted, psych yourself up: Get out and move around, talk to someone, or work yourself up emotionally.

4. If you tend to seize up with anxiety whenever the chips are down, train yourself to relax at will: Learn Progressive Relaxation, meditation, or self-hypnosis.

5. Another solution to the same problem: Before any important test of your ability, settle on some positive and neutral thoughts and be ready to substitute them for the intimations of doom ("I'm falling too far behind!") that could panic you. In addition, decide in advance how you'll cope with different things that could go wrong.

6. Use mental rehearsals to practice new physical skills. First relax completely and then imagine going through the motions.

7. If you're easily distracted when you're under pressure, invent some small ritual that you can use to focus your attention just before you swing into action.

8. Pay attention to the way you *deploy* your attention. Are you preoccupied (focused inward) too much of the time—or not

enough of it? Do you tend to concentrate so narrowly that you miss the broader picture, or can you see so many possibilities in every situation that it's hard to decide on action (broad focus)? To increase your mental flexibility, try meditating or use mental rehearsals to practice focusing and refocusing your attention in different ways.

9. To experience deep flow and enerjoy more often, shop around for a sport, game, or hobby. Choose one that's totally involving and will remain a challenge as your skills develop.

10. Look for more opportunities for flow in your everyday life. When you're doing some routine task, forestall boredom by aiming for elegance or precision. When you're anxious because a task is much too difficult, back off if you possibly can and practice until the work begins to seem like a manageable challenge.

How Weather Affects Your Energy

Food, sleep, exercise: They're the obvious factors that influence your energy. Most people would add weather to the list, for they know perfectly well that there are times when everybody feels draggy because it's hot and humid, bitterly cold, or it's been raining for days.

There's not much you can do about the weather, except perhaps to recognize the way it affects you and make allowances for it. However, it's possible to create an indoor climate that's a real source of energy.

The Search for
an Invigorating Environment

We play out the scenes of our lives against both outdoor and indoor settings. Places have an energy level of their own, a perceptible *energy climate*, and can affect your vitality.

Outdoors the energy climate is, of course, partly a matter of the weather at the time (more about that in a minute). But whatever the weather, a town, a park, a beach, or a room have an ambience of their own that affects different individuals in different ways.

For example, many people are overwhelmed by big cities like New York. The pace of life, the press of people on the streets, the anonymity, and the very scale of the buildings that shut out the sky make it seem an alien world jangling with nervous energy. As such it's devitalizing to some.

To others a city like New York is an energizer; they're turned on by the atmosphere. For instance, ex-disc jockey Ellie Dylan, whose day at a New York radio station began at 3 A.M., says, "It was nice to wake up with the city. I like energy and you could feel it all over the place." There was the night energy in Times Square, which never shuts down; and then, as lights began to bloom in windows, there was the beginning of the day energy. For Ellie the air was charged with all the things about to happen.

Southern California has a different kind of energy altogether; it is less cerebral and perhaps somewhat more hedonistic. "It's really sexual energy," in the opinion of one Brooklyn writer. "In California you spend so much time taking care of your body that you feel you've got to use it in some way." And, of course, other parts of the country furnish environments that have other sorts of energy.

Many people are revitalized by natural settings—the silence of a pine forest, the bite of mountain air at sunrise, or the pounding of surf on a beach. Interior designer Alexandra Stoddard says, "When I'm feeling tired and run down or upset about something, if I can just go to the ocean I'm fine. I turn my face to the sun and walk on the beach, and that's my best medicine."

Once you're aware that places can have this sort of impact on your energy, *you can put yourself, as often as possible, into the environments that you, personally, find energizing.* Your reaction to such places will vary, of course, with the circumstances and the mood you're in, but if you know that Chicago usually sets your adrenaline flowing, or that a day in the mountains makes you feel years younger, then you can set up the energy transaction for yourself, pay attention to it as it happens, and make the most of it. And if you know that a place always gets you down, you can avoid it whenever possible or compensate for the energy drain in other ways.

Feeling Listless? It May Be the Weather

When you're outdoors, the ambience or setting is sometimes less important than the actual weather at the time.

A few years ago I became acutely aware of the impact weather can have on mood and energy. In the course of researching an article on dieting, I studied diaries submitted by nine young women. For purposes of comparison, each had agreed to go on one of three popular diets and to keep a daily record of what she ate, how she felt, and what was happening around her.

Week by week the diaries arrived in the mail. Soon I began to notice a curious thing. On one day almost everyone would report feeling listless and low; three days later all would report feeling full of energy. Since the women were trying different diets, it didn't seem likely that the mood shift was related to food. Nor did it seem a case of shared circumstances and feelings, because most of the women were barely acquainted and they weren't spending time together. They did, however, all live in the same small town. Eventually I realized that their moods were changing with the weather!

By the end of a week of rain, bitter cold, or high humidity our human response to climate is usually quite obvious. Irritability and depression reach epidemic proportions. Tempers are short and people are not kind.

What's more intriguing is that weather also has subtler effects, an impact that often goes unrecognized. The next time you're feeling sluggish and all thumbs for no reason you can think of, take a look at a weather map. You're apt to find that a low-pressure system is passing through and the temperature and humidity are rising while the barometer is dropping.

For years biometeorologists (scientists who study the effect of the weather on the body) have been reporting that *various undesirable things happen when the barometer is low or is falling.* At such times people tend to feel sluggish; their reaction times are slower; the accident rate rises and more people fall ill; schoolchildren behave badly and don't do as well on tests.

The barometric pressure itself is probably not to blame, nor is the change in pressure. Dr. Helmut E. Landsberg of the University of Maryland, a former president of the American Institute of Medical Climatology, pointed out in an interview that someone who works at the top of a tall building, such as New York City's World Trade Center, travels up and down in the elevator two to four times a day, apparently with no ill effects, and that's a faster pressure change than a storm could ever produce. As the elevator ascends, it's as if the individual moved, within seconds, from a polar high-pressure center to the kind of low a hurricane produces.

The real cause, then, may be the temperature and humidity changes that go with a drop in the barometer or even the accompanying electromagnetic disturbances. In fact, one theory suggests that people react as they do because those fluctuating electric fields interact in some way with human brain waves—the minute electric currents generated by the workings of the mind.

"But there are so many possible parameters that it's very difficult to untangle them," Dr. Landsberg said. "The weather is very complex and the human organism is very complex and we don't really know just how they interact."

There's no question that they *do* interact, though; nor is there any doubt that *some people are more weather-sensitive than others*. However, no one really knows why that's so.

Are You Weather-Sensitive?

"A month ago," Beth recalled, "on an ordinary, sunny summer afternoon, I was packing a picnic supper when I suddenly began to feel extremely tense and irritable. I was baffled because there was no reason for it. We were going to an open-air opera that night and I'd been looking forward to it for weeks. We got to the park at around six o'clock and it began to cloud up a bit. At nine the skies opened, there was a terrific thunderstorm, and we had to run for shelter. It occurred to me then that this sort of thing has happened to me before: I start feeling strung out for no good reason, and then later a storm breaks. Could it be that the weather is getting to me?"

It could indeed. In fact, it seems likely that Beth is weather-sensitive, as are many people. Periodically they develop a headache or a vague sense of malaise, and a short time later a storm breaks or the weather changes abruptly because a front is passing through.

Those who are weather-sensitive are especially vulnerable in the face of the world's famous ill winds: the French mistral, Italy's sirocco, the Santa Ana in California, the sharav in Israel, or Argentina's zonda. When the sharav is blowing, for example, about 30 percent of the population suffers from symptoms such as sleeplessness, tension, irritability, headaches, dizziness, diarrhea, nausea, and hot flushes.

What's really intriguing is the fact that these reactions begin to make themselves felt the day *before* the windstorm descends, much as Beth's symptoms developed hours before the thunderstorm broke. Apparently that's because at just about that time an excess of positive air ions develops. By way of explanation: The air we breathe and move around in consists of molecules of various gases. Periodically energy (usually generated by radioactive elements in the soil or by cosmic rays) splits an electron away from a gas molecule. The electron attaches itself to another nearby molecule that instantly develops a negative electrical charge, while the original molecule now has a positive one. These charges attract other molecules, and the clusters that result, called small air ions, are all either positive or negative.

Air ions have a life-span of several minutes, for they're continually forming and breaking apart. Natural forces sometimes increase the number of ions in the air—waterfalls, the pounding of the surf, thunderstorms, and those famous ill winds all do. However, ordinarily half a thimbleful of unpolluted outdoor air contains only a few thousand ions—along with millions upon trillions of uncharged molecules.

Given these proportions, it seems unlikely that ions could be of much significance, and yet apparently they are. Not only do positive ions make weather-sensitive people uncomfortable at times, but there's growing evidence that *ion-depleted air can make you feel drained of energy and can cause drowsiness, discomfort, and a lessening of mental and physical efficiency.* Since pollution, cigarette smoking, and air conditioning all strip ions from the air, there may be cause for concern.

The Benefits of Negative Air Ions

Professor Albert P. Krueger, among others, pioneered the study of small air ions. At the Air Ion Research Laboratory in Berkeley, California, where he has done his research, his studies have demonstrated that ions have somewhat paradoxical effects. Both positive and negative ions will kill bacteria, though the negative ones are more lethal. Both kinds of ions stimulate growth in plants, which apparently can't tell them apart. Negative ions are generally beneficial to both animals and humans, while positive ions aren't.

Negative ions are helpful, in fact, in several different ways. Studies done with rabbits have shown that they improve the protective functioning of tissue in the trachea, or windpipe. (Positive ions actually impair tracheal functioning.) This, added to the fact that negative ions annihilate bacteria, suggests that they should protect people against respiratory infections. And sure enough, in a study done some years ago in a Swiss bank, when three hundred employees were exposed to an atmosphere replete with negative ions for thirty weeks, they had fewer respiratory illnesses than usual; compared to a group who breathed ordinary air, they lost much less working time due to sickness.

But the benefits of negative ions go beyond that respiratory assist and affect mood as well, for it appears that they're somewhat calming. An experimenter at Pennsylvania State University demonstrated their tranquilizing effect by putting rats into a stressful situation (a buzzer sounded and then they received an electric shock) under two different conditions: Either the rats were in a chamber filled with ordinary air or they were in one whose air had been enhanced with negative ions. In both chambers the animals could avoid being shocked if they immediately pressed a lever. They not only learned to use the lever but, in their anxiety, at the sound of the buzzer they tended to press it more than once, the exact number of lever presses serving as a measure of just how anxious they were. In terms of lever presses, then, the rats felt significantly less anxious while breathing negative ions.

Scientists can't yet spell out all the mechanisms by which ions affect mood, but they do know that negative ions lower the level of serotonin (one of the neurotransmitters) in the midbrain while positive ions raise it. In fact, weather-sensitive Israelis, uncomfortable during a sharav, were successfully treated both with negative ions *and* with drugs that discourage serotonin production. Ions also seem to affect brain levels of norepinephrine and dopamine, so they probably act by changing the balance of several different brain chemicals.

As I've said, pollution, smoking, and air conditioning all deplete the air of ions. In addition, in most city office and apartment buildings—even those without air conditioning—the rooms have a very low ion concentration because there is so much steel in the vicinity that electromagnetic radiation can't penetrate. Dr. Krueger estimated that a typical office might have as few as twenty negative and thirty-four positive ions per cubic centimeter of space, compared with four thousand positive and negative ions in the same volume of mountaintop air. Small wonder, then, that so many people find mountain air invigorating and city offices stale and wearying places to be!

Home Generators for Negative Ions

It seems that many people (especially weather-sensitive individuals like Beth) would benefit from owning a negative-air-ion generator. Dr. Krueger estimated that close to a hundred firms make such machines, as well as air-ion measuring devices. Unfortunately, some sell inferior equipment and make extravagant claims about the health benefits of negative ions. Other companies are more reliable—and usually more cautious, too, in their advertising. At any rate, in the spring of 1979 Dr. Krueger estimated that a good, room-sized ion-generating machine ought to cost about ninety dollars.

"Personally," he said, "I've come to the conclusion that ions *can* affect us. The studies done in Israel furnish strong evidence that increased concentrations of positive ions *are* responsible for illness in weather-sensitive people."

Cold Snaps and Hot Spells

Your energy is also affected by weather changes much more obvious than shifts in the ion content of the air. For when the temperature plummets or the humidity soars the body must also change if a person is to remain comfortable, since comfort requires a steady internal temperature of 98.6°, plus a certain balance of water and other things.

All in all, our ability to adjust to different seasons and climates is impressive. In winter our metabolism revs up to produce more heat; in summer it gears down and, in addition, the body cools itself by perspiring more readily. It also begins to conserve more of its own salt. Because these adjustments are gradual, the first

cold or hot days of a new season are harder to take, being more
of an energy drain than similar weather later on.

The onset of cold weather also tends to touch off a rash of
colds and upper-respiratory infections. It's apparently not the
chill in the air that's to blame, because in experiments volunteers
have been deliberately exposed to cold air and they've shown no
greater tendency to catch a cold than other volunteers who
weren't. Dr. Landsberg points out that so far no experiment has
managed to duplicate all the many subtle atmospheric changes
that take place when a cold front passes through. Presumably
some factor there, or a combination of factors, makes humans
more vulnerable to colds and flu.

Sudden Changes in Temperature

Because people create their own indoor climates through heat-
ing and air conditioning, they regularly subject their bodies to
sudden temperature changes regardless of what the weather is
doing. Whenever you're too hot or too cold, the opposite extreme
is seldom more than a few steps—or a flick of a switch—away.
Some people feel that these continual temperature shifts take
their toll, and certainly they have real, physical effects. When
you go from outdoor warmth to indoor cold, for example, the
blood vessels in your skin contract in an attempt to keep body
heat from escaping; your heart speeds up and your oxygen intake rises as your body works to generate warmth. These automatic adjustments may indeed amount to wear and tear for the
elderly and for people who aren't well. However, Dr. Landsberg
suggested that for those who are in good health, stepping from
heat into cold (or vice versa) may actually provide an excellent
workout for the internal systems involved; and, of course, it can
feel as invigorating as finishing up a hot shower with a shot of
cold water.

Your Energy Changes with the Seasons

*For many Americans the "psychological year" begins on Labor
Day with a burst of renewed vigor.* Harvard researchers did a

large-scale, week-by-week survey of people's moods and concerns from July through November of one year. They found that as September rolled around people tended to feel less happy but more involved and excited than they'd felt during the more relaxed summer months. They also spent less time thinking about past accomplishments and more time thinking about their job and the future.

Sociologist Robert Weiss, who worked on the Harvard study, has suggested that fall is, in general, a time for gathering one's resources; that at Thanksgiving and Christmas Americans take time out to reaffirm family and other commitments; that during the long winter months they simply "slug away" at the tasks at hand, but that when spring comes they ease up and begin to think about getting away from it all during the relaxing summer ahead.

This, of course, is not everyone's typical seasonal scenario, though it may be fairly common. There are enormous individual differences in the way people react to the changing seasons. Spring is a tonic for some, but it leaves others feeling dazed and lazy. Winter can be a high-energy time or a severe trial.

Allison, for example, does not feel lighthearted on fine spring days because to her spring is a warning that summer's heat is on the way. "On hot, muggy days I feel miserable," she said. "I can't work. But I have lots of energy in the fall. Even if it's hot when the first of September rolls around, I'm energized just because I know the heat will soon be over. Part of it, too, is all those years I spent in school: Come the fall, I have an urge to sharpen all my pencils and start something new."

Jill, on the other hand, becomes increasingly depressed as the trees turn color and the days grow cool, because obviously winter is near at hand. Jill lives in Toronto, where the winters are long and gray and bone-chilling, and it's often unpleasant to be out of doors. "In the winter I get cabin fever," she said grimly.

Kitty likes brisk fall weather—but only up to a point. Eventually there comes a day when she's sitting at home and a great lethargy descends on her. When she checks, she finds that the building superintendent has turned on the heat and the air has become hot and dry. "In my building I can't control the heat," she said, "and I get too much of it—I have to have the windows open all the time, and even then I'm uncomfortable."

Reactions to the seasons are partly psychological, a matter of personal preference, but body truths are involved as well. *Physiologically, the same weather affects different people differently.* As Dr. Landsberg put it, "We're not like thermometers; we don't all automatically give the same reading. For example, two out of three people react to cold air with a rise in blood pressure, but that third person reacts with a blood pressure drop—and nobody knows why this difference exists."

Your Weight and the Weather

Landsberg pointed out that weight makes a big difference in how well people tolerate heat and cold. In winter a layer of fat is an asset—it's good insulation, since other types of tissue conduct heat out of the body three times faster than fat. A subcutaneous layer of fat one centimeter thick (a little less than half an inch) offers as much protection as a man's suit. However, in summer that same fat means that the body's heat can't escape as easily. In general, if women tolerate cold better than men do and find heat more enervating, it's probably because even the thinnest woman has half an inch more of insulating fat than most men—just because that's how women are built.

Since perspiring is the most efficient way to cool down, the body's water balance also makes a difference in the way we experience heat; the water-balance mechanism varies quite a lot from one person to the next. In addition, people who remember to increase their intake of fluids in the steamy summer months are apt to find the heat less debilitating; so are those who eat less, for when the body metabolizes foods it produces calories of heat, and in summer that heat doesn't dissipate as easily into the air.

Use the Psychological Energy in Sunlight

Though we react to the seasons differently, one thing we all seem to thrive on is sunlight. Psychologically it's a marvelous energizer—as long as temperature and humidity stay within reasonable bounds. Dr. Landsberg believes that's because human beings evolved in hot, sunny regions. Genetically speaking, that was just a short time ago, and so it wouldn't be surprising if we still bore the "mark"—in the form of a hunger for sun-drenched days. At any rate, I know a number of people who say they simply don't work as well in dark rooms or on dark days. One of them, a graduate student who is currently writing her thesis, swears she's been plugging along at twice her normal speed ever since she moved her desk from a dark corner of the bedroom out onto the sun porch.

The Stress of Noise

Since humans first evolved in sunny Africa, they've spread across the planet, adapting not their bodies but their technology to different climates. It is, in fact, this technology that prevents us from having to spend most of our energy just surviving in climates less equable than, say, southern California's. But, of course, there are trade-offs, and one in particular—the noise level that technology creates and that most of us take for granted—can in turn create a drain on energy.

"I was trying to mark exams last year during spring vacation," a high school teacher recalled, "when a crew of workmen started to dig up the street outside my house. By the middle of the morning I couldn't work even when it was quiet for a few minutes. I just sat there, all tensed up, waiting for the jackhammer to begin again and seething with frustration. I finally set up shop in a corner of the local library because I sure couldn't work at home with that racket."

Noise that's unpredictable and uncontrollable is the hardest sort to take. However, loud noise of any kind is a form of stress, and the body reacts accordingly by becoming overaroused in many small ways. Your blood vessels constrict, raising your blood pressure; your heart beats faster; you breathe more rapidly; your muscles tense; and you perspire more. Though you may not be aware of these physical changes, you *are* apt to notice that they leave you feeling tired, irritable, and tense.

Noise drowns out conversation, forcing you to spend more energy to hear or to make yourself heard. Over a period of time it can impair hearing. And it probably affects your sleep more than you know, since even such a relatively quiet sound as a radio playing in the next room can nudge you from deep sleep up to a lighter level. Though you may never quite come to, the body responds to the sound with the same pattern of changes that occurs when you're awake. In fact, experiments have demonstrated that a blip of noise that lasts only a third of a second can cause a sleeper's blood vessels to constrict—and stay constricted for several minutes.

People do sometimes become habituated to high levels of noise, meaning that they no longer pay attention to the sound, but the body never really seems to habituate and always responds by becoming overaroused. Though there's no *proof* that this is dangerous to your health, it's one more stress in a stressful world, and so it's bound to be costly in terms of energy.

Noise and the weather both contribute substantially to the outdoor energy climate—a climate that can slow you down or give you a boost.

The Energy Climate Indoors

"When I was growing up," Alexandra Stoddard said, "I felt that in all the houses I knew, the rooms were serious and dark and gloomy. There were dark rugs on the floors and layers of fabric at the windows, and the draperies were often drawn to prevent dark colors inside the room from fading. There were rules about those rooms, and they weren't inviting or happy places, so I went through my childhood feeling that rooms were places to get out of. I became very interested in gardens and the out-of-doors, but at an early age I also started redesigning rooms in my own mind, fantasizing how they could be better."

We were sitting in the living room of Ms. Stoddard's New York City apartment, and it was as different as it could possibly be from the gloomy interiors she recalled from childhood. The plump, pillowy sofas and chairs were covered in a fabric that was a warm peach in color, the walls and ceiling were a sunny light yellow, and there were white shutters instead of curtains at the windows. All in all, the room looked as delectable as a bowl of summer fruit. As Ms. Stoddard pointed out, life is simpler, less formal, and more comfortable now than it was a generation ago, and so are the rooms we live in.

Alexandra Stoddard—a slim, willowy woman with fine features and grave gray-green eyes—is currently juggling three careers. A well-known interior designer, she recently launched her own firm. She's the author of several books, including *Style for Living* and *A Child's Place*. And she's a wife and mother who takes her family responsibilities very seriously—responsibilities that include three children living at home and a husband who, as a lawyer, has considerable business entertaining to do.

Some people are extremely sensitive to their surroundings, indoors as well as out, and certainly that's true of Ms. Stoddard, who says, "The spaces around us influence us tremendously, much more than we realize."

A Room of Your Own

Stoddard believes, as many others do, that everyone needs a private retreat, a place to be alone. She emphasizes that a room can be more than just a retreat if you put something of yourself into it, so that you come to feel that it defines you in a subtle way. *Energy comes partly from knowing who you are, and it's a help if you can come home at night to a place that affirms your self-image*—that reminds you that you're basically a sunny, upbeat sort of person or that you're a music-loving intellectual with a passionate nature. Accessories are an important part of the effect—those nonessentials that you keep around just because you like the way they look or because they hold memories. As Ms. Stoddard said, they're a form of autobiography.

Sheila never really had a room of her own until after her children were grown and moved out. Then she quietly took over her daughter's room. It took her almost a year to get it fixed up exactly the way she wanted it, and when she was done she was surprised by the effect she'd achieved. "The furniture in the rest of the house is vaguely colonial," she said, "but I found that for *my* room I wanted Swedish modern. Clean lines, clear, sunny colors—and no clutter at all. When I looked around, it didn't feel like the end of a project, it felt like a good, solid beginning for a new life—so I went out looking for a job."

Color It Energetic

Colors make an important contribution to the indoor climate. *Colors are mood shapers—which means that they affect energy as well.* Most people find the warmer colors (purple, red, orange, yellow, and yellow-green) stimulating, while the cooler ones (green, blue, and bluish purples) are calming or actually depressing. Color responses are body responses that can be measured in physiological terms. For example, when a subject in a psychologist's lab focuses on pure red, usually her blood pressure rises; she's apt to breathe faster and her pulse may quicken. Red also stimulates the appetite, which is why restaurants often favor it. It's exciting, warm, and vital, but a small room awash with bright red would give most people the equivalent of coffee nerves.

Yellow also stimulates, though not as reliably as red. Since it's the essence of sunlight, most people find it exceedingly cheerful, which is helpful if you're willing to be cheered. However, Ms. Stoddard noted that sometimes those who are depressed can't stand to be around yellow, apparently because the contrast with their own inner gloom is just too great.

Blue has effects opposite to those of red: It slows the heartbeat, decreases blood pressure, and is peaceful and soothing. It can be tender or conducive to meditation, though the darker shades are depressing—which may be why jazz singers sing "the blues." Green also has well-recognized mood consequences: Most people find it cool, refreshing, even astringent.

Some psychologists believe color responses are universal human reactions while others insist that they're merely cultural biases. There's also a third possibility, namely, that all humans simply share certain very basic associations. Blood, for all of us, is red and so red is alarming or, at any rate, stimulating. Sunlight is cheery and yellow. In fair weather, sky and sea are a soothing blue and grass and other fresh growing things are green.

If you understand what your energy needs are, you can give

yourself a lift by coloring your home from the stimulating end of the spectrum or create a calm, peaceful space for yourself with cooler colors. Some people know immediately which they need to do, but for others the choice isn't so clear. In her book *Style for Living* Alexandra Stoddard suggests that you first close your eyes and imagine a place where you'd like to be and then choose colors to fit your fantasy. You might wind up with the lucid, tranquil blues and blue-greens of a Caribbean seascape; with a room done in pastels like a sunny, secret garden; or with a book-lined retreat as dark and snug as a cave lit by a fire.

Energy Turn-ons

"I get a sense of soaring when I come home and close the door and see my flowers and plants, the paintings that are like old friends, the sunlight striking prisms from a piece of crystal near the window," Alexandra Stoddard said. "You know, I couldn't work in a monastic cell or, for that matter, in most libraries. I need to be able to see a flower or a painting or something else that's personal to me."

For her the energy climate isn't right unless it includes some small delight for the eye. In a sense, she taps into such things for energy. There are people who use music in much the same way and others who turn to sources far more esoteric. In fact, when I began to ask people to tell me about the little things that give them energy, I found that the list was endless. For all of us there are sights, sounds, and activities that are part of the very dailiness of life but that give us a lift when we connect with them. We're happier if they're part of our energy climate. For example:

• My friend Gary (from Chapter 1) says that uncluttered surfaces give him energy: a bare desk top or a dresser with nothing on it except one letter waiting to be mailed. Certainly, if you lead a pell-mell sort of life, evidence of order is reassuring, since to cope you have to be squared away and well organized.

• Others are energized by clutter. I am—at least at times when a deadline looms ahead. As the mail piles up on one corner of my desk and stacks of manuscripts mount on all sides of the typewriter, the message I get from the mess is: You're making progress! You're not frittering away energy on inessentials.

• For writer Wenda Morrone the turn-on is working with her hands—doing upholstery or painting furniture. "It may wear me out at the time," she said, "but the next morning I feel great. I think I've always resented having to put everything into words, because it's so exhausting, though it's what I'm trained to do. I've envied people who can express themselves in other ways—like painters, who can use their hands to go straight from the experience of depression to depression on canvas."

• A historian I talked to feels revitalized whenever he's at sea in a small boat. There are situations, he said, that allow you to redefine yourself at least temporarily. For a scholar with a yen for a life of action, sailing is one of them.

• A college lecturer gets herself off to an energetic start each day by leaving her curtains open at night so that she'll awaken to daylight. "I think it works because it takes me back to childhood," she said, "when I used to wake up every morning to the sun streaming in and I'd think: Wait! Don't start the day without me!"

• At a recent gathering of free-lance writers I chuckled when one woman admitted that it's the morning mail that gets her going. It seems she can't start work without it, and she's in trouble now because she has moved to a suburb where mail isn't delivered until the afternoon. It seemed amusing, that is, until I realized that *I* can't start work until I've skimmed the *New York Times*. Another writer who also needs mail for morning energy had actually found a solution: When her postman makes his afternoon delivery, she reads only what's urgent and saves the rest to satisfy her craving for mail the following morning.

The examples could go on and on and become more and more idiosyncratic. We all have our own private list of turn-ons. If you're in a slump, it sometimes helps to know what's on your list —to realize that you can count on fifteen minutes of needlepoint or of Beethoven. Over the course of a week you might just make a note (mental or otherwise) of the things that make you feel good and those that relax you. Don't overlook the truly mundane matters, like that second cup of coffee in the morning or the way it feels to sink back in a big chair and put your feet up at the end of a long day.

The lift you get from your energy turn-ons may be only a small one, but if you make such things part of your energy climate, over the course of a day or a week they can really make a difference.

Energy Tips

1. Identify the places that invigorate you; when you're feeling really low in energy, take yourself somewhere invigorating.

2. Make allowances, when you can, for the way weather affects your energy. Expect to feel a bit sluggish when the barometer is low or is falling and to feel more tired than usual for the first few very cold or very hot days of a new season.

3. If you're weather-sensitive (you often feel uncomfortable when a storm is coming on) or even if you're not, you might consider buying a negative-air-ion generator for your home.

4. Do you find summer's heat terribly debilitating? Try eating much less and drink a *lot* of water.

5. During the winter doldrums work in natural sunlight as much as possible. Move your desk closer to a window, if you can, for the psychological solar-energy boost.

6. Remember that noise is stress, and stress depletes energy: Stand your ground against noise pollution.

7. Design your own energizing retreat, a private space that reaffirms who you are, and choose the colors you find most refreshing.

8. Keep a week-long record of your energy turn-ons—the ordinary, daily things that give you a lift. Then resort to them more often.

The Company You Keep

Whether you're feeling energized and up or low down and lethargic, you probably take the credit or the blame for it yourself. Most people assume that energy is pretty much internally generated, like intelligence or ambition. Actually it's heavily influenced by outside factors—not only by the weather and the setting but also by the company you keep. For other people have a significant impact on your energy level—for better or worse.

The Company You Keep

Actors, perhaps more than anyone else, are aware that every human encounter has an energy dimension, that people sense and respond to the vitality of others.

In the theater every performance involves an intimate *exchange* of energy between the entertainers and the entertained. I emphasize the word "exchange" because, though it's generally accepted that performers work hard to project their energy and emotions across the footlights, people often overlook the fact that energy also crosses the footlights in the other direction, that the audience has an effect on the performers.

"What I like about the theater is that every performance can be different, because you have a different audience every night," Bill Murray told me. At the time Bill was one of the Not Ready for Prime Time Players, the repertory group featured on the popular TV show "Saturday Night Live." The show is known for its hilarious skits and satirical routines. "You can gauge an audience from the first scene you do," Bill continued, "and depending on how they react, you read your lines differently, you hit them a certain way. If the audience is dead, you really have to pump them up, but if they're hot it's better to play down; you can practically whisper a line and get a huge laugh."

In a sense, *doing successful comedy involves orchestrating the energy flow of the audience.* Rhythm is an important element, for, as Bill explained, "You play an audience according to what they've gone for before, and rhythm is part of that. You can speed up or slow down, and very soon you know what rhythm they're going at, the decibel level and inflections that they're going for. That's real information and you use it."

If every audience is different, one thing that delights a comedian is having a laugher, or a couple of them, right down in front. There are people who come because they badly want to laugh, Bill explained, and they'll respond to almost anything. If they're sitting at the front, their chortles and guffaws will trigger a wave effect that moves the energy all the way back. "They'll push it right through the center for you," Bill said. "It's a strange thing. You don't even have to look at them. Instead, you try to play everyone around them: You play the sides, you play deep. Part of the acting thing is just learning where to aim." He illustrated this for me and it was clear that he "aims" with his eyes, his voice, and the way he positions his body.

The Energy Cycle of "Saturday Night Live"

I was eager to talk to Bill Murray because he obviously has in abundance the kind of zany, off-the-wall vitality that characterizes many of the best comedians. But I was also interested in the whole phenomenon of "Saturday Night Live," because I'd been told that the energy level changes completely between the dress rehearsal and the aired show every week. "Dress," as it was called, was staged in front of a studio audience at 7:30 P.M. Afterward the audience filed out, a multitude of last-minute changes and cuts were made in the show, and at 11:30 P.M. the whole thing was run through again in front of a different audience, but this time it was on the air live. Between "dress" and "air," performances changed, but there was an even bigger change in the energy level of both cast *and* audience—as if the thirty million viewers who typically watched the show each week were somehow having their input as well.

One Saturday night in the fall of 1978 I sat through both the "dress" and "air" shows in an NBC studio the size of a warehouse, high up in the RCA Building in Rockefeller Center, New York City. Lights, microphones, and other paraphernalia dangled from the high ceiling like covens of bats. The audience was accommodated on balconies around the edges of the room and, elbow to elbow, in dainty white swivel chairs crowded around the perimeters of the various sets.

There were half a dozen sets in all, making the show like a six-ring circus. For three or four minutes at a time the action would take place on a stage right in front of my eyes. Then the lights would go out, the actors would quietly depart, the cameramen and their cameras—mounted on huge rolling platforms—would trundle majestically away, and soon a set at the other end of the room would be lit. Once the cameras and production crew were in place, they generally blocked my view completely, so now I watched the proceedings on a TV monitor positioned overhead.

The "dress" show was played before a live audience so that the producer and writers could learn which lines were funny and which ones fell flat. Consequently "dress" was always longer and much flabbier than "air." The night I attended it was clocked at two hours and had to be pruned back to ninety minutes between the shows. There was only about an hour in which to accomplish the surgery.

During "dress" the relationship between cast and audience was decidedly informal. Actors, waiting for the show to begin, sat on the edge of the stage chatting with people nearby. Later the cameraman, lumbering along on his platform from set to set, made clearly audible cracks about the proceedings. Throughout there was a feeling that we weren't just there to be entertained, that we were part of the creative process. Once or twice, when a line got a huge laugh, we could see the actors reacting to the audience reaction—they were delighted with themselves and with us.

It all added up to a kind of intimacy that was absent from the "air" show, for the attitude during "air" was deadly serious. The lines and the pace were snappier. Stagehands hustled furniture on and off the stage between scenes—literally on the run, and actors sometimes actually sprinted from one set to the next, shedding costumes en route. Laughs were louder and built more quickly as the audience, too, responded to the charged atmosphere.

Bill Murray: How to Feed Energy into a Role

A few days after my double-barreled introduction to "Saturday Night Live" I interviewed Bill Murray in his office at NBC. Bill is obviously the kind of person who finds it difficult to sit still for long; as we talked he got up from time to time to prowl restlessly about the room or to shuffle absentmindedly through his fan mail. A tall man with shaggy dark hair and a broad, open face, he got his start in comedy working with the Second City improvisational theater group in Chicago. Before that, he said, "I made pizza, I've been a surveyor, I cut lawns. When I finally hooked onto a part at the Second City, I just did it at first for something to do." But the part expanded and so did the work, which included writing much of his own material. In 1974 Bill moved to New York City to be a writer/actor on *The National Lampoon Show* off Broadway and *The National Lampoon Radio Hour*. After that he made regular appearances for a while on ABC's "Saturday Night Live with Howard Cosell" eventually replacing Chevy Chase on NBC's "Saturday Night Live."

Bill explained that, for the cast, the point of "dress" was "to get your bits on the show. Your obligation to the writer and to yourself is to do the scene well enough so that most of it makes it through to 'air.' I find that the best approach is to barrel through it, so that it seems like more is happening and they may not notice if it's not funny or if you haven't got the character yet."

If an actor was fighting to get his characterization right during "dress," he could slow the scene down and actually sabotage it, which was why Bill felt that at that point it was better not to get into much of what he called "physicalization"—posture, gestures, body movements, subtle inflections of the voice, the touches that bring a part to life. "Often I don't get all that until the 'air' show," he said. "Also, once you know that a laugh is going to be there at a particular point, you can do a little more just before it in terms of physical business, color and shading, facial stuff or whatever. That way, when the laugh does happen you're a little more into it and it's a little richer."

Energy Transactions Among the Cast

*Just as there's an energy exchange between audience and per-
formers, there's one among members of the cast.* Bill mentioned
that Gilda Radner "will really play with you out there. All she
has to do is send out the vibes that we can play around here and
then all of a sudden the whole thing changes. John [Belushi] is a
different thing. He saves his performance until 'air.' He'll just dog
it until then and so he'll give you a whole different performance
—he uses a whole different energy. He'll do all sorts of physical
business, and though it doesn't necessarily help your performance, it does keep you on your toes, because you don't know
what to expect and that means you have to *be* there in the scene.
Because if you don't know what you want to do, if you're just
reading the lines by rote he'll steal the scene away from you."

Because the show is live, because the atmosphere is frenetic
and last-minute changes (including a few ad libs) are simply assumed, "Saturday Night Live" has a peculiar nervous energy of
its own. In fact, its unevenness and unpredictability seem to be
at the root of its appeal for cast and fans alike. In an age in
which almost everything else on television is impeccably smooth
and often bland, "Saturday Night Live" is the real thing.

To Bill the epitome of the "Saturday Night Live" experience
was the evening he played a customer at a Burgermaster, a fast-
food restaurant that "promised to serve this goofy hamburger
any way you wanted it, and I wanted mine with the blood of a
Colombian frog all over it."

Bill recalled that he had been worrying all week about an impression of Walter Cronkite that he was also supposed to do that
night. It came immediately after the Burgermaster scene, with
only a break for commercials in between, so Bill walked on the
Burgermaster set already made up to look like Cronkite. "They
were doing my makeup by committee," Bill recalled, "and they
said, 'Let's make him look old.' Well, I looked like I was dead,
and I went out for the Burgermaster bit with a hat on my head
so nobody would notice the makeup. I was wearing my favorite
jacket, a gold baseball jacket, brand-new, and suddenly there is

this guy pouring about a quart of stage blood all over the hamburger. He hadn't done anything like that before, not in the dress rehearsal or anytime, and it got all over the jacket and just destroyed it.

"Then afterward there were three people pulling off the jacket and putting padding on me to make me look fat; somebody else was lacing my shoes; there were people gluing a mustache on my face and people pulling my hair back with pins so they could stick a wig on me, and all the time the band is playing 'Contusion' by Stevie Wonder, incredibly loud.

"Finally they pushed me out on stage and I realized that I was so padded my jacket wouldn't even come close to closing. Here I'd been worrying about this particular bit all week and now I'm sitting there with this ridiculous-looking stomach, with the padding showing and the coat that won't close, and I've got stage blood all over my hands. The band is pumping me up to an incredible high and suddenly it stops and somebody shouts, 'Five seconds,' and there's total silence. The whole thing was so absurd that I started cackling hysterically and then the audience began laughing because I was going nuts.

"But, you know, I did real well with the Cronkite impression, because the thing with comedy is *you've* got to have fun for it to be funny. The more fun you have, the better it is. That's why I got into acting, really, because I found that in order to be good you had to have fun, and I'd never had a job before where you had to have fun."

When I asked Bill how he saw his future, he replied, "I can't see the future, but there will always be work for me. I can always get a job writing comedy, because we won an Emmy last year. I can walk into an office, throw that on the table and say [here he assumed a quavery voice and hunched his shoulders, becoming, suddenly, Bill Murray aged 80], 'So you want to know how to make your show funny? I can tell you—I won this back in the seventies.' "

Understanding Your "People" Needs

At performances of "Saturday Night Live" energy flows between cast and audience and among members of the cast. The same sort of thing happens in everyday life, for other people do affect your energy level just as you affect theirs. To make the most of the "people" factor, then, you have to recognize what's going on.

That doesn't mean simply taking note of the fact that Aunt Millie is a live wire and Uncle Ed is a stupor inducer. That may be true enough—we'll come back to that point later—but the people factor is much more subtle. To begin with, sheer numbers matter; you need to have enough people in your life, but not too many. Then again, you also need contact with others whose interaction rhythms mesh with yours, whose propensities for speech and silence, animation and inaction are a comfortable fit.

The People Factor: Sheer Numbers

Everyone craves both stimulation and solitude—each in its turn and in the right balance. But since this is one of those body truths, what's right for one person might be incredibly wearing for another. Conversations I had with two young women, in particular, summed up for me what I also learned from others: To use the people factor intelligently, you have to know yourself well and acknowledge your own needs.

Getting Energy from Other People

Mary Anne thrives on social stimulation. The mutual friend who introduced us told me beforehand, "Mary Anne is marvelous. She walks into a room and she's witty, articulate. Sparks fly and people are delighted with her. And she's delighted that they're delighted—it's quite a phenomenon. But Mary Anne not only gives off energy, she also *gets* her energy from being with people. In fact, she could probably keep going twenty-four hours a day if once every eight hours or so someone could just feed her a fresh set of people to react to."

When I met Mary Anne, she turned out to be dark-haired and thirtyish, with a round face and enormous brown eyes. A very vivacious person—she talks fast and laughs often—she rates her energy level at 8 or even 9, and it's easy to see why. When I repeated the remark about what it would take to keep her going twenty-four hours a day, she chuckled.

"It's true," she said. "I remember, when I was single, there were nights when I'd arrive home from work so exhausted that I was practically comatose; but if I was having company for dinner, the minute they'd arrive I'd come to life again and thoroughly enjoy the evening. It wasn't a charade—it didn't take any effort on my part—it was just that somehow the juices started flowing. At the end of the evening, when the guests left, of course I'd collapse."

Mary Anne is married to a hard-working New York City journalist who is himself more likely to be revitalized by getting away from people than by seeing more of them. In the beginning this difference between them took some getting used to. "Norman's ideal Sunday is to sit around and read all day, preferably in his pajamas," Mary Anne told me. "He was fascinated to find that when I open my eyes on Sunday morning I immediately think of nineteen things we could do that day. At first he thought I liked to get out because I was easily bored with my own company, but it's not that. I simply find people—the right kind of people—tremendously stimulating."

Over the years this couple seems to have arrived at a workable compromise: They go out enough for Mary Anne to feel stimulated, while she has accepted the fact that sometimes Norman "likes to be unencumbered by things for a couple of days at a time."

Why is it that some individuals get their energy from being with people while others get it from being alone? Assuming that it's probably a predilection learned in childhood, I asked Mary Anne whether as a child she turned to other youngsters for excitement. But it seems that when she was small she was so fond of being alone that her mother was concerned about her. "It

wasn't that I didn't like the other kids," she said, "but I was perfectly contented to stay home alone and play with my dolls or
read."

Mary Anne grew up in a small town in Pennsylvania in a
close-knit family. She describes it as "a pasteurized background."
People she knew didn't have rough edges, she said; they either
conformed or they weren't accepted at all. But from the beginning she was drawn to those who were different. "I remember a
whole shelf of books at the library," she said, "with titles like
Nanook of the North and *Zelda from Zaire*. They were about
children growing up in exotic corners of the world. I read them
all and loved them." Once she left home, she was finally free to
be "different"—to marry a Latin American, live in New York
City, and pursue a career; but to this day to her family she's
"the weird one, the oddball." What Mary Anne enjoys most are
other oddballs, other people with a strong self-image. Even if
she doesn't agree with their opinions, she loves talking to them
and hearing what they think about things.

Are You Energized by Solitude?

In terms of the people factor, Jan Gosar operates quite differently
from Mary Anne. At the time I interviewed her, Jan was assistant
to the producer of "Saturday Night Live," and her working days
were full of a constant bustle of people. Though she loved her job,
she found that to keep her energy from being depleted she had
to set aside some private time and guard it carefully.

Jan was recommended to me as a low-key sort of person who
was definitely not high in energy, though she could handle a high-
pressure job beautifully. She was a slim young woman with straight,
shoulder-length blond hair and a wide, generous mouth. She spoke
slowly in a warm, quiet voice, and she did indeed strike me as relaxed and low-key. I interviewed her in her New York City apartment
in a living room where a wall of windows framed a skyful of tall
buildings. As we talked, Manhattan was like a third presence
in the room.

For "Saturday Night Live," shows were not so much written as evolved. Over the course of a week they were beefed up, pruned back, switched around, and generally tinkered with many times, right up until literally minutes before air time. Each rewrite could require dozens of adjustments in everything from wardrobe and props to graphics, and as assistant producer it was Jan's job to make sure that when a change was made everyone who needed to know about it was told. She was also responsible for scheduling, making sure people were there when they were needed.

The actual work, she said, was fairly mundane, but the atmosphere was far from it and the pace on any given day varied wildly. One minute she might be sitting around without anything to do, waiting while writers and producer conferred; the next moment she was racing the clock. Sometimes everyone around her was semihysterical—performers tend to be rather volatile—but she knew that *she* must stay calm.

Often, when she had to tell an actor that some of his lines had been cut or changed, she bore the brunt of his initial angry reaction. "You have to remember that it's not really *you* he's mad at," she said. "You just tell him to go see the writer." Jan was well aware, too, that production assistants often get the blame when, in the general melee, the lines of communication break down and the wrong prop, for example, turns up on a set. "Somebody may have forgotten to tell you that that part of the script was changed," she said, "but it's still your responsibility."

Though at times it was nerve-racking, Jan thoroughly enjoyed her job. She loved the atmosphere and the challenge: the need to work against time, to cope with different personalities and, above all, to stay cool under pressure. When I asked her whether she paid a price for her self-control, she said, "The people I'm closest to probably pay the price. I know there are times when I'm apt to blow up over some perfectly innocuous remark.

"Having time to be alone is very important to me," she continued. "It's like sleep—very restorative. If I can be alone for a while, that slows things down so that I can think them through rather than being pulled in all directions. I get a better perspective. When I'm alone I usually read and then after a while I'll just sit quietly and reflect."

Like Mary Anne, Jan was something of a loner as a child. Growing up in a small town in Utah, she was dominated by three older brothers who were supposed to keep an eye on her. Often they were off somewhere else, involved in their own activities. Since her mother was at work, she had the house to herself. "I never minded that at all," she said.

Caught up now in the quick pace of New York City life, Jan wondered at times about her own need for privacy. "Perhaps I'm somewhat antisocial," she said. For, whereas she withdrew from the world periodically to restore her energy, many of her friends, including the man she cared about, seemed to turn outward instead. They liked to be constantly on the go; their idea of relaxation was a game of tennis, and when they needed energy they reached out to other people as Mary Anne does.

"For some people socializing seems to be totally effortless," Jan mused. "But when I force myself to do more of it, it's very depleting; it costs me energy and I feel drained by it. I have a small group of very close friends and I do spend a lot of time and energy on them, but if I go much beyond them it cuts into the private time I need."

How was it, then, that she enjoyed the frenetic atmosphere at work, the continual contact with volatile personalities? That, it seemed, was different. She could close the door on it at the end of the day and, in any case, "I don't expose much of myself to the people I work with."

When I asked her how she'd rate her own energy level, Jan wasn't sure. She was aware that other people often had the impression that she was low in drive, though she maintained that was due mostly to her "physical exterior"—to the fact that she was soft-spoken and seemed somewhat cool and aloof. In her job she felt she operated at a high level of energy and in her free time at a low one. However, in an important way Jan was different from the hurdlers I described in Chapter 1 since their energy swings aren't under their control.

Jan's job brought her into contact with a lot of people, while as a free-lance writer Mary Anne worked alone much of the time. Nevertheless, there were very basic temperamental differences between them.

Why is it that one person turns outward for energy while another turns inward? *There's growing scientific evidence that some individuals need much more in the way of stimulation than*

*others (human contact is, of course, one sort of stimulation) and
that this need is at least partly inborn.*

How the Brain Handles Sensory Overload

Much of the research in this area has been done by a National
Institute of Mental Health (NIMH) scientist, Dr. Monte S.
Buchsbaum. For over a dozen years Dr. Buchsbaum has been
using an electroencephalogram (EEG) to study the way the
brain responds to sensations of various sorts—to light flashes,
sounds, electric shocks. In a typical experiment a subject hooked
up to an EEG relaxes in a darkened room while a light is flashed
in front of his eyes once every second for several minutes. The
light is sometimes dim, sometimes bright—four different intensities are used—and the brain's electrical responses to it are recorded and then analyzed by a computer. With some people
(the "augmenters"), the brighter the light, the bigger the brain
wave reaction will be. With others (the "reducers") the response
begins to lessen with the very bright intensities; they seem to be
equipped with a natural protective mechanism that allows them,
in effect, to turn down the volume when incoming sensations become too intense.

Buchsbaum suggests that the brain may contain a "sensoristat"
that helps the person stay alert. In the face of monotony it tunes
up perceptions so as to make the most of the few sensations that
are available. In the face of sensory overload (including pain) it
dims perceptions somewhat. The overload mechanism seems to
be set to cut in at different levels for different people.

Are You a Sensation Seeker?

Augmenters not only tolerate higher levels of sensation, many
of them actually crave stimuli of all kinds, according to Dr. Marvin Zuckerman, a psychology professor at the University of Dela-
ware who has worked with Buchsbaum. Zuckerman calls this
trait "sensation-seeking." He has devised a paper-and-pencil test
by which he can score people on their need for stimulation.

High scorers *require* variety, novelty, and excitement in their lives if they're to feel happy and to operate at the top of their form. They generally like spicy foods; they say that they'd love to try skydiving, hallucinogenic drugs, and lots of other relatively risky things. They'd prefer a job that involves a lot of traveling; they get bored seeing the same old faces day after day; and they also like variety in their sexual partners. To me the most telling characteristic of all, though, is the fact that they say that when swimming they dive right into cold water—unlike those who score low on sensation-seeking, who report going in inch by shivering inch. As you might expect, sensation seekers do vary in the kinds of sensations they crave. Some (those who have a yen for risky sports) are primarily thrill seekers; others turn to people as their chief source of stimulation.

Apparently, augmenting and sensation-seeking are traits that are at least partly inborn, for on both Buchsbaum's test and Zuckerman's questionnaire identical twins are likely to come out with relatively similar scores. Of course, upbringing undoubtedly plays a part as well. Still, Zuckerman suggests that the need for sensation may be related to levels of brain transmitters such as norepinephrine and dopamine.

To come back now to Jan and Mary Anne, it seems very likely that Mary Anne is more of an augmenter and sensation seeker than Jan is. She needs more stimulation coming at her and, in particular, she needs people. Both women have developed lifestyles that seem to fit their needs and that help them make the most of their energy potential.

Anyone who has ever felt overstimulated—in a discothèque, perhaps, or a crowded department store—knows how uncomfortable that feels and how energy-draining it can be. Anyone who has ever been understimulated, bored to distraction in a monotonous environment, can testify that this also has an impact on energy. Ultimately it, too, is wearing.

At any rate, *it seems important to realize that different people do need different amounts of stimulation, and to give some thought to how much you need and what kind.* If you're like Mary Anne and your favorite type of stimulation is lively people, then you'll give your energy a lift if you can shape your daily routine accordingly. If you've been leading a frenetic, highly populated sort of existence and you're feeling worn out, you might ask yourself whether, perhaps, you're more like Jan and need to revitalize yourself with periodic retreats into solitude.

Conversational Rhythms

Not only do you need the right number of people in your life, you need the right *kind* of people as well. Surprisingly, biological rhythms play a part in that, for everyone has a basic "interaction" rhythm, a characteristic way of alternating speech and silence, animation and inactivity. You may find it easy to adapt to one person's rhythm and difficult to respond to another's.

The study of interaction rhythms was pioneered by anthropologist Eliot Chapple. For over forty years Dr. Chapple recorded and analyzed the rhythms of many kinds of human encounters, from military drills to job interviews. His focus was always on the *pattern* of the action rather than on the content, for it's the pattern that reflects underlying biological cycles.

For instance, for many years Chapple used his Programmed Diagnostic Interview to identify the basic rhythms of individuals. In this procedure two people, subject and interviewer, would sit and talk, watched by an observer equipped with a device about the size of a box of kitchen matches that was connected to a computer. Whenever the subject spoke, the observer would push down the "A" button on the box; when the interviewer spoke, the "B" button would go down instead. Sometimes the interviewer himself did the recording, but in either case the end result was an exact record of the pattern and flow of the encounter, showing how long each of the subject's responses lasted, how long he took to respond each time after the interviewer stopped talking, whether he interrupted, where he hesitated and for how long, and so on. Head nods, smiles, and other nonverbal behavior were registered as well, for, as Chapple points out, they actually make up a major part of the give-and-take of conversation.

Over many years computer analysis demonstrated conclusively that *timing in conversation is never haphazard and that every individual has a characteristic rhythm at which he operates most comfortably.* Actually, we all know from our own experience that there are people who are long-winded—once they've got the floor, it's hard to get a word in edgewise—and others who are almost monosyllabic; most of us fall somewhere in between these extremes. Such characteristics don't seem to change much over the years, and they're a significant factor in the way relationships develop. For instance, imagine a conversation between a woman who always responds at great length, and only after a thoughtful pause, and a man whose remarks are generally brief, to the point, and delivered in rapid-fire succession.

What accounts for the difference between the monologist and the person who's monosyllabic? Most people assume that the former is an egotist who likes to hear the sound of his own voice, while the latter just hasn't much to say. However, Dr. Chapple believes that these traits actually reflect something more basic, an inborn activity rhythm—which might as easily be called an energy rhythm. He says this basic beat is already there at birth but that it can be modulated by upbringing or by traumas that occur before the rhythm is "set" at the age of three or four. At any rate, the beat is a body truth, one that lays some of the groundwork for personality.

How Flexible Is Your Energy Pattern?

Actually, almost everyone has several subrhythms in addition to the basic one that they're most comfortable with. A man may habitually operate at one rhythm while he is with family or close friends and at quite another when he is with his employer. Chapple compares the subrhythms to harmonics in music, because computer analysis has shown that they tend to be mathematical multiples of the basic beat, a doubling or a halving, for example.

People vary greatly in the number of harmonics that they have available and thus in their flexibility. Chapple notes that two individuals may appear to spend the same amount of energy in an interaction—measured in terms of stops and starts, conversational activity and silence—and yet the patterning for one may be much more subtly organized. She may be able to operate almost equally well at a very fast tempo, a very slow one, or at several in between; the other person may be hopelessly loquacious or inevitably and boringly laconic.

Some people are very much aware of their own interaction rhythm because it's fairly extreme. I have one friend who has been teased all her life about the fact that she's an enthusiastic nonstop talker. This creates real problems for her, since friends and acquaintances sometimes want to run the other way when they see her coming—especially if they're in a hurry. She's aware of this reaction, for she called me one night and began the conversation by saying, "You're in luck. I can't talk for long because my husband is expecting a long-distance call . . ."

The person who is highly taciturn may also be aware that he's different from other people. However, most of us have no idea what our basic rhythm is like, nor could we do anything much to change it (assuming that we wanted to) even if we could identify it. But just knowing that such rhythms exist can help you to understand and tolerate some of the discomforts of everyday encounters.

It's easy to understand, for example, why a conversation with a complete stranger is often rather awkward; for when strangers come together they must almost always begin by groping for a comfortable, mutual rhythm. One person may start by speaking for about sixty seconds; if there is then a five-second silence while the other individual gears up to reply, then the next time around the first person may speak for sixty-five or seventy seconds before pausing for a response. Similarly, if individual number one is only fifty seconds into his remarks when his listener interrupts, then he may subsequently make shorter statements.

People do this kind of adjusting all the time without ever being aware it. However, there are limits to how far anyone can adjust. And *that* helps to explain why your encounters with some people are always bumpy and uncomfortable, filled with unintended interruptions and awkward pauses—despite the fact that there are warm feelings on both sides. You simply operate on very different rhythms.

"Complementarity": People Whose Rhythms Dovetail

Rhythms also help to explain why there are people with whom you feel at ease immediately, though you have very little in common: Your basic beats mesh nicely. *It's a real energizer to talk to someone whose interaction rhythm dovetails with yours.* You have a sense that energy is flowing effortlessly, for as soon as you finish speaking, he's ready with a reply, and just as you're primed to speak up again he pauses to allow you to respond. Chapple calls this phenomenon "complementarity" and says it's one of the greater pleasures in life. Studies have shown that it tends to happen much more often between close friends or between a husband and wife who are happily married than it does between strangers. That may be partly because we can anticipate the interaction patterns of those we know well and partly because we choose people whose rhythms mesh nicely with our own as mates and friends.

Rhythms Change Under Stress

When you run into an old friend and your conversation is unaccountably full of awkward stops and starts, though ordinarily you fit comfortably together, it may be because one of you has been under stress and that has distorted your natural rhythm. Most biological rhythms are susceptible to stress, and interaction is no exception.

In fact, conversation itself presents certain stresses. I'm not referring to subjects that make you squirm but rather to matters of timing, to kinks in the normal flow of statement and response. Suppose you're talking to someone, for example, and you finish what you have to say—and silence ensues. You're expecting the other person to pick up the thread of the conversation and instead he sits without speaking as the seconds tick away. Some people aren't bothered by nonresponse, but others inevitably feel uneasy and take it as a rejection.

Or suppose you've got the floor and the other person repeat-

edly interrupts you. In this sort of situation you may simply
shrivel up and find it harder and harder to think of anything at
all to say; or you might swing into verbal combat instead and interrupt right back. In studying the same people over and over
again, Dr. Chapple found that everyone has consistent and characteristic ways of responding to conversational stresses. Thus,
though you may not be able to identify your basic beat, if you
watch for it you can figure out how you typically react to being
interrupted, or to not getting a response, and that kind of knowledge can be useful.

For instance, Alicia always felt somewhat intimidated in conversations with her next-door neighbor. "It wasn't really anything she said," Alicia recalled, "but somehow I always felt
gauche and a little uneasy. One day I was talking to her on the
phone and I suddenly realized that whenever I stopped talking
there was a long pause before she said anything. I'd never noticed it before, but right then it occurred to me that that's the
way she always talks. I also realized that I have a horror of awkward little silences. Whenever they keep happening in a conversation, I get a little tense, and when I'm tense I have a tendency
to talk a whole lot, almost as if I'm trying to drown out those
silences. Anyway, I'm still not 100 percent comfortable talking
to my neighbor, but I no longer wonder whether she's secretly
looking down her nose at me."

Alicia's tendency to start chattering when she doesn't get an
immediate response is a fairly common one. Other people grow
sullen or else they speed up the tempo: Each time a pause occurs, they break the silence a little sooner than they did the last
time, but their remarks become progressively briefer; it's as if
they're trying to prod the other person into a reply.

The Interrupter

Interruptions present a different sort of problem. Though they
do sometimes happen because the other individual misread your
signals and thought you'd finished talking, they're often an attempt to dominate. Recognizing that that's what you're responding to can help you temper your response when necessary; for,

again, people react in characteristic ways. For instance, one man may raise his voice and simply override the interrupter. Most people instead develop a stepped-up tempo: They hesitate and then interrupt back, and then if they're interrupted again they react even more quickly. This, of course, is how quarrels develop. Then there is the person who simply wilts in the face of attempts to dominate him and has less and less to say.

Conversational stresses such as nonresponse and interrupting not only trigger an immediate reaction but in many cases produce a lingering effect and distort the individual's normal interaction rhythm for some time afterward. Thus, the next time you run into a friend and she somehow doesn't seem herself—she's too abrupt or too taciturn or too full of nervous chatter—you can guess not only that some sort of stress has thrown her off her stride but that it may have been something as hard for her to identify as a conversation that was uncomfortable, despite the fact that nothing of significance was said.

Your Daily Supply of Energy

From his studies of interaction Dr. Chapple has come to some provocative conclusions about energy. He believes that *over the course of a day any individual has only a certain amount of energy to spend. Periods in which the energy is discharged alternate with periods in which it's built up again,* an ebb and flow that finds expression partly in the interaction rhythms he has recorded.

"But you have to recognize that factors like dominance determine whether a person has an outlet for the energy that builds up inside," he explained. "Many times I've seen people whose energy is normally so high it could drive you crazy; but if they're around others who are more dominating they'll just sit there and not say anything. So what price energy?

"You can also have someone who reacts to nonresponse by talking and talking and talking. What you see as energy there has been triggered by a particular kind of stress. It doesn't reflect the individual's natural energy level at all."

Obviously, interaction rhythms are enormously complex as they're expressed in day-to-day behavior.

The Ninety-Minute Conversational Peak

Most of us like to think that we talk when we have something to say, and that we say what we have to say and then fall silent. It's somewhat disconcerting to be told that our conversational excursions are directed by underlying biological rhythms.

It's just as disconcerting to learn that *the urge to converse is apparently cyclical, and that if all distractions are removed it will strike about once every ninety minutes.* Yet there's experimental evidence that this is so.

You may remember (see Chapter 5) that other ninety-minute rhythms exist. At night we dream approximately once every ninety minutes, and during the day alertness, the tendency to fantasize, and the urge to eat or put things in your mouth all seem to peak at ninety-minute intervals, perhaps because a basic rest-and-activity cycle is at work.

To find out whether there are similar cycles in human interaction, Professor Donald P. Hayes, chairman of the Department of Sociology at Cornell University, and his colleague, Loren Cobb, paid couples to live in an isolation suite together, cut off from all time cues, free running (see Chapter 5) for periods of from two to thirty days. Whenever the subjects were awake they wore microphones that broadcast a signal to equipment in an adjoining room. There a computer kept a running record not of the conversations themselves but simply of whether from moment to moment the individual was speaking or was silent. In a series of such experiments most couples soon settled into living a "day" that was about twenty-five hours long; and for most, interaction peaked about once every ninety-two minutes.

One study was particularly interesting because it demonstrated once again the way stress can affect interaction rhythms. The subjects were a couple in their twenties who had been living together for some time. They remained in the isolation suite for 30 days, and for the first 12 the computer recorded conversational peaks both at 94-minute and also at 166-minute intervals (approximately).

Three weeks into the study the woman developed a yeast infection; though she was supplied with medication, she was rather uncomfortable. At about the same time the couple had to be told that their landlord was evicting them. The experimenters found them new housing and actually moved all their belongings for them, but in the meanwhile the couple's rhythms were completely disrupted. They began sleeping for shorter periods of time; the 94-minute conversational rhythm disappeared altogether, while the 166-minute cycle also faded a bit. During the final week of the experiment, however, with the infection and the housing situation taken care of, all of the rhythms began to re-emerge.

Dr. Hayes believes that under normal conditions the 90-minute interaction rhythm is distorted beyond recognition as people respond to what's going on around them. (It may often be distorted by stress as well.) The rhythm surfaces in an isolation suite with most distractions removed. For people who live together or work closely together it could be important to have rhythms that are in synchrony. If one person often feels like talking just when the other doesn't, that could be a problem.

No one knows for sure whether the various 90-minute rhythms —daydreaming, snacking, "readiness to converse"—coincide; nor whether they're controlled by the same body mechanisms; nor whether they really are related to a basic rest-and-activity cycle, a rhythmic ebb and flow of energy. In the thirty-day experiment a camera automatically snapped still photos at regular intervals and the time of day was recorded with each. When the photos were compared with the records of speech and silence, there was no indication that the couple became more active every ninety minutes or so at the same time that they grew more talkative. Nevertheless, Dr. Hayes says it stands to reason that a basic activity cycle might exist.

Every human being harbors whole networks of rhythms. It should hardly be surprising, then, if some of them affect our social relationships on several different levels. On one level there is the rhythm that operates for a period of seconds or mere minutes and governs the ebb and flow of conversation. On the next level there is the ninety-minute rhythm that primes us to reach out verbally to others every hour and a half or so. And on a broader scale, if Dr. Chapple is right, there is the beat to which we march, the highly individual rhythm that affects the way our energy is distributed—and expressed—over the course of a day.

People Who Energize or Drain You

It's time now to get back to Aunt Millie, the live wire, and Uncle Ed, who's a drag to have around—or, at any rate, to the fact that *specific people do have an effect on your energy, for better or for worse.*

Dr. George E. Vaillant commented on this in his fascinating book *Adaptation to Life.* Dr. Vaillant is the current director of the Grant Study, an ambitious long-term project that has traced the personal growth and development of several hundred American men over a period of about 40 years. The men, 268 of them in all, were chosen in the early 1940s because they were among the healthiest and most promising undergraduates at a leading American university. Since then they've filled out detailed questionnaires about themselves at intervals. Starting in 1969, Dr. Vaillant reinterviewed 94 of them in depth. This is his perceptive comment on the impact different personalities had on him:

"I soon discovered that whether the men liked me or I liked them had far more to do with their lives than with mine. The men who had always found loving easy made me feel warmly toward them, and led me to marvel at both my tact and my skill as an interviewer and at their good fortune to belong to such an enjoyable project. I left the office of one such man feeling ten feet tall; but he had had the same effect on others all of his life. In contrast, men who had spent their lives fearful of other people and had gone unloved in return often made me feel incompetent and clumsy. With them I felt like a heartless investigator, vivisecting them for science. During his interview one such man had confessed that he was afraid of dying and leaving nothing of worth to the world. Afterwards I, too, felt drained and depressed, as if I had done all of the work in the interview while he took much and gave nothing."

Some people are a tonic: They come into a room like a breeze fresh off the ocean. It's tempting to conclude that vitality itself is what makes them so stimulating to be with, but actually, in another individual energy per se is not energizing—in fact, it can grate on your nerves. As Dr. Vaillant suggests, it's the person's ability to love that plays the major part in the impact he has on you, for *when emotional energy is expressed as warmth and openness even the briefest contact with it can be revitalizing.* People who manage to have a lot of fun also make invigorating company.

As for those who leave you feeling drained, there are a number of different explanations for that, and a first step in coping with the reaction is to understand what's behind it. Sometimes, as Dr. Vaillant noted, the problem lies in the personality of the individual himself. If he's fearful and suspicious and you sense his basic hostility but don't understand where it comes from, then you may feel tense and uncomfortable yourself. Once you realize that the relationship is an uneasy one simply because he is the way he is, you may find it less wearing.

But often when another person depletes your energy it's because of feelings that *you* bring to the situation. Perhaps contact with the person reactivates old conflicts or brings back a muddle of memories. For instance, one young man explained, "Whenever I go back to visit my parents I spend an awful lot of time sleeping, and even when I'm awake I feel absolutely lethargic. I tell myself it's the altitude—they live in Montana—or the fact that we no longer have anything much to say to one another, which means the visit is bound to be boring. But sometimes I wonder if I'm using sleep as an escape, to avoid remembering the old times when we were close and the other times when I fiercely resented the way they tried to stifle me."

Complete strangers can also reactivate memories and conflicts simply because they remind you (perhaps subconsciously) of someone out of your past. For instance, if a woman in some ways resembles your carping, hypercritical older sister, just being with her may be enough to make you feel angry and depressed, though those are feelings that really belong to the earlier sibling relationship. Then there's the man who reminds you of your dead brother, so that the sight of him generates a dull ache that you're barely aware of and don't recognize for what it is: grief.

You're shaped by the relationships you form early in life with parents, brothers and sisters, and your immediate family; in later years those patterns surface again and again, and without meaning to you re-enact them with new people playing the old, familiar roles. A physical resemblance can trigger the phenomenon, but so can a psychological resemblance or some factor in the situation itself. Thus, the next time you find yourself reacting negatively to someone or some situation for no good reason—so that your emotional responses are out of proportion and a drain on your energy—you might try asking yourself what the person or the situation reminds you of.

You Can "Catch" Others' Emotions—and Lose Energy

Sometimes people deplete your energy because they themselves are feeling down and you can't help sharing their feelings; for *to a degree emotions are contagious.* A dental surgeon I know says that working all day long with patients who are tense and frightened leaves him feeling exhausted. Then there is Judy, who is now divorced. Recalling the last year or so of her marriage, she said, "The thing that really got me was that Dick was constantly depressed, and though I tried to get him to see a therapist, or the minister, or someone else who might help, he wouldn't. He hated his job and he was sure the other guys at work were out to get him—but, then, in all his working life he'd never had a job he was satisfied with. Whenever he was at home, it was as if a cloud of gloom settled over the house. In the end *his* depression had *me* feeling so low that it was one of the reasons I decided to leave him."

Sometimes other people's emotions are all too obvious, as they were with Dick; but even when they're not obvious, they're communicated nonverbally. By the slump of her shoulders, the listlessness of her gestures, and the brevity of her responses one woman expresses discouragement, while the high spirits of another are visible in every vigorous movement she makes. We're all enormously sensitive to such messages whether or not we ever get as far as identifying, in so many words, the other person's reactions.

Face to face, we not only observe these signals but we actually imitate them without being aware that we're doing it, thus embodying the same emotions ourselves. During moments of rapport we share postures with a friend, perhaps sitting with knees casually crossed and arms hooked over the chair back, as relaxed as he is; or we stand with shoulders slumped and hands in pockets, thus mirroring his dejection. Most of the time, when people echo postures they're not aware that they're doing it. However, the late psychoanalyst Frieda Fromm-Reichmann would quite deliberately imitate a patient's postures during a session to get a feeling for what the patient might be experiencing. To the extent that it's difficult to feel vigorous and alert when you're physically toned down to match a friend, this special nonverbal sensitivity does have an impact on your energy.

Guilt Trips Are a Waste of Energy

Nevertheless, in and of itself the impact is mild. It becomes debilitating only when other feelings come into play—when you feel somehow responsible for the other person's reactions. Judy, for example, couldn't help feeling that if she really loved Dick (by that time she no longer did) she'd be able to help him or at least persuade him to get help, and so she not only "felt for him" in his distress but was torn by guilt besides.

Susan Shor does group therapy with depressed patients (see Chapter 4). She admits that she does sometimes "catch" their depression—but only in certain circumstances. She explained, "If I'm in a position where I feel I have to help, either as a therapist or as a friend, and then the person doesn't get better, I can feel helpless and depressed myself. But if I'm around somebody who is depressed and I'm not responsible for helping, I don't feel down."

If you're at all sensitive, inevitably you empathize with other people's troubles, you do feel for them. But those sympathy pangs only really begin to get *you* down when you add a healthy helping of guilt, a sense of inadequacy ("If I were any good I'd be able to make him feel better"), or an uneasy desire to atone for the fact that you're better off than he is.

Emotions can be irrational, inconvenient, or overwhelming, but you still have to deal with the fact that they exist and that they are yours. The same thing is true of other individuals: They, too, have to be allowed to have irrational and painful feelings and to take the responsibility for them. Yet, especially with those who are closest to you, you may have trouble knowing where to draw the line that says, "This is where I stop and you begin." When the other person is happy, you may be tempted to take the credit for it, and when he's depressed or angry, you may feel that you're somehow to blame; but at such times you pay for this blurring of psychic boundaries with depleted energy.

What's the bottom line, then, when it comes to the people in your life who are a drain on you? Since avoiding them completely is seldom a workable answer, your best bet is to try to understand why they affect you the way they do and then to work on your own feelings.

Jean Houston: Energy Comes from Getting Involved

I've said elsewhere that to get energy you have to spend energy. That's true, too, with the people in your life. Ultimately, emotional commitment is as energizing as anything there is. *When you're deeply involved with others, when you invest your vitality without stinting in the give-and-take of close relationships, you almost always get back more than you give.*

"I think a lot of human energy has to do with sharing," says psychologist Jean Houston. "We are not islands, we are interdependent systems." Jean Houston is an energist who also is something of a spellbinder. A tall woman with long, dark hair and the kind of stage presence that instantly captures and holds the attention of an audience, she's one of the leaders of the human potential movement. She's also a director of the Foundation for Mind Research in Pomona, New York. With her husband, Dr. Robert E. L. Masters, she has coauthored several books, including *Listening to the Body*. At the workshops, seminars, and lectures that Jean gives around the country, she explains to rapt audiences that human beings typically use only a fraction of their true potential. Then, with a series of exercises, she demonstrates some of the physical and mental abilities her listeners have that they were unaware of (see Chapter 15).

Jean lives in a seventeen-room house in Pomona. I interviewed her there in a living room so large it seemed almost cavernous. An enormous friendly dog sat in on our conversation, while another dog—bitter enemy of the first—was penned in the kitchen. At the end of the room an archway framed a startling sight: a carved wooden effigy, brightly painted and over eight feet tall, recently arrived from Bali.

Jean herself was just back from a trip, and as she described her travel schedule it became obvious that her energy really is quite extraordinary. She's on the road a great deal, traveling about 150,000 miles annually. On this most recent jaunt she arrived in California on a Friday and went straight from the airport to tape a TV show and a couple of TV interviews. The next day, Saturday, she made several short films about her work and then delivered a lecture in Pasadena to an audience of 3,000. On Sunday 200 people attended an advanced workshop she taught from 8 A.M. until 5 P.M. Then at 6 P.M. she caught a plane to Texas, arriving at midnight. For the next four days she taught, lectured, gave seminars, and attended meetings virtually nonstop, until Thursday night, when she flew on to Chicago to open the annual Carl Jung lectures and to run seminars for two more days. She arrived home again on Saturday.

Jean says that she can trust sheer momentum to keep her going for about three weeks at a time. "I can do, say, twenty days of teaching seventeen or eighteen hours a day, getting four to six hours of sleep at night—I never get more than six—and then I'm wiped out. But I come back very fast—within about a day." High energy runs in her family, she says. In fact, some of her ancestors were famous for it, starting with her great-great-great-grandfather, Sam Houston, who was the first president of the republic of Texas.

Acknowledging—and Empowering—Others

Counting off some of the things that energize her, Jean noted, "I'm doing what I want to do. There have been times in my life when I've had very little energy, because that was not true. And being intensely caught up in the world of ideas and making those ideas concrete is enormously refreshing."

But she believes that commitment is more important, and "a sense of communion," a feeling that you're just part of a process, a piece of the whole. It's also vital not to take yourself too seriously, she said, because otherwise you become self-conscious. "I have very little personal ambition," she explained, "but I have an enormous amount of concern that the world work better. That means I'm not encapsulated in my own bag of skin."

Some aspects of Jean Houston's life *are* exhausting, especially when she's on the road. She can't go to a major meeting without strangers lying in wait outside her room, knocking on the door, or calling her on the phone. These people are generally unhappy, frustrated, depressed—even suicidal. As a result, wherever she goes Jean takes her notebooks with her, because she knows a lot of people in different cities; when someone approaches her for help, she gets out her lists to try to find a resource in the local community.

"If you're out in front as a general helper," she explained, "then people you've never heard of will show up, desperate to talk. It's a very difficult time to live. People today don't have the family or the communal sources of support, so someone who appears on television or is written about in a magazine or newspaper becomes a kind of archetype of a support system. Their coming to you may not be for who you are at all, then, but just because you're someone and you're *there*. But it may also be a critical event for them, so you have to be careful to say the right thing, and careful that because of exhaustion you don't close off. You have to really *be* there in a real human exchange; you have to care."

In an odd way Jean Houston seems to combine great strength with great vulnerability. She's the pied piper, but probably any child who was in need could lead *her* astray. The vulnerability may have taken root during one particularly troubled period in her life. She was eighteen at the time and she had had what she calls "an excessively successful adolescence." Having grown up in a theatrical family, she had more poise and more presence than most of her contemporaries. Since she was a natural leader, she was elected president of practically everything she joined. She was also up for the Olympics in fencing, and she had won a major drama award. Then one day when she was onstage a piece of scenery fell on her head and she was partially blinded. For months afterward she could make out colors, light and shadow, and some forms, but she needed a cane to get around. Then, in a devastating series of events, someone whom she loved very much died; her marks went down because she couldn't see and couldn't concentrate; she lost all her offices; and there was talk that she might have to drop out of college because she couldn't do the work.

"I took one last course," she recalled, "and the professor was so brilliant that I found I started to ask questions again. One day he caught me by the elbow when I was finding my way to the bus stop and he said, 'Miss Houston, let me talk to you. You have an interesting mind.'" He asked her opinion on a philosophical question and when she said, "I don't know," he replied, "Oh yes you do. You couldn't ask the questions you do without knowing."

Jean had many other conversations with him after that and, as she put it, she was soon "off and running. And I haven't shut up since," she added cheerfully. "What he did was, he *empowered* me. I was acknowledged. I swore afterward that, wherever I could, if I found people who were in the process of acute disacknowledgment and who were falling away, I would stop and find out where and who and what and find some way to acknowledge them."

That troubled time, now long behind her, left Jean Houston with a tragic sense of life and the conviction that we are all vulnerable. "I had been very cocky," she said, "but that experience democratized my psyche quite radically. Afterward I had a real sense that we are all of the same piece.

"There are people who go through their whole lives without a real meeting and sharing," she continued, "and sharing is important. I personally believe that the greatest human potential there is is the potential we have to yeast the other person and be yeasted: to acknowledge and empower."

The German poet Rainer Maria Rilke once wrote: "Love consists in this, that two solitudes protect, and touch, and greet each other." His is a haunting but rather lonely view of love, for it *is* possible at times to reach out to another person and to "yeast" him, as Jean puts it, to find and respond to the best that's in him. And that's a gift of energy that spills over in all directions.

In a deep and enduring way vitality springs from connectedness and, as Jean said, from commitment. When you feel that you're a secure part of a close social network, and when you commit yourself to working for something that is bigger and more important than you are, you contact wellsprings of human energy. However, many people today instead feel *dis*connected and alone, having no commitment to anything except themselves and their own narrow day-to-day concerns. Individually they're apt to fall short of their potential in many ways. Cumulatively they affect the energy level of the culture itself.

In a newspaper interview Lord Kenneth Clark, the noted British art historian, once pointed out the ramifications of cultural energy. "Now that we only believe in material products," he said, "we are in danger of losing the sense of humility that comes from imagining something beyond and larger than oneself. . . . Civilizations are fragile things and a feeling of hopelessness can overtake people even with a high degree of material comfort." Lord Kenneth believes that *energy is what* makes *a civilization.*

Energy Tips

1. How much stimulation do *you* need? how much social contact? If you're happiest when you're surrounded by a cast of thousands, then that's what you require for energy. But if a constant bustle of people wears you out, then you may have to acknowledge and honor your own need for periods of real solitude.

2. Give some thought to your rhythm of speech and silence and the way it meshes with, or fails to mesh with, the rhythms of some of the people you know. Watch out for and enjoy comple-

mentarity when you come across it, the sense it can give you of effortless communication and an effortless flow of energy.

3. How do you react to being interrupted or to not getting a quick response from someone you're talking to? Knowing what makes you feel uptight and how that affects your energy rhythm may help you react less strongly.

4. If there's someone in your life who's a drain on your energy, ask yourself why that's so. Is it just that you're responding to his (or her) basic hostility? Does he remind you of someone, so that his very presence reactivates feelings you have trouble dealing with? Are you "catching" his emotions? If you are, is it because *you* feel somehow responsible for the way *he* feels? Once you understand your own reaction, the relationship should become less tense and irritating—and less wearing.

5. Don't hesitate to spend your emotional energy on the people and causes you believe in. There's nothing more energy-sustaining than the feeling that you have a place in the scheme of things; than knowing that there are people who care for you and will be there when you need them; than knowing that you're committed to something bigger than you are.

6. When you acknowledge and celebrate the best that's in others, that's energizing both for them and for you.

Other Kinds of Energy

So far I've been talking about energy in the most general sense —as your experience of your own potential from moment to moment. But what about your sense of your sexual or creative potential? And what about nervous energy, mental energy, and the psychic sort?

The third section of this book will move on to consider specific kinds of energy that are obviously related to everyday vitality but that aren't quite explained by it. We'll also discuss what to do in an energy crisis, when your vitality has somehow evaporated, and how to cope if you can't keep up with the man (or the woman) in your life—or if they can't keep up with you.

The next chapter, however, will analyze the sort of energy many people would rather have less of—nervous energy.

III
VARIETIES OF
HUMAN ENERGY

Making Peace with Nervous Energy

Ellie Dylan: How to Ride an Adrenaline High

Ellie Dylan, ex-disc jockey, is a sprig of a woman, barely five feet tall. She's dark-haired, green-eyed, with an infectious smile and a warm southern drawl. She weighs just eighty-two pounds, and when she's dressed, as she often is, in Levis and running shoes she's punk-sized and looks like somebody's kid sister.

When I met her, Ellie Dylan already had her own show on New York City television, though she was still in her twenties. Called "You," it had a magazine-type format, and so each week Ellie reported on subjects ranging from high-tech furnishings to discos. On camera she sampled food in Chinatown and roller-skated with the pros. She even donned climbing equipment once to tackle the side of a New York City skyscraper.

"I always feel on edge before I go on camera," Ellie said. "It's a real adrenaline high, and it's good, because if you felt relaxed—as if the show was nothing—you'd be boring. But while you're waiting to go on you have to do something with the energy. My favorite thing is paper clips—I bend them—and I chew about five packs of sugarless gum. Johnny Carson paces back and forth—I've seen him."

When a show went really well, Ellie said, the adrenaline continued to flow throughout and then afterward there was an incredible high. "Coming back from a shoot, when you know you've done something really good, you go from being high to infinity, and that's what makes the whole thing worthwhile."

Ellie grew up in Columbus, Georgia, a town of about three

hundred thousand. "I'm Jewish," she said, "and I was one of the few Jews in Columbus. I've always been a little different." When she was fifteen she was a thoroughgoing rebel—she was even suspended from school once for wearing skirts that were too short. But Ellie went on to graduate Phi Beta Kappa and magna cum laude in 1974 from Tulane University, in New Orleans.

The next step was supposed to be law school, but the summer after graduation Ellie took a job with a talk show on a Georgia radio station to fill the time. "I played devil's advocate," she recalled, "with all these southern guests, like the young guy who's the head of the Ku Klux Klan. But I was making eighty dollars a week, so I asked for a raise. When they said no, I left." Before she left, though, she heard that NBC in Chicago was looking for a disc jockey. She sent in a tape she'd made and landed the job—at a starting salary of forty thousand dollars a year!

As "the queen of country music," Ellie was an immediate success and was soon shifted to a better time slot. By 1977 she'd been moved to New York City to become what radio people call the "morning man" on WNBC-AM. She was, in fact, one of the few woman disc jockeys ever to work the 6 A.M. to 10 A.M. "drive time" shift, which attracts lots of advertising money and is almost always handled by men.

With the move to New York, Ellie also switched from playing country music to rock, but that didn't bother her. "Country music let me be me," she explained. "All my life I've tried to conform, but I felt shackled and I just couldn't do it. I love rock 'n' roll, too, though—it's pure energy." After eight months as the "morning man" Ellie left to try her luck on television. The very first show she made for "You" was nominated for three Emmys.

Asked about her energy, Ellie said that she doesn't really do anything special to keep it up: "The most exercise I get is walking out the door to catch a cab, and I only get about four hours of sleep a night. All my life everybody has always told me, 'You have so much enthusiasm, you're so energetic.' I don't really see it. But I know I do have this incredible ambition, incredible drive. Sometimes I can feel it—it vibrates, I get so into it."

Obstacles Can Generate Energy

Ellie's drive is actually fed by challenges and opposition. She recalled, "Everyone said I'd never make it in radio because I had a southern accent and I was a woman. So many people were telling me I couldn't do it that I said, 'God damn it, I can!' Then, later, people in radio told me that disc jockeys can never cross over into television. Well, I did. The first obstacle most people have is that they say to themselves, 'I could never do that,' and then it's no longer a possibility.

"I'm a real uphill or downhill sort of person," she continued. "I have highs and lows but no in-betweens." About 90 percent of the time Ellie is at the high end of her spectrum, but even her lows are filled with vitality, though it's a different sort of drive. "They're cosmic lows," she said, "and they happen because I'm trying to reason out what's going on in the world. Why am I here? What's my purpose in life? My lows are full of energy, because I'm searching for something; I'm confused and wondering what's going on. They have the same intensity as the highs, but they're just different." When I asked her whether they interfered with her working schedule, she was surprised at the question. She allowed that it might be nice to lie back at times and puzzle things out, but her life-style doesn't permit time out for brooding.

"I think basically I want to be loved," she said. "Most people who are in front of the camera instead of behind it want to be loved." But Ellie had found that becoming a celebrity was something of a mixed experience. She was beginning to be recognized when she was out in public. Sometimes, when she was having dinner at a restaurant, people would stare or they'd come over and speak to her. The stares occasionally made her uncomfortable, but in general she enjoyed the recognition: "It's like instant friends. I love all the parts of it except the wondering sometimes whether people are being nice to you when they wouldn't otherwise, so that you have to think to yourself, 'Does this person really like *me*?' "

Fame can generate its own brand of insecurity, for success

doesn't necessarily banish all self-doubts. In fact, Ellie noted, "There are lots of people in this business who seem to function totally out of insecurity. They're constantly pushing to prove themselves and to be loved."

She believes that energy is a product of both security and insecurity, or of the balance between them. As time goes on, and as she becomes more secure within herself, Ellie draws more and more of her own energy from self-assurance. But since insecurity can also generate a lot of inner drive, she wouldn't knock it for a minute.

Nervous Energy: A Symptom of Stress?

The adrenaline high that Ellie experiences when she's on camera is undoubtedly nervous energy. The sort of inner push that's generated by insecurity is probably also more nervous than not, while the energy she associates with feelings of self-assurance is enerjoy.

As I suggested in Chapter 3, nervous energy seems to be part of the so-called fight-or-flight response that arouses the body in emergency situations. At such moments—when a speeding car is bearing down on you, for example—that energy and the body changes that go with it can save your life. In fact, they're standard human survival equipment, handed down from the days when escaping from predators and capturing prey were what living was all about.

But that hum of nervous energy is also a sign that you're under stress, and most Americans know now that *over the long run* stress can be dangerous. Medical studies have demonstrated that it can lead to asthma, headaches, ulcers, high blood pressure, heart disease, and innumerable other health problems. It may even be to blame when you catch a cold, the theory being that first stress makes you vulnerable and then the next virus that comes along lays you low.

Prolonged stress also drains away vitality. Partly that's because of the anxiety that so often accompanies stress. It makes itself felt as an intense apprehensiveness that interferes with the ability to concentrate and can produce distracting psychosomatic symptoms. Then, too, people under stress often keep their muscles tensed, almost as if bracing themselves against some threat. Usually they're not aware of their own tension, nor do they realize that it prevents them from moving freely, so that it costs more in energy to move at all. (To feel for yourself what's involved here, grip a pencil as tightly as you can and then try to write with it.) And there's the fact that when the body is kept combat-ready for too long, with internal systems racing, eventually it must slump into exhaustion.

Of course, there's no such thing as a stress-free life, and even if there were it would be a colossal bore. The trick is to organize your life so that you live with just enough stress—which also means just enough nervous energy—though what's "just enough" will vary tremendously from one person to the next. To Ellie, for example, the stress of being on camera is exhilarating; someone else might find it practically paralyzing.

It's worth noting that there are at least two different kinds of stress. There's the kind you generate yourself when you opt for a hectic, high-pressure life. Some people, like Ellie, seem to crave that kind of life, or at least they thrive on it. Then there's the grim kind of stress (associated with death, divorce, and taxes) that's visited on you by circumstances beyond your control. Again, people are different: Some go through terrible ordeals and emerge unscathed while others in similar circumstances buckle under and become very ill. The question that most intrigues stress researchers right now is: What makes the difference?

But before we consider that question, let's take a closer look at the people who generate their own stress.

Are You a Stress Seeker?

It's a safe bet that most, if not all, of those who reach the top in any really competitive field, like television, must thrive on stress. But they're not the only ones. There are stress seekers in almost every occupation and at every level of society.

Peggy is a case in point. A woman in her thirties and a mother of two, she recently went back to work as an insurance broker.

She puts in long hours at the office and even longer ones at home, trying to keep her house as spotless and her children as happy as they were before she became a working mother. Peggy is unwilling to lower her standards in any way. "I'm running full-time and [I'm] exhausted all the time, but it's great fun and I love it," she says enthusiastically. However, she's often so tense that the very air around her seems to tingle with nervous energy.

Theoretically Peggy's life will become less harried once she settles into her new job; but, in fact, she's the kind of person who generates her own pressures. Even before she went back to work, she was constantly on the run, heavily involved in community activities. "My husband says I'm perennially overcommitted, but I think I'm happiest that way," she said.

Mel is like Peggy, only more so. A full-time college student, he also holds a full-time job as a reporter on a local newspaper. In his "spare time" he's involved in extracurricular activities on campus. Mel typically gets by on about four hours' sleep a night, often hasn't time for meals, and has seldom been known to crack a textbook until just a week or so before exams. "I scrape by," he said. "I learn fast. Of course, I forget fast too, but who has time to do it any other way?"

What makes Melvin run? How can he maintain a schedule, month after month, that would exhaust most people within a week? The simplest explanation is energy: He may be just a sprinter capitalizing on his own exuberant vitality. If that's the case, then his life-style, which looks so pressured, really isn't—for him.

It's also possible that he's a sensation seeker who needs a lot of stimulation (see Chapter 12). The odd thing about the negative emotions is that in small doses they're rather enjoyable: Everyone likes to feel a little frightened, a little anxious, a little angry. Books, movies, and television exist to provide those pleasures. Some people—sky divers for example—like a lot of intense emotion. They literally get a charge out of that adrenaline high. The sensations they seem to be seeking are internal ones, but for people who are constitutionally rigged to need a lot of stimulation internal arousal may fill the bill.

Whether Mel is a sprinter, a sensation seeker, or both, his penchant for high-pressure living would be a matter of basic temperament, something inborn. And that's more or less the explanation favored by Dr. Hans Selye. Dr. Selye was the first to suggest to a skeptical world that stress can be dangerous and can lead to physical illness. Today, when his groundbreaking insight is no longer questioned and the word "stress" has come to have an ominous sound, Selye himself often emphasizes the fact that some people actually seek stress.

"There is the racehorse type of person and there is the turtle," he said, "and the difference is inborn. If you force a turtle to run like a racehorse, it will die, and if a racehorse is forced to run no faster than a turtle, it, too, will suffer." Selye would never condemn a racehorse like Mel to a quiet vacation at a secluded beach. He explained that for racers inactivity is stress, though for turtles, of course, beaches are fine. Obviously, Selye spoke from firsthand experience, for he himself was most definitely a racehorse. Though he was in his seventies, he still kept himself as busy as possible. When I talked to him early in 1978 he was contemplating with pleasure a schedule that would have him delivering lectures in four different cities in four days.

"Every person has to find his own best stress level, the highest level of activity that is pleasant for him," he said.

Stress Seekers Who Shouldn't

Unfortunately it's not that easy. Some racers run, not because they have an energy surplus and can afford to, but because it's a way to avoid facing their own emotions. As long as they're frantically busy they can hold anxiety and depression at bay. Others arrange to be continually under pressure because they need to feel punished. Deep down they're convinced that they don't deserve a chance to relax and enjoy life. Peggy's nonstop schedule, for example, may be her way of doing penance because she feels guilty whenever she escapes the domestic routine.

Then there are the Type A's. Research shows that people who are aggressive, competitive, and hard-driving—dubbed the Type A personality—are much more likely to develop heart disease than are the more relaxed Type B's. Mel may actually have a bad case of "hurry sickness," the classic Type A urge to accomplish more and more in less and less time.

How can you tell—if you're someone with a high-pressure schedule—whether you're doing yourself damage or whether you're simply a high-energy type and that's the right amount of stress for you? The way you feel ought to be a clue, since most people believe they can distinguish between nervous energy and the more productive sort. However, a study done at Eckerd College in St. Petersburg, Florida, indicates that though Type A's actually react more strongly to stress than most people—in terms of blood pressure and heart rate—they're generally unaware of how agitated they've become. Apparently they're so used to being strung out that they no longer recognize the feeling when it occurs.

Until there's a sure-fire way to tell the sprinters from the people who are simply driven, all anyone can do is suggest that racers like Peggy and Mel read their bodies as carefully as they can and remain alert to the difference between the energy that flows from a sense of well-being and the nervous energy that's a by-product of stress.

People Who Seem to Be Stress-proof

Every life sees its share of calamities, situations that would seem guaranteed to devastate any human being. Yet some people seem to be born survivors—they come through symptom-free.

This is the great mystery of stress research. Why is it that, faced with a cataclysmic event such as bankruptcy or a death in the family, one person suffers a heart attack, another gets headaches, and a third has no health problems at all? If science could just deduce answers to that question, we might find ways to prevent stress-related illnesses. (Incidentally, we'd also be better at prescribing the right amount of stress for ourselves.)

The chances are, though, that the answers to the puzzle are highly complex, as complex as human beings themselves and the psychological defenses they evolve for dealing with life. For we respond to stress in at least four different and interrelated ways: by what we do, by what we feel, by what we think, and by the way we react physiologically. These responses combine into patterns that vary greatly from one individual to the next.

This is evident from the work of Dr. John Mason of Yale University, a psychoendocrinologist who's interested in the way stress affects the body's hormones (see Chapter 3). Some years ago, back in 1960 and 1961, Dr. Mason was involved in a study of men and women facing the most terrible kind of pressure there is: They had children who were dying of leukemia.

While the children were being treated at the National Cancer Institute, the parents were invited to take part in the study. By analyzing their psychological and physiological reactions to stress, researchers hoped to learn how to help others.

Forty-six parents eventually participated. Except for a few who lived nearby, they stayed at the hospital, so that they could spend as much time as possible with their children. They lived together on a special ward, sharing quarters and often providing emotional support for one another. They filled out brief daily questionnaires, were interviewed by psychologists at regular intervals, and were quietly observed by the staff throughout their stay. In addition, urine samples were frequently collected to get a measurement of the amount of 17-hydroxycorticosteroid (17-OHCS) the body was producing. It's known that during times of stress the 17-OHCS level usually rises, a sign that particular hormones, including cortisol, are circulating in quantity.

Psychological Defenses Against Stress

In all of the literature on stress, few other studies point up so clearly the way psychological defense mechanisms can affect the bodily response to stress. For, though some of the parents, as expected, ran 17-OHCS levels that were chronically high and that spiked higher whenever their child was in a medical crisis, in others the 17-OHCS level was consistently low and actually dipped even lower during crises. It was as if the defense mechanism that was operating overcompensated at times.

Many of the parents who had unusually low levels of 17-OHCS were those who worked hard to deny the seriousness of their child's illness. Blindly optimistic, they would continue to talk about which college the youngster would go to, for example, even though they'd been told he was terminally ill. When an interviewer inadvertently breached the defenses of one such mother, so that she poured out painful thoughts that she hadn't confided to anyone before, her 17-OHCS level immediately rose from the low to the middle range. Soon after the interview, she reverted to blind denial and her 17-OHCS level sank and didn't rise again—even on the day of the child's death. *Obviously, what a person tells herself—or allows herself to know—in a desperate situation can affect the way her body registers the stress.* This fact has important implications that we'll come to in a minute.

There were also parents who *showed* little emotion, though their 17-OHCS output was high. In spite of this physical evidence that they were feeling the pressure, some seemed unaware of their own distress. And there was one woman who reacted in exactly the opposite way: Though she appeared to be almost constantly upset, her 17-OHCS level was generally stable and low. The researchers noted that several times she was sitting quietly alone when someone walked into the room, and she immediately became very agitated. She was small and frail; the staff on the ward tended to protect her. It seems, then, that her defense was *expressing* emotion, perhaps partly as a way of manipulating others and partly as a way of handling the feelings involved. Two days before the end she suddenly became calm and settled down to attending to her child's needs. Simultaneously her 17-OHCS level shot up.

Obviously, hormones don't just respond automatically to a stressful situation. In fact, Dr. Mason states that it's not the stress itself but the *effectiveness* of the individual's defenses that is reflected in the 17-OHCS level.

Titillating though they may be in small doses, at full strength negative emotions are painful to experience, and so we all learn ways of moderating such feelings as fear, anger, and grief. In the process some of us also learn not to betray our emotions by our behavior; others learn to suppress all awareness of the emotion even though the visceral changes that go with it still occur; and some seem able to suppress both the awareness and the physiological reaction.

What Happens When You Deny Reality?

Since denial is regarded as a primitive sort of defense—in fact, psychiatrists maintain that we pay a high price for denying feelings—I asked Dr. Mason whether he thought it was a good idea to shut off emotions, to be unable or unwilling to experience them, and to have a body that doesn't register them either. He pointed out that the answer to that question depends on what your values are. In any situation denial can prevent you from dealing realistically with problems. In the context of this particular study, a mother who denied the seriousness of her child's illness would be no help at all if the youngster guessed the truth and needed to talk about it. On the other hand, her denial exists to help her tolerate the situation, and it's possible that without it she couldn't function at all.

"Whether denial is a good or bad thing to do *physiologically* is a different story," Dr. Mason said, "and we only have pieces of that so far." The evidence is, in fact, somewhat contradictory. Several researchers have looked at the way denial seems to affect the course of a disease, asking whether the patient who denies the seriousness of his condition has a better or worse chance of recovering than the patient who faces reality. Though one study found that hospital patients who fail to do "the work of worrying" before an operation are slower to recover, several other researchers have come to the opposite conclusion. On the basis of preliminary evidence from one such study, Dr. Richard Lazarus of the University of California at Berkeley said, "In a hospital the avoider/denier types seem to recover faster and more smoothly than do the vigilants, who keep searching for information. Vigilants might do better in other contexts, but there's something particular about a hospital. They want information so that they can control events, but in a hospital there's nothing you can control." It seems, then, that to say whether a defense is a good or bad way to cope with stress, you have to ask how it works in a given situation.

Whatever effects denial has on health, you do pay a price for it emotionally. The parents from the leukemia study who showed no signs of grief in the period before their child's death suffered more and for a longer period afterward. As noted in Chapter 4, denial also seems to be expensive in terms of mental energy, for it's not easy to turn off negative or painful thoughts. When you do so deliberately it's called suppression, and psychiatrists believe that suppression is one of the more useful defense mechanisms. *Denial, on the other hand, buries an idea or emotion so deeply that the individual is unaware of its existence. That would seem to be even more difficult to do than simply refusing to dwell on the matter, and more costly in terms of energy.*

How Infants Deal with Stress

Defenses are at the heart of the way we cope with stress. They put in an appearance so early in life that it seems likely that *the particular defenses we adopt may be partially determined by the temperament we're born with.*

Support for this speculation comes from a study done by three University of Colorado researchers who looked at separation anxiety in infants just eleven to thirteen months old. The experimental situation itself was disarmingly mundane: An experimenter simply called at the baby's home and baby-sat for an hour while the mother went out. The infant's urine, collected in a plastic bag tucked into the diapers, was later analyzed for the level of cortisol. Urine collected on days when mother and child were not separated provided a reading on what the baby's cortisol level normally was.

Though most of the twenty infants studied tolerated the separation relatively well, a few didn't, showing their distress in two quite different ways. Four of the babies burst into tears when their mothers departed, their agitation continuing throughout the time that she was gone. These children not only produced an increased amount of cortisol because of the separation, but even on the days when they weren't under stress they ran a relatively high level of it. Two other babies cried when their mothers disappeared and then withdrew and became completely inactive, refusing to look at or respond to the experimenter. Under stress their cortisol levels remained low; in fact, under normal circumstances they were low compared to the other infants. The pattern was similar to that of the parents in the leukemia study who used denial as a defense.

Withdrawal is an unusual reaction in an infant, but it's not considered abnormal. Mrs. Katherine Tennes, who headed the Colorado study, estimated that perhaps 10 percent of all babies behave that way. Though it's conceivable that such withdrawal is a forerunner of the adult defense of denial, year-old infants probably don't know enough about reality to deny it. Mrs. Tennes suggested that their behavior might better be described as regression: They were either regressing physiologically to a drowsy state that would protect them from overstimulation or they were regressing psychologically into the total helplessness they felt at an earlier age.

Mrs. Tennes was surprised that babies so young already exhibited such clear-cut patterns in the way they reacted to stress. The fact that some infants ran a high level of cortisol even on nonstress days—and they were the ones who became most agitated—suggests that they were in some way biochemically primed to respond. Perhaps they were born with a highly reactive endocrine system. "It may be," Mrs. Tennes said, "that we learn different ways of coping according to what we have to work with constitutionally."

If all this seems to suggest that human defense systems are deep-rooted and immensely complex, it's meant to. Though defenses may be crucial to the way we handle stress, they're not easy to change. Mostly we're not even aware which defenses we use, and long-term psychotherapy is about the only way to change them.

Stress Is What You Think it Is

However, I don't mean to say that it's impossible to improve on the way you cope with stress, that if it's a significant drain on your energy there's nothing you can do about it. Stress is very much in the mind of the beholder: What you tell yourself about a situation determines how pressured you feel.

I first realized just how true this is—and how important—when

I had the chance to interview two air-traffic controllers. Theirs is said to be one of the most pressured jobs there is: One mistake in judgment or one significant lapse in attention and two planes may collide, killing hundreds of people. Understandably, controllers are prone to high blood pressure and ulcers. However, as in virtually any other situation, some seem magically immune to the stress that's the undoing of others.

In 1978 I approached the Federal Aviation Agency (FAA) and asked to interview a couple of healthy, contented controllers. I talked first to Lynne DiGillio, a vividly attractive young woman in her twenties.

Lynne: "I Think I'm a Strong Person"

"The stress I feel is from the other people who work here, not from the airplanes," Lynne said emphatically. She was the second woman ever to work in New York City's Kennedy Airport control tower and the first woman to become a fully qualified controller there. Yet some of the male controllers were still hostile to her. She was frequently harassed and criticized for everything from the way she dressed to the way she handled planes.

Lynne refused to react to the personal remarks and the disparaging comments about women, though she did defend herself if someone derided her skill as a controller. She reminded herself that part of the problem was the atmosphere in the tower, which tended to be tense, frenetic, and emotionally charged: People were always blowing up at other people. "The tower is very small and there could be fifteen of us working there at a time," she said. "Personalities are magnified. Everything is magnified the way it is on [the] stage."

Yet she enjoyed the excitement and felt that she worked better under pressure. She preferred summer days, when the air traffic increased by half and the job was tougher than ever, rather than the midnight shift, when controllers worked less traffic.

Lynne had a healthy sense of her own self-worth. "If you have more respect for other people's opinion of you than you have for your own opinion," she said, "that holds you back." She explained that hers wasn't an easy childhood, but that it taught her that she *could* cope well in difficult circumstances. "I think I'm a strong person," she said.

She made a great point of not taking her work home with her, although occasionally she couldn't help it. After one clash with another controller it took her four hours to unwind. She spent most of that time talking on the phone to friends—about almost anything except her work.

Charlie: "Attitude Is the Answer"

Charlie Nichols was in his sixties and had been a controller for over twenty years. A short, wiry, white-haired man, he jogged ten miles a day and commuted an hour and twenty minutes each way to his job at Kennedy Airport. Charlie, like Lynne, believed that "the controllers who run into trouble are the ones who take their work home. I learned early in the game to leave my problems on the far side of my front door."

In fact, he felt that attitude is the whole answer. "For example, when I'm talking to a pilot I dissociate," he said. "It's just me and the pilot; I don't think about the passengers." Dwelling on the passengers, on the fact that he was responsible for all those lives, wouldn't help. Charlie also refused to become irritated over pilots who gave him an argument, demanding a shorter route, or over the occasional arrogance of the young. "Sometimes trainees look at me as though I'm an old fuddy-duddy," he said cheerfully, "but that doesn't bother me. I know I've been there and back and they haven't started yet."

In Dr. Selye's terms Charlie and Lynne are both racehorses: They enjoy the fast pace of a job that's never the same two days in a row. In any high-pressure job it makes all the difference if you love your work; Selye says that the trick is to find work that, for you, is play.

But these two controllers also had other factors in their favor that seem equally important. They both had a strong sense of their own self-worth—they're not easily put down by other people, though apparently that's one of the psychological hazards of the job. And they had great mental discipline, which showed in their ability to forget about the work as soon as they got away from the airport.

Mental discipline is also what was involved when Charlie dissociated and when Lynne spent time talking on the phone to friends
rather than dwelling on her problems.

These and a few of the other tactics Lynne and Charlie used
jibe well with the theories of stress researchers. For though no
one has yet discovered a sure-fire way to prevent an overdose of
stress, I've come across a number of constructive suggestions
that can help most of us to cope with it more intelligently than
we do.

Energy Tips: A Dozen Ways to Cope with Stress

1. Whenever you're feeling pressured, *examine the situation
realistically.* Sometimes tension and persistent psychosomatic
complaints are a message from mind and body that something is
very wrong. If you feel that the pace and the pressures at work
are "killing you," for example, the solution may be to change
jobs, though of course that's seldom an easy decision to make.
You have to ask yourself whether the job is worth the price
you're paying in stress and misspent energy. As California stress
researcher Richard Lazarus put it, "People have internalized
commitments, things they believe in that give meaning to their
lives. What we're talking about are conflicts in values."

Sometimes a situation is stressful and yet there's no way you
can escape it. You may have to stick it out for a while in an impossible job. You may have no choice but to wait days for the results of medical tests that will tell you whether your health problem is serious or trivial. In situations such as these, meditation
and relaxation techniques can help to make life more tolerable.

2. *Practice worry control.* If your problem is job-related, learn
to leave your worries at work the way Lynne and Charlie do.

As noted in Chapter 10, the best way to suppress worries and
thoughts you'd rather not have is to concentrate on something
else. In other words, the trick is to distract yourself; and for
many people human contact provides the most effective distraction. Lynne knew what she was doing when she spent the evening chatting with friends after a bad day at work.

But if, despite your best efforts, a particular worry keeps nag-ging at you, it may help to ask yourself: What's the worst thing that can happen? One woman I know, concerned because she'd made a foolish mistake at the office, asked herself that question and the answer that popped into her head was, "I'll be fired." This snapped the problem into perspective, since her mistake simply wasn't that serious. More important, she realized that even if she were fired it wouldn't be the end of the world.

At times it may also help to remind yourself that not everyone has to like you. "I once said something tactless to one of my colleagues," a social worker recalled, "and from that day on she was down on me. I apologized, but it didn't help. I agonized until it finally occurred to me that I'm not a terrible person just because she dislikes me. Since I grew up feeling everyone had to like me, that was a revelation." At times it's vital to be able to do without the good opinion of others, as Lynne and Charlie can.

3. *Try exercising regularly.* It's not just that strenuous exercise can relieve anxiety and depression and burn off anger. In addition, if you're physically fit you're better able to withstand life's pressures. Dr. Robert Rose, a stress researcher at the University of Texas, suggested, "If we did the simple things our grandparents talked about—getting enough sleep, not drinking too much, smoking very moderately (if at all), and exercising daily— we'd decrease the risks of stress just because the body would be in better shape."

4. *Use your leisure activities to lower your stress level.* The things you do in your spare time offer one of the simplest ways to manage stress. Some years ago scientists discovered that the 17-OHCS level responds sensitively to many ordinary activities (see Chapter 3). We recognize this when we turn to violent action films or sports events for a mildly strung-up high. We can also reverse the process and use activities such as reading or daydreaming to tone down physiological arousal.

5. *Choose activities that match your own particular stress response.* Recent research suggests that everyone reacts to stress either mentally, physically, or in both ways simultaneously. If you know what your own pattern is, you can choose an appropriate remedy. For instance, people who react mentally often find it difficult to concentrate when they're under pressure. They're plagued by indecision and they worry over unimportant

things; they sometimes have terrifying fantasies or find that they can't fend off thoughts that make them anxious. What they need are activities that distract the mind: a good book, a game of bridge or chess, or a crossword puzzle.

Others express the stress reaction through the body. If this is your pattern, then when you're under pressure you tend to perspire a lot; your heart races, you feel jittery, and you're driven to pacing the floor. Sometimes you can feel the tension in your stomach, and you may develop diarrhea. A physical response to stress calls for a physical remedy: a brisk walk, a long swim, or some other strenuous activity.

There are also people who react to stress with mind and body in almost equal proportions: They're jittery, sweaty, *and* easily distracted. The best solution is a physical activity that also demands concentration, such as tennis or handball.

6. *Watch for your limits where stress is concerned.* If you've had a number of major changes in your life within the past year, don't push yourself too far by adding more. Research indicates that any major change that is either good or bad—a promotion, a marriage, a divorce, a death in the family—can be stressful and that the cumulative effect of too many changes in a short time can be devastating.

7. *Value—and take advantage of—your social network.* Many studies have shown that people with family and friends to fall back on are less likely to develop stress symptoms.

8. *Try not to fritter away energy when reacting to daily hassles.* In Berkeley Professor Lazarus has tested the theory that hassles—small, everyday stresses—can be as harmful in their cumulative effect as major life changes. Together with a group of University of California graduate students, Lazarus studied one hundred ordinary people who periodically returned to him forms on which they had checked off, from a long list, the hassles they'd undergone in the previous month. The list included such items as: having an argument with your spouse; commuting in heavy traffic; an overload at work; friction with a coworker; and so on.

Hassles are very much an individual matter—what makes one person tense may not even register with another—and so it's clear that attitude makes all the difference. If, then, you can identify situations in your own life that leave you feeling uptight—

perhaps by keeping a record for a week or so—you may be able to avoid some of them altogether. Others can be defused by a change in attitude. For example, some people are compulsive about being on time. If that's your problem, the next time you're tense and unhappy because you're running behind schedule, ask yourself: What's the worst that can happen if I'm late? Usually the consequences aren't that terrible. It's also smarter not to look at your watch if you're late and stuck in traffic, since looking at it won't get you there any faster and it *will* make you nervous.

For many people time is a form of pressure; there never seems to be enough of it. As one woman said ruefully, "I'm just waiting for someone to invent the nine-day week." One way to ease that sort of stress is to remind yourself that you can only go as fast as you can go and then avoid looking at clocks whenever possible. I've found that at times when I'm really pressured I'm better off if I don't wear a watch at all.

9. *Pay attention to your uplifts.* Uplifts are the small, ordinary things that make you feel good. Dr. Lazarus has studied them, too, because he suspects that the balance between uplifts and hassles may be important. Uplifts, he says, are "the things that sustain people." His list of examples is long and just reading it was enough to make me feel good: receiving a compliment; getting enough sleep; eating out; being lucky; saving money; gossiping; feeling healthy; daydreaming; good weather; meeting a challenge; exercising; and so on. (I'm sure uplifts count for more if you slow down long enough to notice and enjoy them.)

10. *Try to identify and improve on your own coping patterns.* The next time you're involved in a hassle, sit down afterward and think how you handled it. Researchers agree that coping skills make a crucial difference in any stress situation. (Incidentally, they're not to be confused with defenses, which are pervasive approaches to life and are almost always unconscious. Coping skills are more superficial and also easier to identify and change.)

In any difficult situation there are at least four basic tacks you can take: research the problem; try to change things; avoid taking any action even though your first impulse is to act; or try to relieve stress by what you tell yourself—for example, by reassuring yourself that you've solved similar dilemmas before. Most attempts to cope, according to Dr. Lazarus, attack the problem in one or more of these ways.

More specifically, Lazarus has produced a list of sixty-eight items—representing ways to cope—and most are at least a possibility in any situation. For instance, if you think back to the last time you lost your temper, did you: blame yourself? just concentrate on what you had to do next? go over the problem again and again in your mind to try to understand it? turn to work or a substitute activity to take your mind off it? go on as if nothing had happened? concentrate on something good that could come out of the whole thing? sleep more than usual? try to forget the whole thing?

Many people develop patterns of coping and use them again and again in particular situations. When a pattern doesn't work well, sometimes just realizing that there are alternatives can help you break out of it.

11. *Learn from the times when you cope badly.* Make it a habit at bedtime to review the events of the day. Congratulate yourself on small triumphs (that's an uplift), but don't waste energy blaming yourself for mistakes. Instead, think how you might have handled the situation differently. One woman who does this regularly calls it "good exercise for the psyche."

12. When you're feeling pressured, *try seizing control of your life in some new way.* Make an effort to say "no" more often to the things you don't want to do, give up smoking, or go on a diet. I know a man who had been depressed for months—overwhelmed by both internal and external pressures—when he suddenly decided to lose some weight. "I felt I just had to make some kind of change in my life," he said, "and I knew that losing weight was one thing I could do." In the end, he managed to shed thirty pounds and ended his diet not only thinner but charged with new energy.

Dr. Leonard Syme of the University of California at Berkeley pointed out that nothing makes you feel happier with yourself than successfully changing your behavior, a fact that ties into a theory of his. Research indicates that people who are part of a broad and complex social network are generally much healthier than people who are more solitary. Presumably those with friends and family they can count on are less stressed, but Dr. Syme takes this one step further. It's his hunch that our relations with others provide us with a sense of self-worth and a feeling that we can *control* our destiny and environment, not in a dramatic way but in little things, "like being able to get done this afternoon what you need to get done."

Build Confidence to Build Energy

These, then, may be the main reasons why some people handle stress so much better than others: They value themselves and go into most situations convinced that they can cope. (I'm reminded of Lynne's sober statement, "I think I'm a strong person," and of Charlie Nichols' cheerful, "I've been there and back.")

Of course, you can't simply conjure up that kind of confidence. In fact, most of us spend our whole lives trying to generate, maintain, or regain it. Interestingly enough, one route to a really heady sense of assurance is to meet a difficult challenge successfully—in other words, to overcome stress. A rock-climbing enthusiast once explained to me why he liked dangling from mountains: "I do it for the moment when I look down and I'm scared out of my wits," he said, "and for the moment after that when I conquer the fear and feel there's nothing in the world I can't do."

As Dr. Selye said, stress is the spice of life. In the very short run, if you can handle it well it's an energizer, even if it's nervous energy that's produced. More important, *stress is the way we grow, and in the right circumstances and the right amounts it can be downright exhilarating.*

Understanding Sexual Energy

Just as everyone knows what nervous energy feels like, everyone has had some experience with sexual energy as well. People usually refer to it as "sex drive," and it is perhaps the most talked about and least understood form of human energy.

The next chapter will take up the subject of sexual energy. Among other questions, it will ask: What is sexual energy? Why do some people have so much more of it than others do? And are there ways to liberate your sex drive?

14

How to Liberate Sexual Energy

• Do people who are low in energy have less sexual energy as well? Are all sprinters highly sexed?

• Does lovemaking generate energy or is it merely a way to spend energy?

• If two people are mismatched in their sexual appetites, how can they negotiate that particular energy gap?

• Are there ways to increase your sex drive?

• What *is* sexual energy, anyway? How is it different from the more general sort?

Our sex drive is powerful, unpredictable, and mysterious. Sometimes we experience it as an inner urgency that can't be ignored and that's difficult to suppress. Sometimes it's elusive; we try to will desire into existence and it just isn't there. Most of us have known both the power of the sex drive and its waywardness; in this permissive age we tend to feel good about the former and uncomfortable about the latter. As we move into the 1980s, *there are probably very few Americans who are concerned about being oversexed and a great many who sometimes worry that they may be underendowed with sexual appetite.*

It's important to understand more about sex drive and the way it operates because *it's the ultimate body truth.* We've all experienced sexual energy and so we tend to assume that everyone else feels it—and ought to express it—in the same ways that we do. Faced with the fact that someone else is different, we either assume that there must be something wrong with the *other* person or else we wonder why we're not normal ourselves.

Actually, not only do sexual preferences vary a great deal, but

—as with the general energy level—people are undoubtedly born with very different sexual-energy potentials. Certainly they grow up to be different.

Do Sprinters Have More Sexual Energy?

However (to tackle the first of the questions I've posed), there's no evidence that sprinters are necessarily highly sexed, nor that strollers have less sexual appetite than most people. Of course, there's no evidence to the contrary, either, for this is a question that has never been researched—and never will be unless someone finds an objective way to measure energy levels of both the sexual and the general sort.

Nevertheless, common sense suggests that, at least in adults, *sexual interest probably does not correlate with the general energy level, for upbringing has an extraordinarily powerful influence on sexuality—in some cases it can suppress drive altogether.* Thus, a puritanical sprinter dedicated to his career might be a lot less sexually active by choice than a sensual stroller for whom sex and intimacy have a high priority.

Sex therapists have sometimes noted that there *are* people who have little energy for anything, including sex. In fact, in trying to help someone whose drive is very low, clinicians often look first for other kinds of energy, for angry energies or assertive energies. As one therapist put it, "We ask: Does this person put his energy into anything? It's almost like basic fuel, and if he has a very low level of energy all around, then you know it will be difficult to help him."

However, the therapists I talked to didn't feel it was likely that in such cases the individual had simply been born with an overall energy deficit. They suggested that some of those who are lethargic are actually suffering from long-term, low-level depression. Others are out of touch with their own bodily reactions and with their emotions as well. They've learned to protect themselves from the knowledge that they're sexually aroused, or that they're angry or upset. In turning off their feelings they turn off their enerjoy as well.

In addition, sex therapist Leonore Tiefer, an associate professor of psychiatry at Downstate Medical Center in Brooklyn, noted that the patients who seem to be low in every kind of energy also tend to be overweight. She suggested that perhaps they're less active in general because they're carrying around more weight, and they're less active sexually because they feel unattractive.

Can You Generate Energy by Making Love?

Melanie and Phil have a good marriage and a highly satisfactory sex life. They consider themselves well matched in virtually every way. Whenever they make love, though, Phil is galvanized; afterward he's wide awake and full of energy—and usually ravenously hungry as well. While he gets up to raid the refrigerator, Melanie sinks contentedly into sleep, because after lovemaking *she* feels utterly relaxed and is unable to keep her eyes open.

Once again, people are very different, though no one knows why. Not only that, but sex varies in the effect it has from one experience to the next. Even Phil sometimes feels sleepy after intercourse if it's very late at night and he was tired to begin with.

But Phil's typical flush of energy and Melanie's drowsiness are, of course, short-term effects. *In the long run, if having sex makes you feel good about life in general and yourself in particular, it's bound to be energizing.*

One Couple's Differing Sex Drives

Differences in sex drive are much harder to reconcile than other bodily differences. In fact, they're often involved in the breakup of a relationship.

Liz and Carl, for example, lived together for four months and then parted with some bitterness. Looking back on their affair, Carl suggested that they might have married and lived happily ever after if they hadn't been mismatched in their sexual appetite. However, in retrospect Liz was sure that it wasn't the sexual-energy gap itself that was to blame but the way they both reacted to it.

"Sex was one of our many problems," she explained. "Carl was a once-a-night guy and I'm a twice-a-week woman. He made it very clear that he was unhappy because I didn't want to make love more often. He said that I must be very inhibited, and after a while I began to wonder if he was right. In the end all he had to do was mention sex and I felt pressured, angry, and insecure. He, in turn, reacted with anger and hurt feelings whenever I said 'no' to him. There were other problems between us as well, but the sex issue finally loomed so large that it seemed a waste of time to try to resolve our other differences."

According to the statistics, American couples make love, on the average, two and a half times a week. As usual, the statistics obscure enormous differences both in behavior and appetite. Premier sex researcher Alfred Kinsey was very much impressed with differences in appetite and with the fact that they seemed to be lifelong. From an early age some people have a strong and virtually unflagging sex drive, while others almost never feel the stirrings of desire. Most people, of course, fall somewhere in between.

Still, it's rare to find a couple perfectly matched in appetite, so that she's in the mood for lovemaking just as often as he is—or vice versa. And because the sex act comes decked out in strong emotions, the potential for misunderstanding is tremendous.

But before considering what can be done about a sexual-energy gap, let's go back a step and ask: What *is* sexual energy? Where does it come from? What is the physiology of desire? And why are people so different?

Nobody Ever Died of Sexual Starvation

It's hard to say exactly how sex and energy are related. In fact, sexual energy itself is difficult to define. Psychologists today think of it as a "drive"; thus, they lump physical passion in with the other basic animal requirements—the need for food, water, sleep, warmth.

However, in fundamental ways sex is quite different from

those other drives. For one thing, you can live without sex. You may feel starved for it, but the condition isn't fatal. The other drives are necessary if the individual is to survive; the sexual urge insures the survival of the species.

In addition, the need for sex doesn't come from any physical deficit we've yet been able to measure, and it doesn't feel uncomfortable, or downright painful, as hunger and thirst can. Unrelieved lust is usually a sweet sort of torment.

When you satisfy the need for food, water, or sleep you're taking energy in, but to satisfy the need for sex you have to *spend* energy. Sexual arousal feels as if the body is geared up to act and needs an outlet; in some ways it seems akin to nervous energy. In the daily flux of energy it exists as a node in the flow, a swelling of the tide. *If, in general, your energy is low—if you're depressed or physically exhausted—your sex drive falls off as well.*

Can Sex Deplete Your Energy for Other Things?

Not only does sexual desire feel like a kind of energy, but the building up and discharge of energy are inevitably a part of the experience of orgasm. As a result, some people develop strong feelings about the way sex affects their basic vitality. They define for themselves—sometimes in a fairly eccentric way—the sex-and-energy connection.

Some, for example, are convinced that sex drive has to be hoarded, that if they have sex too often they won't have the energy to do other things. Just a few generations ago this was a common belief. Athletes were urged to abstain from sex the night before the big game so that they'd have the drive to play well the next day. Opera tenors were supposed to remain celibate as opening night approached to preserve vocal energy.

New York psychotherapist Leah Schaefer, author of *Women and Sex,* remembers an actor who would give up sex entirely whenever he was deep into rehearsals. "He really felt that he had a limited amount of energy, that if he used it up in sex he wouldn't have it for his performance," she said. On the other hand, she has known other actors who liked to have sex before a performance, so that sexual thoughts wouldn't distract them and they'd be free to concentrate entirely on their part. And then there are the people (like Phil) who find that lovemaking generates energy.

Why do people react to sex so differently? "If you think sex takes something from you that you'll never get back, you tend to save it up," Dr. Schaefer suggested. "A lot of people feel that life rationed out to them a finite number of orgasms, or compliments, or money, or good times, or whatever, so they're reluctant to spend what they've got."

In addition, there's a surging power to sex that is frightening to some people. In her book *On Love and Sexuality* psychotherapist Dr. Edrita Fried points out that sexual arousal is accompanied by many strange sensations. The sense of equilibrium is affected, and so the body seems lighter; some people feel as if they're floating or actually flying. This can be a great pleasure or it can be quite terrifying. The loss of control that occurs with orgasm is a source of panic, too. Some people are afraid they'll never get back to feeling like themselves again, that they'll lose control permanently and go crazy. Small wonder, then, that they feel depleted in the wake of an orgasm.

The Sexual Side of Creativity

There are also people who experience sexual undercurrents in other forms of energy. Creativity, in particular, sometimes feels sexual. One writer I interviewed explained that when she's sitting at her typewriter and her work is going really well, she feels quite "horny." She's aware that her nipples are erect and there's a warmth in her loins, a tingling in her genitals.

Another writer put it differently: "Just after you've made love you feel universal," she said, "as if you've somehow touched everyone in the whole world. I think you can get the same feeling from creative effort. To do one thing well, so that it really rises above the ordinary, you have to have passion, just as you have to have passion in sex. When you put passion into your work, sometimes you can accomplish something that is so satisfying that you get a release, and it feels just as rich and deep and stilling as if you'd just finished making love with someone you care about."

Creativity is similar to sexuality in another way, too: You can't force either experience and, in fact, trying too hard can short-circuit the whole business. Creative solutions can't be willed. Often they emerge after a kind of falling together of various elements, and you have to know how to relax and let that happen. Similarly, you can't force yourself to become sexually aroused or to have an orgasm; in fact, trying too hard creates tensions that can prevent arousal. Perhaps this, too, helps explain why creative effort sometimes feels sexual.

Be that as it may, when you're working at peak capacity, totally caught up in what you're doing—having a flow experience—you feel exhilarated, and energy surges within you. You may or may not choose to label it "sexual energy," but there's no question that it's an emotional high.

Actually, *the tidal flux of energy—the building up and falling back—is basic to life. Sex is only the most dramatic and emotionally loaded example of the pattern.* Small wonder, then, that the ebb and flow of energy in other situations can have sexual echoes.

Freud and the Primal Instincts

Sigmund Freud had a lot to say about sex; he also had some rather elaborate theories about energy. Although many people today feel that he overemphasized the importance of the sexual and aggressive drives, he was an astute observer of the inner experience—of the way sexual energy *feels*—and so his theories suggest some interesting body truths.

To Freud all energy was basically either sexual or aggressive; those were *the* human motivations and an urge toward any other goal was simply a matter of sublimation. Freud believed that energy was generated, to begin with, by the physical and chemical processes of the body, but then it was channeled into the aspect of the psyche that he called the id, where it was placed at the service of the two primitive and dangerous instincts, sex and aggression. Though the instincts were different—in sex the thrust was for life and in aggression it was toward death—Freud felt that they couldn't always be separated. As he saw it, the energy was fluid and flowed between them, so that sometimes they fused.

Human energy made itself felt, Freud observed, as a constant pressure. The individual felt a strong need to find an outlet in sexual or aggressive acts. Freud noted that infants expressed these drives directly while adults didn't. He suggested that as people matured and were confronted by the civilizing demands of family and society, they grew an ego whose job it was to manage the energies of the id. In his analogy the ego was like the rider of a powerful horse, helpless to control the id and "obliged to guide it," to suppress, repress, or rechannel its energies.

Because the id was the source of all vitality and because it was ruled by those two primitive instincts, Freud felt that when human beings spent energy on anything other than sex or aggression they were sublimating. Needing a socially acceptable outlet, they turned to substitute goals. In the Freudian view, virtually every human interest and activity began, back in the dim recesses of the subconscious, as lust or as simmering aggression. Even intellectual curiosity could be traced back to the sex drive, if one assumed that it was only sexual curiosity bent in a different direction.

Many people today feel that Freud took too narrow a view of human motivation. Humans have many different needs, and sex drive is just one kind of energy. However, in other ways his shrewd observations have held up over the years.

For instance, there's no question that some people do sublimate their sexual energy (though others who lead an active sex life virtually never do). I'm thinking, in particular, of a young man I know, a sports car enthusiast who feels intensely happy whenever he's careening around a race course at high speed. He told me once that he loved racing for the same reason that he loved sprinting when he was in his early teens. There were times then when he felt that he just had to get out and run as fast and as far as he could until, strained to the utmost, he finally collapsed, completely spent, wherever he happened to be. He spoke of the way his energy seems to build up to the point where he has to find some release. As a slightly lapsed Catholic, he isn't re-

ally comfortable with singles sex, and so he uses racing to sublimate. In the more repressive era in which Freud lived many people probably did a lot of sublimating.

Can Anger Fuel Sex Drive?

When Freud wrote of the occasional fusing of sexual and aggressive feelings, he seems to have put his finger on something
many of us experience at times: the ease with which sexual stirrings can turn into anger, and vice versa.

Psychologists have actually demonstrated the phenomenon in
laboratory experiments. They've invited subjects to watch an
erotic film or read an erotic passage in a book; then they've given
them the chance to deliver an electrical shock to another individual as punishment because he'd guessed wrong in a game they
were playing. (The other person was actually a confederate of
the experimenter, and no real shocks were delivered.) The subjects who had presumably been sexually aroused chose to shock
more severely than did other subjects who'd been shown a
neutral film or given nonsexual material to read. In speculations
reminiscent of Freud, some psychologists have suggested that
those given the erotic treatment were in a state of high arousal
and so their energy had to have somewhere to go. However, that
doesn't take us back to the concept of the id, for apparently people also become more aggressive if they're aroused first by loud
noises or vigorous exercise.

Other experimenters have demonstrated the reverse proposition, namely, that those who are feeling aggressive are more apt
to become sexually aroused. In everyday life, however, that gen-
eralization probably hides substantial individual differences.
For some people anger is often sexually stimulating—they really like to fight and then make up in bed—but for others angry
feelings cancel out sexual ones. Dr. Schaefer suggested, "If you
were raised to be accepting of your own anger and your sexual
feelings, you'll probably find that it's very energizing to express
either one freely; but if you were raised to believe that anger
was not acceptable or that sex wasn't, you'll feel compelled to

suppress those feelings or deny them, and that's a drain on your energy."

Surprisingly, it seems that in some circumstances fear can also be transformed into sex drive. Two psychologists from the University of British Columbia used a couple of footbridges as settings for an intriguing experiment. One bridge was narrow, rickety, and swayed in the wind hundreds of feet above a canyon; the other was a solid span a mere ten feet above a shallow stream. Men crossing both bridges were waylaid by an attractive young woman, who asked if they'd help her with a study she was conducting. She showed them a picture and explained that all they had to do was write down their thoughts about it. Those accosted on the shaky suspension bridge not only included more sexual imagery in the stories they wrote but were also most likely to telephone the young woman later, ostensibly because they wanted to find out more about the experiment.

Why should fear or anger feed into sexual feelings? Few psychologists today would maintain that Freud's instinct theory holds the answer. A more recent explanation is suggested by the work of Dr. Stanley Schachter of Columbia University. Professor Schachter believes that every emotion has two basic ingredients. The first is bodily arousal: Your heart pounds, you breathe faster, you perspire, and so on. These symptoms of arousal may differ somewhat from one emotion to the next, but the basic components are similar. The second ingredient is the label you attach to the symptoms, the way you explain them to yourself, which may depend on your analysis of the situation you're in or on what you expect to feel. Thus, the men on the suspension bridge, stimulated by fear, may have relabeled their bodily responses and experienced them as signs of sexual attraction.

Where in the Body Does Sexual Energy Come from?

Let's turn now to the question of where sexual energy comes from and why some people have more of it than others.

It seems certain that such differences are not just a matter of sexual upbringing but are partly inborn, for individual animals differ just as people do: Some laboratory rats are sexually active throughout their lives, while others seem more or less indifferent to rats of the opposite gender. You might think that hormone levels are responsible, and it's true that if researchers castrate a male animal it usually loses all interest in sex, and that if they then inject it with large doses of male hormones its interest revives. However, Dr. Leonore Tiefer of Downstate Medical Center suggested that something else must be involved as well, perhaps cells or tissues—a kind of foundation laid down during fetal development—that the hormones act upon. She explained that when injected rats take up sex again, though they're given similar doses of hormone, each displays the same amount of interest in sex (high, medium, or low) as before! There's no clear evidence as to what the foundation might be; Dr. Tiefer suggested that it could be in the brain or spinal cord, in peripheral tissues, or it might be something that controls the speed with which certain neurons fire. The brain seems a likely location, though, since experimenters can produce sexual activity in animals by stimulating particular sites in the hypothalamus with a mild electric current.

When it comes to human beings, we know surprisingly little about the way hormones influence sexual energy, or even about which ones do the influencing, though many researchers suspect that the male sex hormone testosterone may generate desire in both men and women. Women's bodies do produce testosterone, though in much smaller quantities. (This does not mean that women have less sex drive. Presumably testosterone operates differently in men and women.)

Numerous studies have tried to establish a connection between testosterone and desire in men. In one beautifully simple experiment a researcher, who elected to remain anonymous, weighed the hair he shaved off his face every morning, because beard growth is an index of testosterone level. At the time he was having sex only on weekends, and he found that his beard growth peaked just *before* the weekend, the time when he was anticipating the sexual activity to come. Another experimenter showed brief pornographic films to male subjects and reported that the amount of testosterone in the bloodstream began to rise within sixty to ninety minutes of the end of the film. Both these studies suggest that testosterone may be turned on by thinking sexual thoughts; however, another researcher who also did a study using erotic films found no rise in the testosterone level.

And that, unfortunately, is the way it's been with hormone studies. For every experiment that seems to demonstrate a clear relationship between sex drive and biochemistry, another that set out to reproduce the results failed. Consequently, *no one can really say for sure whether testosterone affects the sex drive and, if it does, whether it generates desire or whether the reverse happens and sexual activity generates testosterone.* One team of investigators actually suggested that perhaps a drop in the testosterone level below a certain critical point triggers desire, which leads to sexual activity, which raises the testosterone level, which cancels out desire!

Research on sex drive in women has tended to focus on the menstrual cycle, since it involves regular and dramatic hormonal shifts; it seems logical that these shifts might have an effect on sexual energy. Though some experiments seem to show that sex drive peaks for women at the time of ovulation, other studies turned up peaks either just before or just after menstruation.

Sex Is Partly in Your Head

If hormone research is still at sixes and sevens, it may be because it takes several different hormones to set sex drive going, or it may be because in humans psychological factors play such a major role.

You don't become sexually aroused unless you put your mind to it; and, of course, you can put your mind to it quite a lot of the time and still choose not to do anything about your sexual impulses. All this makes it hard to know how to gauge sex drive. Does it refer only to standard heterosexual and homosexual sex acts or should sexual fantasies and masturbation count as well? If we're trying to take the measure of the urge, then masturbation and fantasies might actually be a better way to judge it than frequency of intercourse, since to make love you have to have another person available and willing.

Take the difference between Carl and Liz, for example. Carl is a short, wiry man in his mid-fifties with a shock of grandfatherly white hair. He still masturbates about once a day when he's not involved with a woman. He grew up in a fairly puritanical family and didn't have sex with a woman until he was in his early twenties. He subsequently married her. Eighteen years later they were divorced, and since then he's had a series of affairs.

Carl feels that he's highly sexed and believes that the physical side of a relationship is extremely important. However, he concedes that he equates sex with affection, so that if a woman says "no" to sex he's apt to take it as a personal rejection. He also uses masturbation at times as a way to relieve tensions generated by nonsexual situations. He appreciates the fact that it's guaranteed to take his mind off his problems, even if only temporarily, and he regards it as one of life's simplest and most reliable pleasures. Carl is a television producer and his work keeps him frantically busy; when Liz once asked him, half jokingly, how he could find the time to masturbate once a day, he said dryly, "It's a matter of priorities."

Liz, on the other hand, masturbates only about twice a month when she's between men. At such times she avoids sexy books and movies and anything else that might be arousing, because she prefers to masturbate as seldom as possible since she suffers paroxysms of guilt afterward. "One of my earliest memories is of the day I learned to masturbate," she recalled. "I must have been about three and I couldn't wait to show my mother this marvelous thing I'd discovered about myself. She was horrified." The sexual urge was irresistible to Liz then, as it is now. Over a period of a week or two the need builds up until she feels she simply must have release.

For Liz, making love with a man isn't loaded with guilt in the same way that masturbation is, and whenever she's had a steady man (she's in her late thirties and was married for five years), she's been ready and eager for sex about once every two or three days. She enjoys it and reaches orgasm almost every time. Why, then, doesn't she want it more often? "I think it's just my natural rhythm," she said. "Also, I work long hours in a tough job and I often go out in the evening besides, so by the time I get to bed I'm tired. I guess what it boils down to is that I often choose to do other things with my time and energy."

It's possible that Liz suppresses her drive to some extent and that Carl's appetite isn't quite what it seems, since he uses sex for general tension release. Be that as it may, there was enough of a discrepancy between them to cause problems. The sex-energy gap seems to be much trickier to negotiate than the more general energy gap. As you'll see in Chapter 18, couples who have very different energy profiles can usually adjust to one another and may even turn the difference into an advantage.

What to Do About a Sexual-Energy Gap

What can you do about a difference in sexual appetites? Many married couples, of course, resort to the age-old solution: The more highly sexed spouse quietly has affairs.

For example, sex is very important to the woman I'll call Jane. She has been married for many years, and she and her husband make love now only about once every ten days. For him that seems to be often enough. It's enough for Jane, too—it's all she wants from him—but for the past five years she has been involved with another man.

Jane says that though her marriage isn't completely satisfactory, she's fond of her husband and respects him. It's a rather distant relationship. "We don't discuss very personal things," she said, yet she's dependent on him in many ways. His need for her is even greater, since he's very much a family man and hasn't many friends. If they ever split up, it will be because Jane has decided to make the move. "He expects less of life than I do," she explained. "I know he can't feel that our marriage is great, but he'd say that that's just how marriage is. I have more illusions and more imagination."

Jane spends several afternoons a week with her lover at his apartment (he works nights). She wouldn't want to marry him, but she appreciates the fact that he's much more attuned to what she wants and needs than her husband, and she can be more open with him. However, sex is definitely the main bond between them. "That's about 80 percent of it," she said.

Jane is and always has been both energetic and athletic. She spends an hour or more a day roller-skating, swimming, or jogging. She also has a part-time job. It's a full life, and she's really quite happy with it.

Sex wasn't always so important to her. She feels she had a healthy, uninhibited upbringing, but it wasn't until she was in her late thirties that she became overwhelmingly aware of her own sexual needs. Now forty-two, Jane recently attended a high school reunion and had a chance to compare notes with former classmates. "I discovered that my sex drive seems to be stronger than most," she said. "I'm very sensitive to touch, I climax easily, I really enjoy it. When I'm not with my lover I masturbate and I fantasize about sex a lot. Meeting a man for the first time, for example, I look at him and imagine what it would be like to make love to him. I think fantasy is a big part of sex."

Despite her daydreams, Jane has so far been faithful to her husband and her lover. However, not long ago she met a new man and at the time I talked to her she was, she felt, on the verge of a new and perhaps even more satisfying affair. "He's very bright," she said, "and there's real rapport between us, but all the same I'm sure it's going to be very much a physical relationship. I'm not looking for a companion. Some women are, I know, but that's not really my need. I'm meeting him tomorrow, and we'll probably have dinner together, but I won't be there for the dinner or for the companionship. It's nice to be courted, but if we're not going to be good for each other in bed I want to know about it now."

How to Narrow or Negotiate a Gap

Jane's method of coping with a sexual-energy gap is perhaps typical of the kind of marriage where emotional exchange has broken down—but not completely. Her solution will have little appeal for close-knit couples who want to solve their problems within the marriage itself. Troubled by differing sexual needs, most couples work out their own compromises. However, some have begun to turn up at sex therapy clinics, hoping for help.

To find out how the clinics handle a sex gap, I talked to Dr. Tiefer and to Dr. Maj-Britt Rosenbaum, director of the Long Island Jewish–Hillside Human Sexuality Center in New Hyde Park, New York.

In deciding what kind of treatment might be called for, sex therapists look first at the relationship between the couple, for *anger and hurt feelings can depress the sex drive, and so a sex-energy gap is sometimes merely a symptom of other problems.* "The sexual relationship tends to be scapegoated," Dr. Rosenbaum explained. "It's used as *the* reason, the concrete symbol of what's wrong, of all the other resentments and unfulfilled needs. The problem may have more to do with sharing and pleasure in general, but it's expressed not as 'You don't hear me' but as 'All you want is sex.'"

Some couples become so focused on their sex problem that what started out as a small difference in drive becomes larger over time. Like Carl, the more highly sexed partner feels rejected and so he (or she) actually escalates sexual demands; the other person reacts by becoming even less enthusiastic about sex.

The individual who is not getting enough sex often feels unattractive and undesirable as a result. Sometimes all that's necessary is to convince such a person that there really *is* a body truth involved, that the partner's appetite simply is what it is, that it's always been relatively low and it wouldn't be different with anyone else.

In other cases a compromise is worked out in much the same way as compromises are negotiated in other areas of life. However, it's seldom a matter of splitting the difference—of deciding, for example, that instead of making love four times a week (her preference) or twice a week (his) they'll settle for three times. Dr. Tiefer has found that often the high-drive person really doesn't want to have less sex and the low-drive person would be willing to have more if he (or she) could work up the interest in it, but simply can't. So a couple may agree that from time to time the husband will stimulate the wife to climax even though he's not in the mood for sex himself. Or they may simply accept the fact that the high-drive partner will have an active masturbatory life. If both regard this as a straight sexual-tension release, and if they spend enough time cuddling so that no one feels deprived of intimacy, for many people this is a comfortable solution.

Other couples agree that the answer is to try to increase the

sexual appetite of the low-drive partner. Actually, at Dr. Rosenbaum's clinic the therapists are seeing more and more patients
whose chief problem is that they have little interest in sex. Dr.
Rosenbaum estimates that perhaps as many as half her patients
have a sex-drive problem. Sometimes they come in because
they've been urged to by a more highly sexed partner. Often
they are themselves dissatisfied, convinced that they're missing
something. Some have never had much desire for sex, but for
others the drive has mysteriously dried up. To the therapist, lifelong low drive is one thing and a sudden loss of appetite is quite
another.

"I've Never Been Much Interested in Sex"

Some people can get by quite comfortably without sex from
one month to the next, or even from one year to the next. Dr.
Rosenbaum has found that it's more difficult to help men who
have had that kind of history than it is to help women. "Women
tend to come alive in therapy in a very different way," she said.
"Often we can awaken something there." Perhaps the difference
is that the culture is more permissive about male sexuality, so it's
less likely that a man with low drive has simply repressed it.

With female patients the first step is usually to do a general
physical checkup, since poor health can diminish sexual interest.
Dr. Rosenbaum doesn't order a hormone workup, because scientists still don't know very much about the way hormones affect
sexual appetite in women. Though substantial doses of testosterone do seem to generate desire, they're seldom prescribed
since they're also masculinizing.

With male patients Dr. Rosenbaum generally checks the level
of testosterone in the blood. In rare cases it turns out to be relatively low and so she prescribes treatment with the hormone.
Testosterone is not a guaranteed aphrodisiac—it has no effect at
all on men whose bodies are already producing normal amounts
of it—but where the level is low it can generate a surge of sexual
interest, thus putting the man in touch with the fact that he *does*
have sexual energy. Dr. Rosenbaum explained, "We try to get a
new pattern going. It gives him encouragement, especially if he's

had difficulties with erection and has become afraid of failing." The welling up of desire can last for weeks or sometimes months, but eventually the body adapts to the drug and begins to suppress production of its own natural testosterone. Therapists hope that by that time the new pattern of sexual activity will have become established.

Low testosterone is a factor in very few cases. In fact, ordinarily therapists are unable to find any physical explanation for low sex drive, and so they go to work on the assumption that the problem is psychological, using a course of treatment that has often been effective.

Unshackling the Sex Drive

Clinicians sometimes speak of "freeing the sex drive from its shackles." Dr. Tiefer explained that when fledgling sex therapists train at the Masters and Johnson clinic in St. Louis the first thing they're taught is that sex is a natural function. "By the time you leave, you can see 'Sex is a natural function' written in front of your eyes whenever you close them," she said. Amplified, the statement means that though therapists can't cause sexual desire and can't take it away, they *can* disinhibit it, and when they succeed in doing that *desire flourishes as a matter of nature*. As Dr. Rosenbaum put it, "The life-force is on our side."

In general, sex therapy focuses on a few tried-and-true techniques. Dr. Tiefer explained, "First of all, we try to encourage people to do those things that seem to have worked in the past, like just being nice to each other and telling each other what they like in sex."

Often abstinence is suggested for a time. Couples are shown how to caress, but told to stop short of intercourse. The caressing exercises are sometimes a revelation: Couples are able to talk honestly for the first time about what they enjoy and how they prefer to be stimulated. Masters and Johnson have always emphasized that people have to take responsibility for their own sexual response by explaining or demonstrating what they like.

Treatment also involves regular sessions with a therapist, so that sexual histories and sexual attitudes can be explored. One of the easier tasks during these sessions is to debunk some of the myths that have been invented or perpetuated by the media. "Many people feel that their own sex lives are dull in comparison with what they read about or see in films," Dr. Rosenbaum said. "They're relieved to hear that nobody in real life has intercourse for two hours at a time."

Dr. Rosenbaum generally encourages fantasies as part of the treatment, since she believes they're an important element in sexuality. By fantasy she means "anything that will take you out of the present moment," whether it's daydreaming about sex beforehand, imagining what might come next during sex play, or remembering afterward. There are, of course, more dramatic fantasies, too; couples sometimes learn to share them, perhaps pretending that they're alone together on a desert island or that they're animals. Fantasy can also be used to practice something ahead of time. The therapist will ask, "How far can you imagine yourself going?" or "What would you do next?" and the patient rehearses mentally.

People often use fantasies during lovemaking to ease their anxiety or to turn off negative thoughts. However, fantasizing can also be a defensive maneuver, a way to escape the present moment or to screen out the feelings you have for your partner. When you pretend to yourself during sex that you're making love to someone other than the person you're with, it's not *necessarily* hostile or defensive. However, according to Dr. Rosenbaum, "We perk up our ears when we hear about it and wonder what's going on."

Sometimes sex therapy solves old problems only to create new ones. Dr. Rosenbaum treated one young couple who came to the clinic because the wife was eager to have a baby. She was also frightened of sex and insisted that she didn't enjoy it. She'd been raised to believe that it was "dirty." Her husband had never had much sexual appetite himself and, though he was willing to have a child, he wasn't pressuring his wife at all.

With therapy the woman became much freer. Obviously her fear had held back a strong, basic drive; but now the problem was the husband's lack of interest. Soon she was again wondering whether there was something wrong with her—this time because she wanted sex and he didn't. "He was a rather unemotional man in other ways, too," Dr. Rosenbaum recalled. Apparently he tuned out both his own emotions and the sexual messages from his body. It wasn't that he didn't function well and enjoy lovemaking once he got involved in it; it was just that it was hard for him to work up any interest in the first place. "We tried almost to force a structure on them," Dr. Rosenbaum said. "We had them make dates for lovemaking and that seemed to work. He's never going to be a fireball, but they have a good relationship in other ways. I suppose he might respond to long-term insight therapy, but he's not motivated to try that. He's happy with things the way they are."

Sometimes Sex Drive Suddenly Vanishes

Lifelong sexual apathy is relatively rare. Much more common are the people who come for help because they've mysteriously lost their sexual appetite. In such cases treatment depends on what has caused the dry spell.

Actually, it's normal for sexual energy to fluctuate somewhat over the course of a lifetime. For men, for example, the drive is strongest in late adolescence or in their twenties: Those are the years when it feels most urgent. A woman's peak is more apt to occur when she's in her thirties or forties.

Life events also have a fairly predictable impact on the drive. The early years of child rearing are a time of lower interest for many women. Dr. Rosenbaum believes that in nurturing babies and small children a woman may, to a large extent, satisfy her own need for closeness and for touching and hugging. Then again, after menopause many women experience an upsurge of sexual interest. They feel freer and much more energetic, perhaps because they no longer need to worry about becoming pregnant—though it's also possible that, with female hormones out of the way, the testosterone produced by the adrenal gland has more of an impact. However, there are other women who lose all interest in sex after menopause. Did they need to know that pregnancy was at least a possibility to feel comfortable about sex? Nobody really knows the answers to such questions.

Career changes, a death in the family, and money worries can, of course, have an effect as well, and depression is another possibility. Someone who is depressed rarely has much interest in sex. In such cases the solution is to treat the depression, since sexual apathy is only a symptom of it.

Therapists also ask questions about drugs, because some drugs can hold down sex drive. Though it's not at all a common problem, there are women who react to the Pill by becoming lethargic and depressed or simply irritable. For them the Pill is a mood depressant and as such diminishes interest in sex.

"In addition, the major tranquilizers put a straitjacket on sexuality," Dr. Rosenbaum said, "while the minor tranquilizers work in much the same way alcohol does. One Valium is relaxing and may free sexual energy, but if you take more you become drowsy, and if you abuse the drug you'll have less interest in life *and* in sex."

As for marijuana, it has a reputation as an aphrodisiac. Though some find that it has no effect on the sexual experience one way or the other, others come to feel that they must smoke before they make love, because otherwise they may not be able to function. Pot loosens inhibitions and also tends to intensify sensations. However, some people find that sex under the influence of pot is a surprisingly lonely experience. As one man put it, "I'm less aware of the other person. In fact, I become so self-centered that it's almost as if I'm by myself."

Drugs, depression, a relationship fraught with anger and tension: These are relatively simple and obvious explanations. Sometimes, though, desire simply vanishes for no apparent reason. When that happens it's important not to panic, since anxiety cancels ardor. It's important, too, to have a partner who is loving, patient, and supportive.

In his book *Becoming Partners: Marriage and Its Alternatives* the famous therapist Carl Rogers described just such a time in his own marriage and his wife's reassuring reaction: ". . . during my forties," he wrote, "there was a period of nearly a year when I felt absolutely no sexual desire—for anyone. No medical cause was found. Helen was confident that my normal urges would return and simply 'stood with me' in my predicament. It is easy to think up possible psychological causes, but none of them 'clicks' as far as I'm concerned. It remains a mystery to me. But her quiet, continuing love meant a great deal to me and probably was the best therapy I could have had. At any rate, I gradually became sexually normal once more."

When do you sit out a dry spell and when do you go for help? Surprisingly, the therapists I talked to didn't advise hurrying off to a sex clinic. The first step, they suggested, would be to talk to your mate, to see if together you can figure out what has gone wrong. Talking to friends might help, too. If they report similar experiences, that may be all the reassurance you need. If not, you can always consult a doctor, minister, or psychotherapist. Head for a sex clinic, then, only if the dry spell really drags on, or if it seems to be damaging your relationship with your partner.

Energy Tips: Sexual Appetizers

Short of therapy, there are a few things you can do to try to increase your own sexual appetite.

1. Talk more openly to your partner—try to air issues instead of burying them. It's hard to feel physically aroused when you're angry or feeling emotionally distant.

2. Don't expect the other person to read your mind. Say what you like in sex play and what you don't. It's easy to blame your own lack of response on your partner's lack of skill, but unless he (or she) absolutely refuses to listen to suggestions, that's scapegoating.

3. If you've been leading a very sedentary life, try getting more exercise. When you feel healthy, active, and vividly alive sex has more appeal; if you see yourself as lithe and attractive, that's a turn-on, too. Desire wells up out of good feelings for the other person, but it comes from self-confidence as well.

4. Realize that you have to spend energy to get energy, and that this is especially true of sexual energy. The less often you make love, the less desire you're likely to feel. The more sex you have, the more you're apt to want.

5. Set time aside for tenderness and sex. Make it a real priority.

6. Raise your sexual consciousness. Spend more time talking

about sex. Try books and movies to see what arouses you. Allow yourself—remind yourself if you must—to daydream about sex. Fantasize about it beforehand; savor the memory afterward; picture the next time. Turn yourself on.

Massage: A Lesson in Sensuality

Here is one last suggestion, slightly more offbeat: You might try taking a course in massage at one of the human growth centers. Dr. Jay Mann, a California sex therapist, told me that he often suggests that couples who consult him should learn massage, because he feels it teaches valuable principles that apply to sex as well.

Growth centers usually teach what's called Esalen massage rather than the brisk, thumping Swedish sort. The Esalen type is easy to learn and it's enormously relaxing and pleasurable, based as it is on long, slow strokes. As for the principles Dr. Mann had in mind:

First lesson: *It feels as good to give as it does to receive.* If you're the giver of the massage and you focus on how marvelous that warm, smooth skin feels under your hands, you'll communicate your pleasure to the receiver with every stroke. You also won't have time to worry about your "technique," and what you do is almost bound to please, since what feels good to you is apt to feel good to the other person as well.

When you're the receiver of the massage, in this setup you have the chance to become, as Dr. Mann put it, "a human sponge soaking up sensation." And you'll learn that your body can give pleasure to another just by being there. "That's an important message," said Dr. Mann, "because couples so often are too concerned about taking care of one another during sex. In taking responsibility for the other person's pleasure, they become unable to focus on their own." Thus, massage not only teaches new ways of touching but demonstrates that it's all right—in fact, at times it's great—to take turns.

Second lesson: *A lot of the fun is in getting there.* Many people tend to end-goal in sex—they develop a kind of achievement drive toward orgasm. Then they worry over whether they're going to achieve or not, which turns lovemaking into an anxious experience, and that, of course, leaches away desire. It's worthwhile getting back to basics, back to total concentration on the flow of pleasure in the present moment. That's a lesson that can be learned from massage, much as it's learned from the caressing exercises prescribed by sex therapy clinics.

Love—the Ultimate Energizer?

It would be rash to write a whole chapter about sex and energy without at least a sidelong glance at the relationship between energy and love.

Many people believe that falling in love must be the ultimate energizer. Most of us have occasionally felt love's galvanizing effects and we've seen them in others. Certainly it's true that romantic passion does have an impact on energy. However, the impact is not quite what one might expect.

Take my friend Pauline, for example. When she fell in love—not for the first time—at the age of thirty-four, she acquired a kind of inner glow that I couldn't help envying. Her eyes sparkled and her short, curly red hair actually seemed to have more spring to it and more sheen. Overnight she acquired a whole new wardrobe; crisp pantsuits replaced the jeans and baggy sweaters that had been her trademark.

When Pauline and her man, Will, were together, their awareness of one another created a sexual aura that was almost tangible. It was as if the air in their immediate vicinity were warmer and more humid. They were always finding excuses to touch each other and they held whole conversations with their eyes. As another friend remarked, there was so much energy in their relationship that one could almost bask in the glow.

Eventually I got around to talking to Pauline about love. "I suppose you'd say that falling in love is a tremendous energizer," I began. "Oh no," she protested. "I wouldn't say that at all."

It seems that ever since she fell in love with Will her energy has been all ups and downs, "like a roller coaster." A trotter in most circumstances, Pauline turned hurdler overnight after she met Will. "It's true that there are times when I'm practically spinning with energy," she said, "but it's not much use for getting things done. At work these days I simply putter and hope that nobody will notice how much time I spend staring off into space, daydreaming. I count the minutes until the evening when I can be with Will again.

"But it's a very rocky relationship right now and so there are also days when I'm afraid I'll never see him again and even days when I believe I never want to. When that happens I get to feeling so down that I have no energy at all."

Psychologist Dorothy Tennov spent ten years studying the phenomenon she calls "limerence," or the state of being in love. A professor at the University of Bridgeport, in Connecticut, and the author of *Love and Limerence: The Experience of Being in Love*, she believes that, *"it's probably true that* initially *limerence mobilizes. It motivates, and when you're motivated you do feel energetic."* Falling in love also tends to produce a sense of elation. Over and over again lovers told Dr. Tennov that they felt as if they were walking on air. "That's not an analogy," she said. "That's exactly how it feels."

And yet, when you look at the symptoms of limerence, it's clear that, as Pauline reported, some of them can short-circuit energy. For example, Professor Tennov noted that limerents become preoccupied with their "limerent object" and often suffer from intrusive thinking: Whether they like it or not, they find it difficult to concentrate on anything else. In addition, limerence thrives on uncertainty; in fact, it wouldn't exist without it, and so there are bound to be emotional ups and downs. Dr. Tennov discovered that limerence actually begins to fade when certainty sets in: You fall out of love once it becomes clear either that there's no hope at all or that the object of your affections is just as limerent as you are. In the latter case limerence is sometimes replaced by something more enduring—a deep mutual love and respect. But whether it ends with heartbreak or wedding bells, limerence never seems to last very long; Dr. Tennov estimates that it's usually over with in about six months to two years.

There are people who never experience limerence—and Tennov emphasizes that this is quite normal. Others experience it often. Some eventually learn to think of it as a self-limiting disorder—a delicious momentary madness that eventually cures itself.

The Flow of Creativity

Most people don't think of creativity as a form of energy. And yet there are those who are literally driven to make use of their considerable talents. For others the urge may not be as imperative, but still there's the sense that something is missing if the individual has no creative outlets at all.

These days some psychologists are beginning to suggest that probably almost everyone has creative potential, but that it's educated out of people as they're growing up. There are, however, ways to revive creative energy, and they're the subject of the next chapter.

15

Your Creative Drive

One of the best ways to get energy is to spend energy in some creative effort; when you produce something good that's original and all your own, there's a phenomenal payoff in terms of self-esteem and redoubled vigor. Psychiatrist Rollo May has written, "We express our being by creating." We celebrate it as well.

Though in many people creativity lies dormant, it's part of the human potential, and psychologists today believe that people can be taught how to tap into it. But before we consider ways to do that, let's look at two highly creative energists and ask: How do *they* make the most of their own natural abilities? What do they know about creative energy that most people don't?

Alexandra Stoddard: Life at Maximum Intensity

Alexandra Stoddard (see Chapter 11) leads a busy triple life as an interior designer, author, and wife and mother. She's not only high in energy, she's highly disciplined as well; *like many energists I've met, she knows just what her priorities are.*

"I think I was born with a certain visual ability," Stoddard said. "God gave me certain talents. I'm not good at chemistry and science and lots of other things, and I'm not interested in them, either. What I try to do is put all my energy into the things that I enjoy and that I'm really good at. That's where my high is—where I live and dream and soar.

"To me energy isn't *just* physical health and well-being. It's a flowing of your whole self, a welling up. I think it makes you feel strong, and when you feel strong you say 'yes' to life. And you want to do something with that feeling, to use it to create something of your own."

Other people, too, experience energy as a strong creative force, but few are more skillful at managing that force. Ms. Stoddard seems to be able to bring her considerable vitality to bear on everything she does: She works hard, plays hard, and when she's with her children she's totally with them. ("I don't see why any afternoon we spend together shouldn't be as much fun as a birthday party.") She's 100 percent *there* in the present moment. And yet she's involved in many different things, and she plays them off, one against the other, thus building her own momentum. *She deliberately intensifies the natural rhythms that are there in all of us, the swings from gregariousness to solitude, from energy intake to outflow* (described in Chapter 12).

She explained that one way she manages this is through planning and a schedule that's carefully thought out: three days out of every week for stimulation and two days for solitude.

On the stimulation days she's constantly on the run. "I try to see as many clients as I can," she explained, "so that in one day I might accomplish fifteen different nonrelated things—talking to clients and tradesmen, going to meetings. I make nonstop appointments and I use all my in-between time, too. I never go anywhere without paper and a pen, so I can be planning a color scheme for someone's living room when I'm in a taxi. If people keep me waiting, I don't get frustrated—that would only dissipate my energy. I use the time to think or make notes. Those days when I'm out seeing people are exhausting, but I find that once I'm started it's far better to keep going." She builds a momentum and uses it to help sustain her energy level.

The other two days of the week Ms. Stoddard works at home, in solitude, on her writing or designing. "I guard this time alone against interruptions," she said, "and that gives me an emotional space much bigger than the actual hours of the day.

"If I keep to this schedule—being very outgoing and then stepping aside—if I maintain that rhythm, I'm able to go at a pretty regular energy level," she continued. "You can't design or write in a vacuum. You have to have something to charge you with ideas. But I can't be creative if I overdo it—if I'm with other peo-

ple constantly. The days when I'm out with clients are exhilarating, but that's a building-up, not a release. Creativity is
released for me only in solitude. It comes when I'm absolutely
filled to the brim with life, and then I go away from it and have
time alone."

How Ideas Grow

As for the creative effort itself, Stoddard said, "It's usually
preceded by a tremendous amount of puttering and brooding,
getting things set. You have to be disciplined and work right
ahead every day whether ideas come easily or not."

Sometimes in her designing they do come easily—all the basic
elements will occur to her instantaneously while she's first looking over an apartment or a house. But at other times they take
longer to jell. She works by visualizing and uses her excellent
memory for what she has seen. Sitting in her studio at home, she
can close her eyes and picture a client's house in minute detail.
She can conjure up the living room, stripped of its present furniture, empty and colorless; then she'll visualize putting a sofa
here, a chair there, adding colors and textures. "My dreams, too,
are so vivid and colorful that they literally solve major problems
for me," she said. "Sometimes I wake up and I just can't wait to
go to my studio and get things down."

Small details are the hardest and take the most time, but she
doesn't worry about them; she simply waits until they "pop in."
She explained, "I'm an old-style Christian and in my prayers I
pray for others and for myself, but I also pray for a deepening. I
pray for being receptive and more aware, so that I'm really listening to the stillness, I'm right there at the edge, waiting to
have something happen to me. Usually it does; I am moved."

There are certain days, she said, that are special days, when
she feels absolutely on top of things and work is total joy. When
I asked her whether she had any idea what brought those times
on, she said she thought they were sometimes related to her
menstrual cycle. "A few days before my period there's a buildup
of tension. I keep dropping things, I'm nervous and short-tem-
pered, and the whole world is a problem that needs to be dealt

with. Then all of a sudden there's a sort of letdown and a calming. I see very clearly all the little pieces that have been floating around as fragments. I'm very philosophical and optimistic, and in my writing I make more sense." Other women I talked to also spoke of a surge of energy at menstruation, though many aren't aware of any such thing.

Ms. Stoddard equates energy with euphoria. "My energy is all positive. It goes away completely when I'm miserable." However, she also believes that *she can usually control both her moods* and *her energy*. "*I try to make all of my life creative,*" she said, "so that I don't have those dark moments when I'm 'doing the housework,' 'doing the cooking.'" She concentrates on setting a pretty table and preparing an irresistible meal, thus denying the humdrum elements in such tasks. When she goes to the market, she notes that the fruits and vegetables delight the eye; though she doesn't like going to the dentist (who does?), she enjoys the marvelous view from his window. In short, she has an unusual ability to generate flow (see Chapter 10).

Ms. Stoddard's crowded schedule would exhaust most people, and, of course, sometimes it exhausts her, too. But she enjoys her life so much that she doesn't complain. "I believe energy is derived from a personal philosophy. It's deeply rooted in who you are, what your values are, and what you hope to get out of and give to life. I expect a tremendous amount from myself because I think life can be exquisite and I want to be part of it in a very vital way."

Alexandra Stoddard is obviously a singularly focused person, with clear ideas about what is important to her and what's not.

Phyllis Whitney: Dispensing Energy Intelligently

Intense focus was just as evident in the way Phyllis A. Whitney marshaled her energy. Miss Whitney is something of a literary phenomenon: She's one of the world's foremost writers of romantic suspense novels, otherwise known as Gothics. Her books have been translated into eighteen languages. They're so popular in the United States that she has yet to have one of them go out of print. She writes for children, too. Throughout most of her long career she has written two books a year. When I talked to her she was hard at work on her sixtieth novel!

Phyllis Whitney is a slender woman of medium height, with smooth skin and gray hair worn neatly coiled. Her eyes dance with interest, and there's no way anyone could guess her age: When I interviewed her she was going on seventy-five. We talked for a few hours at her home, a snug, ranch-style house on a quiet street in small-town Long Island. The house couldn't possibly be more unlike the brooding mansions featured in many of her books.

"I certainly don't feel that I'm a person of extraordinary energy," Miss Whitney began as we settled down in her living room. "Actually, though I'm healthier now than I've ever been before, I've been sickly for most of my life. Even now, if I didn't work at it I'd fall apart."

She explained that her energy came from four things: exercise, sleep, good nutrition, and the fact that she stays active. Nutrition particularly interests her. Five years ago her husband died. "I started to fall apart," she recalled, "which one does in reaction. I was grasping for something—I wanted to get back to work because I knew that the best thing for grief is to get back to work as fast as you can." So she began to read about nutrition and to experiment with vitamins, minerals, and diet. "I take a very strong B-complex vitamin now," she said, "and a good multivitamin and a good multimineral. I also take dessicated liver— that's my favorite source of energy; it's full of B vitamins—and brewer's yeast, plus wheat germ and bran and all those good health food things."

As for exercise, she jumps rope three times a day, persevering for fifteen minutes each time for a total of forty-five minutes in all. "I don't actually use a rope because I don't want to knock the bric-a-brac around," she said. "And because it's a terrible bore I do it in front of the television; I put on some interview program that's interesting." She got up to demonstrate, swinging the imaginary rope with great panache, as light on her feet as any eight-year-old. "Not bad for seventy-five, is it?" she said with some satisfaction as she sat down again.

Miss Whitney also makes sure she gets enough sleep— "enough" is about seven hours a night, plus a half-hour nap in the afternoon. In addition, she's active and loves her work. "I'll have nothing to do with slowing down," she said. "That's a horrible thought. As long as I'm eager to get back to that typewriter, that's what keeps me young. *Activity generates energy.*

"You know, I've always been a liberated woman," she added, "because I always went my way and did what I wanted to do. And I think the drive and the determination and the wanting to are terribly important. I'm sorry for the person who doesn't want to do anything, because he's going to be tired all the time. When I taught writing, students would sometimes complain that they hadn't any story ideas; they weren't interested in anything. I'd tell them to start working on an idea, that you don't have to be interested to begin with. As you work and find out more, the interest will come, and with it the energy, because energy is part of enthusiasm."

"Discipline Is My Middle Name"

Though food, sleep, exercise, and an active life are all undoubtedly important sources of energy for Phyllis Whitney, other factors seem significant as well. For one thing, she's highly organized, which is all the more notable because writers frequently have a hard time organizing themselves without the nine-to-five office day to help structure their lives. Procrastination is an occupational hazard—but not for Phyllis Whitney. "Discipline," she said, "is my middle name."

A Whitney novel begins when the author picks a setting for her story—for example, *The Glass Flame* takes place in the Great Smoky Mountains in Tennessee. After thoroughly researching the area, she contacts someone who lives there—a friend or perhaps a librarian or teacher who knows her books—and arranges to visit for a week.

At this point she generally knows nothing at all about the story, since it grows out of the place; but she does know more or less what she wants to see during her visit. "I need a variety of local settings that are rich and different," she explained. "I need a wonderful spot for a murder, a backdrop for the climax or the final chase scene, and more besides."

Once she has selected a setting, she visits it on a number of occasions to see it at different times of the day and night, as well as on rainy days and when the sun is shining. Eventually she comes to know these few places intimately. She takes lots of color photographs and makes copious notes. She also manages to visit several houses in the vicinity so that she can see what they look like inside. The house in a Whitney novel, with its mysterious, threatening presence, is a central character.

While she's on location, she paces herself carefully, budgeting her energy. She takes an afternoon nap, warning her host beforehand not to plan anything for her in the evenings. "I want to be sure I have enough energy for all the things I need to do," she said. "On the first day of a trip I'm very tired, but then, as I become interested and involved in what I'm doing, I get my second wind. Being with people, plus the flow and exchange of ideas, are energizing."

After just a week at the scene of the crime, Miss Whitney returns home and settles down to organize her photographs and notes; then she begins the actual writing. Again, she paces herself intelligently. Her day starts at six in the morning and by eight she's at her desk. From eight to eleven she writes, with time out for a mid-morning snack. Then she exercises, has lunch, takes a nap, and returns to her desk from two to five—though not to write. "I've found that three hours a day is enough time to spend with my characters," she said. Instead, she does research or writes to her "protégés by mail"—the former students from her writing class, and others, who keep in touch with her. She adheres to this schedule six days a week and on Sundays she also puts in desk time, though she doesn't do any writing. She works in a book-lined room where the desk faces *away* from windows that look out on a tidy backyard.

Tactics for Outflanking Writer's Block

If she runs into a problem with a book and the writing temporarily bogs down, Phyllis Whitney has several strategies for getting things moving again. She may simply switch over for the morning to the fat notebook in which she plans the novel; it has one section for plot and another for characters. "You can always talk to yourself on paper about something," she said. So she puts in her three hours anyway.

Another method she uses is incubation: She feeds the problem in—reading everything she's written of the book up to the point at which the block has occurred. Then she leaves all that information to "soak," refusing to think about it at all for a day or so. Sooner or later she comes back to it and often she finds that the solution has now become clear.

If it hasn't, she tries a different approach. "Perhaps I've known for several days that I was approaching this scene, but I still don't know what I'm going to do with it," she explained. "So I go and lie down and relax all my muscles—I've learned how to do that. I take with me the question, because you have to put something in for your subconscious to work on. I close my eyes and wait and pretty soon the scene just happens on the screen of my mind. I see it like a movie, in color, and I think, 'Oh my goodness, what a good idea! Where did that come from?' And I get up and write it. It's a little like meditating, a clearing of the mind, and then letting this thing come in. I've been doing it for forty or fifty years, ever since I began writing." Sometimes she discovers that her subconscious has already planted characters or incidents earlier in the story that now play a part in the scene.

In a variation on the theme, if she's feeling very tired Miss Whitney will sit down in a chair, close her eyes, relax, and then she'll conjure up an inner vision of a place she loves—a grassy, sun-drenched island. In her imagination she sits in the grass or walks on the shore and thinks to herself, "Energy, energy" or else, "Resting, resting"—words that will help. "If I can do that for five minutes, I can get up and I'm rested, though if I just sat for five minutes it wouldn't be the same thing," she said. "It helps, too, if you tell yourself that there's a source out there that you can draw from. I'm not particularly God-oriented, but I think there is something there that we don't understand; so you tell yourself that you don't have to be all-powerful, you don't have to do it all yourself, that there's something outside yourself that can help you."

Creativity

Phyllis Whitney's problem-solving techniques—her periods of incubation and the movies she watches in her mind—reminded me of the way Alexandra Stoddard works: puttering—lining up all the information she needs—and then opening herself up so that solutions can come to her. By these methods both women are able to tap into their own subconscious. That's important because *most creative insights originate as sparks thrown off by the subconscious mind—they're not produced by ordinary, logical thinking.*

Creativity, as psychologists use the term, is the ability to push aside assumptions that most people make and come up with ideas that are entirely new. Somehow the logical mind is prone to go along with old assumptions—it has its ingrained ways of thinking. The subconscious, on the other hand, is crammed with half-forgotten facts and outlandish images and ideas—in other words, with just the sort of raw material that might coalesce to produce a scientific breakthrough, a scene for a novel, or a theme for a designer.

However, an ability to tap the subconscious is only half the battle. The fact that both women are highly disciplined is equally important, for it's not enough to produce something that's simply original. "Original" might also be crazy and irrelevant, and then the insight it was based on wouldn't be considered creative at all. *Creativity actually requires a nice balance between the rational and the irrational.* It requires a leap of the imagination and then, after the fact, sound judgment as to whether the leap was worthwhile. Thus, the second significant fact about both Stoddard and Whitney is that they know how to sift and shape what they dredge up from the subconscious to create something that other people can instantly connect with.

Has Your Creativity Been Undernourished?

As I suggested earlier, virtually every human being has creative potential. However, our culture fails to nourish it. Schools teach youngsters to absorb and faithfully regurgitate factual information. Teachers insist on logical, linear thinking and often actively discourage flights of imagination. They ignore the dark treasures of the subconscious.

And yet *many people experience creativity as a kind of energy. They feel a real need to express themselves in this unique, risky, and self-affirming way.* Whether an individual sets out to write a poem or paint a sunset, to invent a self-cleaning garlic press or to come up with a truly innovative solution to a stubborn problem (for instance, how to motivate tenants who don't pay for their own heat or electricity to save energy), to some extent he lays his ego on the line in what he does. If he succeeds, the rewards—in terms of pride and self-confidence—will be commensurate with the risks.

What Researchers Know About Creativity

Almost since the birth of psychology psychologists have been keenly interested in what makes the truly creative person tick. They've closely examined the working habits of scientists, artists, writers, composers, the "idea men" of the business world, and others. Though the creative process remains difficult to analyze and describe, some things do seem clear.

The first is that creativity isn't a rare gift enjoyed only by the fortunate few. It is indeed part of the human potential, though some people—those we call geniuses—have so much more of that potential that they seem almost a race apart.

Secondly, psychologists are beginning to suspect that creativity may not be synonymous with intelligence—or, at any rate, not with "intelligence" as measured by the standard IQ tests. For example, most researchers agree that one of the hallmarks of the highly creative individual is an easy, prolific flow of ideas. This ability is not picked up by IQ tests and, in fact, it seems to be independent of IQ. In recent years psychologists have designed new instruments to measure creativity itself, tests that feature instructions such as: Write down all the uses you can think of for junked automobiles. (Six to fourteen uses is an average response, while fifteen and up is said to demonstrate superior creativity.)

Many psychologists also believe that there are four basic steps to the creative process. Though the four don't always occur in the same order, and an individual may do quite a bit of backing and filling before she's finished, the steps are:

• *preparation,* which includes everything the person has learned over a lifetime that's relevant, plus any special work she has done on the problem.

• *incubation,* which occurs when the individual steps back from the problem for a time and, in Phyllis Whitney's words, leaves it to "soak" undisturbed.

• *illumination,* which is a flash of insight that solves the problem or clarifies part of it.

• *verification,* the checking stage that proves out (or fails to prove out) the insight.

Plainly, there are two key questions about the steps in the process: What *is* incubation? How do the first two steps lead to illumination?

The Benefits of "Primitive" Thinking

The kind of mental activity that goes on during incubation is the sort that also occurs in dreams and psychoses. Freud called it "primary process thinking." It's primitive, emotional, and loaded with symbols, expressing a side of the self that many people tend to disparage.

When a person incubates and shoves a problem down, out of awareness, into the subconscious, for the time being she shuts off the disparaging, logical mind. Thus, while logic is busy looking the other way, the subconscious has access to all kinds of memories, fantasies, and images that might seem totally irrelevant if glanced at in the light of day. But if some of them aren't irrelevant, connections will be made, and a spark of insight may flare. Darwin's theory of the survival of the fittest is often cited as an example of the kind of sudden, stunning connection a creative mind can make; for Darwin hit upon the theory after he combined Thomas Malthus' description of the way humans would have to struggle to stay alive if there were a population explosion with his own observations of animals in the Galapagos Islands, of the way they competed for mates and the chance to survive genetically by reproducing.

As to the second question—What makes illumination happen?—though there's no certain answer, it's obvious that one can't simply will insight to occur. As Brewster Ghiselin points out in *The Creative Process*, willpower "cannot enable us to move in directions that have not yet been discovered." Thus, incubation is necessarily a state of suspense, a time of inner chaos and uneasy searching.

How to Be More Creative

The fourth and final thing that seems clear about creativity is that to some extent it *can* be taught, though there's controversy over just how that should be done. Some psychologists believe that the creative process operates in much the same way in novelists as it does in subatomic physicists, and so they focus on general principles and on ways to set a stream of ideas flowing. Other researchers maintain that creativity can only be fostered in the context of a particular activity. They say that painters can be taught to bring fresh ideas to their work, and that business executives can be trained to take a more innovative approach to problem solving, but that the methods used won't overlap.

In putting together the following suggestions, I've sided with those who believe in teaching a common creative process. Here, then, are some *creative energy tips:* six basic ways to tap into your creative potential.

1. When in Doubt, Incubate

Though you can't will illumination, you *can* back off from a problem when you're stymied and turn your attention to something else while your subconscious does its bit.

One of the simplest ways to do this is to "sleep on the problem," since solutions can occur almost magically on the heels of a good night's sleep. Public relations writer David Hackler sometimes actually programs himself to produce an overnight answer.

When he needs a good, strong headline or an angle for a story, before he goes to sleep at night he instructs his subconscious to come up with ideas the next morning. Sometimes when he first gets up he doesn't even remember that he's incubating a problem, but while he's in the shower answers will begin to occur to him.

Some people find that they can occasionally pull inspirations out of their dreams, as Alexandra Stoddard can. There are even individuals who can decide in advance what to dream about. The remarkable anthropologist Margaret Mead would assign a problem to her dreams by concentrating on it just as she was falling asleep. The solution was apt to come through in symbolic form and to need interpretation—for example, a dream she once had about a fishnet provided a clue to the way a culture's kinship system was structured.

Some sports provide an opportunity for incubation. Many runners, swimmers, and bikers find that their activity occupies just enough of their attention so that if they let their minds range freely there's a chance for illumination to occur. Household tasks can work in much the same way. Malka Rosen went back to college after taking time out to have children. She found that when she was stuck on a term paper, if she set the work aside while she tackled the laundry, when she returned to the paper the words usually began to flow again. Another way to incubate is to have several projects going simultaneously, so that you can switch back and forth between them, leaving one to "soak" while you focus on another.

2. Suspend Judgment

Some psychologists believe that incubation can be forced or, at any rate, simulated if a person can learn to let his imagination flow freely, tossing out possible solutions to a problem without judging or rejecting any of them no matter how bizarre they seem. Judgment can come later.

When a group uses this procedure, it's called "brainstorming." The technique was invented by advertising executive Alex F. Osborn back in the 1950s. He laid down four basic rules. First, group members weren't allowed to criticize each other's suggestions. Second, the wilder the ideas tossed out the better. Third, the group was to strive for quantity. And fourth, members were to try to improve on what others suggested and to combine ideas.

In a book called *Guide to Creative Action*, by Sidney J. Parnes, Ruth B. Noller, and Angelo M. Biondi, I found this example of the way one idea can lead to another. It seems that some workers in a plant were less productive than they could have been because they wasted time reading the newspapers they used to pack the company's products. When a group of supervisors tried to come up with a solution to the problem, the first suggestion was to switch to newspapers printed in a foreign language. The next idea was to hire people who couldn't read to do the job. The third was to blindfold the workers. The fourth suggestion—to hire blind people—was actually considered a feasible solution.

Those who teach creativity have found that with training people do become freer with their ideas. If you want to practice limbering up your imagination, you might try reeling off lots of possible solutions to the following dilemmas. (Answers—the solution actually used in each case—are provided at the bottom of the page.)

• Your eyes are so sensitive that peeling onions is torture for you, but no one else is available to do the job. How can you escape the pain?*

• Your house is in the middle of a wildlife park and an overly tame moose keeps hanging around, trampling your azaleas. Short of investing in tall fences or standing guard continually, how can you discourage the moose?†

• As chairperson of your church's repair committee, some time ago you lined up volunteers to paint the outside of the building. But now the church's hundredth anniversary is rapidly approaching and little or no painting has been done. How can you get the volunteers moving?‡

---

* Tara Tayyabkhan (age thirteen) found that when she wore swim goggles to peel onions she never shed a tear.

† Dr. David Hellyer of Tacoma, Washington, drove away the moose by opening all doors and windows and playing—at top volume—a recording of wolves howling.

‡ As reported in *Guide to Creative Action*, Earl J. Ferguson measured off an equal area on the side of the church for each volunteer and then painted each one's name in huge letters in the middle of "his" area. The volunteers turned up in short order to paint over their names.

• You're the mayor of a small town that has plenty of potholes and no money available for filling them. What can you do?*

Though brainstorming seems to work well enough in many situations, people whose creative drive finds its outlet in the arts—in writing or designing, for example—need to use a slightly different approach. The trick is to aim for quantity rather than quality in your initial efforts: to produce, as rapidly as possible, a whole stack of rough sketches, getting ideas down as fast as they occur to you; or to race through a first draft of something you're writing, spilling out thoughts without regard to logic or grammar. Sorting, discarding, organizing—judging—can come later.

3. Balance Imagination with Discipline

Creative effort is seldom just a matter of lucky insights; it's hard work. Without the first and last steps of the process—preparation and verification—you may produce nothing worthwhile; in fact, the whole exercise can turn into a form of self-indulgence.

Bear in mind that the initial effort may be painful, especially if you have in your mind some fairly clear idea of what you want the end result to be like. To begin with, you may fall far short of it. The postimpressionist painter Vincent van Gogh once wrote, ". . . the thing has already taken form in my mind before I start on it. The first attempts are absolutely unbearable."

Note, too, that bogging down is always a possibility where the creative process is involved. Your logic blocked, you may relax and incubate and—maddeningly—get nowhere at all with it. That's when brainstorming or Phyllis Whitney's imaging technique can help. But *the point is to keep plugging away until somewhere, somehow a connection is made and the creative energy begins to flow again.* Both Stoddard and Whitney work right through even when ideas don't come easily.

---

* Mayor John McGee of Falls City, Oregon, sold the potholes as Christmas gifts for "people who have everything." The purchaser received a gift certificate, and those who paid for the twenty-dollar deluxe job could have the recipient's name inscribed on top of the patch.

4. Pictures in the Mind

Creative people tend to resort to imagery quite a lot in their thinking, as Stoddard and Whitney do. Both women are highly visual—they see pictures in their mind. Some people are more inclined to imagine sound or movement.

Visual images are fleeting, unstable, and—if they're complex—hard to grasp as a whole. The way to bring them into sharper focus is to relax completely, as Phyllis Whitney does when she uses her deep-relaxation technique before mentally screening a new scene for her novel.

Psychologist Jean Houston (described in Chapter 12) calls imaging an "alternative energy system" because of the way it opens up creative potential. She points out that the brain can process images much faster than words, which is why during times of great danger people sometimes watch their entire lives flash past them in a matter of seconds. It's also how pianists and skiers, rehearsing mentally, are able to practice a concerto or a slalom event in a fraction of the time they'd spend rehearsing in the flesh.

Margaret Mead was an extraordinary imagist. Jean, who had an opportunity to do a formal study of Mead and the way she worked, found that she'd often plan a speech or a paper she had to write by reviewing a sequence of images. For instance, in an article on Mead published in *Quest* magazine before the anthropologist's death, Jean included this description of the way Mead marshaled her thoughts for a speech on the human uses of science:

"She remembers an appalling exhibit in Copenhagen: A man tried to create human beings and instead made grotesques. Her body responds to the degradation of treating people as objects—'target populations' . . . 'human inventories.' She recalls dozens of scientific studies that objectify the human condition. She thinks of her audience and sees them as strangely deficient in music and art, eyes veiled, ears stopped up. A sweep of Beethoven races through her, a sense of standing before the *David*, and then looking up at the Sistine ceiling. These images give way to pictures of Early Man, pitiful, helpless, with his arms full of sticks; then to a memory of a New Guinean friend, savage in 1928, intellectual in 1953. Images join images, words appear suited to form, and a complex and potent speech unfolds."

Most people's mental pictures wander, but Mead's were organized and coherent. She had learned that when you observe images long enough, they generally cease to be random and arrange themselves into narratives, or problem-solving sequences, with beginnings, middles, and ends. Mead also used imagery to review situations and to plan and analyze. Jean recalled, "Margaret would say, 'If this should happen, then what would follow?' And then she'd think in images, watching the story unfold."

Most children are good at imaging, but as they grow up they give up their active fantasy life. As a result, some adults have difficulty thinking in pictures. "All they can see are two blue dots," Jean said. She herself has found that visual images don't come easily to her, "and when they do come they're not very interesting. I see the tax collector or the tiles on the bathroom floor, whereas my husband is extraordinary. As a result, in fourteen years of marriage we have rarely been to the movies, because he says, 'Why should I go when I can close my eyes and watch a multibillion-dollar production?'" Jean believes that *anyone can learn to think in pictures*. Though some people may be better at it than others, the skill is like a muscle: It's just a matter of exercising it, of putting in the time.

IMAGING CAN BE DISCIPLINED OR FREE-FLOWING

There are at least two different ways of imaging: You can either direct and control the flow of images or you can simply let them happen. Each method has its uses. Controlled imagery is, of course, handy for rehearsing a skill mentally, but it's also a way to preset a pattern for other kinds of action. Jean Houston believes that imaging primes the brain's motor and sensory circuits; she says it's almost as if you've laid down tracks in the brain, so that when you're finally through rehearsing and ready to act the energy flows more easily.

Be that as it may, if there's something you can't quite face doing, it's surprisingly helpful to run through it in your head using imagery first. Perhaps there's a phone call you must make that you've been postponing for days, to the point where you actually feel helpless in the face of your own reluctance. To get past this particular mental block, close your eyes and imagine lifting the receiver, dialing the digits one by one, and hearing the sound of the phone ringing at the other end. If you now open your eyes and approach the telephone, the rest will follow almost automatically.

Dieters can sometimes reinforce their willpower before they get out of bed in the morning by reviewing in mental pictures what they plan to eat that day and rehearsing scenes in which they successfully resist temptation. Imagery can even be used to forestall disappointment and the sharp drop in energy that goes with it. When I'm expecting an important letter, before I open the mailbox I visualize a stack of mail inside that does *not* include the envelope I'm hoping for. Then, if the letter is there I'm pleasantly surprised; if it's not I'm not disappointed.

Creative insights are more likely to occur during uncontrolled imaging, for when you simply let the mental pictures flow you loosen the reins on the subconscious and the result may be ridiculous, bizarre—or illuminating. Phyllis Whitney uses uncontrolled imaging when she closes her eyes, empties her mind, and waits for a mental movie to materialize. Another writer I know had decided that it was time to do a new nonfiction book but had no idea what she wanted to write about. In the aftermath of a Jean Houston workshop, she was experimenting with visual imagery one day when into her head—clear as a snapshot—popped a picture of a book jacket, title and all. Anxious not to break the spell, she carefully opened the book and "read" the table of contents; then she dashed to her typewriter to get it all down.

But uncontrolled imaging is not only useful; it's also great fun, a way to entertain yourself on a commuter train or while you're waiting to fall asleep at night. Another woman I talked to had never really experimented with imaging before she attended a Jean Houston workshop. She says that it has become one of her favorite pastimes. Sometimes the pictures in her mind are faint and relatively uninteresting; at other times they're vivid and rather bizarre. (This variability may be due to the ninety-minute fantasy cycle—see Chapter 5.) She has even found that she can image at times with her eyes open. "I was walking down the street one day," she recalled, "sort of doodling in my head with images, when I happened to notice the way the parking meters were lined up in a row along the curb. Suddenly I 'saw' the whole row of them start to hop away ahead of me, like riderless pogo sticks. I had no feeling that I had thought up the idea—it simply clicked on in my head. It didn't lead to any creative insights, but it *was* great fun."

HOW TO THINK IN SOUNDS AND MOVEMENTS

As I mentioned earlier, imaging doesn't have to be visual; it can be auditory or kinesthetic instead. In most people one of the three types predominates. Since almost every adult thinks in terms of words and "hears" those words with the mind's ear, it would seem that auditory imaging is more common. However, *if you don't count words, then most people are more apt to think in pictures than in sounds or movements.*

Musicians, of course, hear inside their head the music they're composing. Mozart said that his ideas simply came to him when he was alone. He didn't know where they came from or how, and he couldn't force them, but when they were flowing nicely the experience was like "a pleasing, lively dream."

As with visual imagery, the person who hears inner music sometimes feels that the creative act is almost involuntary. Composer Aaron Copland once wrote, "The inspired moment may sometimes be described as a kind of hallucinatory state of mind: one half of the personality emotes and dictates while the other half listens and notates. The half that listens had better look the other way, had better simulate a half attention only, for the half that dictates is easily disgruntled and avenges itself for too close inspection by fading entirely away."

With kinesthetic imagery you "feel" yourself going through the motions of some activity. As noted in Chapter 10, though to all outward appearances you may seem perfectly still, minute electrical impulses can be recorded from the muscles you imagine you're moving—which proves that you really do think with your body as well as your mind. Actors often focus on movement as they observe other people; they mentally "try on" postures, gestures, and facial expressions. When kinesthetic imagery is combined with auditory or visual imagery—in mental rehearsals, for example—it adds a great deal to the vividness of the experience.

Jean Houston is a kinesthetic thinker. In fact, she frequently thinks on her feet, for she is convinced that "if you disinhibit the motor cortex by movement, you disinhibit so many other things as well: thinking, feeling, sensing, knowing." In her workshops she often has participants identify a particular personal problem and then put it out of their heads and dance in the aisles or wherever they can find space. At the end she asks each to recall his problem and to see whether a solution occurs to him or whether he feels differently about it.

Jean herself sometimes dances out her own problems in an even more dramatic fashion. She begins with free, rhythmic movements until she has built up momentum; then she starts to imagine what it is she wants to do and she dances that. "I will dance it," she said, "I will talk it, I will yell it until I am no longer the dancer, I am the danced; I am no longer the talker, I am the spoken; until I have broken through the barriers, and then I'll sit down at the piano or the typewriter and the energy will flow. If I'm dancing and almost enacting something in a dramatic form, then I am becoming the mouthpiece for secondary parts of my personality. Things that are normally submerged can come forth."

IMAGING WITH ALL FIVE SENSES

Another way to use imagery to tap your creative potential is to learn to think with all your senses. That's what Margaret Mead did. For her it all began with the method she used for memorizing poetry when she was a child. Instead of just learning by rote, she tried to see and hear in her mind whatever the poem described. She also felt its textures and experienced its emotions. "It's the rule of memory," Jean said, "that if I add more than two senses—if I hear you, I see you, and your ideas impinge on my skin—I'm not likely to forget."

As an adult Mead had a phenomenal memory and could recall scenes from the past in vivid detail. Jean explained that if someone asked the anthropologist how the people of Manus expressed sympathy, Mead would call to mind a specific incident, perhaps placing herself on the veranda of a particular house in New Guinea. Mentally she would assume the same posture and feel the same sensations as she had experienced decades before, and she would then "watch" as a child fell down and was picked up by someone nearby. As with the poems she'd learned, her memory was tied to bodily feelings and sensory images.

Mead was also capable of synesthesia, or cross-sensing: She could "hear" colors, "see" sounds, and "touch" aromas. There are people who do this sort of thing all the time; often they're surprised to learn that everybody doesn't. Anyone can learn synesthesia with a little practice. For example, the next time you're listening to a record, close your eyes and see what colors, images, and textures it brings to mind.

In her work with children who are problem learners Jean has developed teaching methods that make use of all the senses. The child is taught to think with his whole body: dancing, touching, and tasting information as well as seeing and hearing it. She's found that a youngster can learn spelling as rhythmic patterns and math as a rhythmic dance; he can easily be taught to think in images as well as words.

5. *Solitude*

To be creative you must allow your inner life a fair chance to unfold. When Alexandra Stoddard arranges to work at home, uninterrupted, for two days a week because she creates best in solitude, she recognizes the fact that someone who is too busy to turn inward is too busy to have many moments of insight.

But solitude is not enough. In his book *Creativity. The Magic Synthesis* psychiatrist Silvano Arieti also lists inactivity, daydreaming, and free thinking as conditions that will foster creativity. Thus, if you schedule periods of solitude, it's as well to make sure there's nothing on hand to claim your attention. You can use the time to indulge in the autobiographical fantasies we

call daydreams and to ruminate—to let your mind roam aimlessly
in "free thinking."

6. Focus on the Here and Now

Like many creative people, Alexandra Stoddard has a gift for
being fully *here* in the present moment and for bringing all of
her vitality to bear on whatever she does. That's important as a
kind of counterbalance to solitude and contemplation, for the
person who is too preoccupied with her inner life to notice
what's going on around her will overlook much of the raw data
that art, science, and invention feed upon. An important part of
problem solving, for example, is simply identifying problems that
need a solution.

The most talented writers, artists, musicians, and actors are
generally very much tuned in to their surroundings. The great
modern painter Pablo Picasso once explained in an interview,
"For me, creation first starts by contemplation, and I need long,
idle hours of meditation. It is then that I work most. I look at
flies, at flowers, at leaves and trees around me. I let my mind
drift at ease, just like a boat in the current. Sooner or later, it is
caught by something. It gets precise. It takes shape—and my next
painting motif is decided."

Surprisingly, many people find that it's not easy to be fully
present in the here and now for any length of time. To begin
with, so much of what we do in the course of a day is virtually
automatic. We stand up, sit down, eat, brush our teeth, drive a
car, and all the time our minds are elsewhere and we have very
little awareness of anything except end results: The teeth are
clean and we've arrived at our destination, though we've paid
scant attention to how this came about.

This automatic pilot that exists in all of us is extraordinarily
useful. It's handy to be able to plan dinner while en route to the
supermarket rather than having to concentrate on how hard to
press down on the gas pedal or even on whether to turn right or
left at the next corner. However, some people take the time and
mental energy that automatic responses save them and invest too

much in their inner lives: They're always "away" somewhere inside their heads.

Jean Houston has sometimes done something she calls "timetapping": She simply taps people on the shoulder and asks them whether they're thinking at that moment about the past, the present, or the future. Most of the time she finds that they've been rummaging in the past or trying on the future. To help people focus on the here and now Jean has developed several exercises. Two of them are not only an antidote to woolgathering, they're among the most energizing tactics I know.

Exercises for Intensive Living

The first exercise is called The Stop. It works by temporarily disconnecting the automatic pilot. You choose any ordinary fifteen-minute period in the day and for that length of time you pay attention to every move you make—you deautomate and do everything consciously. For instance, if you're about to pick up a chair and move it, stop first for a fraction of a second and then deliberately direct each movement with your mind. You'll be much more graceful. You'll also discover one of the few drawbacks of the automatic pilot: When you're on automatic you often spend more physical energy than is necessary. Ordinarily, even as you approach a chair to lift it you have already tensed the muscles in your arms, back, and neck in anticipation; as you lift you apply more force than is necessary. But if you're doing The Stop and you approach the chair with no preconceptions and lift it by using only as much strength as it takes—responding sensitively to the weight of the chair—you'll spend less energy and the experience will feel entirely different. The Stop is surprisingly refreshing and will generally leave you feeling very focused and clearheaded.

The second exercise is a form of calisthenics, a workout for your kinesthetic (or imaginary) body as well as the flesh-and-blood one. Here's the general idea: First you move some part of your body—very slowly raising and lowering an arm, for example. Then, when the arm has returned to your side, you raise and lower it again in your imagination. Next, you might repeat the procedure with the other arm, first the real one and then the imaginary arm. You go on to "exercise" both real and imaginary legs and other body parts, finishing up with a movement that involves the whole body: You jump forward and then back, first in body and then (in effect) in spirit. After just a few minutes of exercising your kinesthetic self, you'll feel somehow denser, fuller, more real. Jean explained, *You've put your awareness into different parts of your body. Where there is more awareness there is more energy.*

Neither The Stop nor the kinesthetic exercise will convert you on the spot into someone who makes a habit of living intensely in the present, but they will remind you of how good that can feel; you may decide it's worth the effort to try to strike a better balance between focusing inward and focusing outward.

Creative Energy Springs from Creative Tension

Striking that balance is important because creative energy flourishes where a person is able to reconcile opposing tendencies of various sorts. As Parnes, Noller, and Biondi point out in *Guide to Creative Action,* creativity requires both judgment *and* imagination; logic *and* emotion; insight *and* action; periods of being open to the environment *and* periods of deep self-searching; times for making things happen *and* times for letting them happen.

Small wonder, then, that creativity is experienced by many people as creative tension. And yet there's no challenge quite like it, no better way to stretch your abilities, exploit your potential—and generate energy.

Doing More by Doing Less

When you're absorbed in the creative process and it's going well, you have a sense of energy flowing effortlessly. Everyone would like to feel that way more often, both while making a creative effort and at other times; yet the tensions and frustrations of day-to-day living too often interfere.

Meditation is one way to defuse such tensions. Paradoxically, it teaches you that in the long run the way to get more done is by easing off first and doing a little less.

Mental Energy:
Doing More by Doing Less First

Sophy Burnham: Meditating Generates Energy

"I never meditate at night," Sophy Burnham told me, "because if I do I can't go to sleep. A couple of times I tried meditating at seven or eight at night, and it was so energizing that I was still up, padding around, at two in the morning, wide awake. I suppose it sounds crazy—I mean, why would anyone choose to sleep rather than being awake and full of energy? But my body was tired even if my mind wasn't, and of course it's hard on my husband if I'm up half the night."

Sophy is a Washington, D.C., author and playwright whose creative energy usually flows in half a dozen different directions at once. At the time I talked to her she was involved in starting a new theater in Washington modeled after New York's famous Actors' Studio; her first play, *Penelope,* had recently been produced; she'd had a nonfiction book (*The Landed Gentry*) published a few months earlier and would soon have a children's novel, *The Dogwalker,* in the bookstores. Meanwhile, she was already hard at work on a new play and a new adult novel.

It had been seven years since Sophy first discovered meditation, and she still meditated virtually every morning. Either she got up early to do it or else she waited until her husband and children had left for the day and the house was empty and quiet. In times of strain she also meditated as an emergency measure to calm herself. She recalled, "When *Penelope* was being produced in Washington, I was in a terrible state on opening night, so I went upstairs and meditated for half an hour. I came down again feeling fine."

The technique Sophy most often used was *thera vada* or *vipássana,* a breathing meditation. As she explained it, "You sit quietly with your eyes closed and simply 'watch' the air going in and out of your nostrils—you concentrate on the tip of your nose." She learned the technique from a friend, Jane Hamilton Merrill, who was the first American woman to study in a Buddhist monastery.

Sophy also used a mantra meditation, in which you sit with eyes closed and repeat aloud an ancient Sanskrit word or phrase. Transcendental Meditation (TM), the technique Americans are most familiar with, is the mantra sort. However, Sophy never learned TM, she had her mantra given her by a Hindu master whom she met. "I sometimes do the mantra meditation instead of the *thera vada,*" she said, "because *thera vada* meditation is extremely difficult. It requires an incredible amount of concentration. On the other hand, maybe for that very reason I feel it's purer, so I feel a little guilty chanting the mantra. But both bring you to the same place—and achieve the same result."

Sophy explained that for her the inner experience of meditation has changed over time. When she first began to meditate she was primarily aware of the physical sensation of the air rushing in and out of her nostrils. Distracting thoughts kept intruding and pulling her mind away from her breathing, but whenever she became aware that her attention had wandered she refocused it quietly and without judging herself, beginning again.

One day she found to her astonishment that as the meditation progressed she could "see" a small white form floating at the end of her nose even though her eyes were closed. Later she began to have visions—mad, brilliantly colored psychedelic ones. Extraordinary! No one had told her meditation would be fun. Then this, too, passed and she meditated for a while in blackness and finally in white light. "That's about where I am now," she said. As each meditation progresses, ordinary thinking fades away and she achieves a profound inner stillness sometimes bathed in light.

If that were all meditation meant to Sophy, it could be written off as a form of very provate entertainment. However, she observed, "The meditating doesn't stop when you stop meditating—the effects of it continue all day long." She felt that meditation had changed her in a number of ways. She used to swing (rather violently sometimes) from euphoria into depression and back again. *After she began meditating, her moods evened out and she no longer sank into the depths.* "Neither have I had any great swings into ecstasy," she said, "but it's better this way, for I am usually high—but calmly so."

Moreover, she found that things didn't disturb her as much now; she felt as if she were more attuned to her environment. She was hesitant to speak of what she called "the deep spiritual experiences" that are the real substance of the meditative life. However, her attitudes had changed: She felt differently about herself and her ambitions, about other people and her relationship with the world. For instance, if a magazine editor had asked for changes in an article she had written, it was no longer an ego-bruising experience. Her writing, she said, came more easily, and she believed she thought more clearly. "Things are given to me now," she said. "My job is merely to observe." When she hit a snag in her writing, a solution would sometimes occur to her in meditation.

Sophy differentiated, therefore, between two different things that seem to occur in meditation. Sometimes she sank into the center of herself, arriving at a silence deep inside. It was this meditation that was often accompanied by either blackness or light. She received a calm assurance and sometimes arose afterward with a solution to a problem that had been bothering her.

At other times her thoughts seemed to take on a life of their own. Like Phyllis Whitney, who used a relaxation technique to achieve a similar mental state, Sophy just watched the thoughts that passed before her, almost as if she were watching a movie. In this meditation characters and situations would appear to her, sometimes including whole scenes with dialogue. Many of the scenes from her last play came to her this way. "At first I was tempted to push them away because, after all, I was supposed to be meditating, not writing," she recalled. "But in the end I just watched. I was grateful for what I got."

Over the years there had been other changes in Sophy's life since she had started meditating. She rarely ate red meat anymore, and she stopped drinking. She never did drink much, but now she gave it up altogether because alcohol simply didn't appeal to her. Meditation enthusiasts would say these changes are due to meditating, and they do indeed sometimes overtake meditators. Sophy herself said she didn't really know why they'd happened.

If she stopped meditating even for a few days, however, she could feel herself beginning to revert. "The idea that I have too much to do falls in on me again. There are all the cars honking and the people rushing around asking me to do this, demanding that. I start to worry unnecessarily about things. I am out of tune."

But it was rare for her to skip a meditation. Most of the time she lived with the quiet conviction that whatever had to be done would be done. "The major thing is that through meditating I have a sense that everything is working the way it should be working," she said. "The universe is, and so am I, because I'm just a piece of the whole."

Slowing Down as a Way to Get More Done

Sophy Burnham is not alone. Meditation has made profound changes in the lives of many Americans since it first began to creep into the public consciousness in the mid-sixties. For some, like Sophy, it has a direct and immediate effect on energy: Twenty minutes of meditation work better than a caffeine booster. For most people the energy gain is long-range and not as dramatic. Immediately after meditating they feel unusually relaxed. That's not the end of it, though; they're apt to find that throughout the rest of the day they're both less tense and more vigorous and alert. *Apparently meditation accomplishes a kind of unstressing that allows natural energy to flow more freely.*

All creatures cycle continually between activity and inactivity. Ideally we should let ourselves coast with this natural flux of energy and make the most of it. However, we live in a competitive culture that, on the one hand, praises activity and anything that resembles energy and, on the other, seems to regard inactivity with suspicion. And so we push ourselves, nagged by the feeling that if we just tried a little harder we could do a little more.

I believe that for many people, particularly those who are strung out on stress, *the way to do a little more is to do a little less first*—to opt for inactivity in the form of regular meditation. Ultimately it's a waste of energy to try to run hard all the time. Meditation is in some ways uniquely invigorating, because it produces deep physical relaxation even as it quiets the swooping and darting of an overly busy mind.

How Meditation Affects the Body

Though it's a simple mental exercise, meditation generates a complex, involuntary physical response. Some years ago a physiologist named Walter R. Hess found that if he applied a mild electrical charge to one area of a cat's brain he could produce in the animal all the symptoms of the fight-or-flight response, while if he stimulated another area nearby the bodily reactions were in the opposite direction and the cat suddenly became very relaxed. It was Boston cardiologist Herbert Benson who dubbed this second reaction the "relaxation response."

Of all the changes that constitute the relaxation response, the most impressive is a drop in metabolism. The metabolism rate is a measure of the total amount of oxygen the body's cells consume in burning nutrients. It's highest during intense exercise and it dips during sleep. However, it takes four or five hours of sleep to lower the metabolism significantly, while an experienced meditator can achieve the same effect within a couple of minutes.

During meditation the heart beats more slowly, the rate of breathing slows, and the galvanic skin response (GSR) rises, as it generally does when anxiety subsides. These and other responses combine to produce a general quieting down and tuning up of the body.

However, meditation is more than just a route to deep relaxation, for in the long run it seems to alter the meditator's basic response to stress. Some years ago two experimenters, Daniel Goleman and Gary Schwartz, tested the effects of meditation by asking volunteers to watch a stress film that showed a series of grisly accidents in a woodworking shop. The film is often used in psychological experiments because virtually everyone finds it alarming.

The volunteers in the Goleman-Schwartz study were of two sorts. Either they were people experienced in meditation who taught it to others or they had never tried it but hoped to learn. All saw the film, but in the twenty minutes preceding the screening some volunteers were asked to meditate while the rest were told to relax for a while. Thus, there were teachers who sat and relaxed and other teachers who meditated, and there were non-meditators who relaxed and others who were given on-the-spot training and then had a chance to meditate for twenty minutes.

The results were quite striking. Those who had meditated showed more signs of alarm just as an accident was about to happen on the screen—their hearts raced and they perspired more—but once the film was over they returned to normal faster than did the nonmeditators who had simply relaxed. Even the novices who were meditating for the first time recovered relatively quickly. Since a body that stays aroused long after the danger has passed experiences unnecessary wear and tear, the short-term benefits of meditation were clear.

There were long-term benefits as well, for the teachers assigned to the relaxation group responded in much the same way as did the teachers who were allowed to meditate—with pronounced alarm signals during the film and a fast recovery afterward. Meditators often note, as Sophy did, that they've become more even-tempered. As one man put it, "A lot of things don't seem as earthshaking now as they once did." The Goleman-Schwartz study suggests that *there may be a physiological basis for the change in temperament that meditators experience.*

Problems for Which Meditation Is Prescribed

In the short time since meditation became popular in this country, medical people eager to experiment have prescribed it as a treatment for any number of physical and emotional ailments. Evidently they reasoned that it seemed unlikely to do any harm, and they actually found that in a surprising number of cases it did cure or at least improve patients. At any rate, these days meditation is being recommended for everything from epilepsy to writer's block. Though it's not guaranteed to work for everyone (what treatment is?), if you have any of the following problems, it may well be worth a try.

• High blood pressure: Though blood pressure doesn't ordinarily decrease *during* meditation, over a period of time—say, two months or more—regular meditators can often bring their pressure down by five to ten millimeters, which is enough to permit some borderline hypertensives to do without medication and others to manage with less. However, as soon as the patient stops meditating the pressure begins to ease upward again.

• Pain control: Dr. Donald Morse of the Department of Endodontology at Temple University School of Dentistry has taught dental patients to meditate. His studies show that after just ten minutes of meditating most find injections relatively painless and can get by with less local anesthesia or sometimes none at all.

• Diabetes: Diabetics who meditate can sometimes reduce the amount of medication they need.

• Epilepsy: Seizures occur less frequently for some epileptics who learn to meditate.

• Tension headaches: Princeton University psychologist Patricia Carrington says that she has never seen a case where tension headaches weren't relieved in severity or frequency once the patient began meditating regularly. (However, for migraines biofeedback is sometimes a more effective treatment.)

• Sleep disorders: Meditation can be helpful for insomniacs, poor sleepers, and people who suffer from night terrors or hypersomnia, which is an excessive need for sleep.

• Depression: You can be depressed and agitated or depressed and totally, helplessly passive. Those who are agitated often benefit from meditating, though people who are passive generally don't, perhaps because it takes a certain amount of mental energy to be able to meditate in the first place. Mild depressions —such as those the normal person often experiences in the course of everyday life—may respond extremely well to meditation.

• Anxiety: In the long run meditation usually reduces anxiety, often dramatically.

• Addictions: It has also been used quite effectively to treat addicts of various sorts, including cigarette junkies. Often people who have been meditating for two or three years will suddenly stop smoking; they report that it took very little in the way of willpower to do it. Meditation has also been used with some success to help those hooked on barbiturates, amphetamines, alcohol, marijuana, and LSD.

• Research suggests that meditation is also worth trying if your problem is asthma, chronic fatigue, chronic pain, irritability, blocked emotions, or blocked creativity!

Why Meditation Works

Meditating seems like such a simple thing to do that it's easy to underrate it. In fact, skeptics have suggested that twenty minutes of meditation may be no more beneficial than twenty minutes of sitting quietly. However, for several reasons the kind of rest the meditator achieves is not much like the kind he'd get from mere inactivity.

To begin with, it's clear that conditioning is involved. Just as an animal, once it associates the ringing of a bell with feeding time, will soon automatically salivate at the sound of the bell alone, so meditators become conditioned to their mantra or whatever device they use until it can trigger relaxation almost instantly.

Then again, meditation produces unusual mental states. By now many researchers have used an electroencephalograph to study the brain waves of meditators. Though sometimes the record shows brief snatches of sleep, more often the recorded brain waves look like those of someone just on the verge of sleep. Yet the meditator usually reports afterward that he felt alert throughout, and it's clear that he never actually dozed off. *Time spent hovering deliberately, deliciously, somewhere between sleep and wakefulness is almost bound to be revitalizing.*

Brain wave studies have also turned up evidence of something even more unusual. When an EEG is done, electrodes are stuck to the scalp in several different places to pick up electrical activity in different parts of the brain. With experienced meditators, the EEG has sometimes recorded very fast and completely synchronized beta waves coming from all the electrodes at once, as if the whole brain were pulsating to a single, coherent rhythm. (Ordinarily beta waves occur when an individual is wide awake and active; and they're uneven, unpredictable, and unsynchronized.) When questioned, meditators identified those moments of synchrony as times when they were in deep meditation or in the state TM teachers call "pure awareness"—with a mind completely conscious but completely still, unblemished by even a wisp of thought.

Obviously there's more to meditation than the relaxation response. In fact, it's the mental experience that attracts most people, for meditating is quite different from everyday thinking. That difference has consequences of its own.

How to Tame the Scrambling Mind

To begin with, meditation requires a narrowing of attention that's sometimes called "one-pointedness." The individual is asked to focus on a single repetitive device, such as a mantra.

Many people are surprised to find that this isn't at all easy to do. Ordinarily the mind plays chords, not single notes, and so it's perfectly capable of conscientiously chanting a mantra while planning dinner and simultaneously worrying away at some problem. Thus, though it's not difficult to sustain a mantra, it *is* hard to keep other thoughts from shoving it into the background. Swami Rama, an Indian yogi, once compared the mind to a drunken monkey; and psychologist Lawrence LeShan has pointed out that if we had as little control over our bodies as we seem to have over our minds we'd never make it across the street alive.

In his book *How to Meditate* LeShan describes everyday thinking this way: "If I am talking to someone, I am usually not only talking. I am also thinking about where the conversation is going, what has already been said, how I feel about the person I am communicating with, and what the time is. In the background of my thoughts are memories of the earlier parts of the day and plans or concerns for the later parts. In addition, I am conscious of my posture, the feelings of my body, my fatigue level, and whether or not I have a drink or cigarette in my hand or want one. Each of these aspects of my mental activity is sending signals to my physiological apparatus as to the general state of things and how to respond. Each of these signals is different. In meditation we are in the state—or moving toward it—of sending only one set of signals at a time. The effect of this on our physiology is positive . . ."

You may remember that total involvement is part of the flow experience. During deep flow the mind apparently sends only one set of signals. Humans seem to find this state of mind intensely pleasurable regardless of whether they're meditating at the time or inching their way up a rock face. Evolution presented us with an invaluable gift when it gave us the ability to think about several different things simultaneously, but perhaps we've paid a price for it.

Meditating for Creative Insights

It's not easy to strip down to just one set of mental signals. However, the effort itself—the process of turning inward and *trying* to strip down—has its own value. It's a way to flush out creative ideas, and it can also set in motion the healing experience called desensitization.

Because we're intent on the world outside our skins, we ordinarily register only one of the mind's many babbling voices— the rational inner monologue that occupies the forefront of consciousness. But once we shut out the world and attempt to stifle the monologue by focusing our attention on a device such as a mantra, we become aware of some of the half-formed fantasies, bizarre ideas, and dim desires that have lurked in the background all along. We're able to make connections, as we do in dreams, between ideas, connections suggested not by logic but by intuition and our own emotional truths. As I pointed out in Chapter 15, Freud called this primary process thinking, and it's where creativity begins. Thus, *meditation can indeed generate a sudden insight or a vivid fantasy that can be shaped into a scene for a play or a novel.*

The thoughts and images that constitute primary process

thinking can sometimes be quite disturbing. However, meditators are instructed to deal with "distractions" by refocusing their attention on their mantra or whatever device they've used; and so the same uncomfortable ideas may come up again and again, only to be casually dismissed each time. Eventually they lose their power to disturb; the meditator is desensitized and may even come to accept many of his own quirks and secret impulses.

Meditating to Feel More Fully Alive

Meditation is different from everyday thinking in another way as well. It requires the individual to concentrate either on a device that's rhythmic and repetitive, such as a mantra, or on something that's completely monotonous. (For example, some people meditate by gazing steadily at an object such as a vase or a candle flame.) Whether it's repetition or monotony that's involved, the effect is the same: The meditator is cut off from the varied sensations that her mind is used to handling.

That's important, because humans have been programed by evolution to respond to change and to tune out sameness. The world presents so much information to the senses that the brain is forced to edit out what's insignificant. Both opportunity and danger are most apt to appear as a change of some sort—a sudden sound, a stealthy movement—and so for the sake of efficiency the mind damps down the rest. Thus, we cease to be aware of the ticking of the clock across the room and we no longer really register the sight of familiar people and places.

When we bombard the mind with sameness, presumably that helps to produce one-pointedness, but sometimes it also succeeds in disengaging the mental censor, the dampening down device. At such times the individual emerges from meditation to find that suddenly everything looks fresh and new. Colors are more vivid, sounds seem sharp and clear, and for just a few minutes the ability to see, hear, and feel is greatly heightened. It's a marvelous experience and quite energizing.

Experienced meditators can sometimes achieve a similar state in a more direct way. The technique they use is called the Yoga of the Householder and it's as difficult to do as it is simple. The meditator tackles some task of daily life—working in the garden, perhaps, or washing the dishes—with quiet absorption and a completely silent mind. As long as he succeeds in keeping his mind empty, he will feel intensely alive, as if he were thinking with his whole body and not just his head.

Of course, there's more to meditation than one-pointedness and the kind of inner stillness it can lead to. Americans are only beginning to learn about their mental potential. Sanskrit has about twenty different nouns that we can only translate as "consciousness" or "mind," because we haven't the experience to grasp the distinctions among them.

Meditation Dropouts

Meditation isn't for everyone. The dropout rate, in fact, is fairly substantial. Estimates vary, but the best guess seems to be that of the millions who have learned TM, 30 to 50 percent eventually stop using it. Some simply lose interest or can no longer find the time to meditate, but others quit because they discover it has uncomfortable side effects.

Lucy, a TM dropout, is a middle-sized, middle-aged woman with short, straight brown hair. "I took the TM training about five years ago," she said. "For three months I meditated pretty regularly and I found it a very mixed experience. Most of the time it really did make me feel good—I'd come out of it very calm and deliciously relaxed. But there were also days when I became increasingly tense and twitchy as I meditated, and twice I wound up in tears, overwhelmed by memories of my mother, who died some years ago. And it was always difficult to find the time to meditate. The TM people said it had to be twenty minutes twice a day. That was hard to fit in, and when I missed a meditation I was nagged by guilt afterward.

"Then I broke up with the man I'd been seeing. I felt terrible and I soon discovered that meditating made me feel even worse. I couldn't keep my mind on the mantra and so I spent the time locked up inside my head with my own anger, confusion, and regrets. After a couple of days like that I gave it up. I was sorry afterward, and I've often thought about beginning again, since for a while it really felt like a good thing; but I've got a new job now and a new man, and my life is absolutely frantic—I'm on the run from the moment I get up in the morning. These days I can't see where I'd find the time to meditate."

Meditation is not a completely innocuous activity. Some people do discover after a while that they need to take a vacation from it because it's making them uncomfortable, at least for the time being. The desensitization process simply isn't working and instead of bypassing disturbing thoughts they're locking in on them.

Others run into trouble because they can't resist the temptation to overmeditate. Instead of the forty minutes a day that most of the modern forms of meditation recommend, they soon begin to spend several hours, and as a result they become withdrawn, anxious, or depressed. Overmeditating doesn't create their emotional problems from scratch, but it does seem to trigger them. Professor Carrington suggests that meditation be limited to no more than an hour a day for the first year and no more than an hour at a sitting, nor more than two hours a day, thereafter.

But bear in mind that for most people meditation is entirely beneficial. If anything, they meditate too seldom, and they experience no side effects at all.

Techniques

In the beginning there was TM. Then, as the American interest in meditation mushroomed, people began to try other techniques as well, and some soon found that there was one system that suited them better than another. This was puzzling, since the differences among methods often seemed small. However, they can be significant, for a system of meditation that suits one person admirably can be hard going for another. *The way to get the most out of meditation is to experiment until you find the kind that feels right to you.*

There is, for example, the meditation technique that Dr. Herbert Benson invented for treating high blood pressure. The instruction couldn't be easier to follow: You relax in a quiet place with your eyes closed and concentrate on your breathing. Each time you exhale you think to yourself the word "one" or some other word of your choice. If distracting thoughts occur, you try to ignore them and return to your mantra.

Dr. Benson's method is quite structured. You can learn it without the help of a teacher; in fact, it's especially suited to that because it's so simple that you don't need anyone to reassure you that you're doing it right. However, some people feel that it somehow takes more mental effort than TM, and the lack of detailed instructions can be a disadvantage, too. It may mean that the meditator is unprepared to meet and cope with some of the common problems that arise with meditation practice and so may be unnecessarily discouraged and may even stop practicing, when a little more know-how could have meant success.

Dr. Patricia Carrington, the author of *Freedom in Meditation,* believes that one of the significant characteristics of any system of meditation is the kind of concentration it requires. Dr. Carrington, who has done research on meditation and has also used it with patients in psychotherapy, pointed out that most Americans are only familiar with active concentration—the sort you work at. "That's the kind we know and practice from the time we start school," she said. "For most people in our culture, to be able to say, 'I concentrate well' means that they get an A plus."

However, there's also passive concentration, in which the attention is quietly and effortlessly absorbed by whatever you're paying attention to. "It's as natural and easy as water finding its own level," Dr. Carrington explained, "but it's tricky trying to teach it to Westerners who want to meditate, because the first thing they do is try to force concentration. They tell themselves, 'I've got to keep thinking that word!'"

Meditation is actually a calm, almost dreamlike state in which you simply let things happen. For the beginner some techniques seem to produce that state more easily than others. For example, in TM the mantra isn't linked to breathing as it is in Benson's method. Instead, the word is allowed to proceed at its own pace. Sometimes it drifts through the mind slowly; sometimes it speeds up; it can become louder or softer, or it can fade away altogether, but the meditator simply lets it go its way—which is passive concentration. He's also told to expect distracting thoughts to intrude, since they're a natural part of the process. When they occur, he's not advised to "ignore" them, which would take active concentration; he's simply told to "favor" the mantra over them. TM teachers stress that effort is what keeps one from reaching "the restful depths of the mind."

Transcendental Meditation (TM)

TM training itself is generally excellent, and the group support it provides can be important for a beginner, though the price seems steep to many—at this writing four lessons plus a follow-up "checking" session cost two hundred dollars, though there are discounts for students and families.

However, TM is also replete with mystical trappings that please some people and make others extremely uncomfortable. There is the ceremony at which the initiate receives his own secret mantra while he kneels before a portrait of a white-haired guru and his instructor speaks and chants in Sanskrit. Then there is the mantra itself, supposedly chosen for its affinity to the trainee's particular nervous system, though it's assigned on the basis of a ten-minute interview. Many people are skeptical about the special properties of such a word. Some quietly compare notes with friends and become disillusioned when they discover that a number of others share their mantra.

Dr. Carrington explained that an individual studying with a guru in India is given a mantra carefully chosen by his teacher, who knows him well, to suit his current stage of spiritual development. Presumably this was the origin of the TM practice of presenting each trainee with his own Sanskrit word. However, the TM mantras (there are said to be about sixteen in regular use) are apparently assigned solely on the basis of age.

Some meditation enthusiasts believe it's possible to use virtually any word as a mantra. One new graduate told me, "I've actually meditated using the word 'Nixon,' and Nixon is anathema to me." However, for most people the word does need to be meaningless, since it's easy to become distracted by the meaning. Some psychologists are convinced that there are indeed some words that make better mantras than others.

Laboratory studies have demonstrated that sounds that are resonant and rise slowly in pitch can slow the heart rate and relax the listener. It's not surprising, then, to find that many Sanskrit mantras end on a resonant, nasal note, an "n" or "m" or "ng" sound that seems to reverberate inside the head. Incidentally, the fact that the meditator seldom speaks the mantra aloud is probably immaterial, for other studies have shown that muscles within the middle ear react to sounds we only dream about. Presumably they also respond to sounds we imagine; thus, a mantra repeated silently can have both physical and emotional impacts.

Dr. Carrington once tested the effects of several nonsense words she invented. Working with Douglas Moltz, one of her students, she asked volunteers to meditate using her homemade mantras. She expected to find that some of the words were more soothing than others, but to her surprise she learned that they actually evoked much more specific moods. Those who used the word "grik" as a mantra, for example, reported (on a checklist of adjectives) that they felt more angry and irritable afterward than they had before, and they were also less depressed! That reaction was intriguing in the light of the widely held belief that depression is often simply anger turned inward. On the other hand, the words "lōm" and "noi" seemed both relaxing and mildly energizing. Those who used "lōm" as a mantra said they felt less sluggish afterward, and those who tried "noi" felt less fatigued.

There are hundreds of ancient Sanskrit mantras that have stood the test of time. Someday research may tell us more about the probable emotional impact of many of them. It may become possible to choose one mantra to lift depression and another to revive energy—though even then there may be individual differences in the way people react to particular words.

CSM: A New Technique

For researchers the TM technique has one major drawback. To study meditation in the laboratory they either need to find experienced meditators or novices who can be trained to meditate—or sometimes both. The TM organization has often been quite willing to supply teachers to do the training or to take part themselves in studies, but it has insisted that the TM technique can't be altered in any way, even for experimental purposes, nor will they co-operate if TM is to be compared to some other system of meditation.

Feeling the need for something more flexible that could be used both for research and in therapy, Dr. Carrington developed her own method. Called Clinically Standardized Meditation (CSM), it's a classical form of mantra meditation that can be taught in two one-hour lessons over a period of a week. It is usually learned by means of cassette recordings and an instruction book, with only minimal supervision from a meditation counselor. (Often none is needed at all.) CSM deliberately avoids the overlay of mysticism that so charms or irritates those who learn TM. As in TM, the mantra sets its own pace, but CSM is even more permissive: Trainees are told that when thoughts intrude they can flow with them if they like, simply keeping in mind the possibility of returning to the mantra periodically to touch base.

It's difficult to learn meditation from instructions in a book, since there are always questions one wants to ask. It's also too easy to get off on the wrong foot—for example, to judge the success of each meditation by how well you hold distracting thoughts at bay, thus opting for active rather than passive concentration. Ideally, meditation should be learned from an experienced teacher, although, as indicated, Dr. Carrington has been able to teach it very successfully by using tape recordings (see Bibliography). However, for readers who want to experiment with CSM or who are simply curious about how it's done, here, in abbreviated form, are Dr. Carrington's instructions as presented in *Freedom in Meditation* and later elaborated upon.

The first step is to choose a mantra. The list of sixteen that Dr. Carrington offers in her course includes the following:

> may-yam
> shi-rim
> ha-sam

If none of these words suits you, you can combine a syllable from one mantra with a syllable from another, as long as the end product is meaningless. You might choose "may-sam," for example, or you can make up a word of your own with soothing properties.

Once you've chosen your mantra, find a dim, quiet, pleasant place where you won't be interrupted. Sit down in a comfortable position and then close your eyes and relax as you begin to repeat the mantra. In the beginning say it out loud, but then gradually allow it to become softer and softer until you are saying it silently in your mind. If it speeds up or slows down, grows louder or softer, or links up with your breathing or your heartbeat, let it, but don't try to make any of these things happen. When distracting thoughts occur, flow with them if you like, but keep in mind the possibility of returning to the mantra.

At first try meditating for just ten minutes at a time (later you may wish to extend this to twenty minutes). Don't use a timer because it might startle you unpleasantly when it goes off. Instead, squint at a clock from time to time. At the end come out of it slowly.

For the first three weeks try to meditate twice a day, allowing a minimum of three or four hours between meditations. Later you can work out for yourself how much time you want to spend. For many people once a day is enough. Don't meditate too soon after having a meal; the meditative traditions say you should wait an hour, because experience indicates that, for whatever reason, you won't get the benefits of meditation if your stomach is full. It's also difficult to settle down and meditate if you've just exercised vigorously or have recently had a stimulant such as coffee, tea, alcohol, or even a Coke.

Dr. Carrington believes that beginners shouldn't meditate each time in the same place, nor should they *always* burn incense or meditate in the company of the same person. Meditation *is* a conditioning technique and you don't want to condition yourself so that you can only meditate comfortably if you're in a particular room, with a particular person, or can catch a whiff of incense. For the same reason—because conditioning is involved—it's not wise to use your regular mantra for pain control or to combat insomnia, since eventually you might come to associate it

with pain or with falling asleep. Instead, make up an auxiliary
mantra.

In the first few weeks of meditating some people experience
some odd side effects as the body adjusts to living with less tension. These occur most often at the beginning of a meditation
and usually disappear as it proceeds, though they can happen
between meditations, too. They may include heavy or tingling
feelings; floating sensations; warmth in different parts of the
body; numbness in the hands or feet; vague, floating aches and
pains; an urge to laugh or cry, or a welling up of anger or anxiety. For most people such reactions are quite mild; once they realize that it's common to experience temporary side effects
(other relaxation techniques, such as Autogenic Training and
Progressive Relaxation, produce them, too) they're easy to tolerate. However, others find them distressing. Professor Carrington
suggests that in such cases the meditator reduce meditating time
to ten minutes a day or even just five, so that tension reduction
can proceed at a more leisurely pace for a few days; but she suggests this only where the symptoms are distinctly uncomfortable
and last throughout a twenty-minute meditation.

How to Meditate if You Hate to Sit Still

Unfortunately, some of the people who could benefit most
from meditation are those least likely to try it. I'm thinking particularly of the Type A's, the people who are frequently strung
out on nervous energy, and of Dr. Selye's "racehorses," who are
forever trying to cram eight days' worth of activities into the old
seven-day week. Some of these individuals wouldn't consider
meditating because they simply hate to sit still; others find in-
trospection uncomfortable, even threatening. Then there are the
sensation seekers (see Chapter 12) who really need a lot of stimulation. Yet *most of these people could gain an edge in energy if
they could just learn to manage their own tension.*

Over the years Dr. Carrington has often worked with the
highly active. She has found ways to modify the CSM procedure
to suit their needs. Actually, anyone who is too busy to invest the

conventional forty minutes a day in meditation may find her ideas worthwhile.

For the intensely restive Dr. Carrington sometimes suggests a course in t'ai chi as a prelude to meditation. Derived from the Chinese martial arts, t'ai chi teaches a sequence of exercises that are so slow and graceful that they're like movements made underwater; yet because they're also the motions one makes in fighting an enemy, they can be a way to release aggression as well.

Once an individual is ready to try meditation, Dr. Carrington suggests that he practice it with absolute regularity for at least three weeks so that the conditioning can take effect. Those who are too restless to be comfortable with the standard procedure sometimes find that it helps if they make some small, rhythmic movement as they sit, perhaps rocking slightly. Others learn that they can meditate comfortably provided they keep their eyes open.

Once the three weeks are up, the individual can switch to meditation in motion: He can combine the mantra with some solitary, repetitive activity such as running, swimming, or walking. Most people find that the activity itself becomes more enjoyable; they achieve a meditative state of mind, with all the benefits this entails. *Those who try mantra swimming, for example, report that the swimming suddenly requires less effort and is somehow soothing. Runners sometimes gain new stamina.* One jogger Dr. Carrington worked with was uncomfortable meditating and also complained that he was bored with trotting around an indoor track in the wintertime. When he combined the two the running became a much more intense experience. He perspired more and he felt as if he were using his whole body to run, though his heartbeat was actually slower than it had been before.

Then there was Lucy, who, you'll remember, gave up meditation in a fit of depression and never found time to take it up again. One day she tried a walking meditation. "I focused on the mantra," she recalled, "and within seconds I felt tense muscles in my legs let go. Suddenly my stride was longer and springier, I was walking faster, and it all felt quite effortless. At first thoughts kept crowding in around the mantra as I walked, but after about fifteen minutes my mind became quieter. Then the mantra itself faded away and suddenly inside my head it was completely silent. Yet I was sharply aware of everything around me, of the wind in the trees and the faces of people coming toward me. The silence didn't last long, but I got quite high on it. Since then I do walking meditations often. Walking has become a real, physical pleasure to me—it's no longer just a way to get to the bus stop."

Dr. Carrington explained that when a person does a moving meditation the rhythm of the mantra probably helps her to move more smoothly. It may also relax muscles that aren't being used, muscles that may have been obstructing movement before.

How to Meditate in Snatches

The other tactic Dr. Carrington recommends for the very active and the very busy is the mini-meditation. A mini is a very short meditation, just two or three minutes long—five minutes at most—done for strategic reasons to relieve stress. It doesn't require a quiet room; in fact, you don't even need to close your eyes. You simply repeat the mantra silently and, because it triggers relaxation, you derive benefits on the spot.

Minis are particularly effective for Type A's. Dr. Carrington recalled, "I've taken some very active people who can't bear to hold still for long and proved that they *can* sit down periodically during the day and meditate for two minutes with their eyes open. And that begins to pull the tension level down right there on the spot. I'm more and more impressed with the effectiveness of mini-meditations."

Though it's probably better to continue to do one or two longer meditations a day and tuck in minis as extras, some people find that minis are all they need, while others say they're all they have time for.

There are several different ways to make use of minis. You can think through your schedule and plan to fit them in at particular times—while you're waiting for a red light to change, for example, or while you're waiting for an elevator. Some people find it stressful to be forced to wait for anything; for them minis can work like safety valves. An alternative is to paste a small red dot on the face of your watch; whenever you glance at it you'll be reminded to do a mini.

There are also people who have trained themselves to monitor their own tension level and to tuck in a mini whenever they're feeling stressed. The whole sequence can become virtually automatic: Tension reminds you to do a mini and that relaxes the tension.

You can use a mini to psych yourself down when you're facing a high-pressure situation—an exam or a job interview, perhaps—and you're feeling very anxious; and, of course, you can use it again afterward to relieve accumulated tension. Though it's possible to do so many minis that you overmeditate, Dr. Carrington has found that most people do too few rather than too many. In any case, five a day would be perfectly safe even in conjunction with one or two longer meditations.

Incidentally, minis are most definitely not a modern invention. Yogis think their mantra many hundreds of times a day, returning to it again and again, and the same thing is true in other meditative cultures. A former member of the Peace Corps who lived for a time in Nepal was told by Tibetans there that they tried to keep a mantra going constantly at the back of their minds, like a heartbeat. In fact, he noticed that when old people sat down they would breathe out a mantra instead of letting out a sigh.

Energy Tips

1. Learn to meditate. Unless you're already a very relaxed sort of person, you're almost certain to experience a freer flow of energy. Try Dr. Carrington's CSM method (see Bibliography for information on the recorded course), or take the TM training.

2. Experiment and work out for yourself how much time you want to spend meditating every day.

3. Even if you have no inclination to meditate regularly, it's worth conditioning yourself to relax whenever you repeat a mantra. That's a handy thing to be able to do—in sports competitions,

in the doctor's office, anytime you're feeling uptight, or when you're trying to flush out a creative insight.

4. If you're the kind of person who finds it impossible to sit still, condition yourself to a mantra and then try meditating in motion—while you're running, swimming, or walking.

5. When you're in a hurry try a walking meditation. As your leg muscles relax, your stride will become longer, brisker, springier. You'll even look more energetic!

6. In fact, do a walking meditation when you want to create the impression that you're someone dynamic and full of energy.

7. If you're pressed for time, too restless to meditate for long, a very tense sort of person—or all of the above—try mini-meditations. Do them at preset times or in particular situations, or use a mini whenever you're aware that you're becoming tense.

What Can You Do for "the Blahs"?

Nobody is full of energy all the time. In everyone's life there are periods when vitality simply seems to evaporate. Day after day you wake up feeling so tired that you have to drag yourself out of bed. Everyday tasks suddenly seem to take a lot of effort.

The next chapter will describe some of the things that can cause such an energy crisis and what you can do to pull yourself out of one.

What to Do in an Energy Crisis

"I recently went through an odd sort of energy crisis," Dorothy said. A tall woman, prematurely gray, she has just gone back to work as a secretary after years as a wife and mother. "When I was in the midst of my divorce two years ago," she continued, "I felt tense and anxious most of the time. I knew that was hardly surprising under the circumstances, so I didn't worry much about it until I began to find that I couldn't jog. I was used to running a mile or two a day and suddenly I couldn't even do a quarter of a mile without feeling desperately tired, almost leaden. When I ran, and also at other times of the day, I sometimes felt as if my heart were beating too fast and I was hot and uncomfortable.

"For a long time I assumed that I was just reacting to the unpleasantness of the divorce. Finally I went to see a doctor, and I discovered that my thyroid gland was inflamed and was overproducing hormones. Apparently that's a rare sort of problem that's only recently been recognized. Fortunately it's like a cold: It's self-limiting and cures itself in time. All I had to do was stay in touch with the doctor and wait it out; but while it lasted that off-again, on-again exhaustion was really hard to take."

Meg also experienced a period when her energy inexplicably failed. "I would wake up in the morning," she said, "and I could barely drag myself out of bed. Everything I did seemed an effort, and sometimes I was so tired I just sat in a chair and stared at the wall for half an hour at a time. My husband wanted me to see a doctor, but I didn't even have the energy to do that. At any rate, I was pretty sure my problem was depression.

"I'd had my first child just three months earlier and he was a difficult baby, colicky and tense. We were living in an apartment building in the city and I didn't know any other women who had babies. I felt isolated and trapped, and I was sure I wasn't a good mother. I was used to working for a living, earning good money and being independent, and now suddenly it was as if I no longer had any control over my life.

"Eventually, of course, things got better. The baby settled down and so did I. But I've never forgotten the terrible tiredness, the sense of overwhelming inertia that I felt in those first few months after Sam was born."

When to Start Worrying About Chronic Fatigue

Up to a point, lapses in energy are normal—nobody feels peppy all the time. However, sometimes a down period drags on and turns into a case of chronic fatigue. If this fatigue is accompanied by other, more dramatic symptoms such as an extremely sore throat or a fever, we tend to think of it as a normal part of feeling ill. But occasionally there are no other symptoms and low energy is really the only noticeable problem. At that point many people begin to wonder whether they're actually sick or whether they're experiencing some kind of emotional reaction. Often it's difficult to tell what's going on, because *though poor health is always accompanied by exhaustion, anxiety and depression can also undermine your energy*. It's hardly surprising, then, that in the beginning Dorothy assumed that her problem was due to stress, while Meg's husband was convinced that Meg must be physically ill.

If you've been feeling chronically tired, it's important to find out what's causing your fatigue, since the tiredness is only a symptom and to get your energy back you'll have to get at the underlying cause. Your problem could be entirely physical, entirely emotional, or a debilitating blend of the two; it could be a reaction to stress. The solution might be something quite simple or it might be as drastic as revamping your life-style or your whole outlook.

In hunting down the cause, the place to start is with a visit to your doctor—even if, like Meg, you have good reason to suspect that your energy crisis is entirely psychological. It's wiser to play it safe.

According to Dr. Jack Richard, a New York City internist and endocrinologist, *fatigue is worth consulting a doctor about when you can't explain it on the basis of the activities you've been involved in, and when it's so debilitating that it interferes with your daily routine.* He added that though loss of energy may be the only problem *you're* aware of, a discussion with a doctor will often make it clear that you have other symptoms as well.

Different Kinds of Fatigue

When a patient comes in complaining of fatigue and low energy, Dr. Richard often begins by asking exactly what she means by "fatigue," since the word apparently means somewhat different things to different people. One person may explain that she just feels terribly draggy, that it takes immense effort nowadays to keep up with her normal routine. Another will say that she's not only draggy but sleepy a lot of the time; *she* may well have a thyroid gland that's underproducing.

Dr. Richard also asks questions about the pattern of the fatigue, since different problems produce different patterns. The typical insomniac, for example, feels poorly when he gets up, is much improved by the middle of the morning, caves in again at about three or four in the afternoon, but then gets his second wind after dinner. The person who has some physical disease generally feels more and more tired as the day wears on. When he wakes in the morning he's at his energy peak for the day and from there on it's all downhill. On the other hand, the person whose fatigue is generated by emotional problems often wakes up feeling terrible but by noon is somewhat improved.

Even when Dr. Richard suspects that it may be depression and anxiety that are sapping a patient's energy, he tests carefully for physical causes. There is, he said, "an obligation to investigate. In any case, there's no law that says a person can't be depressed and have a physical illness as well."

Thus, Dr. Richard takes a careful history and does a general examination. He inquires whether the patient has been running a fever and whether the fatigue first occurred in connection with some illness that has since cleared up. He's alert for physical changes, because a persistent cough, weight loss, or poor appetite might suggest a serious illness. As part of the physical exam he does a blood count to check for anemia, since people who are anemic often come in with complaints as vague as low energy and chronic fatigue. Blood samples are also used to screen for infections and for thyroid disease and other endocrine-gland pathology.

Some of the people who consult a doctor because of a lapse of energy are convinced in advance that low blood sugar is the problem and that they're suffering from hypoglycemia. However, Dr. Richard noted that as serious medical pathology hypoglycemia is quite rare, though there *are* perfectly normal people who do sometimes experience a dip in blood sugar several hours after eating a starchy meal. When that happens they may briefly feel nervous, shaky, sweaty, and cold. But that's a far cry from chronic fatigue, depression, and the other symptoms that are sometimes attributed to low sugar.

Thyroid Disease: The Energy Disorder

Thyroid diseases, on the other hand, are true energy disorders, for their chief symptoms are changes in the energy level. A person who is *hypo*thyroid—who has an underproducing thyroid gland—is apt to feel listless and depressed twenty-four hours a day, while someone who is *hyper*thyroid, a condition due to an overproducing gland, tends to be abnormally active, though she, too, may complain of periodic fatigue.

The thyroid gland is located just below the voice box, in front of the windpipe. The hormones it dispenses, traveling through the bloodstream, affect most of the cells of the body, controlling their metabolism—the rate at which they burn foodstuffs. When thyroid production is chronically high, it's as if the body's thermostat were turned up: Metabolism is faster, mental processes are speeded up, and other glands also become more active. When the thermostat is set too low, as it is in the person who is hypothyroid, everything moves more slowly. The patient feels tired all the time and she may actually sleep for fourteen or sixteen hours a day. She's overweight, constipated, and she may develop a husky, froglike voice. She's also extremely sluggish mentally. In fact, sometimes the change in personality is dramatic when hormone replacement is begun—as if a mental fog had lifted.

Hypothyroidism tends to develop very gradually over a period of years. Dr. Richard believes that it's one of the most commonly undiagnosed conditions. Very often hypothyroid patients are seen first by a psychiatrist and are treated for depression. It may be quite some time before it occurs to anyone that their problem might be primarily physical rather than emotional.

With *hyper*thyroidism the energy pattern is different. As Dr. Richard explained, "These individuals wake up in the morning raring to go. They move at a fast pace, but they burn out very quickly. They have short-lived periods of great energy alternating with periods of fatigue." Women are much more likely than men to develop either hyper- or hypothyroidism.

Because the symptoms of an overactive thyroid are very much like the symptoms of anxiety, hyperthyroid patients, too, may be seen first by a psychiatrist. Or sometimes they don't see a doctor at all because they assume that anxiety is the whole problem.

"Hyper" as in Hyperthyroid

That's what Amanda thought. A widow in her thirties, she had recently married again. She and her new husband, Tom, had combined two households and half a dozen teenage children. Within months of the wedding they found themselves caught up in the suburban homeowner's nightmare: They'd sold Tom's house, the new owners were due to move in, and the house they were building still wasn't finished. In the end they had to store their furniture and rent living quarters temporarily. They wound up camping—two adults, six children, four cats, and two dogs— in a two-bedroom apartment for ten days.

Throughout this period Amanda felt strung out and simmering

with nervous energy. She was on the go from early in the morning until late at night, but she'd always been a sprinter and it never occurred to her that anything might be wrong with her. "I did feel at times that I seemed to be running in too many different directions at once, but that was all," she said. "However, my family said afterward that they'd noticed a personality change. Suddenly I'd become extremely irritable, and I think Tom began to feel that he was finally seeing the real me. But we were all under such stress at the time that that seemed to account for everything."

As it happened, just before the move to the apartment Amanda had had a routine medical checkup; blood samples were taken and she was told to call back in a week for the results of the blood tests. When she called, she learned that her thyroid gland was overproducing "to a horrifying extent. The doctor suggested that all the stress in my life might have precipitated the disease," she said.

"Precipitated" is not the same as "caused," and Dr. Richard cautioned that he doesn't believe stress *causes* hyperthyroidism, though it may make it develop earlier than it otherwise would have. But, in any case, Amanda's experience neatly illustrates a point Dr. Richard made. Even if you've been under enough stress to generate half a dozen energy crises, it's not safe to assume that there isn't something physically wrong with you as well. In fact, stress can trigger all kinds of medical problems. That's why it's wise to see a doctor if you're suffering from chronic fatigue *or* if you're chronically strung out on nervous energy.

Fatigue When Nothing Is Medically Wrong

When a medical examination turns up negative, you have to look to your life-style and your emotions to explain your lack of energy. Actually, in Dr. Richard's experience long-term fatigue *is* more often caused by emotional problems than by physical ones. In fact, he believes that *boredom may be the single most common reason for exhaustion!* He pointed out that an individual tired to death of his job often begins to feel literally tired.

However, there are other possibilities as well, and the list of
questions that follows covers quite a number of them. As I mentioned earlier, what you do about your fatigue will depend on
what's causing it. Once you've identified the cause, you'll find
energizing suggestions in the appropriate chapters in this book—
indicated after each question by the number in parentheses.

Energy Tips: How to Find the Source of Your Fatigue

1. Are you sleeping well and getting enough sleep? Is it possible that you have one of the subtler forms of insomnia? (6)

2. Have you become dependent on sleeping pills? If so, they
may be affecting the quality of the sleep you get. (6)

3. Have you been trying to lose weight on a diet that's very
unbalanced? Or have you cut back so far on calories that you're
not eating enough to keep up your energy? (7)

4. Have you been overdosing on vitamins? (7)

5. Have you been drinking too much alcohol? Or have you
come to lean on some other drug (such as Valium) that may be
depressing your energy? (8)

6. Have you just lately cut back a lot on the amount of coffee
you drink? (8)

7. Are you overweight to the point where it's a real effort to
get around? (7)

8. Have you been leading an increasingly sedentary life? (9)

9. Is there too little stimulation in your life? too much? (12)

10. Have you been under a lot of pressure of one kind or another? (13)

11. Are you depressed, desperately bored, or frustrated? Or is
it possible that you're angry and can't admit to yourself that
you're angry? (4)

Coping with an Energy Gap

In the next chapter we'll take a look at the way energy
differences affect human relationships. What happens when
someone who has an enormous amount of energy marries some-

one who has a great deal less? For that matter, what happens
when two people who are alike live together? Would two
sprinters inevitably run each other ragged? The answers to these
questions may surprise you.

Can Two People Be Incompatible in Energy?

The Trotter Who Married the Sprinter

"My husband has much more energy than I do," Amy said. "That's something that became uncomfortably obvious to me when we were on our honeymoon years ago. I was exhausted from all the wedding preparations and I just wanted to lie on the beach and rest, but Arthur was all set to swim and play tennis, to do snorkeling and scuba diving; in the evenings he wanted to go dancing until all hours. I trailed around after him, but it was hard. In fact, I thought we were so mismatched that I was ready to leave him."

That was twelve years ago, and at times Amy still has trouble keeping up with Arthur. Yet it was partly his energy that attracted her to him in the first place. "I did have boyfriends who were more sedate," she recalled, "but they didn't have enough gumption for me. There was a time when I thought I really needed Arthur's energy to get going myself, though now I don't think that's true."

Amy believes that on the energy scale she's a 7 and Arthur is probably a 9. However, he denies that he has a lot of energy, nor does he feel that his wife has any less vitality than he has. In fact, the evening I telephoned to interview Arthur, he and Amy were in the middle of an argument about her energy. He had come home from work unusually early to find her in bed watching television. "I was really tired," she said, "so I was resting." Arthur was indignant. "Her idea of a good time," he complained, "is to lie in bed watching the tube."

Arthur's attitude is typical of many of the sprinters I talked to (see Chapter 1). He assumes that *his* pace is normal and that his wife is moving in slow motion. In fact, he has two different explanations for Amy's behavior. If she can't keep up with him, he says, it must be either because she isn't really trying or because she simply doesn't want to do what he expects her to do.

"People who are doing things they want to do have tons of energy," he said. "People who are unhappy about doing something cop out, and then they *claim* their energy is low. Amy has plenty of energy to fight with me tonight but none to do anything disagreeable, like clean the house."

It was hard to tell whether or not Arthur was completely serious. At any rate, Amy didn't seem particularly disturbed by the argument; but then, they'd been over the same ground many times before. Up to a point she agrees with him that she does have more energy for the things she likes to do; however, that's true of everybody.

Amy explained that she has tried to accommodate herself to Arthur's faster tempo. Six months ago she took up jogging because she hoped it would give her more energy, and it has helped. But part of the problem is that Arthur doesn't just judge by results—whether the house is clean and the children seem happy. "I don't really know why," Amy said, "but he doesn't like to see me sit around, so I save the bulk of my housework for the weekends. He's always jumping around himself—he can't sit still —and he likes to know that I'm active, too."

By anyone's standards Amy works hard. A short, sandy-haired woman, she teaches at a junior college and also manages a house and two school-age children. Her days are full, though they're seldom really hectic. "There would be no point in my running around constantly the way Arthur does," she says. "I can't do everything, so it's a matter of priorities; the least important things give. If I keep the house looking decent, if everybody has something to wear and they're fed, I can't do more than that. But when Arthur is very nervous about something he wants everybody else to jump, too. He carries a lot of people's burdens with him, and it seems that when he's agitated it's not reassuring to be around someone else who's calm."

Amy is generally a relaxed sort of person. She can only recall two or three times in her life when she was so worried or so excited about something that she couldn't sleep at night. "And I like to let things go sometimes," she said, "so that I can chew them over and figure out a solution. I have a real need for contemplation."

Arthur, on the other hand, is physically very active. He runs regularly and goes in for tennis, swimming, and waterskiing whenever he can find the time. A stockbroker, he likes to get off to a fast start on any working day, because he believes that he sets his pace for the day by what he does first thing in the morning. If he begins his day by lingering over the newspaper, he feels that he loses so much momentum that the whole day may be wasted.

To people who know them it seems obvious that Arthur has more drive than Amy. Still, their energy gap isn't really a substantial one, so it's surprising that of all the couples I interviewed they were among the few for whom an energy difference had created real problems. However, I think the gap itself isn't to blame.

Good and Bad Energy Gaps

When I began researching this book, I expected to find that energy differences are often a hazard, especially for married couples. Instead, to my surprise I learned that a difference can be either a liability or an asset, and that in and of itself it's not necessarily either a good thing or a bad one. *Which way it works depends on what it* means *to those involved.* Where a gap creates difficulties, then, you have to ask how people are interpreting it and what other problems it's playing into.

Amy, for example, values Arthur's greater energy—except when he insists that she conform to his pace. Arthur denies that there's any difference between them. When his wife has a lapse of energy, what it *means* to him is that she's saying "no" to things he wants her to do. And actually, to some extent he may even be right about that. Like most people, Amy can't always tell whether she's genuinely worn out from all that she's been doing or whether the tasks that face her are so unappealing that the very thought of them saps her energy. A lot of the time it's probably a little of both.

But there may also be other factors involved here that have nothing to do with energy. It may well be that Arthur envies Amy because she's a more relaxed sort of person than he is, and because she doesn't work under the kind of pressure that he has to cope with. Arthur has a way of taking other people's problems to heart; he does, as Amy said, carry a lot of burdens. When he arrives home after a grueling day at the office, he may feel irritated and envious when he finds his wife relaxing in front of the television set, though like most people he probably wouldn't acknowledge the envy even to himself.

Then again, there's the friction that develops when he's all nerved up and Amy isn't. Whenever two people come together there's a kind of leveling off that has to happen before comfortable communication can take place. If one person is high, either on enerjoy or on nervous energy, and the other is very much wound down, prolonged contact is apt to be jarring. Other people I talked to also commented on this fact. One man explained, "When I'm feeling anxious and hyped up, it's not at all helpful if my wife is unshakably calm and relaxed. The questions that occur to me then are, 'Doesn't she care?' and 'Is there something wrong with me that I'm so upset about things she obviously doesn't consider important?'"

Another couple have worked out a solution to the problem: When they meet after being separated for a time, instead of immediately exchanging news they begin by talking about how they're feeling ("I'm a little tense tonight" or "I had a marvelous day and I'm so high on it that I'd like to go out and run around the block"). Once each has acknowledged the other's feelings, tensions somehow dissolve and the person who is up no longer resents the one who is down, and vice versa.

The Hurdler and the Stroller

What was true of Amy and Arthur—a trotter married to a sprinter—is true of other kinds of gaps, too: It's the meaning of the gap, the way people take it, that determines whether it's a problem or not.

Laurie, for example, is a hurdler (she was described in Chapter 1). She lived for a time with a stroller and felt that the energy difference was definitely one of their problems. Later she became involved with a sprinter and once again had trouble adjusting to the vitality gap. Yet in both cases other issues were really at the root of her difficulties.

The stroller, Tim, was a professional musician. Placid almost to the point of lethargy, he made an uncertain living. Laurie herself was working as a lab technician at the time, and so for the most part it was she who paid the rent. Her job was dull and undemanding, and she often came home at night hungry for stimulation, eager to get out and see friends.

"Tim was very wound down," she recalled, "and he spent most days just hanging around the apartment. He didn't seem to put much effort into finding work, so you'd have thought he'd be eager to get out in the evenings; but most nights all he wanted to do was stay home and watch television."

Eventually Laurie began to feel chronically irritated with Tim. Part of the problem was the cultural stereotype that makes Americans feel that men should be more ambitious, active, and energetic than women. Laurie was not only partially supporting Tim, she was also the one who made most of the decisions and supplied the impetus for most of the things they did.

Thus, it wasn't so much Tim's lack of energy that annoyed her —although at first she thought it was—as the fact that their sex roles had been reversed. On an even deeper level, his passivity disturbed her, perhaps because of the corresponding passivity that she recognized in herself. "We both wanted to be taken care of," she said, "but because I was more competent and had more drive I wound up taking most of the responsibility, financially and otherwise, and I resented it." With Laurie and Tim the energy gap played into an unacknowledged struggle between them over who was to play the role of parent in their relationship. Thus, for Laurie the gap began to look like a serious problem.

The Hurdler and the Sprinter

Within a year after she broke up with Tim, Laurie ricocheted to the opposite extreme: She fell in love with a man who's a classic example of a sprinter (see Chapter 1). A well-known trial lawyer, David travels a lot, and his schedule, whether he's traveling or at home, is one that even Laurie can't keep up with. For a while that worried her.

"When we first started living together I thought I'd go crazy," Laurie recalled. "We were racing here and there, seeing people every single night. I found that David had to have something scheduled for every minute he was awake, and it seemed as if we were never alone together, never had a chance to sit and talk. I felt that all that tearing around was a way to avoid real intimacy.

"Things are much better now. He's finally slowed down a little, and he even does things sometimes to relax, like taking a bath. Do you know, it had never occurred to him before to do something just because it was relaxing! I guess I understand him better now, too. I realize that if he's not doing something he feels guilty. This is, after all, a man who grew up in a very poor family. His father held two jobs, his mother also worked, and still there wasn't enough money. He went through both college and law school on scholarships.

"It's also possible that some of his racing around comes from not wanting to face himself—he's not the introspective sort. Besides, the more there is in your life the more you're forced to live in the present, and that allays anxieties about the future.

"But even so, David isn't the sort of man who keeps busy simply for the sake of being busy—he's seldom just racing his engine; he uses his energy to the utmost. He says his schedule gets to him sometimes—he does feel pressured; but where the pressure would paralyze me, he just keeps plugging away and gets it all done. He's super-organized and he knows when to stop, too. He'll say, 'I can't do any more on this tonight,' whereas I'm inclined to persist even knowing that I'm so tired I've become inefficient."

Hurdlers sometimes sense that what they need in a spouse or a lover is a stabilizing influence. For most that means someone with a more even temperament, without the ups and downs of energy and mood. For Laurie it means someone who is consistently up. "I feel so much better when I'm revved up myself," she says, "and it helps me to be around people who are revved up, too, as David usually is."

Other hurdlers need someone who is relatively low in energy. One woman told me, "I have my ups and downs, but basically I'm an incurable optimist, and it's my high-energy periods that are sometimes a problem. For a while I'll go around feeling great, and then pretty soon I'm staying up later and later, or getting up earlier and earlier in the morning, taking on more stuff than I can really do. Once I get beyond a certain stage, I get sort of swept away by it all; that's when my husband sits me down and has a talk with me. I sometimes give him an argument, but really I need him to pull me back down again before I exhaust myself completely."

Energy Opposites Often Attract

Obviously for some couples an energy difference is a solid asset. In fact, *it seems probable that when they fall in love many people subconsciously pick someone whose energy and temperament will balance their own.* Thus, some sprinters actually wind up married to strollers. This pairing of energy extremes can work out beautifully, though again the determining factor is the way both partners feel about their differences.

The Stroller and the Sprinter

Martha (the psychiatrist I described in Chapter 1) is a stroller happily married to a sprinter. "Al has two jobs," she told me. "He's a stockbroker and he also coaches a basketball team. He thinks no day is complete unless he buys a few million dollars' worth of stock, goes to a team practice, and gets in a couple of hours of tennis. Any one of the things he does would be a whole day's activity for me."

Martha believes that her awareness of time passing is different from the sense of time of people like Al. The hours coast by more sedately for her and she responds rather slowly to the flow of everyday events. "I read the newspaper on occasion," she explained, "but to read it every day would overload me. People who like up-to-the-minute news reports—that blows my mind. I keep track of changes month by month, not hour by hour." Sometimes that slow response of hers is an advantage, for Martha notes that Al gets upset about little things "that just don't last long enough for me to bother about them. And when Al is in a bad mood, that rolls right off me; it's not a big number unless he keeps it up.

"It takes a relaxed person to live with my hyper husband," she continued. "I can't keep up with him, but I realize when he's away that I miss his energy. I can't quite generate enough of my own."

Al agreed that most of the time their energy difference is an asset. "Sometimes it's a drag if I think something needs to be done and Martha is just going off to have a nap," he said. "But if I occasionally experience my energy as too high it's a help to be slowed down."

Other stroller-sprinter couples had similar things to say. However, that doesn't mean for a minute that strollers and sprinters inevitably need one another. Energy matches also occur, and people who share the same tempo often say that *that's* an asset, too. Once again, many other factors play into the energy equation.

When a Sprinter Marries a Sprinter

Julia is a sprinter married to a sprinter. Both she and her husband are so busy with their own activities that they spend very little time together. Some women would find the situation frustrating, but it suits Julia very well.

Julia is a research physicist with a university post. She occasionally chairs conferences, she has edited several books, and she's the mother of five teenage children! Her life, she said, has the kind of organization that's born of desperation. "By eliminating a lot of the things that take up people's time I get more done," she explained. "We don't have a TV set—I threw it out years ago. I hardly ever read the newspaper. My husband knows what I'm interested in and he reads items to me. I don't clean the house—I pay someone to do it. And my kids are terrific. They all do their own wash, and I've trained them to order their clothes from Sears every fall."

Julia's husband, Peter, is a corporate executive, a professional musician who's a co-owner of a small nightclub, and an amateur builder besides. "He's turning our summer place into cement city," Julia explained. "Last summer he added a second story to the house; then he poured a huge cement breakwater along the lakefront. He's a real whirling dervish. On a weekend he'll play at his nightclub until two in the morning; come out to the lake—it takes an hour to get there; sleep from three until six; pour cement until eight at night; and go back to the nightclub until two in the morning. When he gets home again he's ready to make love."

An Energy Match May Suit Your Needs

Julia estimates that, of their waking time, she and Peter probably spend an average of half an hour a day together, even on weekends. "People say, 'Don't you miss him when he's at the nightclub?' and I say, 'Hell, no!' I love to read late, and I've got a million things to do, and there are the kids. When he shows up we're probably just about ready to see each other anyway. We're lucky in that we seem to need each other at the same rate. I think if he were extremely energetic and I weren't there would probably be a lot of evenings when I'd be bored and expecting him to entertain me, but neither one of us need entertainment from the other. We do like being together, but we don't miss each other in between.

"Peter has a marvelous philosophy: He believes that communication destroys a marriage. We don't see each other often enough to really talk things out. For example, we had five children before I had any idea how many he wanted, and at that point it became obvious how many he considered were too many. Because we haven't gotten around to discussing an awful lot of things, I never know what he's going to do next, though we've been married for twenty years. I know I'm not predictable either, because he's always sort of stunned by things I'm doing. It makes for a delightful marriage.

"We're very lucky in that everything sort of jibes. Our basic outlook on life is very different, and that's something we both need. He's the perfect foil for me because he's a pessimist—he's my own private Woody Allen. If I were married to a person like me—an optimist—we would have spent every penny we had by now and borrowed besides, because my attitude is: Let's buy this now and we'll find the money to pay for it later. His attitude is: Let's never, ever spend a penny because we'll always need more money than we've got."

People look for different things in a marriage—or, for that matter, in any relationship. So an energy match, like a gap, is an asset only if it jibes with the needs of the particular couple. If Julia were the kind of woman who hungers for 100 percent of her husband's attention, who needs to be reassured that she's the most important thing in his life, and if she applied her own formidable energy to trying to wring such concessions from him, their marriage would never have lasted.

A Gap Need Not Create Problems

Sometimes an energy gap appears to be a formidable problem. If you are the more energetic half of a pair and your partner sometimes hangs back when all your systems are "go," you may feel impatient and even suspect that the hanging back is a form of passive resistance rather than a true lack of energy. If, on the other hand, you're the one with less energy, you may find that you resent it when you have to struggle to keep up and are equally resentful when you're left behind.

I believe that energy is, or should be, a nonissue in a marriage or love affair. *Where a gap seems to be creating problems, you need to ask yourself what it means to you and what else is going on.* Here are a few suggestions.

Energy Tips: How to Negotiate a Gap

1. It helps tremendously if you can accept the fact that energy is a body truth, that many people—including your partner—do experience their vitality differently from the way you experience yours.

2. There's an obvious solution where a substantial gap exists: If the person who has more vitality feels free to go off on his (or her) own periodically, and the person who has less energy feels free to stay behind, the problem evaporates. Unfortunately, where one or both people are insecure, this solution doesn't work. Insecurity is often at the root of an energy controversy, as is the larger question: Just how much separateness can you tolerate?

3. It may help to realize that in choosing someone whose energy level is very different from your own, you were probably looking for a balance. As with everything else, there were bound to be trade-offs; as the price of the balance you may need to settle for less togetherness than you'd really like.

The Generational Energy Gap

An energy gap between parent and child is probably a universal problem. *All children seem to have much more energy than adults can muster,* and so virtually all parents have trouble keeping up.

No one really knows why children have so much energy. However, Dr. Jay Tepperman, professor of experimental medicine at the Upstate Medical Center in Syracuse, New York, suggested that the body machinery generally "just works better in the young than it does in older people. Children are in positive nitrogen balance, they're synthesizing a lot of protein because they're growing, they're active and mobile."

Even at the cellular level kids have an advantage. Dr. Tepperman explained that living cells display impressive resilience: They'll respond to changes in their environment by altering their own biochemical machinery. In the cells of the young these adaptive changes are very striking and quite brisk, but in cells taken from older individuals they're sluggish and not so extensive. "All-around adaptability is the distinguishing feature of the young, rapidly growing animal," Dr. Tepperman said.

Though most children have the edge on adults when it comes to energy, some kids, of course, are much more active than others. Parents do face different problems raising a sprinter than they would with a stroller, a hurdler, or a trotter. However, where a really substantial energy gap exists between parent and child, it operates in much the same way as it does between adults: Whether or not it creates a problem depends on what it means to the parents. As I mentioned in Chapter 2, the way parents feel about their own energy colors their reactions. If a woman who is proud to be a sprinter sees her energy level reproduced in her small son, she's apt to be pleased; but if instead she feels that she's almost a freak because she has too much energy, she may be far from happy. There's nothing more painful than watching your child display traits that you feel are your own worst qualities—except, perhaps, watching him repeat your mistakes!

The Gap Between Siblings

Where the children in a family have sharply different energy levels, the parents need to be careful, since those differences are apt to aggravate the natural rivalry that exists between siblings.

Jenny, for example, grew up in the shadow of an older sister who had tremendous energy. When I asked her what that was like, she said: "In a word, it was awful. I felt all wrong. Whatever I could do only with tremendous effort Karen did easily, so it was impossible for me to excel at anything. When we tried to do something together, I could make no contribution that she hadn't thought of first and couldn't do better. She was often impatient with me and she didn't really approve of me. I always had the feeling that she was determined to improve me whether I liked it or not."

Both sisters had an artistic bent, but each expressed it differently. Jenny recalled the time when Karen, aged twelve, painted life-size murals on her bedroom walls. Though her mother was angry with her because she hadn't consulted anyone first, the murals were extremely well done. "She painted them freehand in just one day," Jenny said, "and that was what got me. I would have made it a six-month project, starting with preliminary sketches on graph paper.

"The contrast between Karen and me shaped the way I saw myself," she continued. "I knew I could do small, neat things and I tried to stick to that. Karen was sometimes sloppier, but she was at her best on a grand scale. Looking at things she'd done, people would exclaim, 'Oh, isn't that beautiful!' The response to what I did was usually, 'My, that must have taken a lot of work.' "

Jenny and her sister were very different in both energy and personal style, and these differences became a focus of their competitiveness. Their mother, who was somewhat intimidated by Karen, tacitly fostered the competition. Jenny recalled, "She'd say to Karen, shaking her head, 'Oh, my, it exhausts me just to watch you,' as if there were something unseemly about all that energy. Yet at the same time she made *me* feel that I was a slouch because I couldn't keep up with Karen." The net result was that Jenny grew up feeling that she had too little—of energy and many other things—while Karen grew up feeling that she had too much. Where siblings are very dissimilar in their energy, parents need to accept and value each child for what she is.

Energy Tips for Parents

1. If you feel that your child is "too active" or "hasn't enough drive," ask yourself what the child's energy level represents for you. Is she (or he) just like you, or is she totally different? How does that color your feelings?

2. Try to accept your child just as she is, energy level and all, especially if she has siblings who are quite different.

Energy as the Mystics See It

In the final chapter we'll explore some ancient ideas about energy to see what validity and meaning they might have today.

Some of the Eastern traditions share certain notions about energy. They conceive of it as a life-force that flows through the body. They say that that force can become blocked, and that when it's blocked we fall ill. Acupuncture, t'ai chi, Indian chakra psychology, and psychic healing all work with energy in this sense of the word. But *is* there such a thing as "psychic energy"?

The Life-force: Psychic Energy

Some years ago I was asked to write a magazine article about energy massage. At the time I knew only that it was a form of massage that was supposed to generate energy, and so I got more than I bargained for the day I went to see Cherie McCoy for an interview and demonstration.

Cherie is a psychotherapist who works out of Cambridge House in Milwaukee. I soon learned that to her energy massage is partly a form of psychic healing. She began by teaching me to feel my own energy: I sat with my eyes closed and my mouth slightly open and breathed slowly and deeply. As I inhaled, Cherie told me to imagine that I was drawing the breath all the way down to my navel; then, as I exhaled, I was to imagine that I was sending energy up from the navel and down my arms to my fingertips. When I had been doing this for several minutes, she had me bring my hands slowly together in front of me while continuing to send energy into them.

As my fingertips came closer and closer together, I was startled to discover that there was a kind of static in the air between them, a tangible force that alternately pulled them together and pushed them apart. I played with it for a while, feeling puzzled, intrigued, and a little uneasy. Eventually Cherie told me to turn my hands palms up; she held her own hands above mine, palms down. An even stronger force—something that felt to me like electricity—seemed to crackle in the air space between our hands. Then we got down to the massage itself. It involved some of the usual stroking and kneading, but again there were times, especially while Cherie was working on my feet, when I felt that a current of energy—or something—was traveling from her hands up my legs and throughout my body.

Was it just the power of suggestion? I simply don't know. Cherie explained that we *are* energy fields, that our energy extends beyond our bodies and that one person's energy field can stimulate another's.

I found it very difficult to believe that. Actually, I find it difficult to believe in anything I can't see, hear, taste, smell, or feel. I *did* feel the energy in my hands and in Cherie's, of course, and it wasn't just the kind of mild tingling that's easy to imagine into existence; the sensation was intense and unpredictable. Yet it was still easier for me to assume that I'd imagined it.

What Is Psychic Energy?

Psychic energy is a venerable concept that's currently attracting a lot of new interest. *According to the basic premise, there's a kind of energy in the body that we can't yet measure or even detect, and that can be passed on from one person to another.* Many people believe that if that energy becomes blocked in some way the individual will fall ill. Techniques for removing such blocks range from acupuncture to psychic healing, and include t'ai chi, various kinds of massages, and such modern psychotherapies as bioenergetics.

If extrasensory perception (ESP) and psychokinesis exist, then presumably they operate on the basis of some form of psychic energy. Many people believe they do exist, that there is sometimes an extra dimension to human communication that's not verbal or even nonverbal, but is more like the connectedness of a set of tuning forks resonating on the same wavelength. When they speak of "good vibes" and "bad vibes," these people mean it more or less literally.

To date, modern science has invested very little effort in the search for psychic energy or for something that might answer the description. Partly the problem lies in the connection to the paranormal: Most scientists don't want to risk the ridicule or even the censure of their colleagues, to say nothing of the committees that hand out research grants. So far no one has been able to record anything emanating from the human body that's clearly the basis for a mysterious energy system.

Nevertheless, a few studies that have been done recently on psychic healing and on acupuncture have come up with provocative results. Though there's no hard evidence that psychic energy exists, to my surprise some of the recent research makes the basic idea seem quite plausible.

Gone Respectable: Paranormal Healing

There is, for example, the work of Dolores Krieger. Dr. Krieger, who is a professor of nursing, does paranormal healing. She has taught her technique at the graduate level at New York University and at workshops and seminars around the country. In fact, over a period of five years she instructed more than four thousand health professionals in this ancient method of healing and wrote a book about her work (*The Therapeutic Touch*). She has also demonstrated experimentally that the laying on of hands has a real and measurable effect on human physiology.

I interviewed Dr. Krieger at her house in Port Chester, New York. She's a short, solidly built woman with gray hair and a strong, highly expressive face. We sat in lawn chairs inside the little greenhouse that bellies out from the front of her home. The room was crowded with plants, there was a large dog literally underfoot, and a couple of cats wandered in and out.

How to Do "Therapeutic Touch"

Dr. Krieger explained that she calls her technique "therapeutic touch" and that it's basically a healing meditation. The healer must first take a moment to become "centered," to achieve a state of passive concentration so that her mind is empty of distracting thoughts and her attention is focused effortlessly and entirely on her own hands. Once she is centered, she scans the patient's energy field. Though she may make actual physical contact with him, that's not necessary; usually she simply holds her hands four to six inches from his body as she feels for areas of tension. She checks both sides of the body simultaneously, looking for places where the right side and the left side feel different.

When she encounters such an area, she said, the sensation in the palms of her hands is usually a bit like a pressure front, a sort of resistance. However, it might also be sensed as tingling or pulsing, as heat or coolness, or it could feel like faint jabs of electricity. The goal is to balance out the energy, to make that part of the field feel the same as the rest. Thus, where Dr. Krieger senses tension she uses a stroking motion to try to push it out of the field altogether and get the energy flowing again. If instead the problem area felt cool, she would try to warm it; if it were too warm, she would work to cool it; and if she sensed tingling, pulsing, or electricity, she'd attempt to dampen down and quiet that part of the field.

The next step is to focus her own energy and transmit some of it, through her hands, to the patient. The aim now is to raise his energy level sufficiently so that his own recuperative powers can take over and his body can begin to heal itself.

The whole process, from centering to conclusion, takes anywhere from about five to fifteen minutes; by the end of that period of time the patient is often profoundly relaxed. His voice is apt to have dropped in pitch, his face may be slightly flushed, and all visible signs of tension will have disappeared. *Laboratory studies have confirmed that therapeutic touch does generally lead to deep relaxation, and it often relieves pain as well.* It also creates a highly personal relationship between patient and healer, something that's all too rare in the often depersonalized atmosphere of a busy hospital. The patient can't help but feel that someone cares intensely about him, and that in itself has value. Dr. Krieger says that the healer acts as a "human support system."

She noted that she's not talking about miraculous cures. "I don't know of many miracles," she said. As a rule, therapeutic touch does not produce lightning recoveries or totally unexpected cures; it simply seems to help the healing process along.

Healers

Having taught her technique to several thousand people, Dr. Krieger has discovered that not everyone can successfully master it. Students must be able to direct and modulate their own energy. Dr. Krieger believes that "man is an open system. Energies of many different kinds constantly enter and leave the body, but normally the output occurs in a very random way." *To do therapeutic touch, then, you must know your own body, learn to discipline it, and use it to focus energy.* "I call that the yoga of healing," Dr. Krieger said.

Beyond that, a healer must have a particular attitude. When she deliberately transfers energy, she must do it in response to the needs of the patient rather than as a personal ego trip. "There's no getting away from it," Dr. Krieger said. "The laying on of hands, cloaked as it has been in mystery, is a power tool. It has always been looked on with awe. You have to be very clear about why you want to get into it."

Janet Quinn, one of Dr. Krieger's NYU students (they call themselves "Krieger's Krazies"), recently described one of the ways the ego can interfere with healing. Writing in the *American Journal of Nursing*, she reported that when she first took Dr. Krieger's course she was full of self-doubt because she couldn't feel the physical cues that others seemed to be able to pick up; when she tried and failed she would become quite anxious.

"One day," she wrote, "I was working with a client with a more experienced member of the group, and suddenly I felt *connected*. I started picking up the elusive cues from the client in our assessment, and my partner validated them. My hands somehow seemed to know what needed to be done, and I let them lead me. I felt the energy of the client balance and even out, and again my partner validated. My interaction had finally been therapeutic and beneficial . . . What I learned that day was to stop thinking about me. I had been so caught up in worrying about myself—was *I* sensitive enough, could *I* do it—that, of course, it was impossible to make contact with anyone else."

Ms. Quinn has found since then that when she is able to be

completely centered and open, so that energy from outside can simply flow through her, she herself feels peaceful and energized afterward, and she believes the patient also gets the maximum benefit. Occasionally she's not really open and so "much of the energy I am giving is my own. I am then left feeling tired, a bit sad, and ineffectual."

In addition to training nurses, Dr. Krieger has taught doctors, psychiatrists, psychotherapists, physical and occupational therapists, and even veterinarians. She noted with some amusement that when doctors first start doing therapeutic touch, they often feel self-conscious about it. So some of them use an ingenious ploy: They get out a stethoscope, put the earpieces in place, and hold the bell against the patient's chest—going through the motions of the traditional medical routine while all the while they're actually doing therapeutic touch.

Supporters and Skeptics

Dr. Krieger has been pleasantly surprised by the extent to which professionals in the health field have accepted her work. Undoubtedly the fact that therapeutic touch is such a safe thing to do has helped. Neither she nor anyone else has ever suggested substituting it for regular medical care, to which it bears little relation.

Some medical authorities have remained entirely skeptical. Dr. Virginia Saddock, head of the American Psychiatric Association's Committee of Public Relations, made the following statement in a newspaper interview: "I am unwilling to believe in [therapeutic touch] unless I can see scientifically validated studies. I believe there is a very strong psychological component involved and it should be kept in the proper perspective. I'm especially skeptical of anything involving the so-called 'energy fields.'"

Though other doctors also doubt that a transfer of energy occurs, they assert that, all the same, it can't help but be good for patients to get the feeling that someone really cares. Some suggest that if healing *is* facilitated it may be because therapeutic touch acts as a placebo. In effect, they are saying that the power of suggestion is responsible. Dr. Krieger herself believes that a

placebo effect could be involved. She suggests that even if that
were the whole explanation, it would be useful to know more
about how to turn it on. However, she's convinced that there *is*
more to therapeutic touch—that in some undefined way it actually helps to rebalance human energy.

Measuring the Healer's Impact

Dr. Krieger can't prove that therapeutic touch speeds healing
because it's usually done in conjunction with regular health pro-
cedures and the placebo effect can never be entirely ruled out.
However, she *has* proved that *the laying on of hands causes a
real, measurable change in body chemistry: It raises the hemoglobin level almost every time.*

Dr. Krieger didn't come across this effect in the course of a
wide-ranging investigation of the way the body responds to therapeutic touch. She guessed that the hemoglobin level might
change, and it turned out that she was right. This seemed extraordinary to me, especially since hemoglobin isn't directly related to healing; and so she traced the development of her
theory for me.

Her interest in unconventional methods of healing began in
the late 1960s during a period when she was looking for a problem on which to do postdoctoral research. Several times she had
had the chance to work as a nurse in the temporary clinics set up
by Oskar Estebany, a well-known healer, on his annual visits to
the United States. She was impressed by what he was able to do.

She was also intrigued by some of the research that had been
done on psychic healing. The studies that particularly interested
her had actually involved Estebany. A Montreal biochemist, Bernard Grad, had asked him to "treat" water that was to be used
to irrigate barley seeds. Estebany simply held the containers in
his hands and attempted to transmit energy to them. Grad found
that seeds irrigated with that water sprouted sooner, grew taller,
and developed more chlorophyll than did seeds given water that
had been held by ordinary people or that hadn't been held at all.
This was true even when all of the water was kept in commer-
cially sealed containers throughout the experiment.

In another experiment Grad took three hundred laboratory mice and wounded all of them slightly in exactly the same place and the same way. The mice held by Estebany recovered faster than did mice held by medical students or mice simply left to heal on their own. Another biochemist, Sister M. Justa Smith (a nun), asked Estebany to treat test tubes containing trypsin, a human enzyme manufactured by the pancreas; the enzyme solutions he held were chemically more active afterward than others he hadn't treated.

Evidence of a Universal Energy

Dr. Krieger put these studies together with what she knew about the yogic concept of *prana*. The word refers to a kind of universal force or energy that supposedly permeates everything from rocks to humans. Healthy people are said to have more *prana* than they need, and sick people don't have enough. In fact, it's a deficit of *prana* that makes them sick, and they can be healed if energy is passed along to them from someone who is well. Though the ultimate source of *prana* is the sun, we also absorb it through foods, liquids, and especially in the air we breathe. Actually, to Dr. Krieger the literature seemed to imply that *prana* was intrinsic in what Westerners call the oxygen molecule.

On the basis of all this, she decided that it might be worth finding out whether Estebany could affect the level of hemoglobin circulating in the human body. Hemoglobin is the component of the red blood cells that transports oxygen to all the tissues. Several important enzyme systems are involved in its synthesis and functioning, so in the light of Sister Justa's research it seemed a logical thing to study. Dr. Krieger was also struck by the fact that in Grad's work the plants treated with healer-held water developed more chlorophyll. Like hemoglobin, chlorophyll carries oxygen to the tissues; in addition, biochemically it's similar to hemoglobin.

In 1971 Dr. Krieger did a small pilot study. She asked Estebany to treat nineteen sick people by the laying on of hands, and she recorded hemoglobin values before and after. She found that the values rose to a significant extent. What's more, a smaller control group of patients—selected because they were similar in many ways to those in the first group and who were not treated—showed no real change in their hemoglobin over the same length of time.

Elated, Dr. Krieger proceeded to do two large-scale studies that also produced positive results. As she went along she kept improving her experimental design, so that with the last study she was able to rule out a number of extraneous factors that might have affected the hemoglobin value. She could say for sure now that the rise did not occur because her patients had been smoking, exercising, meditating, doing yogic breathing exercises, or because of medications they'd been taking or some quirk in their diet.

Dr. Krieger's results have held up in the follow-up studies that she herself has done, and her work has also been replicated by others. Though it's not clear just how the hemoglobin level might be related to healing, there seems to be a kind of rebalancing involved. After a laying on of hands, in almost every case the hemoglobin value rises. In general, the lower the value was to begin with, the greater the rise, with dramatic increases seen in patients actually suffering from anemia (which is, of course, caused by a shortage of red blood cells and the hemoglobin they contain). There is such a thing as too much hemoglobin—the condition is called polycythemia—but patients whose level is already quite high experience only a small increase and stay within the normal range.

Personally Dr. Krieger is convinced that the hemoglobin increase is beneficial not only because it means that the body is better oxygenated but because she believes that a special kind of energy is bound up in the oxygen molecule; so an increase in hemoglobin would mean that more of that energy was supplied to the tissues.

Are We All Potentially Healers?

Once she had proved that a healer does have a demonstrable effect on hemoglobin, Dr. Krieger became personally curious.

She decided to see whether she herself could learn the laying on of hands. When she discovered that she could do it—that her experiences and those of her patients fitted the descriptions in the literature on healing—it occurred to her that, as she put it, *"Perhaps healing isn't something only a few specially chosen people can do but rather is a natural human potential."* So in another study conducted in 1974 she trained thirty-two registered nurses to do therapeutic touch.

The hospital patients involved in this particular experiment all knew that they were taking part in a study of psychic healing, but none knew whether they themselves were part of the group being given therapeutic touch or whether they had been assigned to the control group. Half the nurses used the technique Dr. Krieger had taught them, while the other half assumed similar positions with their patients but made no effort to transfer any sort of healing energy. Since the patients didn't know who was getting special treatment and who wasn't, it seems unlikely that the power of suggestion could have caused the rise in hemoglobin level that occurred in the healer group and not in the other.

One can't completely rule out the possibility that by some subtle, nonverbal signal the nurses unintentionally tipped patients off to whether they were in the healer group or not. Those who were trying to project energy might have had an air of concentration that the others didn't quite have. However, Dr. Krieger has also done studies to see whether people who believed in psychic healing were more apt to show a rise in hemoglobin than people who didn't, and she found that belief apparently had no effect.

Dr. Krieger's research, even taken together with the work of Bernard Grad and Sister Justa, doesn't prove that psychic energy exists. But in each case something happened that's difficult to explain in conventional scientific terms.

How Acupuncture Works: The Chemical Theory

When acupuncture was first introduced in the United States, many American scientists scoffed. The very idea seemed outlandish—the claim that a therapist could eliminate pain and promote healing by inserting long, thin needles into the skin at specific points and twirling them. The theory behind acupuncture was just as hard to accept, for it asserted that the universal energy (the Chinese call it *ch'i*) flows through the human body along twelve meridians that connect organs deep inside to a network of several hundred acupoints on the body surface. Illness supposedly occurs when the flow of *ch'i* is somehow obstructed. The needles are used to remove these obstructions.

Very few American scientists scoff at acupuncture today. It's clear that it works. The only question is why? We'll probably have some good, logical explanations for it in the not-too-distant future; they may even describe a kind of energy system. So far we have a chemical explanation for the way acupuncture relieves pain and an electrical theory that could also account for pain relief and a good deal more besides.

The chemical theory involves endorphins. It seems that *when acupuncture needles are twirled in the right acupoints they stimulate peripheral nerves. The nerves signal the pituitary gland and the brain to release endorphins, which then presumably shut down the brain cells that normally respond to pain.* Endorphins are also released into the spinal fluid, so they probably interfere with incoming pain messages at that level as well.

The evidence for all this is quite solid. For example, Dr. Bruce Pomeranz, a University of Toronto researcher, has demonstrated that naloxone, the drug that blocks endorphins, also blocks acupuncture's pain-relieving effects. When Dr. Pomeranz injected a local anesthetic into acupuncture sites, he found that nearby nerves no longer sent signal volleys when an acupuncture needle was inserted, and that the needling was no longer effective against pain.

Unfortunately the endorphin theory doesn't explain why acupuncture has been so successful in treating medical problems other than pain; it's being used in the United States these days to treat everything from ulcers to insomnia, from schizophrenia to drug addiction. Dr. Pomeranz said it's not very likely that endorphins would be involved except in the suppression of pain. "We have some evidence," he said, "that acupuncture raises cortisone levels, and cortisone is anti-inflammatory and suitable for healing." But even if cortisone turns out to be involved, it still leaves a lot unaccounted for.

The Electrical Explanation

Dr. Robert O. Becker, of the Upstate Medical Center in Syracuse, New York, approached the acupuncture puzzle from a different direction, bringing to it a complex theory he'd developed through his own research on healing.

The process by which the body heals itself is little understood, but it appears to operate by a kind of feedback system. Somehow, when an injury occurs a signal goes out that repairs are urgently needed, and the body then does exactly what is required. As Dr. Becker has pointed out, the control mechanism is remarkably efficient: Healing occurs only when there's an injury; what takes place is always appropriate to the injury; and the repair work ends as soon as the job is done—as soon as the fractured bone has mended or a new layer of skin has formed beneath a scab.

Clearly, the key to all this is the signal system that initiates and maintains the healing process and then shuts it off. There's no evidence that nerve impulses of the traditional sort are involved, and scientists have been unable to find a chemical explanation, either.

Dr. Becker has suggested that an electrical current may be responsible. His theory harks all the way back to the eighteenth century, when the so-called current of injury was discovered. It's a direct current (DC) electrical potential that appears suddenly at the site of an injury in both animals and plants. Once it had been detected, scientists concluded that electric currents must flow in all living things. However, as they learned more about physiology and electricity, and failed to find any mechanism in the body that looked as if it could carry current, "animal electricity" was discredited. (Regular nerve impulses operate not by an actual flow of current but by a much more sophisticated process.) It's only very recently—thanks to the electron microscope—that physiologists have discovered complex crystal-like structures in living tissues that could conceivably carry current, much as crystalline materials carry it in solid-state physics.

Dr. Becker's theory suggests, then, that healing is regulated by a very faint DC current that travels not through the nerves themselves but through the nerve sheaths. The so-called Schwann cells that encase peripheral nerves and the glia cells that surround neurons in the brain seem to form a complex, continuous network; they could be a relic of a primitive "nervous system" that still serves some functions.

Dr. Becker reports that you can measure DC potentials on the surface of all living animals and that DC current also produces an electromagnetic field around the organism that's very low in magnitude. Within just the last few years scientists have finally developed an instrument sensitive enough to pick up that field in the areas of the brain and the heart.

Dr. Becker produced dramatic proof that there is indeed something to his theory when he solved a famous puzzle: Why is it that when a salamander's leg is amputated it's able to grow a complete replacement, while when a frog—or a human—undergoes the same sort of amputation, healing consists of the stump scarring over? Becker not only discovered that the current of injury is quite different in frogs and salamanders, he was able to duplicate the salamander's current of injury and apply it to a frog amputee, the result being that the animal's limb regenerated completely. More recently he has been able to accomplish partial regeneration in rats.

Acupoints

As for acupuncture, it occurred to Dr. Becker some years ago that the DC signal might just possibly be the equivalent of *ch'i* and the meridians might correspond to the DC network. Taking into account the fact that DC current fades out over time and distance, he suggested that the acupoints could be amplifiers, spaced out at intervals to boost the signal. Such amplifiers would be quite sensitive to disturbances—for example, the insertion of a metal needle.

Dr. Becker tested his theory by recording electrical resistance and conductance along sections of two meridians between the elbow and the fingertips. He found that approximately half the traditional acupoints did register: They were different from non-acupoints in their electrical properties and in ways that supported his theory. As for the traditional sites that failed to register, there are several possible explanations. Their electrical properties might not be as well defined; or they might exist in some people but not in all; or perhaps they never existed and the Chinese were right in describing some points and wrong about others. Of course, it's also possible that there were flaws in the recording technique itself.*

Dr. Becker was able to survey only seventeen acupoints before the funding for his study ran out, but that was enough. As Dr. Maria Reichmanis, one of his coinvestigators, put it, "We demonstrated to our own satisfaction that at least some of the points register in terms of electrical measurements, and therefore physically they do exist. That would imply that there's something more to look at in the whole system."

Becker has suggested that the extra low-frequency (ELF) electromagnetic field that surrounds humans might be the basis for ESP, psychokinesis, and psychic healing. Though the field has a very low strength, ELF signals can actually travel vast distances—a fact of physics the U. S. Navy is hoping to take advantage of with a proposed ELF communication system.

Paranormal phenomena aside, Dr. Becker's theory provides a possible explanation for the way acupuncture relieves pain. So, of course, does the endorphin research done by Dr. Pomeranz and others. However, the two explanations may not actually contradict one another. As Dr. Reichmanis said, "I expect we could tie things together."

Is there such a thing as psychic energy? There are almost too many possible answers to the question. If it exists, it could have something to do with the oxygen molecule; it could be a faint DC current; it could even be some sort of magnetism, as psychics often suggest.

---

* Other researchers scanning for acupuncture points have found virtually all of them. However, most used devices that were pressure-sensitive: If the technician pressed just a little harder, the reading went up. Dr. Becker's meridian scanning probe was designed to avoid that problem.

Or it could be something else altogether. *Some physicists have also begun to talk about psychic energy, pointing out that on the subatomic level the concept of* prana *suddenly, eerily turns into a pretty fair description of the way things are.*

The Reality of the Senses Versus Subatomic Realities

In the twentieth century quantum mechanics has taught us that there is more than one reality. There is the ordinary world of the senses and then there is the very different reality of subatomic events—the world of the very small.

Physicists have learned quite a lot about the subatomic reality, and their knowledge has been expressed in complex mathematical formulas. It has had enormous consequences—we have hydrogen bombs and nuclear power plants to prove that. But when scientists have tried to translate what they know into the kinds of concepts we work with in the world of the senses, the concepts have turned out to be full of contradictions, sounding as vague and mysterious as the pronouncements of any mystic.

Take the whole idea of matter, for example. My dictionary defines matter as "what a thing is made of; constituent substance or material." Certainly, in the world of the senses matter appears to be solid and substantial enough; yet it's not what it seems.

At the atomic level the matter that constitutes a stone, a finger, or anything else turns out to be made up mostly of empty space. No one has ever seen an atom, but because scientists know quite a lot about the way atoms behave, they have a pretty good idea of what they must be like. They say that if we decided to expand an atom until it was large enough so that we could see its nucleus, to begin with we'd have to make it fourteen stories tall. Even then the nucleus would be about the size of a grain of salt, and the electrons that revolve around it at fantastic speeds would be no bigger than particles of dust. What's more, those particles exist not in three dimensions but, unimaginably, in many dimensions.

The familiar, natural laws that govern matter and energy in everyday life simply don't operate on the subatomic level. In the world of the senses, as physicists pointed out centuries ago, matter is indestructible: It can change its form—turning from a solid into a liquid or a gas, for example—but it can't simply disappear. Energy is also conserved. It, too, may change its form, but it can't increase or decrease.

In the subatomic reality none of the above is true, for there mass and energy are the same and change continually into one another. When particles collide, for example, some may be destroyed, and the energy, which was also their mass, may be distributed as energy among the other parties to the collision, or it may become mass, forming new particles. Thus, subatomic particles are not infinitesimal objects that actually exist; physicists say they are merely "tendencies to exist"! They are like knots of energy that come and go, materializing out of an underlying field of energy and then disappearing back into it.

By implication we, too, are simply knots of energy, temporary condensations of the field. In fact, as Gary Zukav has written in his marvelous book about the new physics, *The Dancing Wu Li Masters,* "the philosophical implication of quantum mechanics is that all of the things in our universe (including us) that appear to exist independently are actually parts of one all-encompassing organic pattern, and that no parts of that pattern are ever really separate from it or from each other."

If this sounds similar to the mystical belief that we are all part of the One—ripples on the surface of the same sea—and if the energy field from which all things arise sounds rather like *prana* or *ch'i,* it may be because mystics long ago found a way to experience that other reality that escapes the senses. At least that's what some mystics and some physicists are beginning to suggest. Meditators who manage to achieve that rare state where they feel at one with the universe may (or may not) be in touch with the universal energy that *is* reality in the world of the very small. Meditators who have had the experience are sometimes changed profoundly by it. Though typically they can't even begin to describe what they felt, it becomes for them a body truth as real as any other.

I have never had the experience and so I'm still not sure whether or not I believe in a universal energy. It occurs to me, though, that the kind of energy particle physicists deal with might have nothing at all to do with psychic energy, psychic healing, or the human experience. But then again, it's rather striking the way many physicists have come to the same conclusions that Eastern philosophers and mystics from various cultures arrived at long ago.

And it seems very clear to me that if we all *behaved* as if we were energy fields—local condensations of the life-force—it would be a different and better world. We would start with the assumption that there is a kind of energy that flows through and connects all of us, that we are derived from it and perhaps return to it in the end. None of us are really alone, then, confined though we are in separate envelopes of skin, and anything that happens anywhere ultimately affects all of us.

Furthermore, it's not that we *have* energy. We *are* energy. We have only to learn to direct and focus ourselves and to stay open to the universal flow. Mystical? Yes, but a promising beginning for a gentler life and a more connected existence.

APPENDIX:

How to Chart Your Energy

One way to learn a great deal about the way your own energy operates is to keep a record of your energy level over a period of a week.

Using ordinary graph paper, you can chart your energy flow. Each graph should cover one twenty-four-hour period, and on each you record your vitality with a continuous line whose crests and troughs reflect the way your energy rose and fell on that particular day. Mark off the time of day along the graph's horizontal axis, beginning at 6 A.M. and ending at 6 A.M. the following morning. Along the vertical axis write the numbers from o (at the bottom) up to 10; this is a scale for rating your moment-to-moment energy level.

• At o you would be deeply asleep and thus totally unaware of your energy level.

• 1 would be about as low in energy as you can ever remember feeling.

• 5 represents what, for you, is an average state. At 5 you're not feeling particularly energetic, but neither are you aware of fatigue.

• 10 would be as energetic as you ever feel.

Please note that the point here is not to compare yourself to anyone else. Forget about the scale that expresses the differences among sprinters, trotters, and strollers. On these charts a 10 represents *your own* top energy level; whether your top is higher or lower than anyone else's top is irrelevant.

To be more specific, let's say you wake at seven in the morning and you're a lark—someone who wakes up on most mornings feeling completely refreshed and ready to swing into action immediately. Between seven and seven-thirty your energy score might shoot straight up from 0 to 9 and then stay there until you fell asleep that night, when it would drop again—gradually or sharply, depending on your pattern—to 0.

If there's a sudden change in your energy level during the day and you know why the change has occurred, flag the time when this happens, where the score begins to drop or rise, and then record the reason. For example, if you received bad news at around ten in the morning and your energy instantly plummeted, you might make this note: *"Bad news: Melanie very ill." At the times when your energy feels mostly nervous, make a note of that, too. You may find, as some people have, that you need to chart two energy patterns, one for physical drive and the other for mental alertness.

If you find that your energy peaks at about the same time every day, then that's probably the way your body is programed (see Chapter 5). And if your energy score takes a daily nose dive around mid-afternoon, you're someone who has a problem with postprandial dip (again, see Chapter 5 for details).

When I charted my energy, I learned a great deal about myself. Others who used the charts said the same thing. One man, for example, picked up some unexpected information about what he needs to do to sustain his own momentum. The charts confirmed that he's at his most energetic in the morning—which was not news to him. In addition, the graphs showed that if he has a long, relaxing lunch, that stalls his momentum, so that he can expect to feel lethargic for the rest of the afternoon; and that if he works late at night, his energy will be much lower for all of the next day. Furthermore, when he sleeps late on a weekend morning he's unable to work up any real momentum for the rest of the day.

The point of keeping an energy chart is *to raise your energy consciousness:* to become more aware of the things that give you an energy lift and those that drain you; to pinpoint the time of day when you can expect your energy peak to occur; and, if possible, to learn something about your momentum as well. Several people also noted that after a week of keeping charts they were so much more aware of their own energy that afterward they went right on noticing—and learning.

They were finally—permanently—in touch with an important body truth!

BIBLIOGRAPHY

CHAPTER 2: Energy that "Runs in the Family" . . . or Doesn't

Based partly on interviews with Dr. T. Berry Brazelton, Dr. Stella Chess, and Louis Nizer.

Brazelton, T. Berry. *Infants and Mothers.* New York: Dell, 1969.

——. "Understanding the Person Your Baby Is," *Redbook,* Jan. 1979.

Chess, Stella; Thomas, Alexander; and Birch, Herbert G. *Your Child Is a Person.* New York: Viking, 1965.

Chess, Stella, and Thomas, Alexander, eds. *Annual Progress in Child Psychiatry and Child Development 1979.* New York: Brunner-Mazel, 1979.

Nizer, Louis. *Reflections Without Mirrors: An Autobiography of the Mind.* New York: Doubleday, 1978.

CHAPTER 3: The Physiology of Energy: Your Body and Brain

Based partly on interviews with Dr. Arnold Friedhoff, Dr. John W. Mason, Dr. Jack Richard, and Dr. Baron Shopsin.

Fieve, Ronald R. *Moodswing.* New York: Morrow, 1975.

Greenberg, Joel. "The Brain. Holding the Secrets of Behavior," *Science News,* Nov. 25, 1978.

——. "Memory Research. An Era of 'Good Feeling,'" *Science News,* Nov. 25, 1978.

Guyton, Arthur C. *Textbook of Medical Physiology.* Philadelphia: W. B. Saunders, 1976.

Hubel, David H. "The Brain," *Scientific American,* Sept. 1979.

Iversen, Lesley L. "The Chemistry of the Brain," *Scientific American,* Sept. 1979.

Mason, John W. "Organization of Psychoendocrine Mechanisms," *Psychosomatic Medicine,* Sept.–Oct. 1968.

——. "Emotion as Reflected in Patterns of Endocrine Integration," in *Emotions—Their Parameters and Measurement,* edited by L. Levi, New York: Raven Press, 1975.

——. "Clinical Psychophysiology. Psychoendocrine Mechanisms," in

American Handbook of Psychiatry, vol. IV, edited by M. F. Reiser. New York: Basic Books, 1975.

Mason, John W., and Brady, Joseph V. "The Sensitivity of Psychoendocrine Systems to Social and Physical Environment," in *Psychobiological Approaches to Social Behavior,* edited by P. Herbert Leiderman and David Shapiro. Stanford: Stanford University Press, 1964.

Schildkraut, Joseph J. "Current Status of the Catecholamine Hypothesis of Affective Disorders," in *Psychopharmacology: A Generation of Progress,* edited by M. A. Lipton, A. DiMascio, and K. F. Killam. New York: Raven Press, 1978.

Snyder, Solomon H. *Madness and the Brain.* New York: McGraw-Hill, 1974.

CHAPTER 4: The Thrust and Drag of the Emotions

Based partly on interviews with Dr. Doris Rothman and Susan Shor.

Scarf, Maggie. "From Joy to Depression. New Insights into the Chemistry of Moods," *The New York Times Magazine,* April 24, 1977.

CHAPTER 5: Learning to Flow with Energy Rhythms

Based partly on interviews with Dr. Andrew Ahlgren, Dr. Charles Ehret, Dr. John Hanley, Brian Nakauchi, James Nesdill, Dr. John Palmer, George Plimpton, Deborah Sewitch, Dr. Wilse Webb, and Dr. Elliot D. Weitzman.

Ehret, Charles F., and Potter, Van R. "Circadian Chronotypic Induction of Tyrosine Aminotransferase and Depletion of Glycogen by Theophylline in the Rat," *International Journal of Chronobiology,* vol. 2, 1974.

Ehret, Charles F.; Potter, Van R.; and Dobra, Kenneth W. "Chronotypic Action of Theophylline and of Pentobarbital as Circadian Zeitgebers in the Rat," *Science,* June 20, 1975.

Greenberg, Joel. "Cracking the Cycles of Depression and Mania," *Science News,* Nov. 25, 1978.

Halberg, Franz. "Implications of Biologic Rhythms for Clinical Practice," *Hospital Practice,* Jan. 1977.

Klein, Raymond, and Armitage, Roseanne. "Rhythms in Human Performance: 1 ½-Hour Oscillations in Cognitive Style," *Science,* June 22, 1979.

Lavie, Peretz, and Kripke, Daniel F. "Ultradian Rhythms: The 90-Minute Clock Inside Us," *Psychology Today,* April 1975.

Palmer, John D. *An Introduction to Biological Rhythms.* New York: Academic Press, 1976.

Schmeck, Harold M., Jr. "Manic-Depressive Cycle Tied to 'Clock' Defect," New York *Times,* Dec. 5, 1978.

"Study Finds Health Perils in Rotating Work Shifts," New York *Times*, Dec. 27, 1978.

CHAPTER 6: Sleeping Tactics

Based partly on interviews with Dr. Frederick J. Evans, Dr. John Hanley, and Dr. Wilse Webb.

Altman, Lawrence K. "Study of Sleep Reports Men Stop Breathing Longer," New York *Times*, March 9, 1979.

Evans, Frederick J. "Subjective Characteristics of Sleep Efficiency," *Journal of Abnormal Psychology*, Oct. 1977.

———. "*Hypnosis and Sleep:* The Control of Altered States of Awareness," *Annals of the New York Academy of Sciences*, Oct. 7, 1977.

Evans, Frederick J., et al. "Response During Sleep with Intervening Waking Amnesia," *Science*, April 29, 1966.

———. "Sleep Patterns in Replacement and Appetitive Nappers." Paper read at the American Psychological Association, Washington, D.C., Sept. 1976.

———. "Appetitive and Replacement Naps: EEG and Behavior," *Science*, August 12, 1977.

Schmeck, Harold M., Jr. "U. S. Study of Sleep Drugs Finds Risks and Overuse," New York *Times*, April 5, 1979.

Webb, Wilse B. *Sleep: The Gentle Tyrant.* Englewood Cliffs, N.J.: Prentice-Hall, 1975.

CHAPTER 7: How to Eat for Energy

Based partly on interviews with Dr. Sami Hashim, Dr. Victor Herbert, Elaine Kaufman, and Dr. Fredrick Stare.

"Alcohol: The Starvation Diet," *Science News*, March 10, 1979.

Brody, Jane E. "Researchers Challenge Old Theories on Obesity," New York *Times*, Feb. 20, 1979.

"Clear advance in acne therapy," *Science News*, Feb. 24, 1979.

Eden, Alvin N., with Heilman, Joan Rattner. *Growing Up Thin.* New York: McKay, 1975.

Greenberg, Joel. "The Fat American," *Science News*, March 25, 1978.

Harris, Robert S., and Karmas, Endel. *Nutritional Evaluation of Food Processing.* 2nd ed. Westport, Conn.: Avi, 1975.

Herbert, Victor D. "Megavitamin Therapy," *Journal of the American Pharmaceutical Association*, no. 17, 1977.

Lamb, Lawrence E. *Metabolics. Putting Your Food Energy to Work.* New York: Harper & Row, 1974.

"New therapies, New Forms of an Old Vitamin," *Science News*, March 24, 1979.

Rodin, Judith. "The Puzzle of Obesity," *Human Nature*, Feb. 1978.

Stare, Fredrick J., and Whelan, Elizabeth M. *Eat OK—Feel OK! Food*

Facts and Your Health. North Quincy, Mass.: Christopher, 1978.
"Vitamin C and Immune Protection," *Science News,* May 5, 1979.

CHAPTER 8: Drugs: The Now-and-Future Energizers

Based partly on interviews with Dr. Arnold Friedhoff, Dr. Christian Gillin, Dr. Ernest Hartmann, and Dr. Marcus Reidenberg.
"Anxiety and Pain over Valium, Darvon," *Science News,* Feb. 10, 1979.
Arehart-Treichel, Joan. "The Pituitary's Powerful Protein," *Science News,* Nov. 25, 1978.
Cooper, Jack R.; Bloom, Floyd E.; and Roth, Robert H. *The Biochemical Basis of Neuropharmacology.* New York: Oxford University Press, 1978.
"Do-it-yourself Valium in the Brain," *Science News,* Nov. 10, 1979.
Greenberg, Joel. "The Lore of Cocaine," *Science News,* Sept. 9, 1978.
———. "Memory Research. An Era of 'Good Feeling,'" *Science News,* Nov. 25, 1978.
Hartmann, Ernest. "L-Tryptophan—The Sleeping Pill of the Future?" *Psychology Today,* Dec. 1978.
Hirsch, Madelyn J., and Wurtman, Richard J. "Lecithin Consumption Increases Acetylcholine Concentrations in Rat Brain and Adrenal Gland," *Science,* Oct. 13, 1978.
Iversen, Leslie L. "The Chemistry of the Brain," *Scientific American,* Sept. 1979.
Jones, Ben Morgan, and Parsons, Oscar A. "Alcohol and Consciousness. Getting High, Coming Down," *Psychology Today,* Jan. 1975.
Potkin, Steven G., et al. "Phenylethylamine in Paranoid Chronic Schizophrenia," *Science,* Oct. 26, 1979.
Smith, T. G., Jr. "Three Modes of Intercellular Communication." Paper read at the Ninth Annual Meeting of the Society for Neuroscience, Atlanta, Ga., Nov. 1979.
Snyder, Solomon H. *Madness and the Brain.* New York: McGraw-Hill, 1974.
Timson, John. "Is Coffee Safe to Drink?" *Human Nature,* Dec. 1978.
Wurtman, Richard J. "Food for Thought," *The Sciences,* April 1978.
———. "Brain Muffins," *Psychology Today,* Oct. 1978.
Zimmerman, Earl A. "Immunocytochemical Studies of Anterior Pituitary Hormones in the Central Nervous System." Paper delivered at the Ninth Annual Meeting of the Society for Neuroscience, Nov. 1979.

CHAPTER 9: Exercise: Using Your Body to Fine Tune Your Mind

Based partly on interviews with David Hackler, Dr. William McArdle, Dr. William P. Morgan, and Diana Nyad.

Greist, John H., et al. "Running as Treatment for Depression." Mime-ographed. Department of Psychiatry, University of Wisconsin, Madison, Wis.

Nyad, Diana. *Other Shores.* New York: Random House, 1978.

CHAPTER 10: Tricks of the Mind that Energize the Body

Based partly on interviews with Dr. Mihaly Csikszentmihalyi, Dr. Robert M. Nideffer, and Dr. Richard Suinn.

Csikszentmihalyi, Mihaly. *Beyond Boredom and Anxiety.* San Francisco: Jossey-Bass, 1975.

Gallwey, W. Timothy, and Kriegel, Robert. *Inner Skiing.* New York: Random House, 1977.

Jerome, John. "How High Can a Man Jump?" *Quest,* Nov. 1978.

Morgan, William P. "The Mind of the Marathoner," *Psychology Today,* April 1978.

Nicklaus, Jack. *Golf My Way.* New York: Simon and Schuster, 1976.

Nideffer, Robert M. *The Inner Athlete. Mind Plus Muscle for Winning.* New York: Crowell, 1976.

Nideffer, Robert M., and Sharpe, Roger C. *A.C.T. Attention Control Training: How to Get Control of Your Mind Through Total Concentration.* New York: Wyden, 1978.

Suinn, Richard M. "Body Thinking: Psychology for Olympic Champs," *Psychology Today,* July 1976.

——. "Psychology and Sports Performance: Principles and Applications." Paper read at the Association for the Advancement of Behavior Therapy, Atlanta, Ga., 1977.

——. "Behavioral Applications of Psychology to U. S. World Class Competitors." Paper read at the Congress of the Canadian Society for Psychomotor Learning and Sport Psychology, Toronto, Canada, 1978.

CHAPTER 11: The Search for an Invigorating Environment

Based partly on interviews with Ellie Dylan, Dr. Albert P. Krueger, Dr. Helmut E. Landsberg, and Alexandra Stoddard.

Berland, Theodore. *The Fight for Quiet.* Englewood Cliffs, N.J.: Prentice-Hall, 1970.

Krueger, Albert. "Are Negative Ions Good for You?" *New Scientist,* June 14, 1973.

Krueger, Albert Paul, and Reed, Eddie James. "Biological Impact of Small Air Ions," *Science,* Sept. 24, 1976.

Krueger, A. P., et al. "Electric Fields, Small Air Ions and Biological Effects," *International Journal of Biometeorology,* vol. 22, no. 3, 1978.

Krueger, Albert P., and Sigel, Sheelah. "Ions in the Air," *Human Nature,* July 1978.

Landsberg, H. E. *Weather and Health. An Introduction to Biome-teorology.* Garden City, N.Y.: Doubleday, 1969.

Lipscomb, David M. *Noise: The Unwanted Sounds.* Chicago: Nelson-Hall, 1974.

Rubin, Zick. "Seasonal Rhythms in Behavior," *Psychology Today,* Dec. 1979.

Stoddard, Alexandra. *Style for Living. How to Make Where You Live You.* Garden City, N.Y.: Doubleday, 1974.

CHAPTER 12: The Company You Keep

Based partly on interviews with Dr. Eliot Chapple, Jan Gosar, Jean Houston, Bill Murray, Dr. Susan Shor, Mary Anne Symons Brown, and Dr. Marvin Zuckerman.

Buchsbaum, Monte S. "The Sensoristat in the Brain," *Psychology Today,* May 1978.

Chapple, Eliot D. *Culture and Biological Man. Explorations in Behav-ioral Anthropology.* New York: Holt, Rinehart and Winston, 1970.

Davis, Flora. *Inside Intuition. What We Know about Nonverbal Com-munication.* New York: McGraw-Hill, 1971.

Hayes, Donald P., and Cobb, Loren. "A Physiological Basis of Con-versational Episodes." Paper read at the conference of the Insti-tute for Nonverbal Communication Research, New York City, March 1979.

Vaillant, George E. *Adaptation to Life.* Boston: Little, Brown, 1977.

Zuckerman, Marvin. "The Search for High Sensation," *Psychology Today,* Feb. 1978.

CHAPTER 13: Making Peace with Nervous Energy

Based partly on interviews with Lynne DeGillio, Ellie Dylan, Dr. Richard Lazarus, Dr. John Mason, Charles Nichols, Dr. Robert Rose, Dr. Hans Selye, Dr. S. Leonard Syme, and Katherine Tennes.

Friedman, Meyer, and Rosenman, Ray H. *Type A Behavior and Your Heart.* Greenwich, Conn.: Fawcett, 1974.

Friedman, Stanford B., et al. "Behavioral Observations on Parents Anticipating the Death of a Child," in *Stress and Coping. An An-thology,* edited by Alan Monat and Richard S. Lazarus. New York: Columbia University Press, 1977.

Mason, John W. "Strategy in Psychosomatic Research," *Psycho-somatic Medicine,* July–August 1970.

———. "Emotion as Reflected in Patterns of Endocrine Integration," in *Emotions—Their Parameters and Measurement,* edited by L. Levi. New York: Raven, 1975.

———. "Clinical Psychophysiology. Psychoendocrine Mechanisms," in *American Handbook of Psychiatry*, vol. IV, edited by M. F. Reiser. New York: Basic Books, 1975.

Mason, John W., and Brady, Joseph V. "The Sensitivity of Psychoendocrine Systems to Social and Physical Environment," in *Psychobiological Approaches to Social Behavior*, edited by P. Herbert Leiderman and David Shapiro. Stanford: Stanford University Press, 1964.

Tennes, Katherine; Downey, Karen; and Vernadakis, Antonia. "Urinary Cortisol Excretion Rates and Anxiety in Normal 1-Year-Old Infants," *Psychosomatic Medicine*, May–June 1977.

CHAPTER 14: How to Liberate Sexual Energy

Based partly on interviews with Dr. Jay Mann, Dr. Maj-Britt Rosenbaum, Dr. Leah Schaefer, Dr. Dorothy Tennov, and Dr. Leonore Tiefer.

Feshbach, Seymour, and Malamuth, Neal. "Sex and Aggression: Proving the Link," *Psychology Today*, Nov. 1978.

Fried, Edrita. *On Love and Sexuality*. New York: Grove Press, 1975.

Greenfield, Norman S., and Sternbach, Richard A., eds. *Handbook of Psychophysiology*. New York: Holt, Rinehart and Winston, 1972.

Rogers, Carl R. *Becoming Partners: Marriage and Its Alternatives*. New York: Dell, 1972.

Rubin, Zick. "The Love Research," *Human Behavior*, Feb. 1977.

Schaefer, Leah Cahan. *Women and Sex*. New York: Pantheon, 1973.

Tennov, Dorothy. *Love and Limerence: The Experience of Being in Love*. New York: Stein & Day, 1979.

Yankelovich, Daniel, and Barrett, William. *Ego and Instinct. The Psychoanalytic View of Human Nature—Revised*. New York: Random House, 1970.

CHAPTER 15: Your Creative Drive

Based partly on interviews with Jean Houston, Alexandra Stoddard, and Phyllis Whitney.

Arieti, Silvano. *Creativity. The Magic Synthesis*. New York: Basic Books, 1976.

Douglas, John H. "The Genius of Everyman. Discovering Creativity," *Science News*, April 23, 1977.

———. "The Genius of Everyman. Learning Creativity," *Science News*, April 30, 1977.

Ghiselin, Brewster, ed. *The Creative Process*. New York: New American Library, 1952.

Houston, Jean. "The Mind of Margaret Mead. How She Democratizes Greatness," *Quest*, July–August 1977.

Masters, Robert, and Houston, Jean. *Listening to the Body. The Psychophysical Way to Health and Awareness.* New York: Delacorte, 1978.

Parnes, Sidney J.; Noller, Ruth B.; and Biondi, Angelo M. *Guide to Creative Action.* New York: Scribner's, 1977.

CHAPTER 16: Mental Energy: Doing More by Doing Less First

Based partly on interviews with Sophy Burnham and Dr. Patricia Carrington.

Carrington, Patricia. *Freedom in Meditation.* Garden City, N.Y.: Anchor/Doubleday, 1977.

———. *Learning to Meditate: A Self-Regulated Course in CSM.* Kendall Park, N.J.: Pace Educational Systems, 1979. This kit, containing three tape cassettes and a text, costs $49.95 (postpaid) and can be ordered from Pace Educational Systems, Inc., P.O. Box 113, Kendall Park, N.J. 08824. (New Jersey residents add 5 percent sales tax.) Or you can write for a free brochure.

Goleman, Daniel. "Meditation Helps Break the Stress Spiral," *Psychology Today,* Feb. 1976.

LeShan, Lawrence. *How to Meditate. A Guide to Self-Discovery.* Boston: Little, Brown, 1974.

CHAPTER 17: What to Do in an Energy Crisis

Based partly on an interview with Dr. Jack Richard.

CHAPTER 19: The Life-force: Psychic Energy

Based partly on interviews with Dr. Dolores Krieger, Cherie McCoy, Dr. Bruce Pomeranz, and Dr. Maria Reichmanis.

Becker, Robert O. "The Significance of Bioelectric Potentials," *Bioelectrochemistry and Bioenergetics,* vol. 1, 1974.

———. "An Application of Direct Current Neural Systems to Psychic Phenomena," *Psychoenergetic Systems,* vol. 2, 1977.

Becker, Robert O., et al. "Electrophysiological Correlates of Acupuncture Points and Meridians," *Psychoenergetic Systems,* vol. 1, 1976.

Capra, Fritjof. *The Tao of Physics.* New York: Bantam, 1975.

Krieger, Dolores. "Therapeutic Touch: The Imprimatur of Nursing." *American Journal of Nursing,* May 1975.

———. *The Therapeutic Touch. How to Use Your Hands to Help or to Heal.* Englewood Cliffs, N.J.: Prentice-Hall, 1979.

Krieger, Dolores; Peper, Erik; and Ancoli, Sonia. "Therapeutic Touch. Searching for Evidence of Physiological Change." *American Journal of Nursing,* April 1979.

Quinn, Janet F. "One Nurse's Evolution as a Healer," *American Journal of Nursing*, April 1979.

Zukav, Gary. *The Dancing Wu Li Masters. An Overview of the New Physics.* New York: Morrow, 1979.

Catalog

If you are interested in a list of fine Paperback
books, covering a wide range of subjects
and interests, send your name and address,
requesting your free catalog, to:

McGraw-Hill Paperbacks
1221 Avenue of Americas
New York, N.Y. 10020